REIGN OF
TERROR

REIGN OF TERROR

HOW THE 9/11 ERA DESTABILIZED AMERICA AND PRODUCED TRUMP

Spencer Ackerman

VIKING

VIKING
An imprint of Penguin Random House LLC
penguinrandomhouse.com

LIBRARY OF CONGRESS CATALOGING-IN-PUBLICATION DATA
Names: Ackerman, Spencer, author.
Title: Reign of terror : how the 9/11 era destabilized America and produced Trump /
Spencer Ackerman.
Description: [New York] : Viking, [2021] | Includes bibliographical references and index.
Identifiers: LCCN 2021015357 (print) | LCCN 2021015358 (ebook) |
ISBN 9781984879776 (hardcover) | ISBN 9781984879783 (ebook)
Subjects: LCSH: War on Terrorism, 2001–2009. | September 11 Terrorist Attacks, 2001. |
National security—United States—History—21st century. | United States—Military policy. |
United States—Foreign relations—21st century. | United States—
Politics and government—2001–2009. | United States—Politics and government—2009–2017.
Classification: LCC HV6432 .A336 2021 (print) |
LCC HV6432 (ebook) | DDC 973.931—dc23
LC record available at https://lccn.loc.gov/2021015357
LC ebook record available at https://lccn.loc.gov/2021015358

Printed in the United States of America
1st Printing

DESIGNED BY LUCIA BERNARD

For both Bettes and Sylvia

For the people of New York City

For the hundreds of thousands dead,
whose names we do not know and must say

CONTENTS

The same malignant aspect in republicanism may be traced
in the inequality of fortunes, and the opportunities of fraud,
growing out of a state of war, and in the degeneracy of manners
and of morals engendered by both. No nation could preserve
its freedom in the midst of continual warfare.

—JAMES MADISON

I belong to the generation born with the century, nurtured on
the Emperor's bulletins, having always before its eyes a naked
sword. To us, war seemed the natural state of our country.

—ALFRED DE VIGNY

Sick of living in America
Sick of mass hysteria

—CEREMONY

NEITHER PEACE NOR VICTORY

I
n November 2020, as he deceitfully insisted he had won reelection, Donald Trump gestured at ending the Afghanistan war. After purging his Pentagon of its leadership, he installed, as acting defense secretary, a thematically apt choice.

The new acting secretary was a longtime counterterrorism figure named Chris Miller. A Green Beret colonel before he entered the vast security bureaucracy, Miller personally gave as much to the War on Terror as anyone has. He was among the advance deployment of special operators who arrived in Afghanistan ahead of the October 2001 invasion. His official biography describes "numerous follow-on deployments" to both Afghanistan and Iraq; the precise details are classified. Miller's last-minute elevation to the penultimate position in the chain of command had bypassed the Senate-confirmed deputy defense secretary, and was legally questionable.

Speaking in the Pentagon briefing room for the first time, Miller hailed Trump for having arrived at a "successful and responsible conclusion" to the United States' longest foreign war. He hailed the sacrifices of American troops and left after eight minutes without taking questions.

Trump's primary preoccupation at that moment was not Afghanistan but stealing the presidency. He pursued his task characteristically: through cultivating a mass hysteria and daring the politicians he had bent to his will to challenge him and his movement. No national Republican politician of any stature was willing to tell him to stop his flagrant assault on constitutional governance. So it stood in glaring contrast that several of them, including Senate GOP leader Mitch McConnell, demanded that Trump not go through with the withdrawal. Their Democratic opposition twisted itself in knots to say that while of course they supported a responsible end to the war, Trump was engaged in what Senator Tammy Duckworth, an army veteran who had lost her legs in the Iraq war, called "a reckless, chaotic drawdown."

Amid a war that had lasted an entire generation, everyone played what were by now grimly familiar political roles. Reluctance to end the constellation of post-9/11 military conflicts was bipartisan, broad, and instinctive in Washington. Trump, however obstreperous he was about it, proved no exception. Despite Miller's grandiose rhetoric, the president was not ending the war in Afghanistan at all, but merely cutting the U.S. troop commitment there from five thousand to thirty-five hundred—twenty-five hundred announced, and another thousand added through deceptive, and by now typical, Pentagon accounting—by the time Joe Biden took office. Trump was even undercutting what had been the most valorous act of his disgraceful presidency, an accord with the Taliban that nominally tethered U.S. withdrawal to reciprocal Taliban measures and an inter-Afghan peace process. In Iraq, Trump was removing even fewer forces. Syria went unmentioned. Trump would be the third president to hand the Forever War—a term that was at first derisive but grew more accepted as the point became harder to contest—to his successor.

Throughout his presidency, Trump was often misperceived as being an opponent of the War on Terror. He owed that reputation to his vocal derision of "stupid" Mideast wars. Yet in office he escalated the war dramatically, intensifying aerial bombing campaigns across multiple war zones, particularly in Somalia, where the war had never been fought as intensely as under Trump. One study, in December 2020, found that Trump's accelerated bombing had increased civilian casualties in Afghanistan by 330 percent. Military commanders faced fewer operational restrictions and transparency obligations. In 2019 the president deployed an additional fourteen thousand U.S. troops to the Mideast as part of a pressure campaign against Iran, the War on Terror's white whale, which culminated in the assassination of its senior external security official. Every time Trump proposed withdrawal—even once declaring a still-ongoing war over—he ultimately acquiesced to the objections of the military leadership. Before sensibly suing for peace with the Taliban, he even doubled troop levels in Afghanistan, the Forever War theater he claimed to hate the most.

It was hardly the first time in Trump's career that he convinced people that the truth was the opposite of what the evidence told them. But Trump's durable antiwar persona derived from nothing that he did and only from what he said. For many, the propaganda of "Donald the Dove," as *The New York Times*' Maureen Dowd infamously described him, was convenient. Trump's justifiers, determined to dominate the broad institutional machinery of the state, needed to portray it as bloodthirsty and inept. Their opponents did the rest of the work. Liberals, who tended to identify with that machinery, wanted to view Trump as a deviation from American history, a man in political and perhaps even financial debt to foreign adversaries, someone incapable of acting in the national interest. They used Trump's rejections of the counsel of generals and spymasters to demonstrate their point. Rarely did they pause to consider the merits of continuing wars they had long stopped believing in.

Trump understood something about the War on Terror that they did not. He recognized that the 9/11 era's grotesque subtext—the perception of nonwhites as marauders, even as conquerors, from hostile foreign civilizations—was its engine. As much as Trump shifted his positions on this or that conflict, he never wavered on that crucial insight. Appearing on Howard Stern's radio show for the first anniversary of 9/11, during a period when U.S. foreign policy was the geopolitical equivalent of a psychotic episode, Trump surveyed all the changes to national security and lamented, "I'm not sure things are any tougher."

His problem was that the psychosis he encouraged had revealed not the might of America but its weakness. For those millions of Americans who demanded vengeance for 9/11, and then for the United States' compounded misfortunes in seeking it, the Forever War brought only the pain and humiliation of attaining neither peace nor victory.

The pursuit of vengeance not only created new enemies that America failed to vanquish. It also created more ambitious ones, who had their own ideas about vengeance. Yet it was beyond the limits of respectable discourse to blame the Forever War for giving birth to new generations of forever-enemies. The agony of the war outlasted the enthusiasm of the political, media, cultural, and intellectual elites who had hailed it as the Great War of Our Time, a grand national, even civilizational crusade against . . . something Islamic that hated freedom, or at the very least hated America. In the early years after 9/11, they even treated the open-ended nature of the war as a virtue, a Kennedyesque challenge for a reunited America that was finished with the frivolity of the 1990s, something that could prove America could again accomplish anything, no matter how arduous the struggle. Even after that delusion died in Iraq, the fallback position among the politically powerful was that extrication was more dangerous than quagmire. A circumscribed, managed quagmire could even ultimately comport with America's broader hegemonic position of open-ended foreign deployments pursued in the name of what Washington called the "rules-based international order." Those elites were so implicated in providing neither peace nor victory that it would be easy to discredit them in the eyes of those to whom that was intolerable: the people who had listened to what they said.

Being unable to defeat this something-Islamic was intolerable for a people accustomed to thinking of itself as exceptional, for whom uncontested American supremacy had existed long enough to appear as inevitable as the weather. The painful condition of neither peace nor victory, against an enemy seen as practically subhuman, itself required vengeance. Trump offered himself as its instrument. Declaring his presidential candidacy in his golden tower, he asked, "When was the last time the U.S. won at anything?"

A war that lasted for an entire generation was typically defined in a re-
ductive, misleading fashion. It was not simply something that happened on
the battlefields of Iraq and Afghanistan, or Pakistan, or Yemen, or Somalia, or Libya, or Syria, or Niger. It was something that happened inside the
United States. It was the construction, institutionalization, and maintenance
of surveillance at a scale unimaginable a generation earlier; indefinite detention without charge; remote assassination of foreigners and then of American citizens; law-enforcement infiltration of communities, businesses, and
even houses of worship to generate informants; expansive categories of criminal association, but only for certain people; the treatment of immigration as
a national security threat; a public wealth transfer to the military and associated security services estimated in 2019 to total over $6 trillion; secret
prisons; and torture. The war routinized official euphemisms and outright
government lies about whom it targeted, the scale of its operations, their
second-order impacts, and their prospects for success. It withheld the relevant truths about the war as official secrets. And it encouraged an atmosphere of paranoia that frequently turned conspiratorial.

The effect was to create a patriotic veil of unreality to conceal the
damage done by and to America—particularly the self-inflicted damage.
Long before Trump, the War on Terror revealed how the manipulation of
reality and the normalization of atrocity would proceed. Trump brought
aspects of the war home, but fundamentally the war was *always* home.
For the 9/11 generation, the first generation to be extremely online, the
War on Terror was an early red pill, releasing an omnidirectional, violent
nihilism that viewed itself as the only rational, sophisticated, honorable,
and even civilized option. Its culture was one of manufactured outrage,
self-congratulation, and obedience to authority that convinced itself it was
transgressive. I have to admit that after 9/11 I swallowed that red pill myself. Even after I thought I spat it out over the carnage of Iraq, it took me
years to recognize its lingering effects. In retrospect, any failure—especially
by the war's architects, stewards, and chroniclers—to see that the War on
Terror was seeding the ground for a figure like Trump testifies to the power

of American exceptionalism, which is nothing more than white innocence applied globally.

Occasionally the legal and political structures that, in a mature democracy, were supposed to constrain this apparatus succeeded in rolling back some of its operations. More often they reacted deferentially, leaving the bedrock of the War on Terror intact. As they did, they incrementally hollowed out the institutions all this security machinery was predicated on defending. Trump lay in wait for a brittle America that told itself it was resilient. The same tools that destabilized foreign countries were bound to destabilize America. Trump was the War on Terror's lagging indicator, the promise of what George W. Bush unleashed and what Barack Obama nurtured.

Experiencing neither peace nor victory for such a sustained period was a volatile condition for millions of people. Trump knew how to explain such humiliations: the War on Terror was an enraging story of insufficient brutality wielded by untrustworthy elites. Those elites, he claimed, pretended that America was not at war with Islam, that it was not experiencing a foreign invasion, that it was not at risk, in the final analysis, of being itself lost. If America could not defeat its enemies abroad, there were so many here at home: Muslims, nonwhite immigrants, brown people from what Trump called "shithole" countries, queer and especially trans people, Black people, socialists, liberals, Jews. A war that never defined its enemy became an opportunity for the so-called MAGA coalition of white Americans to merge their grievances in an atmosphere of righteous emergency. That impulse unlocked a panoply of authoritarian possibilities that extended far beyond the War on Terror, from stealing children to inciting a violent mob that attempted to overturn a presidential election. Those options were enabled by how deeply the Forever War had eroded the legal, political, cultural, and economic armor surrounding American democracy. By December 2020, one of the men who could credibly say he had waged the War on Terror at its worst, retired army lieutenant general Mike Flynn, encouraged Trump to suspend the Constitution in order to remain in office.

One of the insignia of that wartime coalition was the racist slander known as birtherism. Birtherism—which held that the first Black president was secretly a Kenyan Muslim noncitizen—was a fortress surrounding white anxiety made of anti-Black racism, Islamophobia, and xenophobia. The mortar of birtherism was the War on Terror, because it cast Obama as an enemy of the United States who had usurped its highest office.

Yet even as he was birtherism's target, Obama perpetuated the War on Terror, as if the politics of one could be separated from the other. He treated the War on Terror like a plane that was unsafe thirty thousand feet above the ground but whose flight could be acceptably steady at ten thousand. Even as he kept the aircraft airborne—and gave it a legacy for liberals to follow—he seemed to recognize its danger. "A perpetual war," Obama observed in May 2013, would "prove self-defeating, and alter our country in troubling ways." A great tragedy of Obama's presidency is that this insight did not guide his actions.

Trump did not hesitate to act on his insights. In the plague year of 2020, he maneuvered the War on Terror onto newer domestic frontiers. He declared followers of popular movements against fascism and for Black liberation to be terrorists. When the military leadership balked at opening fire on Americans, Trump turned to the Justice Department and the quintessential creation of the War on Terror: the Department of Homeland Security. Suddenly, minimally identified government forces, kitted out for war, started conducting widespread surveillance over American cities, shot protesters with "less-lethal" rounds, abducted them off the streets, and, in one instance, executed a man instead of apprehending him. It showed Trump's true intentions toward the War on Terror: not to end it, but to make it an instrument of his will.

The War on Terror was by no means the only factor enabling Trump's rise. But it was a path to power for the others. It revitalized the most barbarous currents in American history, gave them renewed purpose, and set them on the march, an army in search of its general. This book tells the story of that campaign. It is the story of a compounded and often improvised tragedy, rather than an intentional conspiracy, that implicates an entire generation of American leaders through either action or acquiescence. Their central blind spot emerged from the American exceptionalism at the heart of the War on Terror: the belief that the damage they inflicted abroad would not damage their own country. In that they followed a historical pattern. "People are surprised, they become indignant," Aimé Césaire observed in 1950:

> They say: "How strange! But never mind—it's Nazism, it will pass!" And they wait, and they hope; and they hide the truth from themselves, that it is barbarism, but the supreme barbarism, the crowning barbarism that sums up all the daily barbarisms; that it is Nazism, yes, but that before they were its victims, they were its accomplices; that they tolerated that Nazism before it was inflicted on them, that they absolved it, shut their eyes to it, legitimized it, because, until then, it had been applied only to non-European peoples; that they have cultivated that Nazism, that they are responsible for it, and that before engulfing the whole of Western, Christian civilization in its reddened waters, it oozes, seeps, and trickles from every crack.

Trump and MAGA, for now, are out of power. The War on Terror is not. Left alone, it will continue to produce neither peace nor victory; it will remain the soil from which to cultivate more and worse Trumps. Of all the endless costs of terrorism, the most important is the least tallied: what fighting it has cost our democracy. How *like* America it is not to recognize that the true threat was counterterrorism, not terrorism.

Until the entire War on Terror is abolished—not only the foreign military deployments, but the broader entrenched architecture of surveillance, detention, immigration suppression, and the rest—it will propel itself toward greater domestic destabilization. Inertia alone is sufficient to power it. We should not assume the Forever War has reached its final form. If the United States is ever to recover from the destruction it unleashed not only on the world but on itself, and primarily on its most vulnerable, it must first understand the post-9/11 era as nothing other than a reign of terror.

REIGN OF
TERROR

THE WORST TERRORIST
ATTACK IN AMERICAN HISTORY

T he city of God lay deep in the Ozark hills of northeastern Oklahoma, at the end of six miles of dirt road. Young men in thrown-together fatigues guarded the gates to the domed church of Elohim City. The church was the center of community life for the isolated settlement, host to charismatic morning prayers and evening assemblies. It flew Christian banners and Confederate flags. Many of Elohim City's roughly one hundred residents were transients, who drove their mobile homes onto its four hundred acres for as long as they needed refuge from an iniquitous world. Polygamy was encouraged and patriarchy enforced. Nondomestic work for women was forbidden.

"Elohim" is a Hebrew word for God, but those who lived in Elohim City preferred to call God "Yahuah," owing to something a resident once uttered while speaking in tongues. They considered themselves the real Israelites, not those descendants of the devil who called themselves Jews. That was what Christian Identity, the religion practiced at Elohim City, instructed. No one at the compound ate pork, and children at its school learned Hebrew. Knowledge of Hebrew was valuable for demonstrating that the different words for "man" in the Bible proved that Yahuah created races of people, some superior, others inferior. Their faith ordained that the chosen people—descended from the northern European countries that these true Israelites settled—separate themselves in preparation for the reckoning to come. A monstrosity called the Zionist Occupational Government (ZOG), a cabal of Jews, had subverted America, the intended home of the chosen, and empowered their subhuman puppets. A local boy sang visitors a song about murdering Barney the dinosaur. Underneath his costume, the boy explained, Barney was a "nigger."

The patriarch of Elohim City was an elderly Canadian named Robert G. Millar. Millar said that a vision from Yahuah had led him on the path to both America and Christian Identity. A polygamist known to his followers as Grandpa, Millar had founded Elohim City in 1973, and about half its populace at any given time were members of his extended family. "Any equality at all" among races was "against the Bible," Millar explained to a *Dateline NBC* reporter. Yet he refused to label himself a white supremacist: "Let's put, 'We're separatists.'" Asked to account for his racism, Millar replied, "The truth is often offensive." When he died in 2001, the Southern Poverty Law Center ranked Millar among a generation of men "who have led the American radical right for some 30 years."

Christian Identity did not accept the Rapture foretold in Revelation. The Second Coming would instead result from struggle—an armed struggle to racially cleanse the world, probably after an economic collapse that would bring down this mongrel civilization. The heavily armed residents of Elohim City meant to triumph in the rough life to come. Under the tutelage of a German Army veteran named Andreas Strassmeir, they drilled in marksmanship and repurposed old ammunition crates into building materials. That established the community as a safe haven not only for Christian Identity believers but for fellow-traveling neo-Nazis, as well as violent criminals. These included members of a gang called the Aryan Republican Army, which aimed to finance the white revolution by robbing banks across the

Midwest while wearing *Point Break*–inspired masks of ex-presidents. Another was the leader of a white supremacist militia, the Covenant, Sword and Arm of the Lord (CSA), which had forced law enforcement into a three-day standoff in Arkansas in 1985. Two years earlier a CSA member had plotted an attack on the Alfred P. Murrah Federal Building in Oklahoma City.

According to an informant for the Bureau of Alcohol, Tobacco and Firearms, a wiry former soldier, firearms enthusiast, and white revolutionary named Timothy McVeigh was present at Elohim City in July 1994. An infantryman from Buffalo, McVeigh had already begun preparing for the revolution by the time he enlisted in the army in 1988. He called Black soldiers by slurs, perceived their insolence everywhere, and seethed that the army was too politically correct to discipline them. At the same time, McVeigh flagrantly violated army regulations by smuggling at least twenty guns into his Fort Riley barracks. Guns were the nonbelieving McVeigh's religion. He spent his spare time at gun shows, which were not only a means to amass his arsenal but a way to make money. At the gun shows, McVeigh sold copies of a white-supremacist propaganda novel called *The Turner Diaries*, the story of a gun confiscation by the government's Black enforcers and Jewish puppeteers that prompts a white militant vanguard to begin a firestorm to purify America. Service in the initial 1991 ground invasion of Iraq—where he earned a Bronze Star and even a Combat Infantryman Badge—taught McVeigh that the corrupted government would rather use the army to enforce the globalist agenda of the United Nations than to protect America's borders from invasion. While in uniform, McVeigh sent the Ku Klux Klan twenty dollars for a trial membership and a WHITE POWER T-shirt. His army evaluations described him as an "inspiration" to younger soldiers.

McVeigh left the army in 1992, a time when he thought the United States was sending signals of an intensifying persecution of whites. In August the ZOG's ATF and FBI goon squads shot it out at Ruby Ridge, in the northern Idaho mountains, with the white patriot and ex–Green Beret Randy Weaver, leaving his wife and fourteen-year-old son dead, as well as a U.S. marshal. Not long afterward the new president, Bill Clinton, introduced a regime of background checks for gun purchasers and then a ban on semiautomatic rifles and other weapons of the sort McVeigh stockpiled. Barely six months after Ruby Ridge, the FBI and ATF besieged an armed religious compound in Waco, Texas, for fifty-one days before a fire consumed seventy-six Branch Davidians inside. April 19, 1993, became a martyrs' day for those dedicated to resisting ZOG tyranny. McVeigh, working as a security guard in Buffalo, told a colleague that he had driven to Texas to support the doomed Branch Davidians. He was openly talking about avenging them.

Along with his army buddy and lackey Terry Nichols, McVeigh constructed a plan strikingly similar to the CSA's 1983 plot to hit ZOG in its Oklahoma City redoubt. By purchasing massive amounts of ammonium nitrite, McVeigh could construct a forty-eight-hundred-pound bomb. He and Nichols would steal blasting caps from a construction site, rent a Ryder truck, assemble the bomb, and drive it to the Murrah building for detonation. The historian Kathleen Belew, in her book *Bring the War Home*, observed that McVeigh's plan followed "a very specific example of a truck bombing" from *The Turner Diaries*. To prevent any confusion about why the attack was perpetrated, McVeigh chose April 19 as his day of reckoning. With another army friend, Mike Fortier, McVeigh performed reconnaissance on the Murrah building in December 1994. He would later claim that the evening darkness prevented him from seeing that the building housed a day care center on its second floor.

McVeigh didn't plan to die in the bombing. Two weeks before the attack McVeigh placed a phone call to Elohim City. A biography with which he cooperated stated that he was trying to determine if Millar's compound would give him shelter. His other option was another white-supremacist training camp, this one belonging to the National Alliance, the party founded by *Turner Diaries* author William Pierce. He was unable to reach either of them. But McVeigh considered whatever happened to him to be less important than his ability to inspire the revolution that would follow. He left in his car propaganda extolling "the motto of many American militias . . . 'Don't tread on me.'"

It was 9:02 on a clear Tuesday morning when the bomb sheared the façade off the Murrah building. While the blast killed some instantly, many more were crushed and buried alive. Twenty-year-old Daina Bradley was running an errand at the Social Security office when the ground floor caved in. Rubble pinned her arm and her leg as frigid water pooled beneath her. For hours she stared up at a concrete slab whose fall had stopped just short of crushing her skull. Rescue workers who found her had to amputate her leg to extract her before the rubble shifted and killed them all. Bradley's three-year-old daughter, Peachlyn, her four-month-old son, Gabreon, and her forty-four-year-old mother, Cheryl Bradley Hammons, were among the 168 people McVeigh killed. Nineteen of the victims were children. It was, at the time, the worst terrorist attack in American history.

Journalists and their law-enforcement sources immediately knew the culprits of the Murrah bombing: Muslims. Only two years had passed since Ramzi Yousef set off an explosive at the World Trade Center; Oklahoma City must have been a follow-on attack. CNN reported, then retracted, that Middle Easterners were under immediate law-enforcement suspicion. A respectable-sounding conspiracist who saw American Islam through the lens of foreign subversion, Steven Emerson, told CBS that Oklahoma City was "probably considered one of the largest centers of Islamic radical activity outside the Middle East," an assessment never to reappear. Former representative Dave McCurdy, an Oklahoma Democrat who had recently chaired the House intelligence committee, stated that there was "very clear evidence" that "fundamentalist Islamic terrorist groups" were involved.

With culpability established, commentary turned to what action needed to be taken. In the New York tabloid *Newsday*, columnist Jeff Kamen typified the public appetite for a response to jihadists. Foreign students, diplomats, and other "threatening people," he declared, ought to be placed under surveillance, with Navy SEALs and other elite military units dealing with those revealed to be dangerous. "Shoot them now," Kamen wrote, "before they get us." Mike Royko, a titan of Chicago journalism, wrote in the *Tribune* that the country was in denial about the "act of war" launched against it. Treating the bombing as merely a crime would only encourage further attacks. "Because we are so open a society, terrorists can be sent here almost as easily as shipping a package," lamented Royko, who called on the government to "stop admitting people who come from countries that are hostile." Right-wing radio host Cal Thomas agreed that the danger from Muslims proved the larger point that "illegal immigrants are a threat to our democracy."

The presumption of Muslim guilt had consequences. Ibrahim Abdullah Hassan Ahmed, an Oklahoma City man born in Palestine, attempted to fly to Jordan and was questioned by police at his connection in Chicago. When he had to rebook after missing his flight, officials intercepted him in London and sent him back to Oklahoma City. False reports circulated that he had bomb-making equipment in his luggage; the FBI insisted he was never a suspect. Ahmed, the *Los Angeles Times* explained, "had too many similarities to the sort of person the police thought they were seeking." In the wake of Oklahoma City, law enforcement nationwide received 227 reports of harassment against Muslims, *The Christian Science Monitor* reported, ranging from "verbal threats to assaults." Fear gripped Muslim communities far from Oklahoma City. A restaurant owner in Orlando told the paper, "We all phoned each other for support. I'll never forget it."

SEVERAL ELOHIM CITY RESIDENTS, including security chief Andreas Strassmeir, whose card McVeigh carried in his wallet, reportedly decamped from the compound ahead of April 19. Grandpa Millar was in Arkansas to witness the execution of the CSA militiaman who plotted the original attack on Oklahoma City. If they feared arrest, it never came.

The need for a successful prosecution after the Murrah bombing—as well as a strong FBI/ATF desire to avoid another Waco—ultimately drove a narrow investigative focus onto McVeigh and Nichols. An ATF informant, Carol Howe, told a grand jury that Strassmeir discussed taking "direct action" against the government in Oklahoma City. But investigators were unable to substantiate her tip that the compound possessed an illegal M60 machine gun, which was the likeliest way to charge Strassmeir with a crime. McVeigh, to the frustration of his attorneys, insisted that he acted alone, and his plan to decamp to Elohim City was the limit of the community's involvement in the plot. The compound faced little post–Oklahoma City scrutiny beyond the occasional visit from journalists and academics. Whatever his views on the tyranny of ZOG's police, Millar liked to tell reporters about the warm relationship Elohim City had with the local sheriff.

Whether or not anyone at Elohim City had specific foreknowledge of McVeigh's plot—a supposition that remains unsubstantiated twenty-five years later—the compound was part of the broad infrastructure of militant white supremacy in late-twentieth-century America. Belew writes that Oklahoma City was "the culmination of decades of white-power organizing." Along with the CSA's Arkansas base, the Aryan Nations' Idaho headquarters, Jack Oliphant's Hephzibeh Ranch in Arizona, and other white supremacist warrens, Elohim City provided a haven, ideological and spiritual strengthening, connections to people and groups with proven track records of violence, and access to a bounty of weapons. The infrastructure was loose by design, rather than organized into a coherent network. That suited people and groups who preferred living in the rugged country, as far as possible from the reach of the government. It also reflected the influence of Louis Beam.

Beam, an influential KKK grand dragon from Texas, put forward in the 1980s a theory of "leaderless resistance." It envisioned "survival" camps for militants where autonomous patriots could prepare for the coming guerrilla war against a government that had turned hostile to white interests during the 1960s. Its goal was the reconquest of America. Until victory came, these compounds would be microcosms of the "Racial Nation of and by ourselves" they sought to establish. Beam drew on his Vietnam service not only for militancy and authority but to construct what Belew calls a narrative of "stymied grief, constant danger, fixation on weapons and betrayal" by elites whose horrific war had become a "catalyst for American decline." Remaining leaderless was both a tactical necessity and a key component of their political strategy. It would allow for a broad disavowal of any individual act of violence, particularly from their politicians, whose objective was to enter "mainstream 'kosher' associations that are generally seen as harmless." Accordingly, even after McVeigh's conviction, Grandpa Millar "conjecture[d]" to a reporter that the bombing was a government attempt "to frame Christian Identity."

But even if the white supremacists' connection with McVeigh was more ideological than operational, the public discussion of Oklahoma City obscured any association between them. As with Ruby Ridge, the press reported McVeigh's "survivalism" as his most salient feature, and his motivations "antigovernment." Both characterizations made McVeigh's mission seem politically agnostic. You didn't have to be a white supremacist to consider the government tyrannical—you didn't even have to be right wing. A poll taken barely a week after the bombing found that 45 percent of respondents believed the government was a "threat to the constitutional rights enjoyed by the average American." Survivalism sounded defensive in nature. Journalists typically waited until the later paragraphs of their articles to identify McVeigh as a white supremacist, if they did at all. *The Baltimore Sun* asked if the "American love affair with the strong silent type" like the "loner" McVeigh would come to an end. A *Washington Post* profile portrayed the twenty-seven-year-old McVeigh as an "Ordinary Boy" who had "lived the divorce revolution" and turned to guns to fill the void left by his absent mother.

In his interviews with journalists, McVeigh stressed themes that had broad purchase with Americans who might have benefited from white supremacy but did not aver it as a creed. He had acted, he insisted, in the traditions of the Founding Fathers. The guns he'd accrued, as so many Americans had, were his protection against tyranny. America had lost its way in a globalizing world, its government having become alien to the people whose liberty it was supposed to protect. McVeigh, the decorated Gulf War veteran, was disgusted by all the foreign wars his corrupted government was waging. "I don't like going to other nations. I thought the principle was defending yourself," he told reporters Lou Michel and Dan Herbeck. McVeigh's arguments were enough to make him seem almost mainstream. In describing his time in the army, the reporters' biography could hardly ignore

McVeigh's racism, but they explained it away. "McVeigh's enemies weren't blacks, they were the politicians who were pushing more gun laws," they wrote, concluding that McVeigh "was looking for a way to get to patriotism."

There were no calls from newspaper columnists to send elite commandos into places like Elohim City. Shooting suspected white supremacist guerrillas on sight, deporting them, seizing whites from their airplane seats for the misfortune of being the wrong race in the wrong place at the wrong time were unthinkable options. Yet white supremacist terrorism was the oldest, bloodiest, and most resilient terrorism in the history of the United States. Its justifications and its symbolism were rooted in the American national heritage, making its appeal to Americans orders of magnitude larger than Islamic terror could ever claim. Its soldiers called themselves Patriots. Their enemies were America's enemies.

Deemphasizing the role of white supremacy in incidents like Ruby Ridge made it easier for elements of the American right, both fringe and respectable, to interpret and portray them as extreme examples of overreach from a government naturally inclined to trample liberties. They witnessed these sieges and, as McVeigh and his ilk had wanted, imagined themselves to be next to be targeted. In the view of influential conservatives, the government was not acting against fascists stockpiling weapons for the race war but was itself fascist. Six days before Oklahoma City, Wayne LaPierre, of the politically mighty National Rifle Association, cited both Ruby Ridge and Waco as evidence that it was no longer "unthinkable for federal agents wearing Nazi bucket helmets and black stormtrooper uniforms to attack law-abiding citizens." On the NRA's online message boards, internet pioneers swapped conspiracy theories about the coming government disarmament and fantasized about murdering ATF agents. Not long before the bombing, Rush Limbaugh, the most powerful broadcaster on the right in an era before Fox News, told his radio listeners that "the second violent American revolution is just about—I got my fingers about a fourth of an inch apart—is just about that far away." At trial McVeigh's lawyers described him as just the latest conservative to be persecuted by the government. Yes, they acknowledged, he did have "considerable anger about the federal government, but that does not distinguish him from millions of other Americans."

The respectable right expressed outrage at any suggestion that it had anything in common with McVeigh. Claiming so was a cynical, dangerous political gambit by liberals to persecute and muzzle conservatives. Bill Clinton, a centrist whom the right considered a radical, angrily demanded that the "purveyors of paranoia" on the right take responsibility for the consequences their invective could have. But the cautious Clinton spoke against generic "hatred," rather than white supremacy specifically. Limbaugh called the president "irresponsible and vacuous," determined to ensure that the right be "permanently disqualified and silenced" through a campaign of innuendo. Newt Gingrich, the architect of a historic GOP congressional victory based on white backlash to Clinton, denounced as "grotesque and irresponsible" the idea that mainstream conservative rhetoric lent legitimacy to acts of terrorism like McVeigh's.

A political context like that meant there would be no urgency to pass legislation addressing the worst act of terrorism in American history. Although Clinton had promised "certain, swift, and severe" justice for Oklahoma City, no bill was passed until April 1996, largely thanks to the House, led by Gingrich. Congressional hearings on Waco and Ruby Ridge undercut any Republican willingness to give federal authorities more power; four months after Oklahoma City, Randy Weaver and his surviving family won a $3.1 million wrongful-death suit against the federal government. A civil liberties alliance spanning from the ACLU to Larry Pratt, a gun activist who briefly cochaired Pat Buchanan's 1996 presidential campaign, rallied to prevent the law from redefining terrorism to include what one attorney called "so much activity that the section cannot help but be enforced selectively, according to the politics of the day." It was an assertion of bedrock civil-libertarian principle—ideological similarity is not the same thing as operational association—and in 1996 it got an attentive hearing. It helped that one example the ACLU's Gregory Nojeim offered to show the bill's slippery slope to criminalization was the "forcible blocking of an abortion clinic, if that use of force violated any criminal law." Churches lending anti-abortion groups transportation or meeting space could become federal targets. A *Los Angeles Times* poll found that 70 percent of the public feared the new legislation would restrict American freedoms.

By the time of its passage, the bill had changed substantially. Aspects of it that could expand the reach of investigators and prosecutors into the affairs of conservative whites, particularly their financial records and gun modifications, were stripped away. The section that Nojeim warned would broaden the definitions of terrorism was gone. To the consternation of the Justice Department, no expansion of FBI surveillance authority into this domain made it into the final version. That "eviscerated the heart and soul" of the bill, lamented the Michigan Democrat John Conyers.

But what remained in the Antiterrorism and Effective Death Penalty Act was extraordinary. In addition to making the American carceral state more lethal, the bill contained sweeping expansions of government authority to combat terrorism—but only the sort of terrorism that *didn't* involve white supremacists.

Congress used Oklahoma City as an opportunity to give prosecutors greater authority to more easily convict people in the United States of ties to foreign, typically nonwhite terrorist groups, rather than those allied with McVeigh and Millar. A measure known as 2339B, part of an expanding body of law prohibiting "material support" for terrorism, made it a crime to contribute to nonviolent activities and charities of banned foreign terrorist groups. Support for the measure came from the FBI, which had begun investigating American Muslims' donations to jihadist-linked charities after the 1993 World Trade Center bombing. Associations with even nonviolent members of banned foreign terrorist organizations, rather than involvement in actual acts of terrorism, was now sufficient evidence to get someone banned from entering the country. For good measure, a bill ostensibly aimed at responding to Oklahoma City included a congressional finding that Clinton ought to take "all necessary means, including covert action and military force" to destroy "terrorist infrastructure," but only that belonging to "international terrorists," such as "overseas terrorist training facilities and safe havens."

———

THE RESPONSE TO OKLAHOMA City was clarifying. When terrorism was white—when its identity and its purpose claimed the same heritage as a substantial portion of the dominant American racial caste—America sympathized with principled objections against unleashing the coercive, punitive, and violent powers of the state. When terrorism was white, politicians and journalists recognized that such a response consigned their neighbors to an unfair burden of collective suspicion, one from which they might never escape. When terrorism was white, the prospect of criminalizing a large swath of Americans was unthinkable. When terrorism was white, the collective American response was to focus the machinery of its wrath anywhere else, sparing white supremacy the expansive violence America pledged against terrorism that was foreign, Muslim, nonwhite.

Timothy McVeigh was convicted on June 2, 1997, and sentenced to death. He was tried openly, before a jury of his peers, with full access to legal counsel. The warnings he received from law enforcement against self-incrimination ahead of his interviews with federal authorities prompted no outcry about affording legal rights to terrorists. There was no demand for McVeigh to be abused in prison, held incommunicado, or moved to military custody. Putting McVeigh on trial was uncontroversial. No one contended that McVeigh should instead be summarily executed. No one believed that a failure to do so would embolden his fellow white terrorists. White America could recognize the fundamental humanity of the ordinary boy.

Facing execution as the summer of 2001 began, McVeigh selected the William Ernest Henley poem "Invictus" to serve as a declaration of victory. Its final couplet deemed McVeigh the master of his fate, the captain of his soul. He was defiant in the face of an enemy that he had proved was not too mighty to be challenged. Its corruption fed its violence. Its infamous acts would be on display because of what he had done. He wanted white Americans to know that they, like him, could be warriors. McVeigh would not go to death in defeat. He would greet death as a martyr.

CHAPTER ONE

9/11 AND THE SECURITY STATE

2001–2003

Throughout the spring and summer of 2001, the world's most powerful security apparatus collected and issued warnings of what appeared to be a forthcoming attack on the United States, its allies, or its interests. It was more than a threat to America. It was a threat to them.

They were the stewards of American power: the CIA, the National Security Agency (NSA), the uniformed military, the FBI, and all the other intelligence and law-enforcement adjuncts that made the U.S. the dominant global force of the post–Cold War era. Whatever cultural attraction, financial engine, and diplomatic architecture America offered, it was their might that guaranteed America's preeminence. What in turn guaranteed the power of this Security State was its ability to keep Americans safe at home. The Security State had succeeded so thoroughly that America exercised its strength abroad while taking its own domestic safety for granted. America acted. As the global hegemon, it was not *acted upon*. That assumption was part of a civic religion, as old as the country itself, known as American exceptionalism: the prerogative that America, by destiny as much as by right, set terms for the world that it was not itself bound by, a global police-man's doctrine of qualified immunity.

Indications of an emergency accumulated as the summer advanced. "The system was blinking red," the CIA director, George Tenet, would later recall. For more than two years, out of public view, Tenet had consid-ered himself "at war" with the enemy he was tracking, a group called al-Qaeda. By August 6, a briefing prepared for President George W. Bush was specifically titled "Bin Laden Determined to Strike in U.S." The CIA could not provide Bush with a date, time, or location for any potential attack, specificity it considered beyond reasonable expectations for intelligence. The Security State hoped that providing a general strategic warning would be enough to spur Bush into urgency. Yet the president responded to the report by telling his al-Qaeda briefer, Michael Morell, "Okay, Michael, you've covered your ass."

The CIA knew much about Osama bin Laden, an impossibly wealthy Saudi construction scion who had turned religious militant. Bin Laden had declared war on the United States because "for over seven years America has been occupying the lands of Islam in its holiest of places," he explained in his 1998 communiqué. "The Arabian peninsula has never—since God made it flat, created its desert and encircled it with seas—been stormed by any forces like the crusader armies spreading in it like locusts, eating its riches and wiping out its plantations." Since it underwrote the world or-der, America was ultimately responsible for the cheapness of Muslim life worldwide: the Iraqis it starved and bombed; all those tortured and slain by America's allies in Saudi Arabia, Egypt, Jordan, Yemen, Pakistan, and beyond; and even the deaths caused by American rivals or enemies, like Chechens killed by Russians or Bosnian Muslims exterminated by Bos-nian Serbs.

Bin Laden's charisma obscured the conspiratorial nature of his critique. Here was a billionaire who had given up a life of opulence to defend his coreligionists against the Soviet Union in Afghanistan. Miraculously—that is, thanks to the indomitable guerrillas of Afghanistan, and support from

Riyadh, Islamabad, and satanic Washington, something he preferred not to emphasize—bin Laden's side won. Now, as he targeted the only remaining superpower, he told Muslims they could redeem all the humiliation they felt. All it required was violence—violence that wasn't just permissible, but holy. Bin Laden sought to force America to abandon its grip on the Muslim world. Knowing by now how superpowers work, all he needed was to provoke it into unsustainable military campaigns.

If Tenet, a holdover from Bill Clinton's presidency, thought he was waging a war on al-Qaeda, the summer's warnings demonstrated that he was losing. His CIA, the centrifugal force uniting the nation's sixteen intelligence agencies, had failed to notify the FBI and the State Department that it had extensively monitored the travels of Khalid al-Mihdhar and Nawaf al-Hazmi, future 9/11 hijackers who entered the United States legally. FBI officials made their own mistakes, including not knowing how to procure a surveillance warrant on an al-Qaeda target. Some of their inhibitions had the force of law, such as Clinton attorney general Janet Reno's 1994 "wall" edict preventing the bureau from sharing its intelligence information with CIA agents responsible for building criminal cases. The National Security Agency, the brightest star in a global Anglosphere surveillance constellation, did not translate an intercept that referenced 9/11 as the date for the attack. Tenet and White House counterterrorism chief Richard Clarke later traded accusations of negligence over al-Qaeda, responsibility for which Michael Scheuer, the founder of the CIA's Usama bin Laden Unit, ascribed to both of them. After past al-Qaeda attacks, including the horrific 1998 bombings of U.S. embassies in Kenya and Tanzania that killed 224 people, the military leadership assented to missile strikes on al-Qaeda targets in Afghanistan and Sudan. There was little appetite for anything more from the generals and admirals who had grander visions of what warfare in an age of U.S. unipolarity should be.

While the CIA desk that Scheuer founded studied al-Qaeda's motivations and justifications, as did several counterterrorism agents in the FBI, few within the higher echelons of the security services were interested in understanding them. Al-Qaeda's message was to them an indistinguishable blur justifying violence through inscrutable interpretations of Islam, a religion that was primarily familiar to most white Americans as a frightening accelerator of Black resistance, thanks to demonized figures like Malcolm X. None of that was as relevant to the Security State as the sheer fact that bin Laden had declared war. All hegemonies throughout human history have become the objects of violent resistance from those who consider themselves to be unjustly dominated. But because the United States believed itself to be exceptional, it was poorly equipped to understand that the sort of geopolitical, economic, and cultural impact it has on the world would at some point provoke a violent response. Such recognition was too close, for elite comfort, to contending the entirely separate proposition that America *deserved* such an attack. But exceptionalism equipped the nation very well to turn its trauma outward onto the world.

That trauma was real. Live news footage, soon to run on an endless loop, showed two passenger jets piercing the Twin Towers like missiles. Then it televised police officers and firefighters rushing to their deaths in the hopes of saving whomever they could. It showed terrified office workers jumping to their deaths before an icon of cosmopolitan America fell forever. For days afterward New York's skyline was defined by the plume of smoke that replaced the World Trade Center. That inescapable smoke, lingering over the city, smelled nauseatingly sweet, creating the awful recollection that it emerged from the incineration of 2,606 people. Neither the New Yorkers who died agonizing deaths, nor those left behind, nor those persecuted in what was to follow were meaningfully complicit in policies bin Laden expressly attributed to them.

Whatever historical forces led to 9/11, it was an act of mass murder, geopolitical in effect, national in scope, and deeply local in impact. New Yorkers found themselves trapped in a defining experience. There were desperate rushes to post pictures of missing loved ones on lampposts and storefronts by votive candlelight. Police cordons at Canal Street, Houston Street, and Fourteenth Street kept Manhattanites separated from downtown and subjected to spot searches. Viewing the wreckage overwhelming the Financial District, Donald Trump, a real estate developer and New York fixture, called in to a local television show to boast, inaccurately, that his nearby property at 40 Wall Street was now the tallest building in Manhattan. He marveled at all the "easily recognizable" firms "wiped out" by the destruction, adding, "and many of the people are gone with them."

Despite the snap judgment six years earlier that jihadists had bombed Oklahoma City, September 11 came as a horrifying dislocation. "Americans are asking, 'Why do they hate us?'" Bush told legislators nine days after the attack, answering, "They hate our freedoms—our freedoms of religion, our freedoms of speech, our freedoms to vote, and assemble, and disagree with each other." Senator Zell Miller, a Georgia Democrat, articulated the subtext. "I say bomb the hell out of them. If there is collateral damage, so be it. They certainly found our American citizens to be expendable." The ignorant, solipsistic, and ahistorical explanation for the attack that American political and cultural leaders provided spoke to a desire to proclaim the country's innocence ahead of the vengeance to come. Neil Young, who once wrote "Cortez the Killer," contemplated the passenger resistance aboard United Airlines Flight 93 and wrote "Let's Roll."

A traumatized public united behind Bush, granting him approval ratings in the 90s. His advisers moved rapidly to cement his image as a "war president," someone whom it could be politically disastrous to question. If there was going to be a public reckoning over the failures preceding 9/11, its target would not be Bush but the security institutions that had been warning him of an attack. While the Security State typically aligned with the right, now the right presented it with a tacit threat. "The failures in the intelligence are so widespread, so deep, that we owe the American people a searching job," said Bush's ally Richard Shelby, the GOP chairman of the Senate intelligence committee. What Tenet had considered to be three years of war against al-Qaeda was now dismissed by political elites as a failed "law-enforcement" approach to terror. At the same time, Bush was offering the Security State more power than ever before. They were the means through which America would seek revenge. The Security State did not need to be coerced into the War on Terror. It had much to gain from aligning with Bush, and much to lose from rejecting him.

On 9/11, an eighteen-year-old community college student watched anguished NSA analysts evacuate their black-glass headquarters at Fort Meade. "Think of the guilt they were feeling," noted Edward Snowden, whose patriotism was so offended that, unlike most of his generation, he quickly enlisted. The same American exceptionalism fueling the Security State ensured that the response to 9/11 would be *some kind* of war. As the instrument of that war, the Security State would always be implicated in its operations—its successes, its failures, its morality. Often that implication was enough for the Security State to identify with and take ownership of the war.

Still, the war posed an inescapable danger for the Security State. Any failure would be most visibly on its shoulders, and interpreted as the Security State not doing enough—certainly not doing what had been necessary. In this crucial moment, and because it saw itself as the ballast in American geostrategy, it proved that it would present no bulwark against the violent delusions of elected officials. Instead, with energy if not enthusiasm, it built, maintained, and justified the machinery that inflicted those delusions on the world. Some, in keeping with the rhetoric of the 9/11 era, considered it "the great war of our time," as Morell, soon to become a senior CIA leader, titled his post-9/11 memoir. For the Security State, it was a mission of redemption.

THE CULTURE OF 9/11 ECHOED the jihadism it sought to destroy: brutal, messianic, aggrieved, censorious, and eschatological. Conservatives had long used New York City as a synecdoche for the cosmopolitan decadence they saw corrupting America. But now that New York could serve as a rallying cry for war, it was a city of martyrs. On "the Pile," as the ruins of the World Trade Center became known, Bush stood beside rescue workers and shouted through a bullhorn, "The people who knocked down these buildings will hear us all soon." The response was not only political. Americans drove hundreds of miles to Manhattan to stand in solidarity with New Yorkers, donating whatever skills they had to an impromptu rescue effort. Their embrace contrasted conspicuously with how Bush treated New Yorkers' basic material needs. The fires at Ground Zero burned for one hundred days, filling the air over lower Manhattan and beyond with carcinogenic toxins for locals, and particularly firefighters, to inhale. Christine Todd Whitman, the former New Jersey governor who ran Bush's Environmental Protection Agency, blithely assured residents and rescue workers that "air samples we have taken at all levels . . . cause us no concern." The residential deep cleaning that was recommended to mitigate the risk by health experts was left by the government to be performed by landlords, who did the sort of job familiar to generations of local renters. New Yorkers mattered less than did enlisting their suffering for a war that possessed an ominous spiritual component. *The Wall Street Journal* columnist Peggy Noonan marveled at "God Bless America" sung on Park Avenue and concluded, "God is back. He's bursting out all over." Subway trains put on American flag decals that would remain twenty years later. The flag was now a shroud.

It also became a border, segregating those who were authentically American from those who were not. A thirty-three-year-old Palestinian-born woman raised in Chicago, Lina Elayyan, told reporter Tram Nguyen that people who wore hijab, like her mother, felt as if "they had a bullseye on their forehead." Hate crimes against Muslims—or those, like Sikhs, perceived to be Muslims by whites uninterested in distinctions—skyrocketed from 28 incidents in 2000 to 481 in the final months of 2001. A generation of Arab and Desi children were called "Osama" by white classmates. With racism came conspiracy. False rumors spread that Jews who worked in the World Trade Center warned one another to stay home on 9/11. A durable conspiracy theory called 9/11 trutherism, which took root on both the far left and the far right, held that the towers were destroyed by a treasonous globalist government that sought to gin up an imperial war. "Larry

Silverstein, the owner of the WTC complex, admitted . . . that he and the NYFD decided to 'pull' WTC 7," wrote a rising conspiracist named Alex Jones, who twisted Silverstein's words. More respectable versions of the post-9/11 fury were no less vicious. Commentators, and hardly only conservative ones, pathologized Arabs and Muslims, whose critiques of America were proof of *their* conspiratorial thinking. Within days of 9/11, the right-wing radio host Dennis Prager told the Fox News host Bill O'Reilly, "It is very sad to say, but a significant percentage of the Muslim world hates us." Before September ended, O'Reilly urged, "I think we should put troops on the border right now." Enemies were everywhere.

A Palestinian man named Adham Amin Hassoun worked at a Miami technology company. Born in Lebanon, Hassoun had lived through the horror of the Lebanese civil war. A youth spent surviving bombings, beatings, and even kidnappings taught him both the fragility of civilization and the resilience of humanity. Hassoun was active in his mosque, quick to open his wallet to Muslim refugee charities, and he found inspiration in the solidaristic community aid efforts after Hurricane Andrew demolished much of South Florida in 1992. "All that bullshit I used to hear" in the Middle East about the perfidy of Americans lay in ruins, he recalled, since "these people were like us." After 9/11 Hassoun knew that there would be a backlash against Muslims—the lessons Lebanon taught were indelible—but he couldn't accept the enormity of what was coming. "I got phone calls from overseas, 'Leave the country.' All the time I would say, 'No, no, no, they're wiser, it's not like with the Japanese,'" Hassoun recalled.

For entire months afterward, when cable news wasn't rebroadcasting footage of the towers collapsing or the burnt facade of the Pentagon, it documented a cascade of disasters following 9/11. Powderized anthrax spores were mailed to the U.S. Capitol, and around the country, bearing the message *You cannot stop us*; the FBI never did. In December, a college student, Monique Danison, noticed that a fellow passenger aboard an American Airlines flight from Paris to Miami attempted to ignite a fuse in his shoe, but the passengers and crew restrained him. Reports about the fear gripping American Muslims, like Elayyan and her mother, received less emphasis and made little impact on the direction of the country. Particularly in New York, people retreated indoors and watched the unfolding violence on TV in a kind of catatonia. It augured a phenomenon that would last for a generation. The overwhelming majority of Americans—the ones who did not serve in the military or the security services; the ones who were not pursued by the security services—experienced the 9/11 era as a media event. Those Americans could disengage from it when it grew unbearable.

An America in a fugue state went looking for heroes. *Vanity Fair* dispatched Annie Leibovitz to photograph Bush's war cabinet. New York's reactionary mayor, Rudy Giuliani, not three years removed from the police slaying of Amadou Diallo, was apotheosized on the cover of Tina Brown's latest venture, *Talk* magazine, as THE MAYOR OF AMERICA. Giuliani had catastrophically placed his command center in the World Trade Center, the only place in New York known to have been a terrorist target. He echoed Whitman in insisting that the air was safe to breathe—elbowing federal agencies out of the way to get workers back on the job, regardless of the health risks—and passed through Ground Zero with his face protected by what *Village Voice* journalist Wayne Barrett recalled as no more than "a dust mask on his mouth." Brown was hardly the only media figure to wash Giuliani's brutal mayoralty in the blood of 9/11. Giuliani had always been a media creation, propelled by journalists who might have found him incorrigible but generally treated him as a necessity to control an out-of-control city—something that, in practice, meant repressing Black, brown, and poor New Yorkers. In short order the Fox network began airing a smash hit TV show about a counterterrorist who each season combated another imminent apocalyptic attack by torturing its perpetrators. Jack Bauer's more resilient enemies on *24* were the bureaucrats, lawyers, and politicians attempting to prevent him from saving America. Supreme Court Justice Antonin Scalia, the right's guiding legal light, used the show to champion impunity for torture. "Jack Bauer saved Los Angeles," Scalia told an Ottawa legal conference. "Are you going to convict Jack Bauer?"

Never had a people thrust into an avowedly epochal conflict been asked to do less in response to it. The NFL paused its week-two games the Sunday after 9/11, then resumed. Bush urged people to go shopping as a way to stimulate a wartime economy. Vice President Dick Cheney invoked the "wrath" of the United States emerging and, simultaneously, hoped Americans would not "let what's happened here in any way throw off their normal level of economic activity." It was a decisive message that the wealthy would not have to make any sacrifices—Bush pressed on with cutting their taxes in wartime—while the working class would, as ever, be a different story. Manhattan plastic surgeons marveled that rich New Yorkers viewed a tummy tuck as therapy for 9/11-induced stress. One cosmetic surgery consultant explained, "Some of them are telling me, 'I may not have a face-lift this year, but whether there is a bomb or not, I'm going to be a blonde. And I'm not going to give up my Botox.'" Wall Street made sure to hang a giant flag outside the New York Stock Exchange.

The flag was an intellectual border as well, and it would be policed.

Within days of the attacks Susan Sontag, a titan of American literature, wrote in *The New Yorker* that bin Laden had shown that America's global domination sowed the seeds of atrocities like 9/11. She warned that the country was choosing martyrdom over understanding the bitter lesson of the attack. "Where is the acknowledgment that this was not a 'cowardly' attack on 'civilization' or 'liberty' or 'humanity' or 'the free world' but an attack on the world's self-proclaimed superpower, undertaken as a consequence of specific American alliances and actions? How many citizens are aware of the ongoing American bombing of Iraq?" In three paragraphs Sontag summarized the emerging "Soviet Party Congress" mode of American politics that would shape a generation: a faith in the righteousness of violence and a deliberate ignorance of both its origins and its effects.

The vilification Sontag reaped lasted until her death in 2004. Joan Didion recalled reading three separate denunciations of Sontag on a single page of the neoconservative *Weekly Standard.* Eminent conservative pundit Charles Krauthammer devoted a *Washington Post* column to Sontag's "moral obtuseness." The neoliberal *New Republic,* which saw its role as policing a left it considered indecent and unreliably American, sneered at Sontag's "self-flagellation." Sontag was correct that 9/11 was about American power, conceded the magazine's Lawrence F. Kaplan. But rather than dismantling it, the time had come to "wield it effectively in the coming struggle." Rejecting Sontag ensured that no one could respectably argue that stopping the next 9/11 required relinquishing American hegemony. Anything resembling that suggestion would be considered not only anti-American but morally deficient. "In the wake of a massacre that killed more than 5,000 innocent Americans in a single day," Krauthammer sniffed, "one might expect moral clarity."

That funneled American responses to 9/11 down a bellicose and censorious path. The country star Toby Keith released an anthem heralding the epic ass-kicking coming "Courtesy of the Red, White and Blue." It captured the national mood. People in uniform, from the military to police to firefighters, were valorized to the point of civic worship, an impulse most conspicuous in those whose lives intersected with such people rarely. To criticize the national mobilization was to disrespect the troops, to disrespect the 9/11 dead. The Strokes, on the cusp of contending for the title of the city's dominant rock band, pulled their September debut album to remove a song whose chorus went "New York City cops, but they ain't too smart." Being Muslim in public was treated as a disreputable political act. Harvard's 2002 valedictorian, Zayed M. Yasin, was compelled to change the title of a speech about justice from "American Jihad" to "Of Faith and Citizenship"; students protested Yasin anyway. In the months after 9/11, Didion, taking the banner from the canceled Sontag, wrote that "inquiry into the nature of the enemy we faced . . . was to be interpreted as sympathy for that enemy. . . . Pathetic fallacy was everywhere."

One such fallacy concerned the Qatar-based Arabic-language satellite news channel Al Jazeera. In the months following 9/11, al-Qaeda issued its communiques through the channel. Osama bin Laden even granted its Taysir Allouni an interview in October 2001. For years afterward, American political and media classes treated Al Jazeera, a news organization, as little more than al-Qaeda's amplifier, providing critical aid to an enemy. That meant treating Al Jazeera not primarily as a forum where the War on Terror was treated more critically than most, but as a combatant. When the U.S. invaded Afghanistan in November, it bombed Al Jazeera's bureau in Kabul and said it had indications that the building was "a known al-Qaeda facility." The next month, Pentagon communications chief Victoria Clarke claimed that the U.S. did not have indications that the channel operated out of the building, though Al Jazeera had said it provided the Americans with their location.

During the apogee of American geopolitical supremacy in the 1990s, national politics had devolved into a culture war. Now elites, needing to make 9/11 meaningful, treated the trauma as a path to a longed-for national unity. Commentators spoke of a frivolous "holiday from history" coming to a close, as if the country were a young man recognizing the need to put aside childish things. "One good thing could come from this horror," wrote Roger Rosenblatt in *Time*, "it could spell the end of the age of irony." Now it would be an age of iron.

It was in this context—outwardly receiving deference from a frightened public; threatened with scapegoating for 9/11 by fearful politicians; expected to act as an instrument of both vengeance and deterrence—that the Security State constructed what became known as the War on Terror. Its name reflected what both Sontag and Didion had diagnosed: exceptionalist euphemism that masked a boundless, direful ambition.

A BASIC DECISION DOOMING the war from its inception was the result of deliberate indecision. It concerned the war's most fundamental question. Who was the enemy?

On the rainy Friday after 9/11, Bush returned to Washington after his bullhorn speech and put the war in metaphysical terms. "Our responsibility to history is already clear," he declared, "to answer these attacks and rid the world of evil." As Bush spoke, Congress prepared to vote on a fateful document framing the war expansively. Prepared by White House attorney Timothy Flanigan and Justice Department attorney John Yoo, the Authorization for Use of Military Force named no specific enemy, and declared that such identification was a presidential prerogative. The document granted the president the power to direct "all necessary and appropriate force" against "nations, organizations or persons he determines planned, authorized, committed or aided the terrorist attacks," or harbored such participants, "in order to prevent any future acts of international terrorism against the United States." These grants of authority to the president for his exclusive interpretation were unlimited by space or time.

California Democrat Barbara Lee, who called the AUMF a blank check, begged her colleagues to "think through the implications of [their] actions today so that this does not spiral out of control." She was the only legislator to vote against it. Michigan Democrat Carl Levin even claimed the AUMF was "not a broad authorization for the use of military force against any nation, organization, or person who were not involved in the September 11 terrorist attacks." But Yoo vindicated Lee. Precision was not something temporarily lost in the wake of the attacks but was a fundamental obstacle to the emerging enterprise. "[T]his war was so different, you can't predict what might come up," said Yoo. The priority was to give—or as Yoo saw it, preserve—maximum flexibility to the president to wage the war. On September 25 he wrote a memo stating that the AUMF ensured presidential discretion for military force "preemptively" against undefined terrorist organizations or sponsor states, "whether or not they can be linked to the specific terrorist incidents of September 11." Once granted, the president's "broad constitutional power" gave him the right to "take whatever actions he deems appropriate to pre-empt or respond to terrorist threats from new quarters."

The maximal flexibility Yoo etched into law, combined with Bush's increasingly messianic depiction of the coming war, meant that the enemy was never going to be just the specific terrorist network responsible for the 9/11 attacks. At the National Cathedral, Bush spoke of "the enemies of human freedom" attacking America. To restrict the fight against terrorism to al-Qaeda risked exposing America to those who were similarly motivated. And since, as Sontag learned, America was unwilling to view al-Qaeda as having specific political grievances against it, what remained was some vague sense of religious motivation: people who *believed* as al-Qaeda believed. All Americans knew was that al-Qaeda claimed to act on behalf of Islam. The immediate response to Oklahoma City presaged how thoroughly white Americans would accept that.

But *which* Muslims did they think were culpable? Were Israel's Palestinian and Lebanese enemies now America's, as Israel quickly contended? What about Iran, for twenty years an American adversary—and a sponsor of terrorist attacks, no less—but whose Islamist ideology was vastly different from al-Qaeda's? Bush only complicated matters. A deeply religious Christian, he initially insisted that the enemy was not Islam, adding that women like Lina Elayyan's hijabi mother "must not be intimidated in America." He undermined that message days later by calling the emerging conflict "a crusade," invoking a totemic religious war. Bush was criticized for it and didn't repeat it—it played into bin Laden's "Crusader–Zionist alliance" propaganda—though many on the religious right viewed it as a forbidden truth. The result was a vague definition of an enemy that consisted of thousands of Muslims, perhaps millions, but not *all* Muslims—though definitely, exclusively, Muslims.

From that deliberate imprecision came the name of the coalescing enterprise: the Global War on Terror(ism). The name reflected a social compromise. It elided implicating Islam and declared itself formally ecumenical, as if what it considered at issue was a form of asymmetrical political violence. Such a euphemism could simultaneously offend nativists (as a craven, dangerous unwillingness to blame Islam) and leftists (as a capitalist empire concealing its violence and plunder). Distrusting the name "War on Terror" would easily translate to distrusting those who wielded it. Elites simply adopted the term and set aside whatever discomfort they had with its vulgar patriotism. Yet whatever Bush claimed about America not being at war with Islam, the War on Terror's enemies would exclusively be Muslim. Any visitor to Grandpa Millar's Elohim City, or any other white-terror sanctuary across America, seeking to take up McVeigh's banner could sleep easy. Years later, after the consequences became clear, a knowledgeable FBI retiree described white supremacist terror becoming "the lowest priority" for bureau counterterrorism.

Having abandoned the concept of a war against a specific terrorist organization, Americans would never be able to agree on when it could be won. If there was a moment the war was conceptually doomed, it was this. Opposing factions within American politics, as well as within the Security State, would never be willing to accept a rival's definition. That would prevent the war from coming to an agreed-upon end. It would place an enormous burden on the military, especially, yet there is no record of any general or admiral significantly dissenting from this conceptual definition of the war.

There were fateful implications for law enforcement as well. The Justice Department, the FBI, and the immigration services established patterns that would last for the next two decades. They treated Muslim communities within a framework of guilt by association, on the supposition that *someone* must know something about the next attack. They came to treat immigration not as a process for becoming American but as a vehicle for terrorism. The fact that the hijackers had entered the country legally became a scandal, regardless of what implications that would have for an open society waging what Bush was describing as a war for the survival of freedom. Those implications—that an open society was a threatened society—suited many, such as Attorney General John Ashcroft and his immigration adviser Kris Kobach. "Our enemy's platoons infiltrate our borders, quietly blending in with visiting tourists, students and workers,"

Ashcroft pronounced the following spring when he unveiled what was functionally a foreign-Muslim database called NSEERS, a registry of non-citizen entrants from twenty-four substantially Muslim countries and, for window dressing, North Korea. The database would eventually contain information on eighty-four thousand people, resulting in deportation proceedings for fourteen thousand Arabs and Muslims who had voluntarily registered.

Commentary during the first months of the war tended to treat federal law enforcement as an alternative to the military, rather than a domestic supplement, and a "law enforcement paradigm" as the folly that led to the attack. But there was nothing soft about what the Justice Department and the FBI did to Muslim and immigrant communities across the United States. In the eleven months after 9/11, what became known as the FBI's PENTTBOM investigation held 762 people on immigration charges, ostensibly to keep them in the country on suspicion of connection to the attacks. The average length of time it took the FBI to clear them was eighty days. At the federal Metropolitan Detention Center in Brooklyn's Sunset Park, 184 people were held in the most restrictive conditions available. That included cells equipped with what a Justice Department investigation called a "four-man-hold restraint policy, hand-held cameras recording detainee movements, cameras in each cell to monitor detainees, and physical security enhancements." A measure called the material-witness statute was originally created to stop, in extraordinary circumstances, criminal witnesses from fleeing the country. During the weeks after 9/11, the Justice Department used it as one of several roundup tools. It remains unknown, nearly twenty years later, exactly how many people were subject to the roundups; one estimate pegs the number at ten thousand. A San Antonio radiologist from Saudi Arabia, al-Badr al-Hazmi, emerged from thirteen days in material-witness detention to ask a reporter, "Who is this Kafka that people keep mentioning?"

Immigration was the responsibility of the Justice Department at the time. Among migrant communities, the Immigration and Naturalization

Service was infamous even before 9/11. But after 9/11 the roundups were too much for its director, James Ziglar, who rebuked Ashcroft's chief of staff: "I know you're not a lawyer, but we do have this thing called the Constitution." He lost that battle. Soon immigration would formally leave the Justice Department's jurisdiction to become a bureaucratic subcategory of something called *homeland security*.

The result was the erosion, for specific and vulnerable minorities, of the constitutional right of association. For American Muslims, citizens as much as noncitizens, the thinnest of suspicions endangered entire communities. Northern Virginia's prosperous Muslims, proximate to the FBI's powerful Washington field office, garnered suspicion after it was discovered that two hijackers visited the Dar al-Hijrah mosque in Falls Church. Its thirty-year-old preacher condemned 9/11 as "heinous" and conceded that "every nation on the face of the earth has a right to defend itself" even as he condemned the emerging Afghanistan war. The imam did have a permissive attitude toward jihad, including against Russia in Chechnya, but not against America: "We came here to build, not destroy," he explained. But after the FBI launched Operation Green Quest, an aggressive raiding campaign in March 2002 against Muslim charities and businesses, the imam, Anwar al-Awlaki, warned that Islam was in danger of being outlawed. The journalist Jeremy Scahill later discovered evidence that the FBI had attempted to blackmail Awlaki into turning informant. The cleric opted instead to flee to Yemen, where he was part of an influential extended family, and began preaching that an American Muslim identity was untenable: "This is not now a war on terrorism . . . it is a war against Muslims and Islam."

Congress granted the FBI sweeping authorities less than two months after the attacks. It expanded the penalties on material support for terrorism charges, which had been pioneered in the 1990s, and expanded the criminalization of charitable and nonprofit organizations. The chairman of the House Financial Services Committee called it "the most far-reaching anti–money laundering legislation in two decades." To uncover the hidden connections to jihadist organizations—in practice, usually connections to

banned charities rather than terror groups, a distinction that had been collapsing after Oklahoma City—it vastly expanded the FBI's warrantless
access to so-called "business records": financial, telecommunications, and
other highly revealing documents about an individual created and held by
a service provider. Another ominous provision aided the immigrant roundups by allowing the FBI to detain noncitizens for a week without charge;
nondeportable noncitizens, such as stateless people, could be held indefinitely. Yet another blurred the line between intelligence and law enforcement by permitting the FBI to obtain foreign-intelligence warrants from a
secret court on a lower standard of evidence than probable cause, as long as
generating intelligence was merely a "significant" purpose of an investigation, rather than its primary purpose. Senator Russ Feingold of Wisconsin
warned that the FBI would now use the Foreign Intelligence Surveillance
Act "as much as it can," circumventing the Fourth Amendment's protections against unreasonable searches and seizures. On October 25 he was the
only senator to vote against the bill, known as the PATRIOT Act.

After 9/11 the criminalization of association, through the PATRIOT
Act and other means, had a life-changing effect on Adham Hassoun.

Hassoun, a refugee and a war survivor, had donated throughout the
1990s to Muslim refugee charities, including an al-Qaeda-proximate one
called the Global Relief Foundation. Hassoun insisted that he had no idea
that it had terrorist connections; when charities came to the Miami mosque
he attended, he didn't ask questions. The same was true of a convert from
Chicago who attended the mosque, Jose Padilla. Padilla seemed as if he
couldn't quite get his life together, so another congregant who had moved
to Egypt, Mohamed Youssef, offered him a new life there. Hassoun encouraged Padilla to take Youssef up on it. Over the two years that followed,
Hassoun received about four calls from a grateful Padilla. He thought little
of it until June 2002, when Bush declared Padilla, an American citizen
seized as a material witness, to be an enemy combatant, and locked him up
in a military prison with no rights.

On June 12, police and FBI agents approached Hassoun's car. He remembered them coming toward him in plainclothes and wielding pistols. "I'm from Lebanon, these people are like *Toy Story* to me," he said. They informed him that he was being detained on an immigration violation, even after he produced his work permit, rather than charged with a crime. They took him to a city jail and asked why he hadn't told them about Padilla. Hassoun replied that he had nothing to tell. For the next two years he would be held in Miami's Krome detention center, an immigration lockup. "It was the first time in my life I've been handcuffed. Only in the land of the free and the home of the brave," Hassoun remembered.

Over the course of several jailhouse interrogations, it didn't appear to Hassoun that the FBI was attempting to unravel the mystery of Jose Padilla's alleged plot to detonate a radiological weapon. Instead, they were waiting for him to crack and turn informant. Hassoun was indignant. "They would say I could get out, 'We can help you if you help us, we can talk to immigration,'" he recalled. "The way I'm living, my kids were living, they thought I would be extremely desperate, look like a weakling, and cooperate fully, kiss their ass. They were wrong." Several of Hassoun's colleagues from MarCom Technologies wrote to immigration vouching for him. One of them, Valdis Ozols, wrote a lengthy October 2002 statement stating how on 9/11, "I saw a man in sorrow because of the pain his adopted country was experiencing. Never once did I see anything that would convince me he was an extremist." Ozols concluded: "Our reactions to Adham should not be based on the fears and anger arising from the events of September 11, but should be based on the principles that have been a part of our country since July 4, 1776."

Not everyone was as unwilling as Hassoun to inform on their communities. Craig Monteilh, a felon convicted of robbing cocaine dealers, sued his FBI handlers for manipulating him into spying on the Islamic Center of Irvine, California, where he would encourage co-worshippers to visit jihadist websites. By one accounting, such FBI tactics in the course of a decade resulted in a network of fifteen thousand informants. Some operated in mosques, demonstrating the conditional nature of First Amendment protections for Muslims after 9/11.

Untangling webs of association was laborious work for the FBI. Feingold warned that the PATRIOT Act would incentivize the bureau to use foreign-intelligence warrants to make the task easier. But it turned out freedom of association was at greater risk from a different agency. The National Security Agency had secretly built a program to uncover social connections at unfathomable scale.

The day after Yoo issued his memorandum, the NSA's director, air force lieutenant general Michael Hayden, decided that every phone call from Afghanistan to the United States was interceptable. The logic was that any such conversation could theoretically contain evidence of a terrorist connection. It ignored the reality of commonplace international communications, as between relatives; or aid workers and journalists contacting their home offices. In fact, all such phone calls involving people on U.S. soil, citizens or not, were constitutionally protected from interception absent specific suspicion of a crime. Tenet told Bush and Cheney that Hayden would go to prison for what he had done. Cheney reportedly promised to post bail.

In his memoir, *Playing to the Edge,* Hayden suggests that he owed his job to a stint in the White House alongside Tenet's deputy. Now, he was the NSA's director at perhaps the most important moment in its history. On authorization from Cheney, and armed with a legal memo from Cheney's aide David Addington—with another from Yoo soon to follow—Hayden enlisted the major telecommunications companies and internet service providers to help the NSA collect Americans' international communications data, from phone records to email and browser history, as well as domestic call records, in bulk. Doing so violated the Foreign Intelligence Surveillance Act—a reformist 1978 law established to be the "exclusive means" for conducting foreign-intelligence interception within the United States—thereby rendering quaint Feingold's fear that the FBI would *overuse* FISA. The program Hayden activated on October 6, STELLARWIND, was a secret for another four months even from the chief justice of the secret FISA Court. The other members of the court, save his successor as chief, would not learn about the existence of STELLARWIND until they read about it in *The New York Times* four years later.

Emerging technology could not have been more opportune for a panopticon. The turn of the twenty-first century inaugurated a seismic economic phenomenon that the Harvard Business School professor emerita Shoshana Zuboff has termed "surveillance capitalism." Rising tech giants raced to commodify the digital traces of everyone's lives on the internet, recognizing that ever more sophisticated methods of sifting through enormous data sets would reveal patterns useful for tracking purchasing and other behavioral habits. Doing that required the companies to incentivize people into generating ever more data on their platforms. A volume the size of human history's records until 2003 was now generated every two days, according to Google's Eric Schmidt. Sifting through it all and finding patterns—including those that predicted future behavior—was an ambitious task. In 2004, the CIA's investment arm staked $2 million to a company entering the new field of data-mining, with the Tolkien-inspired name Palantir.

The digitization of everything was a gift to the NSA. Once the glut of metadata—records generated by the websites someone visited, emails received, and so forth—streamed into Fort Meade's servers, it entered a tool called MAINWAY, which could reveal an astronomical number of connections between people. Its sophistication increased with the volume of its input, until it could effectively operate retroactively, revealing patterns of communications going back years. Such connections had life-and-death implications. Hayden later observed, "We kill people based on metadata."

THE NSA HAS A GREAT DEAL invested in its image of itself as a law-abiding foreign-intelligence agency. Yet there could be no reconciling STELLARWIND with either FISA or the Constitution. It was committing the first mathematically exponential violation of constitutional rights in American history, to say nothing of claiming for itself the right to steal the records of untold hundreds of millions of foreigners' communications. However much control over the program rested within Cheney's office, STELLARWIND was the enthusiastic creation of the Security State, even if much of the NSA's workforce knew nothing about it. The part that participated in it could have trouble seeing NSA's targets as people instead of data. One internal memo on how to format accounts for surveillance used the placeholder name "Mohammed Raghead." NSA attorneys provided Hayden with the necessary argument for why a secret program collecting Americans' communications records in bulk was constitutional. They interpreted Addington's authorization to mean that "NSA did not actually 'acquire' communications until specific communications were selected" for search, according to an internal history of STELLARWIND. It was akin to arguing that your credit card wasn't stolen until the thief registered a charge.

The case study of the PATRIOT Act, passed three weeks after Hayden switched on STELLARWIND, suggests that Congress would have given the NSA its cherished freedom from FISA. But the unilateral assertion of presidential authority was the point. "Anecdotal evidence suggests that government officials feared the public debate surrounding any changes to FISA would compromise intelligence sources and methods," the NSA inspector general explained. The only members of Congress informed about STELLARWIND were a pivotal body known as the Gang of Eight, a group composed of the political leadership of the House and Senate, joined by the Democratic and Republican heads of the congressional intelligence oversight committees. The intelligence agencies used them as proxies for political support from a legislature it otherwise skirted. On October 1, 2001, a week into the Afghanistan call collection and five days before the activation of STELLARWIND, Hayden briefed the Gang of Eight. Days afterward Nancy Pelosi, the senior Democrat on the House intelligence panel, told Hayden she was "concerned" about his "expansive view of [his] authorities"—seemingly less concerned about the actual interception than about whether he had the proper "legal analysis" and presidential authorization to conduct it. A year and a half later, when Senator Jay Rockefeller joined the Gang of

Eight and was informed about STELLARWIND, he wrote to Cheney to say the technical complexities of the NSA's operations overwhelmed his ability to provide informed consent to the surveillance. Hayden nevertheless considered all this to mean Congress was fully informed and fully on board.

Even while the NSA was secretly violating FISA, Congress was being advised openly that the NSA should be finally free of restrictions on mass surveillance in an age of terrorism. Making that argument was William Barr, a former attorney general turned general counsel of Verizon, which would become one of the NSA's critical telecom partners. Barr contended that notwithstanding the PATRIOT Act's necessary erosion of FISA, the statute remained "too restrictive in a fundamental respect": requiring probable cause to connect an individual to a foreign power. (That would prove to be an ironic objection twenty years later.) FISA decreed that judges had authority over national-security surveillance, but Barr argued that surveillance was a decision "judges are not competent to make or responsible for making under the Constitution." When it came to obtaining a suspected terrorist's records, it was absurd that any judicial process existed at all. "Foreign terrorists should not get rights that no one else in the country has," he told the House Intelligence Committee. For good measure Barr recommended that Congress strengthen immunity protections for "officers involved in domestic security."

One aspect of STELLARWIND contributed to a dramatic showdown between the Security State and the Bush administration. The deputy attorney general, James Comey, and Yoo's replacement at the Office of Legal Counsel, Jack Goldsmith, considered STELLARWIND's bulk collection of Americans' internet records to rest on an untenable legal foundation. In March 2004 Comey, acting as attorney general while Ashcroft underwent gallbladder surgery, refused to recertify STELLARWIND for an additional forty-five days, prompting senior White House officials to race to Ashcroft's hospital bed. Comey and Goldsmith did the same. Ashcroft, deeply unwell, supported Goldsmith. The Justice Department prepared for mass resignations—including those of FBI director Robert Mueller and the criminal division chief, Christopher Wray—as Comey warned Bush that the public would "freak out when they find out what we have been doing." Addington called Hayden and asked if the NSA would continue the bulk collection of internet metadata anyway. Hayden promptly answered that he would.

The denouement of the episode was that the surveillance was preserved. It was easy to overlook that what bothered Comey, Goldsmith, Mueller, and others was not the bulk interception but the poor lawyering supporting it. "Immediately," records the NSA internal history of the episode, NSA and Justice Department attorneys began working "to recreate this authority." They shoehorned the bulk internet collection into FISA, citing references in it for methods of intercepting outgoing electronic communications—a pen register—and for collecting incoming ones—a trap-and-trace device. The attorneys persuaded themselves, and by July persuaded chief FISA Court judge Colleen Kollar-Kotelly, that STELLARWIND's interceptions were methodologically similar enough that the law could overlook the stark difference between specified and bulk interception. "The order essentially gave the NSA the same authority to collect bulk internet metadata," the NSA history reads. Hayden accurately observed that "on the core issues" Kollar-Kotelly had "broadly gone with the White House (and Justice's pre-March) view." They had not made the War on Terror respect the law. They had made the law respect the War on Terror. Such a simulacrum of law was termed the "state of exception" by the Italian philosopher Giorgio Agamben: "The normative aspect of law can thus be obliterated and contradicted with impunity by a governmental violence that—while ignoring international law externally and producing a permanent state of exception internally—nevertheless still claims to be applying the law."

Hayden demonstrated the meaning of the state of exception a year after activating STELLARWIND. On October 17, 2002, Tenet, Mueller, and Hayden were called to testify before a congressional inquiry into how the Security State could have allowed 9/11 to happen. Tenet raged against what he considered a political show trial; Mueller, who as a new director was subject to none of the political danger Tenet faced, soberly pledged improvement. Hayden, instead, lectured Congress to do its constitutional and democratic post-9/11 duty. "What I really need you to do is talk to your constituents," Hayden implored, "and find out where the American people want that line between security and liberty to be. In the context of NSA's mission, where do we draw the line between the government's need for counterterrorism information about people in the United States and the privacy interests of people located in the United States?" If "we fail" to draw the line in the right place, Hayden concluded, "then the terrorists win and liberty loses in either case." The director spoke as if he had not been drawing that line in secret for an entire year, as he would continue to do for three years to come. As long as he did, whatever national deliberation about freedom and security emerged in a post-9/11 world would be no more than a simulacrum of democracy.

THE TRIUMPHALISM OF THE WAR on terror stood in conspicuous contrast with its lack of interest in its first actual battlefield. Having ruled out diplomacy—Bush refused to "negotiate with terrorists"—about 100 CIA officers, joined by 350 Special Operations forces, entered northern Afghanistan with $70 million in cash to rent the anti-Taliban Northern Alliance army. With American bombers overhead, the Taliban that had sheltered al-Qaeda fled Kabul for its Kandahar stronghold in November. Footage of jubilant Afghans shouting praise for the United States for ending an oppressive regime filled cable news. Bush portrayed victory as inevitable. Only a few mop-up operations remained.

The truth was that the most powerful military on earth was still built for armored combat against national armies and had little idea what to do in a war it had not expected. Neither Defense Secretary Donald Rumsfeld nor Central Command's General Tommy Franks wanted a large ground force to police Afghanistan, which they considered a job for lesser nations. Its elite forces were similarly unprepared. A PowerPoint presentation to the White House from the commander of the Joint Special Operations Command (JSOC)—an elite military entity that would prove crucial to the War on Terror—prepared an "outside the box" option, according to the reporter Sean Naylor: "Poisoning Food Supply." A White House staffer had the sense to remove the slide recommending that Bush commit war crimes.

As December began, the Northern Alliance and U.S. forces closed in on Kandahar. The Taliban, having vowed to stand and repel the invaders, prepared terms. They would surrender and demobilize if their leader, Mullah Mohammed Omar, could remain in Kandahar under some negotiated supervision. The United States–designated Afghan leader, Hamid Karzai, moved to secure the opportunity to end the combat before it turned into guerrilla warfare. Rumsfeld instead called a "negotiated end" to the standoff "unacceptable to the United States." More than four thousand marines under the command of a one-star general named Jim Mattis were on their way.

As a predictable consequence of the United States' defining its enemy broadly, its focus on ousting the Taliban and installing a new Afghan regime allowed Osama bin Laden and al-Qaeda to flee. This cost the United States its first chance to win the War on Terror, to the degree the war's conceptional flaws allowed such a possibility.

During the anti-Soviet jihad, a warren of tunnels had been cut through the Tora Bora mountain complex near Jalalabad, sometimes extending as far as 350 yards into its granite. Despite elevations reaching thirteen thousand feet, the area was intimately familiar to bin Laden. He had brought his family's construction equipment to maintain it; one account has him designing its hydroelectric generators. Not only was it the most likely place in Afghanistan to withstand U.S. airpower, but the tunnels emptied onto the southern slope of the mountains in Pakistan. The CIA was also familiar with the tunnels, as Langley had helped finance their construction.

Beginning in December, B-52s rained fire hourly on Tora Bora, yet the mountains absorbed the blasts. The CIA and the JSOC had a force of twenty-five hundred Afghans, who had been conscripted by three warlords, but reasoned they needed substantial American infantry. Bin Laden's highly motivated men, variously estimated at eight hundred to three thousand fighters, held advantageous positions. They launched "nonstop" small-arms fire to repel their attackers, CIA field leader Gary Berntsen recalled in his memoir. But the CENTCOM commander, General Tommy Franks, rejected Mattis's request to divert from Kandahar to Tora Bora. Berntsen witnessed the "gruesome scene" of the first day of fighting, which concluded with thirty Northern Alliance fighters dead and fifty wounded, and requested an Army Ranger battalion that never arrived. Berntsen's ally at CIA headquarters, Hank Crumpton, warned Bush personally that without the marines, bin Laden would escape. Bush backed Franks anyway.

Even if it were a political possibility to invade Pakistan, the Afghan triumvirate concluded that the December snow made it impossible to trek to the southern slope of the mountains to cut off bin Laden's escape. The warlords were in touch with al-Qaeda to arrange a cease-fire on December 12, which bought the group time to flee, with bin Laden remaining behind until the sixteenth to oversee the exfiltration. The CIA, which learned of the cease-fire after the fact, blamed the Afghans. Bush, having once vowed to get bin Laden "dead or alive," now insisted that he "truly was not that concerned about him." In February 2003, bin Laden released an audiotape on which he said with a laugh, "Planes poured their lava on us, particularly after accomplishing their main missions in Afghanistan." Rather than concluding the war three months after 9/11, all the United States gained from Tora Bora were prisoners.

CIA GUARDS ENTERED Gul Rahman's cell in the predawn hours of November 2002 to discover that he had frozen to death during the night. The room in which he was being held was part of an unacknowledged prison in

Afghanistan known as the Salt Pit. During the three weeks after Rahman had been seized in Peshawar on suspicion of knowing something about jihadis, the CIA contorted his body in painful "stress" positions, kept him naked or diapered, and doused him with cold water. His corpse was shackled to the wall and naked below the waist—retribution for what the CIA considered his obstinacy during an earlier interrogation.

Days earlier Bruce Jessen, a psychologist who had been dispatched by the unit within the CIA's Counterterrorism Center that handled al-Qaeda analysis, had departed the Salt Pit. He had provided the staff with instructions for interrogating Rahman. Along with a colleague, James Mitchell, Jessen had recently designed a regimen to reduce a human being to his biological essence. Now that regimen had killed a man.

They had found their first test subject months earlier. A man known as Abu Zubaydah, suspected of being of being the "third or fourth man" in al-Qaeda, was captured in Pakistan after sustaining gunshot wounds through his leg, stomach, and testicles. He was revived in custody, where the CIA obstructed a bedside FBI effort to establish rapport with him, opting instead to use him as a guinea pig at a black site in Thailand. The two psychologists wanted to test inducing "learned helplessness," a traumatic reaction to acute and sustained physical and emotional distress. They proposed locking Abu Zubaydah in a coffin-sized box, and an even smaller "confinement space," and filling the boxes with insects, denying him sleep by keeping his body contorted in painful positions, and inducing the terrifying sensation of drowning, a technique favored by North Korea called "waterboarding." One of the FBI interrogators, Ali Soufan, urgently called the Hoover Building, vowing, "I swear to God, I'm going to arrest these guys."

Instead the fastidious Mueller ordered Soufan and a colleague out of Thailand. Mueller's allies portrayed that gesture as a protest. It amounted to the FBI averting its gaze from years of CIA brutality, sexual assault, and even manslaughter to come.

Years later, in military custody, Abu Zubaydah recalled experiencing "almost forty seizures" induced by the anxiety of imprisonment at the CIA's

Thailand black site. Specifically, his condition peaked as a result of the agency's refusal to grant him access to a diary he had kept for over sixteen years, which he claimed could "refute the accusations against me." At least 118 others would follow Abu Zubaydah into the black sites, where there was no law, no one to whom they could plead their case, no one to convince a terrible mistake had been made, no one to investigate, no one to determine the truth. There was only what their captors decided. His inability to challenge his brutalizers' judgment of him was, to Abu Zubaydah, "another form of torture."

So was the nudity to which the CIA subjected Abu Zubaydah. "I think you know how much it is bad for us as Muslims," he later told a military panel, particularly as he was bleeding from the wound that cost him a testicle. Already humiliated by his nakedness, "they put me in . . . a medical bed. They shackle me completely, even my head; I can't do anything. Like this and they put one cloth in my mouth and they put water, water, water." Between dousings, Abu Zubaydah heard his captors mock him by gasping in imitation. "Again and again, they make it with me," he said, "and I tell him, 'If you want to kill me, kill me.'" By the ninth day of his torture, some of his interrogators were convinced that he had no actionable intelligence; four years later, the CIA concluded he was not even a member of al-Qaeda.

About two months after Jessen left Abu Zubaydah to the other interrogators' mercies in Thailand, he arrived at the Salt Pit in Kabul. He had not been given explicit instructions to administer the same sort of treatment to Rahman, but there was little other reason the Counterterrorism Center sent for him. CIA headquarters soon received notification via cable that Salt Pit interrogators had subjected Rahman to "48 hours of sleep deprivation, auditory overload, almost total darkness, isolation, a cold shower, and rough treatment." Headquarters staff quickly responded by approving "enhanced measures" to "extract any and all information" from him. They appeared not to have anticipated the prospect of those methods killing their quarry, despite the likelihood of hypothermia when keeping a man naked and chained in prolonged cold.

Jessen and Mitchell had been air force psychologists experienced in instructing captured airmen how to survive and evade torture. Now they were CIA contractors tasked with designing and administering techniques of physical and psychological brutality. It made them rich: Langley paid out $81 million to their enterprise over the better part of seven years.

The psychologists adopted a grandiose view of the men they abused, and, by implication, themselves. Mitchell, in his memoir, presented them as the defenders of a faith he delighted in dominating. He "looked into the eyes of the worst people on the planet," and "heard their eagerness to convert or kill millions of people in the process. . . . Islamists who, driven by Iron Age religious beliefs, seek to convert, enslave, or slaughter everyone on the planet who does not believe as they do." Mitchell described Abu Zubaydah possessing the "dignity and grace of a caged cat, similar to the way Star Wars fans might imagine a Jedi Knight would carry himself if held captive by his enemies." Traditional methods of interrogation stood no chance against the Jedi of the Iron Age.

The CIA did not possess an interrogations cadre before 9/11. But it had what it understood as a mandate from Congress and Bush for "the gloves [to] come off," as its counterterrorism chief, Cofer Black, told the joint congressional inquiry. It remains unclear, twenty years later, how exactly it came to rely specifically on Mitchell and Jessen, but their project was clearly amenable. As Tenet indicated before the inquiry, the CIA felt most acutely vulnerable to the political argument that it would be blamed for any future attack. The psychologists assured Langley that their targets were eschatological genocidaires. Such encouragement was likely not necessary, but it carried the benefit of valorizing the brutality. In their view, *not* to torture was a dereliction, a moral vanity that gambled with the lives of those the CIA sought to protect.

Rahman's frozen corpse did not derail the CIA's plans. Its use of torture had progressed past the stage of a pilot program. Internal cables document the extreme discomfort and objections of interrogators and medical staff. But barely two months after the CIA killed Rahman, Tenet institutionalized torture. The CIA could use several of the psychologists' techniques, including "isolation, sleep deprivation not to exceed 72 hours, reduced caloric intake . . . deprivation of reading material, use of loud music or white noise (at a decibel level calculated to avoid damage to the detainee's hearing), the use of diapers (generally not to exceed 72 hours)." He operated on the theory that standardizing the brutality within layers of directives, legal approval, and the presence of medical officers would render torture safe— an absurd concept for the men subjected to it, but certainly safer for the CIA in the coming legal and political battles its leadership anticipated as inevitable.

Tenet put a Counterterrorism Center component, then known as the Renditions Group, in charge of the entire apparatus of torture, including maintenance of its secret foreign locations, loaned out by partner governments and intelligence services; the construction of legal indemnities by its lawyers; the instruction of interrogators; the dispatch of medical personnel; and the coordination of the "intelligence" obtained. When possible, the CIA preferred its partners do its dirty work, and sent captives to the prisons of eager contractors like the Mukhabarats of Hosni Mubarak's Egypt, Bashar al-Assad's Syria, and eventually Moammar Qaddafi's Libya. Michael Scheuer, the founder of the CIA's Usama bin Laden Unit, was an architect of renditions before 9/11. By the time of the attacks, Scheuer, an irascible man who had been sidelined from the unit in 1999, lamented that the United States was unlikely to divest its empire. That left it with no choice but to wage a war it had best fight with maximum brutality, including against civilians.

The soon-to-be-renamed Renditions Group was not about to discipline its people for brutality. The CIA officer responsible for the Salt Pit remained there for eight months after Gul Rahman's death. His name is not known, but before he left the Pit, a colleague recommended him for a twenty-five-hundred-dollar cash bonus for his "consistently superior work." His experience in an enterprise that had frozen a man to death was considered enough of a credential, and his involvement in that death an insufficient obstacle, to certify him in April 2003 as an interrogator for other missions. The CIA's executive director declined any disciplinary proceedings for him in February 2006, writing that torturing a man to death needed to be understood "within the operational context that existed at the time." Early in the War on Terror, the CIA established that its officers could kill a man and its leadership would insulate their officers from any sanction.

They had high-level legal cover. Months before the CIA set up its internal structures for the application of torture, Tenet petitioned the Justice Department to determine exactly how brutally the agency could treat those in its custody. Bush had already decreed that the military's captives in Afghanistan would not be considered prisoners of war with acknowledged legal protections, but rather as unlawful enemy combatants, whose treatment would be at American discretion. That was insufficient to reassure Tenet, as federal law criminalized torture, including torture performed by anyone "acting under the color of law," such as CIA officers. If the agency was going to torture people, Tenet was going to ensure that the rest of the administration was complicit. In August 2002, Yoo, at the Justice Department, issued his most infamous opinion of all. He and colleague Jay Bybee indemnified the CIA of any harm for implementing Mitchell and Jessen's regimen by setting the legal threshold for illegal torture to stand at pain equivalent to organ failure or death and irreversible psychological damage.

The agency was thus now in charge of a hidden detentions complex, a place invisible to any outside oversight, including from any attorney, judge, legislator, or human rights group. Not even the International Committee of the Red Cross, which trades public silence for access to disappeared detainees worldwide, knew of the black sites.

The month before Gul Rahman died in Afghanistan, the Thailand black site received its second occupant, a man named Abdul Rahman al-Nashiri. Nashiri was the rare CIA detainee who had personally committed an act of violence, the November 2000 bombing of the USS *Cole* in Aden. Yoo's memo suggests that the CIA represented to him that the use of torture would occur only after less coercive options failed. Nashiri, captured after the Justice Department memo, was tortured "immediately" upon arrival at the Thailand black site, according to a CIA inspector general's report. The report records that Nashiri provided specific intelligence on "other terrorists" on "his first day" in captivity, but on his twelfth, the CIA waterboarded him anyway.

Nashiri's interrogators instructed him to keep his hands on his cell wall for three days during which the CIA denied him food. While Nashiri knelt, they put a broomstick behind his knees and abruptly bent his spine back, separating his knee joints. They tied Nashiri's wrists with a belt and suspended him from the restraint, arms raised behind him. The CIA staff at the black site feared they would dislocate Nashiri's shoulders, and one unidentified official later recollected that he "had to intercede," but the CIA's inspector general does not record the results.

For the final weeks in fall 2002 that the black site existed, its chief was Gina Haspel, a Kentuckian air force brat with a passion for Johnny Cash. She permitted Nashiri's torture to continue until fears of the black site's location leaking prompted his move to a military base in northeast Poland known as Stare Kiejkuty. There his torture intensified to include a mock execution and the threat of rape of his mother, prompting someone later identified as the CIA's interrogations chief to threaten resignation. "To continue to use enhanced technique[s] without clear indications that he [is] withholding important info is excessive and may cause him to cease cooperation on any level," the chief cabled. Later Haspel took over the interrogation program, according to a memoir by the CIA's top attorney, and later still aided in destroying ninety-two videotapes from her black site documenting Abu Zubaydah's and Nashiri's torture.

Under three directors and over the course of six years, the CIA held and tortured at least 119 men. An unknown number, believed to be far greater, were sent to its partners' torture chambers, a process known as extraordinary rendition. One of the rendered, Abdul-Hakim Belhaj, was a Libyan jihadist determined to overthrow Qaddafi. The CIA gave Belhaj as a gift to its new renditions partner, along with his pregnant wife, Fatima Boudchar.

As the agency transferred custody, it took pictures of her bound and naked body. The CIA institutionalization of torture begun by Tenet in January 2003 required that such records be made should the agency ever have to contest who was responsible for deaths in partner custody. The CIA had sexually violated Boudchar, a violation that its internal guidelines justified. A Senate report later found that when detainees refused to eat in protest of their conditions, the agency would insert pureed food into their anuses, another sexual violation, and one the CIA claimed was necessary for the detainees' nutrition.

The CIA never called this regimen torture. Not only was torture illegal, it was the sort of thing barbaric nations did. All of the CIA's not-torture occurred cynically, down to the diplomatic assurances that the CIA's allies provided that they wouldn't torture the individuals the CIA turned over to them. The agency came up with a euphemism for its actions, one that it expected politicians and journalists to use, as it took umbrage at anyone who would impugn its officials by describing their actions as torture. In what would amount to a years-long fake-news campaign about the nature and efficacy of its brutality, the CIA called it *enhanced interrogation*.

Enhanced interrogation did not remain within the warrens of the black sites. It spread to the Antilles within a year of its adoption.

The Pentagon sent what it considered its highest-value and most dangerous terrorist suspects from the battlefield of Afghanistan to its naval station at Guantanamo Bay. While it characterized a detainee population that would come to include eight hundred people as the "worst of the worst," many, if not most, were suspected only of some nebulous Taliban affiliation, several steps in importance removed from bin Laden. They were not even tactically relevant to the Afghanistan war, which would have prompted the U.S. to lock them up in the enormous prison on the outskirts of the Bagram air field, an hour's drive from Kabul, which held about a thousand people at a time.

Their legal status was nebulous. In February 2002, Bush established that although the United States wouldn't consider al-Qaeda and the Taliban "lawful combatants," they could be held until the end of hostilities. For the purposes of denying its captives access to U.S. federal courts that might free them, Guantanamo—the Cuban base for which the U.S. military annually wrote Fidel Castro a $4,085 check he never cashed—was legally designated as foreign soil. Simultaneously, to indemnify military personnel for any acts of torture conducted on foreign soil, Guantanamo was deemed to be U.S. territory, as the U.S. military flew its flag above the base. What mattered was establishing, by whatever means possible, a state of exception. No one could stop the military from doing as it liked at Guantanamo, much as no one could stop the CIA from doing as it liked at the black sites. There was even a CIA black site at Guantanamo.

By the fall of 2002, with Guantanamo officials under pressure to produce actionable intelligence from a detainee cohort presumed to possess it, the new military command overseeing the detentions called the CIA in for advice, even though the CIA is not subject to the law of armed conflict. A Counterterrorism Center attorney, Jonathan Fredman, arrived in October. Fredman later told the Senate that his guidance had been that the military had to operate within clear, nonsubjective legal guidelines—at the time, those set by John Yoo. Fredman warned that penalties for violating the federal antitorture statute, particularly "should a detainee die," could include capital punishment. An attendee of his briefings, Joint Task Force Guantanamo staff officer Lieutenant Colonel Diane Beaver, recorded her takeaway, one that would be emblematic of Guantanamo, a place beyond law: "If the detainee dies, you're doing it wrong."

Weeks later Guantanamo took on as an interrogator a naval reserve officer named Richard Zuley. He had done similar work on Black people as a detective in the infamously racist and brutal Chicago police. Benita Johnson remembered Zuley shackling her to an eyebolt in an interrogation room for an entire day and threatening her with the loss of her children unless she signed a statement implicating her ex-boyfriend in the murder of a white woman, Renee Rondeau. Another Zuley target, Latherial Boyd, who would be exonerated for murder after twenty-three years in prison, recalled Zuley searching his loft and saying, "No nigger is supposed to live like this." Now, at Guantanamo, Zuley stood before a man named Mohamedou Ould Slahi. Arabic-speaking interrogators put a hooded Slahi on a boat in the bay before stuffing ice in his jacket and repeatedly punching him. Slahi remembered, "I wasn't me after that." Zuley threatened to bring Slahi's mother to Guantanamo, which Slahi's attorneys later understood to be a rape threat. Slahi said he would say whatever the Americans wanted, "I don't care, as long as you are pleased." Torture might have come to Guantanamo from the CIA and the Justice Department, but it also came from American cities like Chicago.

By Thanksgiving 2002, Guantanamo interrogators stripped naked a man thought to have been al-Qaeda's intended twentieth 9/11 hijacker. They denied him sleep for twenty hours a day, menaced him with dogs, and forced him to pray to an idol shrine. Another detainee was sexually humiliated by a woman interrogator, who smeared him with what she portrayed as menstrual blood. One technique for inducing sleep deprivation involved deafeningly loud music, often the nu-metal band Drowning Pool chanting "let the bodies hit the floor." Another involved "stress positions" that rendered sleep impossible, often by stretching detainees so their restraints would hurt them should their muscles slacken. Rumsfeld, who approved torture at Guantanamo in early December, commented in a memo on forced standing, "I stand for 8–10 hours a day." Unlike at the CIA, however, the military's senior attorneys, and especially the navy's, resisted torture, on not only legal but moral grounds. Alberto Mora, the navy general counsel, argued that institutionalized cruelty was a Rubicon from which constitutional government could never return. "If you make this exception, the whole Constitution crumbles," he told the journalist Jane Mayer.

Inside Guantanamo was an Al Jazeera cameraman named Sami Muhyideen al-Hajj. Al-Hajj, arrested by the Pakistanis as he and a colleague tried to cross the Afghanistan–Pakistan border for work in December 2001, said he was interrogated extensively about any relationship between Al Jazeera and al-Qaeda. He claimed that the interrogators asked him over a hundred times just about the war correspondent Ahmed Mansour. It would not be until 2006 that the Pentagon officially acknowledged it held al-Hajj at all. The Committee to Protect Journalists, noting a lack of American solidarity, said that year that he was "virtually unknown in U.S. media circles."

Guantanamo even caged a child. Omar Khadr's parents were Canadian al-Qaeda sympathizers. They took the boy to Afghanistan and introduced him to a life of militancy. They lent him as a translator to a compound that Army Special Forces raided in July 2002. During the raid, a grenade mortally wounded Sergeant First Class Christopher Speer. For years after, the U.S military maintained that the fifteen-year-old Khadr, wounded to the point of losing his left eye, had thrown the grenade. On his arrival at Guantanamo in October, guards hog-tied the boy. Left alone so long that he urinated, the guards threw solvent on the floor, elevated his legs, and used Khadr as a human mop. A Canadian intelligence operative who interviewed Khadr at Guantanamo months later said that he viewed al-Qaeda "through the eyes of a child." Very few people at Guantanamo were ever charged with a war crime. But the U.S. eventually brought a teenaged captive, who would grow into manhood at Guantanamo, before a military tribunal.

It took barely a year after 9/11 for America, in its righteousness, to torture a wounded child. Mora's insight was that once America was willing to do such things, it was willing to do anything to anyone, in a boundaryless war. Its most agonizing battlefield—one created by a show of dominance by the right against the Security State—loomed on the horizon.

CHAPTER TWO

9/11 AND THE RIGHT

2001–2006

Two months after the towers fell, Attorney General John Ashcroft instructed federal prosecutors to conduct an unusual sort of roundup. They and the FBI were to question some five thousand recent immigrants, men between the ages of eighteen and thirty-two who had recently arrived from countries that the Justice Department did not publicly identify. By Ashcroft's admission, these young men were not terrorists. There was no suspicion any of them had so much as overstayed their visas. Instead, as he explained in a November 2001 speech, the point of the questioning was to "expand our knowledge of terrorist networks operating inside the United States." Thousands of Muslim men were thus expected to prove their loyalty by informing on their neighbors.

Reflecting the precarious situation of American Muslims after 9/11, one of their leading advocacy groups, the Council on American-Islamic Relations (CAIR), tempered its criticism of Ashcroft. Executive director Nihad Awad pleaded that "all elements of due process and respect for civil liberties be adhered to" as the "interviews" unfolded. He leavened his statement with an assurance that "American Muslims condemn terrorism in all its forms." The American Civil Liberties Union, more safely positioned, stridently denounced Ashcroft's "blatant racial profiling." Even local police departments were discomfited. Charles Wilson, chief of police in Detroit, said he didn't want his officers to "treat people like criminals, or even go out and find these people." Ashcroft, testifying at a Senate panel soon after, was indignant at the criticism. He had, he insisted, merely "offered noncitizens willing to come forward . . . a chance to live in this country."

Soon after 9/11, criticisms of the emerging War on Terror began taking form in predictable circles: Muslims, lawyers, concerned members of the security community, and anyone else reciting from the old liberal hymnal about how protecting the country risked disfiguring it. Victory in the Cold War was supposed to have decisively refuted what conservative writer James Burnham had termed the ideology of Western suicide. Instead, at a time of danger, liberalism was looking past a terrorist enemy that, as Ashcroft put it, "threatens civilization." Its tactics included "infiltrating our communities," providing journalists with "stories of torture and mistreatment," and "exploit[ing] our judicial process." In so doing, the enemy waged its war not only on foreign battlefields but through the institutions of liberalism in the United States. "To those who scare peace-loving people with phantoms of lost liberty," he told the Senate Judiciary Committee, "my message is this: your tactics only aid terrorists, for they erode our national unity and diminish our resolve."

Muslim immigrants were not the only ones who had to prove their loyalty. That day Ashcroft established a key ideological template: what Muslim terrorists were unable to destroy, many on the right would argue, liberals would. They would do so through respectable means already under their control: so-called "due process" roadblocks from their lawyers, slanders and equivocations in their news outlets, restrictions imposed by their politicians, and obstruction from their shadow state of bureaucrats. Beyond those official mechanisms lay cultural danger: liberals identified not with America, but with its enemies. As long as America tolerated such constraints, it would not be free to win. "The decadent left," burrowed within "its enclaves on the coasts," wrote influential conservative journalist Andrew Sullivan, "may well mount a fifth column." Even college students could apply Ashcroft's template. "There are profound political forces within and without the United States that would like to see us stand down . . . and cease the post-9/11 strategy that has kept the terrorists on the defensive and prevented a second attack inside our borders," a Duke University junior named Stephen Miller argued in 2006. Liberal and left dissent, Miller promised, carries "the possibility of someday being stained with the blood of the innocent Americans whose country they betrayed."

Even as the right assailed liberals for not emerging from their "holiday from history," it drew upon another familiar theme. "There is a religious war going on in this country," the nativist politician and columnist Pat Buchanan had argued in 1992, a "cultural war, as critical to the kind of nation we shall be as was the Cold War itself, for this war is for the soul of America." Buchanan and his antiglobalist foreign policy views were marginal within the Republican Party on 9/11, but the politics of cultural grievance that he practiced—*white* cultural grievance—had kept the conservative coalition united after the end of the Cold War removed its centripetal force. Those politics lent themselves well to a war against a nonwhite foe primarily associated with a non-Christian religion few white Americans practiced and whose ambitions were understood to be global.

For years after the September 11 attacks, these War on Terror politics offered the right what it considered a path to sustained national dominance. Bush's first-term approval ratings averaged 62 percent. "Conservatives saw the savagery of 9/11 in the attacks and prepared for war," his political architect, Karl Rove, explained at a fundraiser, while "liberals saw the savagery of the 9/11 attacks and wanted to prepare indictments and offer therapy and understanding for our attackers." When Bush was popular, the right lionized him as a man of history. But as the war dragged on, it came to consider his definition of the enemy as not just euphemistic, but tragically complicit in liberal orthodoxies about cultural sensitivity that prevented an honest identification of the enemy. All schools of conservative thought agreed on a central point. "Victory in war, and particularly in counterinsurgency wars," wrote the American Enterprise Institute's Fred Kagan, "requires knowing one's enemy." When Bush ceased being popular, he accommodated the dissatisfaction on the right by offering a more explicitly Islamic conception of the adversary.

As a constituency grew on the right that considered Islam synonymous with terrorism, its members came to consider themselves political martyrs of the War on Terror, suffering the censorship of a necessary truth by the nation's internal enemies. After CBS Radio rejected an ad promoting a 2005 anti-Islam conference, one of its speakers announced that he would reveal what the network was afraid of airing. "I will show how jihad violence—in the words of terrorists themselves, including Osama bin Laden—gains its impetus from core elements of Islamic theology mandating against unbelievers and call upon sincere moderate Muslims to confront and repudiate these elements of Islam," vowed an activist named Robert Spencer, who would become influential in the precincts of the right that were contemptuous of Bush's conception of Islam as a "religion of peace." They would create an activist infrastructure of Islamophobia, which doubled as a lucrative industry in enterprises as diversified as media and law-enforcement contracting. If Muslims objected to such things as mass roundups, this infrastructure considered it proof that American Islam had something to hide.

Victory required suppressing not only Islam but the liberalism that kept the borders "open," the courts available to terror suspects, and the culture from equating Islam with terrorism within respectable discourse. Triumph over the left or liberals—two different political traditions that the right often conflated—took on the imperative of national survival, a posture familiar from the right's approach to the Cold War. While the Security State was the instrument of the War on Terror, it could also become an obstacle to the war's interests; and even it, too, could be brought to heel. The right would also need to police itself for insufficient commitment to the war or any misconception of the enemy. After all, defeat, as Ashcroft warned, threatened civilization.

CONSERVATIVES EMERGED from the Cold War triumphant. Sometimes the story they told had the Soviet Union collapsing from the inherent weaknesses of communism, particularly measured against the dynamism of capitalism and the allure of bourgeois freedoms. At other times the United States attributed it to the wisdom and strength of generations of conservative theorists, activists, academics, polemicists, and politicians who confronted the Soviets. Either way, the most important geopolitical fact of the late twentieth century was that the United States had vanquished its rival. Conservative scholars in the West portrayed that victory as the final vindication of the social, economic, and political order they favored.

They believed as fervently that they had achieved that victory despite the liberals. Now identified with the Democratic Party, liberals had opted for containment instead of rollback during the Truman administration, minimized the threat of domestic Communist infiltration and socialist indoctrination, and stumbled into two stalemated wars. Then the liberals capitulated to the even more shameful radicals further to their left by turning against Vietnam and subsequent proxy conflicts. Lacking convictions of their own, liberals—particularly the richer they were—preferred to laugh at ignorant, bigoted right-wingers too obtuse to know that their patriotism was embarrassing. Yet it was the man at whom they sneered the most, sometimes as a buffoon and at other times as a madman, who won the Cold War. Now, in the place of Ronald Reagan, there was George W. Bush.

Bush was the overindulged grandson of a senator and son of a president. Yankee money that had relocated to Texas for personal and political fortunes yielded a frivolous, loutish man-child who drank to the point of embarrassment until he was forty. In 1968, when his father was Houston's congressman, Bush secured a comission in the Texas Air National Guard, sparing him from Vietnam. He went on to become a relative failure in the oil business. But in 1986 the Reverend Billy Graham paid a visit to the Bush family home in Kennebunkport, Maine, that awakened Bush spiritually. It awakened his political ambitions as well. Bush channeled them into a Christian-inflected conservative politics more natural to Reagan than to his father. Once he convinced evangelicals he was one of them, he provided them a viable pathway to the White House and received their enthusiastic support.

Bush seemed, not least to himself, an example of the rewards of faith. Aides and deputies frequently ascribed to him absolute certainty, to the point of indifference to evidence and distrust of those who sought it. His first treasury secretary wrote in a memoir that Bush would simply stop paying attention during policy discussions. EPA chief Whitman recalled that she would be "accused of disloyalty" by asking if there were "any facts to support our case," before retracting her comments. Bush's instincts had gotten him the presidency—through a bitter legal victory secured by five GOP-appointed Supreme Court justices—and they would get him through it. His spokesman, Ari Fleischer, demonstrated Bush's approach to those who undermined certainty in the War on Terror within weeks of the attacks. The provocateur comedian Bill Maher had said the hijackers, whatever else they were, weren't cowards. Asked about it at a White House briefing, Fleischer said Maher's "terrible" comments were a reminder "to all Americans that they need to watch what they say, watch what they do."

To a broader national audience Bush's "compassionate conservatism" defined itself against Buchanan's culture war. Buchanan's distaste for post–Cold War foreign adventurism—having won that conflict, his war was now at home—likewise clashed with how Republican leaders, including Bush, understood American global responsibilities. One such conception "endeavor[ed] to prevent any hostile power from dominating a region whose resources would, under consolidated control, be sufficient to generate global power." So stated a draft strategy document written in 1992 for Defense Secretary Dick Cheney by his undersecretary, Paul Wolfowitz. Their alliance helped define national security conservatism. The neoconservative wing, to which Wolfowitz belonged, furnished the rationale for American global power that people like Cheney, from the Nixonite wing, sought to wield. Cheney believed that the United States had to treat even the least likely "one-percent chance" scenarios of terrorist danger as certainties, reported journalist Ron Suskind, a conviction that opened the aperture of military response. At *National Review*, the magazine operating as the center of conservative intellectual gravity, board member Neal B. Freeman recalled that the consensus was to respond to 9/11 "with disproportionate force and to disproportionate effect." Any objection to invading and occupying Afghanistan was "no more than quiddity."

The split between neoconservatives and nativists represented competing conceptions of American exceptionalism. Both were inclined to civilizational explanations for 9/11. Neoconservativism held that the attacks revealed the cultural and political pathologies afflicting Arab and Muslim societies. Princeton's Bernard Lewis, a guiding light to neoconservatives, blamed 9/11 on what he called the Arab world's "failure of modernity." The neoconservatives treated the legacy of Western imperialism and contemporary American hegemony as tiresome alibis deflecting from what they insisted was the core issue: Islam's failure to be civilized. The true interests of Muslims, they continued, aligned with those of the United States. Essayist Max Boot wrote that the "state-building" functions that would be the result of long-term U.S. occupation of Muslim lands was "a service that we should extend to the oppressed people of Afghanistan."

Nativists viewed the War on Terror less in terms of America transforming the world than in terms of stopping the world from transforming America. In 2002 Buchanan's new flagship, *The American Conservative*, published an article warning that "the deconstruction of America is well underway." That was how its author, Roger McGrath, judged the arrival of Somali Muslim refugees in Lewiston, Maine. While America "send[s] our boys overseas to fight and die, ostensibly to protect the United States," its elites flooded America with foreigners. "We are under no obligation to destroy the ethnic, religious, and cultural traditions that have built this country," he wrote. A line of respectability separated Boot and Lewis from McGrath and pundits like Ann Coulter, who wrote that the War on Terror required the United States to "invade [Muslim] countries, kill their leaders and convert them to Christianity." *National Review* fired Coulter for that piece, while Lewis published his musings about Islamic pathology in *The New Yorker*.

Meanwhile, millions of evangelical Christians were imbibing a message from their religious leaders that Islam had launched something like a counter-crusade. The leaders of the most politically potent religious organizations in America, people with enormous influence in the Republican Party, filled the definitional vacuum at the heart of Bush's War on Terror.

When the Southern Baptist Convention met in St. Louis in June 2002, its former president, the hugely influential Jacksonville preacher Jerry Vines, cited a book published that year that the Hofstra sociologist Richard Cimino placed among the most popular in a new evangelical literature blaming Islam for 9/11. In *Unveiling Islam,* two self-described "ex-Muslims," Ergun and Emir Caner, argued that an "essential and indispensable tenet" of the religion was violence. Al-Qaeda was "following the teachings of Islam to the letter." For good measure, the Caners denied Islam its status as an Abrahamic faith by attributing paganism to the prophet Muhammad. As if to anticipate the inevitable objections, they claimed the godless culture of America would reject these truths, as Christians had by now long expected. But "essential to an effective witness" was defending the truth of Christianity against the falsity of Islam, even though it was "neither popular nor welcome [in a] politically correct, politically charged, postmodern culture." At the convention in St. Louis, Vines denounced Muhammad as a "demon-obsessed pedophile." Islam was something distinct from and inferior to Christianity, Vines preached: "And I will tell you Allah is not Jehovah, either. Jehovah's not going to turn you into a terrorist."

Franklin Graham, the son of Billy Graham, also denied Islam's place in the Abrahamic family, saying, "It is a different God, and I believe a very evil and a very wicked religion." Focus on the Family's founder, James

Dobson, warned that Islam's sharia codes stood in opposition to the "Judeo-Christian" bequest of freedom. "If the Islamic law were the law of this land," the influential Dobson explained, "there would not be that freedom. And if you don't believe that, look at the countries where Islamic law rules." Reverend Jerry Falwell told *60 Minutes* in 2002 that the prophet Muhammad "was a terrorist," a slur that would become ubiquitous in anti-Islam circles. Falwell's influence ensured that his remarks had international consequences: a protest against his disrespect in India escalated into a riot that killed eight people and wounded ninety. CAIR's Ibrahim Hooper defended Falwell's right to "be a bigot" while noting, "What really concerns us is the lack of reaction by mainstream religious and political leaders, who say nothing when these bigots voice these attacks."

It did not escape evangelical attention that a significant number of Taliban prisoners had been Christian missionaries. That fed the anxiety that globally, as *Christianity Today* put it, the Gospels might be "outpaced by Islam." A February 2002 editorial argued that security "in our post–September 11 world" necessitated "respectful and courageous" attempts at converting Muslims. While wide majorities of evangelical leaders in 2003 told *BeliefNet* pollers that protecting American Muslims' civil rights was very important, 70 percent also called Islam a "religion of violence." There was a tendency to consider criticism of such views to be religious persecution, as when it emerged that Rumsfeld's deputy undersecretary for intelligence, Lieutenant General Jerry Boykin, said of a Muslim opponent, "I knew that my God was a real God and his was an idol." Boykin was never in danger of losing his position, but a *Christianity Today* headline defending him preemptively asked: "Should Christians Be Banned from the Military?"

Millions of Americans took their political cues from Bush and their spiritual ones from Vines, Falwell, Graham, and their anti-Islam colleagues. The discrepancy between their public messages led to a sense that Bush was hesitant to acknowledge a shared truth. A different president might not have been able to get away with such vagueness, but evangelicals trusted Bush. His language about "the terrorists" might have been euphemistic, but it included a critical word evangelicals needed to hear: "evil." It touched off a national debate on the importance of "moral clarity," itself a euphemism for asserting the blamelessness of America in any number of foreign policy atrocities. Bush ensured the War on Terror was framed in moral terms that appealed to religious conservatives, even while an undercurrent of conservatism chafed at Bush's language and longed for him to define the enemy in terms of religion.

Layered atop that was a secular conservative and centrist tendency to define Islam as a danger to cosmopolitanism. The Taliban's violent misogyny served as an argument that Islam threatened women, which in turn became a cudgel to demand that feminists support the war or expose their hypocrisy. Overthrowing the Taliban, observed the neoconservative *Weekly Standard*, meant Bush would have "secured the feminists' most worthy goal of the last several years." The article luridly suggested that female genital mutilation might be the wages of Muslim immigration. Christopher Hitchens, a contrarian socialist polemicist, used the anti-cosmopolitanism of "fascism with an Islamic face" to break with the left. "What they abominate about 'the West,' to put it in a phrase, is not what Western liberals don't like and can't defend about their own system, but what they do like about it and must defend: its emancipated women, its scientific inquiry, its separation of religion from the state," Hitchens wrote shortly after 9/11. The ideological defection of the insouciant Hitchens gave the War on Terror important validation: left-wing condemnation of dissent as indecent.

Some heard these messages about Muslims and took matters into their own hands. Just before midnight on February 22, 2003, two eighteen-year-old brothers from Yorba Linda, California, Rashid and Mohamed Alam, drove to San Antonio Park to rendezvous with friends for a late-night movie. By the time they assembled, so did a convoy bearing twenty drunk white teenagers armed with baseball bats, screwdrivers, golf clubs, and beer bottles. At least one had a swastika tattoo. The Alams' crew—Arab, Black, Filipino, and white—fled. Sixteen-year-old Michael Tineo saw the mob tackle Rashid and then form a circle around him to beat and stomp him for two minutes, yelling what the *Orange County Register* recorded as "slurs against Arabs" and, Michael remembered, "Nazi for Life." Police found Rashid lying in the street, barely conscious, in a pool of his blood. Doctors repaired his jaw using a metal plate. The Orange County Muslim community took alarmed note that police did not announce arrests or a hate-crime investigation for nine days, during which activists requested FBI involvement. Rashid's father, Ahmed, lamented not taking his sons' accounts of schoolyard racism seriously. "When I see him now, I think it is my fault," Ahmed anguished. "I should have named him Robert or John."

The Orange County chapter of CAIR stated that Rashid Alam's near-fatal beating was the "direct result of the barrage of pro-war and anti-Islam rhetoric coming from right-wing and evangelical leaders." These charges incensed the evangelical magazine *World*'s Bob Jones, who demanded that CAIR "explain the 'direct' link between evangelical leaders and a bunch of foul-mouthed teenagers." In any event, Jones continued, in the War on Terror, CAIR "sometimes seems to have trouble deciding exactly which side it is on." Jones lamented that evangelicals could "well understand the resentment Muslims feel when they are stereotyped as dangerous and anti-American," but through its censorious ways, CAIR "chose to drive home a verbal wedge."

Evangelicals found uses for Bush's vague conception of the enemy. In October 2002, rallying in Washington to support Israel's violent suppression of the second Palestinian intifada, they portrayed Israel's fight as indistinguishable from America's. "We are in a war on terrorism," said Gary Bauer, the conservative Christian activist. "We are trying to limit and lessen the number of terrorist nations. So under no circumstances should we create a new terrorist nation of Palestine." Texas congressman Tom DeLay, the Republican whip in the House of Representatives, bluntly asked the crowd if it wanted "Israel to look more like the Middle East, or do we want the rest of the Middle East to start looking more like Israel?" Seeking to cement its ties to an American community that enjoyed overwhelming political influence, Israel was happy to portray itself as the tip of the spear in the War on Terror. For decades GOP politicians had marveled at Israel's ability to subjugate Muslims, often using euphemisms like DeLay's. It didn't matter that Bush had declared war on terrorist groups with global reach, which even the most aggressive Palestinian resistance was not. The Reverend Richard Cizik, a vice president of the forty-three-thousand-church-member National Association of Evangelicals, observed, "Evangelicals have substituted Islam for the Soviet Union. The Muslims have become the modern-day equivalent of the Evil Empire."

LATE IN JULY 2002, the State Department's Mideast bureau warned Secretary of State Colin Powell that the United States would sow a "perfect storm" by overthrowing Iraqi dictator Saddam Hussein. What became known as the "Perfect Storm memo" predicted a "horrible wave of bloodletting and private vengeance"; hostility to the U.S.-backed Iraqi government from the Shia clerisy in Najaf; and "U.S. troops com[ing] under attack, especially while patrolling at night, in Shia cities of the south, Baghdad, and the north central towns where Sunnis dominate." Assistant Secretary Bill Burns emphasized that an occupation could last as long as a decade.

Over a year later, in October 2003, the CIA vindicated Burns on the important points. The burgeoning resistance that American troops faced in Iraq, which Rumsfeld had indignantly refused to characterize as guerrilla war, would become a civil war. Its combatants would be not foreign jihadis but Iraqis fighting a foreign army as well as one another. That was the judgment of a National Intelligence Estimate (NIE) that the intelligence agencies issued a year after another one of its reports became a tool that Bush compelled and Tenet delivered to drive the United States into Iraq.

To the State Department and the CIA, such assessments were the first step to prevent or mitigate such a disaster. But to the Bush administration, Burns's memo and the October 2003 NIE were acts of subterfuge by the usual coterie of Security State bureaucrats who failed to appreciate that redressing 9/11 required the profligate use of American power—unsurprising, they added, considering that this wise cohort had failed to thwart 9/11 itself. Such criticism revealed not only a strategic failing, but a lack of faith in American exceptionalism. Those leveling it would have to be dominated.

Among the legacies of the U.S. invasion was a presidency's willingness to treat the Security State as an obstacle to its ambitions, even as it needed the Security State to make those ambitions real. Another was using intelligence to manufacture a fiction—multiple fictions—justifying a war of aggression. Lying about a war is of course nothing new. But lies and delusions inflected every aspect of what would become an agonizing foreign occupation that U.S. elites resisted ending.

The right would cheer lustily for the war, and later denied its many failures, since it believed doing so ensured its power. But the Security State, much of which understood the disaster about to enfold, accepted being used instead of resisting. A marine general on the Joint Staff, Gregory Newbold, and a counterterrorism coordinator in the White House, Rand Beers, were marquee resignations over the Iraq war, and both were obscure. The embodiment of everything the Security State believed it was, national hero Colin Powell, became the most important validator for the sort of war he had devoted his career to preventing the United States from fighting.

Despite the Security State's acquiescence, the right accused it of threatening the constitutional order. It of course *was* threatening the constitutional order, through its surveillance, torture, indefinite detention, securitized immigration enforcement, and other aspects of the apparatus of counterterrorism, but those were all things conservatives applauded. Conservatives' grievance was that the Security State threatened the right's hold on power by contradicting what Bush had proclaimed about the war. "Modern history is filled with intelligence bureaus turning against their own governments, for good or ill," wrote columnist Robert Novak. "The CIA is a long way from those extremes, but it is supposed to be a resource for—not a critic of—the president."

None of the factions that clashed over the Iraq war took into account how an American war of aggression in the heart of the Middle East might actively metastasize global jihad. The Iraq occupation did so not only by supplying the jihad with new recruits but by providing it with motive and opportunity to evolve into something more virulent and more ambitious. Through their compounding errors, the Americans made al-Qaeda in Iraq, which did not exist before the invasion, into the most powerful jihadist franchise in the world. The War on Terror was already a conceptual failure, compounded by the disaster at Tora Bora. But Iraq proved the War on Terror generated its own futility.

Bush had said after Tora Bora that he was unconcerned about bin Laden. That was an understatement. The day after 9/11 he asked White House counterterrorism adviser Richard Clarke to investigate any complicity that Saddam Hussein might have had in 9/11. Clarke responded that the attack was bin Laden's work. "I know, I know," Clarke recounts Bush responding, "but . . . see if Saddam was involved. Just look. I want to know any shred." When Bush assembled his national security team at Camp David that weekend, Secretary of State Colin Powell was compelled to argue that including Iraq in reprisals for 9/11 would cost the United States whatever international support for a military response existed. Rumsfeld agreed to table Iraq, but as an official at the time noted, "He hasn't given up on it."

It remains a matter of dispute when exactly Bush decided to attack Saddam. Bureaucratic machinations in that direction from both the Pentagon and Cheney's office were underway soon after the attack. Shortly after Christmas 2001, Bush's team assembled at his Texas ranch to hear CENTCOM's Franks outline a plan for what the general billed as "regime change" with a force of more than one hundred thousand troops. Three months later, national security adviser Condoleezza Rice was meeting with three senators at the White House when Bush popped his head in to say, "Fuck Saddam. We're taking him out."

Though the outcome was never in doubt, throughout 2002 Bush and his aides publicly denied that they had taken any decision to invade Iraq or overthrow Saddam. They did so even as cable news filled with endless speculation, bordering on enthusiasm, about whether Bush would finally move against the Iraqi leader, whose survival throughout the Clinton years was viewed as an unacceptable defiance of America. In October MSNBC debuted a show literally called *Countdown: Iraq* and a few months later canceled Phil Donahue's program, which had been a rare venue on cable news for war skepticism. The default tone of coverage treated war as inevitable— the wisdom of it debatable within narrow, tactical parameters, but its justice taken for granted. "The part that makes me uncomfortable," pundit Tucker Carlson said on CNN in June, "is that the details of it are being discussed in public. Saddam Hussein watches this. He knows that, having committed to it, the United States must follow through and must topple him." Carlson's guest that day, Pentagon adviser Kenneth Adelman, answered his questions about al-Qaeda and Saddam's relative importance by insisting that "the preponderance of evidence is in favor that Iraq was involved" in 9/11— a lie—before predicting overthrowing Saddam would be "a cakewalk."

Adelman's representation was characteristic of the fabrications and delusions presented to Americans by the war's architects and supporters. They confidently portrayed Saddam as allied with al-Qaeda and voiced the baseless fear that he would give bin Laden a deadly arsenal they were baselessly certain he possessed. "You can't distinguish between al-Qaeda and Saddam when you talk about the War on Terror," Bush said in September. The president's choice of "terrorism" as the enemy rather than al-Qaeda aided his argument. Saddam indeed nurtured ties to terrorist groups, but they were Palestinians fighting Israel, not al-Qaeda; and he had never given them chemical agents even when he had maximal stockpiles and freedom of international action. By September 2003 a *Washington Post* poll found 69 percent of Americans believed Saddam was complicit in 9/11, a claim Bush himself stopped short of making.

George Tenet, weakened by 9/11, observed the administration's efforts and, characteristically, attempted accommodation. In June 2002 his head of analysis, Jami Miscik, prepared a "purposefully aggressive" analysis "seeking to draw connections" between Saddam and al-Qaeda because neoconservative ideologues in the Pentagon and vice president's office insisted both that a connection must exist and that the CIA couldn't be trusted to find it. The result was something called "Iraq and al-Qaeda: Interpreting a Murky Relationship," which suggested a link the CIA had previously written off as unlikely. Miscik had to ignore the agency's Mideast analysts to get there. Cheney's team was hardly appeased. His chief of staff, Scooter Libby, called Miscik to demand she withdraw her insufficient paper. Her successor, Mike Morell, called it "the most blatant attempt to politicize intelligence that I saw in 33 years in the business, and it would not be the last attempt by Libby to do so."

It was not enough merely to reject the CIA's conclusions. Neoconservatives had an explanation for why they were right and the skeptics within the agency and the State Department were wrong. Reuel Marc Gerecht, a former CIA officer, wrote in *The Weekly Standard* that both institutions were proving to be outright obstacles to the entire post-9/11 project. "The State Department and the Central Intelligence Agency have stubbornly refused to see the big picture of Islamic militancy," Gerecht charged. "Our actions toward Iraq, the Israeli-Palestinian confrontation, Egypt, Saudi Arabia, Syria, or Iran should not, in this view, radically change because of September 11." The subheadline purported to lay out "how the CIA unintentionally aids terrorism." His argument had an old pedigree. A conservative intellectual tradition rooted in the dawn of the Cold War considered the State Department and the CIA's analytical arm to be institutional redoubts of liberalism at its most craven. Laurie Mylroie, a conspiracist influential with Wolfowitz who insisted Saddam was tied to the 1993 World Trade Center bombing, claimed the CIA was "trying to stop the War on Terror." Mylroie, outdoing Cheney, noted that "no one has been held accountable" at the CIA for missing 9/11. A substantial cohort on the right contended that the analytic institutions of the Security State were not only untrustworthy but fundamentally hostile.

Within the Pentagon, under the auspices of the neoconservative undersecretary Douglas Feith and allied with Cheney's office, something ominously called the "Office of Special Plans" aimed to bypass the CIA by replicating its function. Asked after 9/11 if he thought Iraq was implicated, Wolfowitz offered a vague answer about how "everyone has got to look at this problem with completely new eyes in a completely new light." The Office of Special Plans was their new lens.

Established in August 2002, the Office of Special Plans went beyond Miscik's "deliberately provocative" paper. It reinterpreted dubious or dismissed material to create enough of an association as to be useful to validate the desired war. The neoconservative David Wurmser, an Office of Special Plans official who apprised Cheney's office on its work, conceded that mapping those connections "looked like that scene in *A Beautiful Mind*" where a delusional man visually depicts an impenetrable mathematical proof. But to Wurmser, the implication of those connections was obvious. Given that the CIA had so much raw intelligence indicating possible contacts, wouldn't it be irresponsible to discount it, in the wake of 9/11? And if the CIA persisted in pointing to the contradictory evidence as being more substantial, wasn't its judgment suspect, since the agency opposed overthrowing Saddam? Shouldn't *someone* be reappraising its work? As Wurmser explained to reporter Barton Gellman, "I was more laboring against obsolete assumptions, rather than cherry-picking." By September Rumsfeld spoke of "bulletproof" evidence connecting Saddam Hussein to al-Qaeda.

Visiting Langley personally, Dick Cheney pelted junior analysts with questions when they presented information insufficiently conducive to invading. Paul Pillar, the senior intelligence officer for the Mideast at the time, observed later that the administration, obsessed with alleged weapons of mass destruction and supposed terrorism links, never asked CIA analysts to forecast the repercussions of an invasion. "[I]ntelligence was misused publicly to justify decisions already made . . . ill will developed between policymakers and intelligence officers, and . . . the intelligence community's own work was politicized," Pillar wrote, describing a sense inside the CIA that Bush had decided on war by mid-2002, rendering contrary analysis futile. That was also the impression of MI6 director Richard Dearlove, who briefed colleagues in the UK government after a June 2002 visit to Washington that "intelligence and facts were being fixed around the policy."

Tyler Drumheller, a CIA operations officer, stated that the administration dismissed a September 2002 warning from Tenet that Saddam's foreign minister, desperate to avert war, assured his secret CIA handlers there were no illicit weapons stockpiles. But the weakened Tenet buckled again. By October the agency's intelligence products became more alarming, in time for Congress to vote for war. As the weapons analysis moved further up the analytic chain, Tenet and his deputies sanded down their doubts into a National Intelligence Estimate, an intelligence product with the aura of rigor, that was full of deceptive language implying surety. Key aspects of the CIA's report on Saddam's alleged biological weapons came from a defector, code-named Curveball, whose German handlers had long dismissed him as unreliable. Curveball later admitted fabricating his account so the United States would invade. "You want it real bad, you sometimes get it real bad. And the Iraq WMD estimate falls in that category," a senior State Department intelligence chief involved in producing the NIE later reflected.

While the administration suborned the intelligence agencies, it also amassed political capital for the Republican Party. Rove had urged Republicans to "go to the country" on the War on Terror "because they trust the Republican Party to do a better job protecting and strengthening America's military might and therefore protecting America." By the fall, it won one Senate race with a television ad that juxtaposed triple-amputee Vietnam veteran Max Cleland, who supported Bush on the war, with images of Saddam and bin Laden. Such successes, buoyed by terrorism anxiety and Bush's commanding approval ratings, created a dynamic where Republicans outdid themselves to back the war. "Some people seem to think there has got to be some new dramatic bit of evidence to justify our action, but frankly the president has stated the facts and they are sufficient for me to support a regime change," judged a nativist Alabama senator, Jeff Sessions. Such sentiments carried over into the broader culture. Supporting the war was not only respectable but came to be regarded as a test of an upstanding person's character. After one of the most popular country-music groups, the Dixie Chicks, expressed shame in their fellow Texan George W. Bush, they suffered a career-shattering backlash, complete with orgiastic public destruction of their CDs.

Unscrupulous people predictably exploited the war fever. "I'm not sure things are any tougher. They sound tougher, but I'm not sure if they are tougher in terms of security," Donald Trump told Howard Stern on the first anniversary of 9/11. Stern asked if Trump supported invading. Trump answered, "Yeah, I guess so. I wish the first time it was done correctly."

Neoconservatives convinced themselves that the war would be a grand act of liberation. The Iraqi émigrés they consulted stoked their American exceptionalism by assuring them that, as Bernard Lewis wrote, "there are democratic oppositions capable of taking over and forming governments" in Iraq and Iran. Wolfowitz spoke in the Arab American community of Dearborn of Iraqis' "dream of a just and democratic society"; admirers like Hitchens called Wolfowitz "a revolutionary." For his part, Bush implied that opponents of the war believed that Arabs must not be civilized enough for democracy: "Are the peoples of the Middle East somehow beyond the reach of liberty? Are millions of men and women and children condemned by history or culture to live in despotism?" When the French government became an obstacle to invasion, two Republican congressmen had the cafeteria menus in the House office buildings offer only "Freedom Fries." One of them, Walter Jones of North Carolina, would soon become one of the premier GOP war skeptics. But that was after Jones said the culinary change was a matter of honor swelling from his respect for the troops in his district. "As I've watched these men and women wave goodbye to their loved ones, I am reminded of the deep love they have for the freedom of this nation, and their desire to fight for the freedom of those who are oppressed overseas," said Jones, who also made the cafeterias advertise "Freedom Toast."

During the peak of the war fever, the neoconservatives moved against the nativists. David Frum, a Bush speechwriter, assailed the Buchananites as "self-described conservatives who see it as their role to make excuses for. suicide bombers." Those who practiced "uninhibited racial nationalism" were now deemed to be "Unpatriotic Conservatives," Frum wrote in a *National Review* cover story, reversing an attack the nativists typically aimed at the often Jewish neoconservatives. "In a time of danger, they have turned their backs on their country. Now we turn our backs on them," he wrote. Such was the promise of the War on Terror: it could adjudicate which factions were and were not authentically American.

IN SUCH AN ENVIRONMENT, perhaps the only voice whose opposition might have prevented the war chose instead to market it. Colin Powell would not be the last eminence of the Security State to convince himself that his complicity in a disaster was in fact internal resistance to it. A Vietnam veteran from the South Bronx, an architect of America's Gulf War victory over Saddam, and the first Black person to serve as national security adviser and chairman of the Joint Chiefs of Staff, Powell was a beloved national figure. A social conservative, Powell retired from the army disgusted with what he considered Clinton's blithe willingness to commit soldiers to solve complex foreign problems but withdraw them at the first, inevitable sign of trouble. The Republicans wanted him to run against Clinton for the presidency, but he declined. His influence was such that Bush made Powell, who considered himself a statesman, his chief diplomat.

Cheney had hated Powell since they clashed over the management of Desert Storm, and was eager to marginalize him. Powell, whose established steadiness diplomats trusted, provided cover in nervous foreign capitals for Cheney's radicalism. They came to know that Powell did not truly speak for Bush. Powell emphasized multilateralism and restraint when discussing a war Bush treated as a matter of American exceptionalist principle. Tragically, in an attempt to avert war, Powell convinced his counterparts on the United Nations Security Council that fall to reestablish an extensive weapons-inspections regime for Iraq. Powell had warned Bush that if he broke Iraq, he owned it, and considered the weapons inspections an alternative to invasion. But the move implied the legitimacy of using military force should Saddam commit a "material breach," thereby virtually ensuring war by making a disarmed Saddam look intransigent.

Finally, in February, Cheney, with a cutting remark over Powell possessing credibility to spare, compelled him to present the United States' specious intelligence case to the United Nations. Tenet provided it, though the intelligence displayed Cheney's influence. Powell; his chief of staff, Larry Wilkerson; and his deputy, Richard Armitage, all Vietnam veterans, stripped out some obviously absurd claims. Yet Powell presented as certainty a collection of flimsy, misconstrued, or manufactured evidence, such as a claim that Iraq had trained al-Qaeda in chemical warfare. That was the work of CIA torture on a captive named Ibn Shaikh al-Libi, who, the Senate Intelligence Committee affirmed in 2006, later recanted the claim as an attempt to avoid further torture or rendition. Powell also presented an al-Qaeda ally named Abu Musab al-Zarqawi, who was active in the part of Iraq Saddam didn't control, as bin Laden's Baghdad liaison. Powell's unimpeachable reputation ensured that wavering elite opinion made its peace with the war.

The month of Powell's speech, another Vietnam veteran, army chief of staff General Eric Shinseki, warned Congress that "several hundred thousand" troops were necessary to stabilize a post-Saddam Iraq. Such a protracted, ugly pacification mission, with significant cost, was the opposite of the message that Rumsfeld and Wolfowitz wished to send. Wolfowitz dismissed Shinseki as "wildly off the mark." But Shinseki, who had clashed with Rumsfeld, was already on his way to retirement, and Powell, who had himself urged a far larger force than Rumsfeld wanted, kept silent at Wolfowitz's rebukes.

Having offered no obstacle to a war that reminded him of the Vietnam disaster that forged him, Powell would by 2004 describe himself as a "patsy" for the hawks. More often, he blamed George Tenet and the CIA for feeding him false and fabricated information. Later, after forty-five hundred

Americans and hundreds of thousands of Iraqis died needless deaths, Powell presented himself as having his hands tied. "What choice did I have? He's the president," Powell told author Robert Draper.

By March 2003 a CIA analyst named Nada Bakos watched Zarqawi materialize in northern Iraq with a jihadist group called Ansar al-Islam, which appeared to be operating a highly crude bioweapons lab. Her colleague Sam Faddis, part of a CIA advance team, recommended an immediate air strike on Ansar's camp, reasoning that the group would disband once the United States invaded. They learned later that the administration rejected the strike. Bakos, who had dealt with Cheney's insistence on an al-Qaeda–Saddam connection, reasoned that Bush decided to spare Zarqawi to preserve an argument for war. "If they killed him prior to the invasion," she later told *Frontline*, "part of their justification is gone."

WHEN U.S. TROOPS CAPTURED Baghdad on April 10, neoconservatives celebrated the dawn of a new era of American power. Writing in *The Weekly Standard*, David Brooks asked readers to see the new world through the eyes of an imaginary college student he called Joey Tabula-Rasa. Glued to CNN, Brooks's twenty-year old "sees a ruling establishment that can conduct wars with incredible competence and skill. He sees a federal government that can perform its primary task—protecting the American people—magnificently." Surveying the intellectual landscape, Brooks noted with delight, "Now that the war in Iraq is over, we'll find out how many people around the world are capable of facing unpleasant facts."

Weeks later, as a patrol from the First Armored Division maneuvered through the Baghdad neighborhood Yarmouk, an Arabic-speaking reporter, Anthony Shadid, loitered behind it to assess the local reaction. "They're walking over my heart. I feel like they're crushing my heart," remarked thirty-four-year-old Mohammed Ibraham. Outside a school for autistic children the Americans had declared under their protection, twenty-three-year-old Saif Din extended no credit to those who claimed to be his liberators: "We're not against the presence of the school, we're against the presence of the Americans." A seventy-year-old, Ahmed Abdullah, promised to fight soldiers young enough to be his grandchildren. "Baghdad is the mother of Arab culture, and they want to wipe out our culture, absolutely," he said.

Yarmouk was the sort of neighborhood that the Pentagon, which ran the occupation, assumed would embrace the new status quo the United States imposed. Located west of the Tigris River, it was a young, planned community, built first for officers in the Iraqi military and later became a redoubt for professionals. There was substantial Baath Party membership in Yarmouk, but party membership was a requirement for the lifestyle that Yarmouk residents lived. Here resided the sort of people that an occupation predicated on establishing a bourgeois republic, governing from the center outward and pro-American in outlook, desperately needed.

What it got, at most, was the reluctant support of those whose interests at the moment coincided with those of the occupation. More often the occupation was accepted with the forbearance of those desperately seeking to survive. It was also met regularly with resistance—violence that the occupying forces recognized, as well as subtler forms that they didn't. Engineers, in pursuit of goodwill, transformed a garbage-strewn lot into a soccer pitch. They soon found that the goalposts and even the dirt off the field had been stolen. "What kind of people loot dirt?" an army captain wondered.

Convinced the war was over, Bush landed on the aircraft carrier *Abraham Lincoln* to infamously declare MISSION ACCOMPLISHED on May 1. By July he installed a powerless Iraqi advisory council mostly consisting of Saddam-era exiles enthusiastic about or acquiescent to the American project. Real power resided with the Pentagon's Coalition Provisional Authority (CPA), run by an autocratic protégé of Henry Kissinger named L. Paul "Jerry" Bremer. In keeping with the Pentagon's fantastical assurances of a transformed Iraq, they disbanded the Iraqi military and banned the Baath Party. These blithe decisions materially disenfranchised millions of Iraqis, removed a military institution through which the U.S. military hoped to operate, and underscored the humiliating reality that the Iraqis were a conquered people. Such indifference to the lives of Iraqis was characteristic of the occupation. Pentagon planning neither anticipated nor prioritized such infrastructural measures as fixing the damaged power grid, collecting trash, maintaining the sewers and the water system, repairing the roads, enforcing the traffic rules, providing for all the aspects of daily life that support normalcy and convince people that their needs matter to those who rule them. They permitted the looting of antiquities from the Iraqi National Museum, resulting in the theft of priceless artifacts of early human civilization, something Rumsfeld shrugged off as the spoils of freedom.

Permissive attitudes toward looting were symptomatic of the grift the CPA oversaw. By the time Administrator Bremer departed, $8.8 billion in reconstruction funds—taxpayer money harvested during a recession while Bush tilted more of the tax burden onto the middle and working classes—had simply disappeared without leaving a paper trail, while American contractors selling the occupation everything from laundry detergent to private security reaped windfalls. One of them, KBR, a subsidiary of the company Dick Cheney had run until the 2000 presidential campaign, provided the 101st Airborne with mobile barracks that cost twice what the division would have paid for building its own lodgings.

Bremer's organization was less interested in hiring professional administrators than bringing aboard twenty-somethings with Republican Party connections. It hired individuals who had submitted their résumés to the conservative Heritage Foundation while denying that such employment arrangements represented cronyism. An experienced diplomat on the CPA staff called it "amateur hour . . . we could not run a country we didn't understand." Iraq could indeed not be understood from within the Green Zone, the four-square-mile fortress in the heart of Baghdad from which the CPA operated. Described in 2004 as home to perhaps five thousand Westerners but "quite simply empty" thanks to its luxurious open spaces, it was a playpen for Americans looking to drink at its seven bars, find sex, enjoy cigars by elegant pools once patronized by Saddam's coterie, and eat a bounty of pork dishes. CPA buildings, protected by seventeen-foot-high concrete walls ringing the Green Zone, were kept at a comfortable sixty-eight degrees, unlike the rest of the sweltering, electricity-starved Baghdad, in what was by default the Red Zone. In the Red Zone, Iraqis looking at the army vehicles that patrolled their streets saw a warning that they could be shot if they came within a hundred meters.

The war allowed a retired Navy SEAL, a scion of Michigan Republican aristocracy, to parlay the law-enforcement "training" services he offered on his North Carolina shooting range into a billion-dollar business. Not a decade into its existence, Erik Prince's Blackwater won a piece of the State Department's contract to protect its diplomats, worth hundreds of millions of dollars. Blackwater's guards, many of whom were former service members, liked to party. Howard Lowry, a Texas businessman who came to Iraq to make money, later said in a deposition that he would supply Blackwater personnel with steroids "by the case." Their behavior reflected it. "Company personnel had large amounts of cocaine and blocks of hashish and would run around naked," Lowry recalled. Coked-up naked gym rats on heavy steroidal doses would run onto Green Zone balconies and, screaming, fire AK-47 rounds into the Iraqi night sky. Before sunrise Blackwater staff would load American diplomats into their armored SUVs and drive them through Red Zone Baghdad roads strewn with improvised explosive devices, the cheap homemade bombs that represented the insurgents' signature technological innovation.

Ill-equipped to govern the country they occupied, the American forces expressed irritation at the high expectations foisted upon them by the subjects of their conquest. "You Americans can put a man on the moon, why can't you give me a job with a salary right now? Why can't you snap your fingers and produce twenty-four-hour power?" summarized the division commander in Mosul, the two-star general David Petraeus. Petraeus's approach was to functionally disregard the direction Bremer imposed and seek to work with the extant Mosul power structure, which the de-Baathification order had criminalized.

It was the exception. Restive villages typically faced crackdowns. The former West Point champion quarterback Nate Sassaman ringed the town of Abu Hishma in concertina wire. He issued cards to Abu Hishma's men, written in English only, informing them they would be shot if they entered or left the town without American permission. Mothers warned their misbehaving children to go to bed before Colonel Sassaman came for them. Sassaman later covered up his soldiers' murder-for-sport of twenty-four-year-old Zaydoon Fadhil, whom they made jump off a bridge into a river; Sassaman lost his army career but not his freedom. In Taji the commander of an artillery battalion, Lieutenant Colonel Allen West, had four of his men beat a restrained Iraqi policeman, Yahya Jhrodi Hamoody, whom he suspected of having knowledge of a supposed assassination plot against him. West placed the bound Hamoody by a nearby weapons-clearance barrel before firing his nine-millimeter service pistol into it. He then ordered his men to put Hamoody's head in the barrel. A policeman who had earlier worked with West stated later that Hamoody spouted names of random people in the hope of staying alive. Major General Ray Odierno, West's division commander (who was also Sassaman's), declined to order a court-martial.

Fallujah, a city of three hundred thousand people in the western Sunni province of Anbar, had a blood debt to pay America. On April 28, 2003, beside the Baath Party headquarters next to its city hall, Iraqis demonstrating against the newly established occupation came under fire from American soldiers, who killed fifteen people. "I am sure that if we had had weapons we would have killed them," demonstrator Ahmad Hatim Karim told Human Rights Watch investigators. Then into the city arrived Abu Musab al-Zarqawi. While Zarqawi, a Jordanian, had spent time in Afghanistan's Arab-jihadi circles, al-Qaeda considered him beneath them. They were men with advanced degrees who believed themselves to be waging an aristocratic jihad aimed at pernicious America. Zarqawi was a tattooed former gangbanger and rumored ex-pimp, a criminal, who wanted to kill "Safavids," or Shiites, to provoke bloody retaliation against Iraqi Sunnis, who would unite under the banner of what he, in a tacit challenge to bin Laden, called al-Qaeda in Iraq. "Our combat against the Americans is something easy," Zarqawi wrote in 2004. "The enemy is apparent, his back is exposed, and he does not know the land or the current situation of the mujahidin because his intelligence information is weak." Even bin Laden considered Zarqawi nihilistic, but the chaos the Americans had unleashed in Iraq only marginalized bin Laden and empowered Zarqawi.

In the waning days of March 2004, Iraqi militants in Fallujah, whose tactics indicated that professional soldiers were among them, ambushed and overwhelmed a convoy of SUVs driven by four Blackwater contractors. Cheering crowds, young boys among them, gathered as the Fallujans set the vehicles aflame and lynched the contractors, hanging two of their charred corpses from atop a bridge. Footage of the carnage, the lead story on American news programs, featured a banner held by a member of the crowd proclaiming FALLUJAH IS THE CEMETERY FOR AMERICANS. The First Marine Division commander, James Mattis, argued that the insurgents wanted to draw the marines into a brutal street fight in their home neighborhood. Overruled, Mattis had his marines advance into a nightmare known as the First Battle of Fallujah. Insurgents fought the marines, using IEDs, rocket-propelled grenades, skillful indirect fire, and maneuvering that weaponized their far greater understanding of the geography of the city. They drew the marines deep into its confines and attacked the roads behind to prevent resupply or escape. Their resistance swelled a wave of Iraqi pride. Baghdad's Shiites in Sadr City and Adhamiya organized blood drives for the Sunnis in Fallujah. "We are with them, in death and killing," said Daoud al-Akoub of Sadr City. When the Iraqis on the occupation council threatened to quit, Mattis had to withdraw from an unfinished weeklong mission that had taken the lives of thirty-nine marines and supporting soldiers. According to a memo that two British Labour Party members of Parliament violated the Official Secrets Act to leak, Al Jazeera's coverage of Fallujah was so intolerable to Bush—who had already bombed its Baghdad bureau during the invasion, as he had the Kabul bureau in 2001—that he mused to Prime

Minister Tony Blair about bombing the station's headquarters in Qatar. The marines returned to the city after the U.S. presidential election for a grueling house-to-house battle, Second Fallujah, that took the lives of eighty-two of them and wounded another six hundred. While Fallujah passed into Marine Corps legend, the city launched attacks on the occupiers for years to come.

Holding such territory was a job for conventional U.S. forces who had never been trained for the task, despite how often the military had performed such imperial work during the conquest of the American West, the Philippines, Haiti, Vietnam, and elsewhere. Whatever civic deference military service was supposed to yield stateside, troops quickly learned how little they mattered to the institutional military once deployed. Their bases hosted massive open-air incinerators, "burn pits" that set alight everything from random trash to human waste, meaning that proximate troops would breathe in the acrid, dangerous particulates. When they left the bases for patrols, their lightly armored vehicles, built for the speed of an invasion rather than for the survivability of an occupation, were little defense against insurgent weaponry. They would fish through scrap heaps for metal to weld on, so-called hillbilly armor of last resort. When they complained about it to a visiting Rumsfeld, the defense secretary shrugged. "You go to war with the army you have," he said.

Hunting forces like Zarqawi's was assigned to a Joint Special Operations Command task force led by the three-star general Stanley McChrystal. McChrystal's raids involved dispatching Americans in intimidating body armor and night vision goggles to kick in doors, round people up, and tear houses apart in pursuit of terrorists, weapons, or information. McChrystal climbed the stairs in one dwelling to encounter a family standing on their second-floor landing to watch the invaders. "I'll never forget their stare," McChrystal would write. "It was controlled, but I sensed pure anger, radiating like heat. . . . We were big men, made bigger with body armor, it was one o'clock in the morning, and our searching of their home was as humiliating to them as if we had stripped their bodies." McChrystal's task force would kill Zarqawi two years later, after innumerable house raids, but would never vanquish his organization. The durability of al-Qaeda in Iraq convinced McChrystal that the bloodshed was futile unless the United States could address the root causes of the violence.

But the Americans, unwilling to leave Iraq, preferred a carceral approach. In the summer of 2003 Rumsfeld's intelligence chief dispatched the Guantanamo commander to Iraq with instructions on "Gitmo-izing" detentions and interrogations. The regimen, modified and implemented by Iraq commander Lieutenant General Ricardo Sanchez by October, was a version of what the CIA had implemented at the black sites. The prison where this would unfold, Abu Ghraib, was staffed with 380 military police to guard 8,000 prisoners; by contrast, 800 MPs guarded Guantanamo's 600 detainees. Interrogators flooded into Abu Ghraib alongside guards who answered to a different chain of command.

Abu Ghraib soon became the site of widespread sexual assault—most of which, a 2004 investigation found, "did not focus on persons held for intelligence purposes." An exception, a detainee assessed to have significant intelligence value, was sodomized with a police baton and photographed nude by two women guards while they threw a ball at his penis. Soldiers took a photograph of a detainee with a banana inserted into his anus. Guards positioned naked detainees into groups and compelled them to masturbate before what an investigator called riding them "like animals." A particularly brutal MP, Corporal Charles Graner, beat a man into unconsciousness and shoved a different detainee into a wall with sufficient force to require thirteen stitches on the man's chin. Graner photographed his assaults for souvenirs.

Exposed in the summer of 2004 as uprisings exploded across Iraq, the brutality of Abu Ghraib resulted in the first instance of the Bush administration and the Security State conceding error. Except the responsibility wasn't theirs: it belonged to junior enlisted personnel acting like what a Pentagon investigation called "'Animal House' on the night shift." A series of Pentagon reports sought to portray the Abu Ghraib abuse as a departure from what went on at the black sites and Guantanamo. "No policy, directive or doctrine directly or indirectly caused violent or sexual abuse. In these cases, Soldiers knew they were violating the approved techniques and procedures," read one. A former defense secretary, James Schlesinger, lamented that such tortures "migrated" from Guantanamo, a formulation that suggested animal compulsion rather than deliberate decisions taken by men like Rumsfeld, Guantanamo commander Geoffrey Miller, and Sanchez. If Rumsfeld resigned over the scandal, Schlesinger said, it would be "a boon for all of America's enemies."

The brutality at Abu Ghraib in some measure provided release for the frustrations of a war that did not unfold as its architects had promised. Ian Fishback, a company commander in Iraq, wrote to Senator John McCain—a fervent advocate of the War on Terror and the Iraq occupation as well as a survivor of torture in Vietnamese captivity—pleading for a ban on military torture. Alabama's Senator Sessions implied Fishback was slandering the military: "Captain Fishback said he had seen at least one interrogation where prisoners were being abused. Now I don't know what abused means. I'm a former prosecutor. What does 'abused' mean?" Sessions would have been appointed as a federal judge had colleagues not come forward with accounts of his racism. These included the prosecution of three civil rights workers, including a onetime Martin Luther King deputy, for organizing Black Alabamans.

McCain immediately demanded Sessions deliver an "abject and deep apology" to Fishback. Affecting innocence, Sessions insisted that all he had done was read Fishback's account in *The New York Times*. It was the Senate's sanctimonious, slanderous opponents of so-called torture who owed the military an apology, he continued. "Those in this Senate who have accused up and down members of the chain of command of the United States Army, the United States Marines, the Department of Defense of being—promoting policies to abuse prisoners, they ought to think about whether they should apologize," Sessions fumed.

Locked inside the unreality it created to invade Iraq, the Bush administration chose to compound the lies to avoid acknowledging the disaster it had unleashed. It insisted there was no substantial resistance from Iraqis. It called Iraqi insurgents "anti-Iraqi forces" and sought to attribute the insurgency to Zarqawi and Saddam Hussein dead-enders. Rumsfeld, increasingly an object of derision from U.S. troops whose lives he had treated so cavalierly, accused reporters of manufacturing narratives of failure and his critics of lacking sufficient faith in America. "The only way this effort could fail is if people were to be persuaded that the cause is lost or that it's not worth the pain, or if those who seem to measure progress in Iraq against a more perfect world convince others to throw in the towel," he said.

The Democratic senator who on 9/12 had pronounced himself sanguine about killing Muslim civilians, Zell Miller, gave a venomous speech at Bush's renomination convention excoriating liberals for the calumny of accurately characterizing the American presence in Iraq: "Today's Democratic leaders see America as an occupier, not a liberator. And nothing makes this marine madder than someone calling American troops occupiers rather than liberators." As the insurgency coalesced into a civil war in 2005, with Shiite parties empowered by the United States operating torture chambers out of the Interior Ministry, Cheney insisted the resistance was in its "last throes." When no weapons of mass destruction were found, Bush was left pleading that there was no choice but to continue with a *mission civilisatrice*. "Iraq will either be a peaceful democratic country or it will again be a source of violence, a haven for terror and a threat to America and to the world," he said in April 2004.

But Iraq's slide into chaos rendered conservatives dissatisfied with the president's rhetoric of obligation. American exceptionalism could never permit them to embrace withdrawal, but there was another option. "I'd like to see one other thing in Iraq," wrote Fred Barnes of *The Weekly Standard* after visiting Baghdad in April 2004, "an outbreak of gratitude for the greatest act of benevolence one country has ever done for another." Six months later epidemiologists from the British publication *The Lancet* estimated that the war and its effects had killed at least one hundred thousand Iraqis.

The Iraq war had been glorious; the fault lay with the Iraqis. Some in the Security State agreed. A military source told *Newsweek* that the Sunni population "is paying no price for the support it is giving to the terrorists . . . we have to change that equation." By 2006 the cable news war promoter Tucker Carlson announced that he had "zero sympathy" for Iraqis, who "don't use toilet paper or forks," thereby demonstrating to Carlson their cultural inferiority. "They can just shut the fuck up and obey, is my view," Carlson said. Neocon defense theorist Danielle Pletka later lamented the Iraqis' "political immaturity" and "embrace [of] sect and tribe over ideas." Evangelicals were reaching a similar conclusion after a war they had embraced in part to convert Muslims unleashed an orgy of violence that endangered missionaries and Iraqi Christians.

There were other villains to pursue closer to home: the liberal media undermining the War on Terror. In 2005 the military acknowledged multiple incidences of desecration of the Koran—though it preferred to describe them as "mishandling"—at Guantanamo. One of the confirmed desecrations was what *The Washington Post* described as a "two-word obscenity" scribbled in a Koran; the military claimed a detainee might have written it. *The Wall Street Journal* pronounced the details "unhorrifying" and the "hullabaloo" around the Koran desecrations as "all about repudiating the Bush administration's approach to the war on terror." Barnes, speaking on Fox News, counteraccused the Muslim world: "Why is it that Muslim terrorists can bomb a mosque in Pakistan and there are not demonstrations anywhere, and yet they think some Koran has been mishandled and there are these demonstrations? I mean, that is spectacular hypocrisy, which shows you how politically bizarre a lot of the Muslim world is." When *The New York Times*' James Risen and Eric Lichtblau exposed part of the NSA's STELLARWIND bulk surveillance, an army captain accused them of "gravely endanger[ing] the lives of my soldiers and all other soldiers and innocent Iraqis here." The next time the captain, Tom Cotton, heard an explosion, he said, "I will wonder whether we could have stopped that bomb had you not instructed terrorists how to evade our financial surveillance."

Bush never abandoned his war. But in recognition of the political threat that anger over it gave rise to, he empaneled a commission to blame the CIA. The Robb-Silberman Commission, whose mandate focused exclusively on WMD intelligence failures, urged politicians to put greater pressure on the Security State. The intelligence community "will not do its best unless it is pressed by policymakers—sometimes to the point of discomfort," it advised. To apply the necessary force, Bush replaced Tenet with House Intelligence Committee chairman Porter Goss, a former CIA operations officer. Goss brought in a coterie of loyalists whom the agency considered political commissars. Alumni leaked damaging stories about Goss's deputies, whom they christened the "Gosslings" and sometimes "Hill Pukes," and about highly regarded agency counterterrorism veterans resigning. Goss's GOP replacement on the House committee, Representative Pete Hoekstra, accused intelligence leakers in 2006 of trying to sabotage Bush "or help al Qaeda, or perhaps both." Adding injury to insult was Congress's 2004 decision to strip the CIA of its centrality within the intelligence community. It created a new position, a director of national intelligence (DNI), as a kind of coordinator, without budgetary authority, atop the agencies. Beholden to none of them, the DNI was in a stronger position to be obligated to the president appointing him or her.

With domestic dissatisfaction over the situation in Iraq intensifying, Bush redefined the War on Terror as something more explicitly anti-Islamic. It was his key to arguing that Americans had to keep fighting, no matter how horrifying what the Pentagon now called the "Long War" became. While Bush said the enemy was "very different from the religion of Islam," it was motivated by a "clear and focused ideology" that he compared to communism, inflating by implication the scale of purchase this ideology had. But the president was not prepared to give it a specific name—only to nod to those on the right who had chafed at his euphemism and longed for him to identify the enemy as Islamic. "Some call this evil Islamic radicalism. Others militant jihadism. Still others Islamofascism," Bush declared. After creating the conditions for Zarqawi to eclipse bin Laden in bloodshed, Bush dismissed as "an excuse" any suggestion that American bellicosity had spurred an appetite for this ideology. As Ashcroft had done four years earlier with his roundups, Bush demanded that "all responsible Islamic leaders" denounce this radicalism, which he said was different from their religion, just not different *enough*. Bush's speech was simultaneously an assertion, providing assurance to conservatives, of both Muslim guilt and American innocence.

The right rejoiced. One of Bush's former security aides, Richard Falkenrath, considered the president's "more sophisticated" depiction of what he called "radical Islam . . . closer to the truth" about the post-9/11 enemy. One of his political strategists, Dan Bartlett, hailed Bush's speech as a matter of national necessity. "If we don't take the enemy seriously, it's impossible for us to defeat them," he told MSNBC. The Republican chairman of the House Foreign Affairs Committee, Ed Royce of California, "welcome[d] the president's move from the generic 'war on terrorism' to the more specific 'Islamic radicalism,'" and considered a "long struggle" against it unavoidable. Bay Buchanan, Pat's sister and a conservative columnist, hailed on CNN that "up to now it's war on terrorists, we're after terrorists. And now he actually called it, it was radical Islam." On Fox, Barnes similarly exulted that "the president over and over again used the word 'Islamic.' It's Islamic radicalism, or it's Islamofascism, and so on." Bush and his aides "don't explain what it is because they said their hands are bound by the rules of political correctness and they can't say it's an offshoot of Islam that's gone crazy, which is exactly what it is," observed Tucker Carlson, by then an MSNBC host.

Stanley McChrystal, by this time leading JSOC and hunting Zarqawi, later reflected that Islam was little more than a "unifying rationale" for the jihadists, a solution to a fundamentally geopolitical phenomenon. "It wasn't why they fought the fight," he said. "The Islamic world felt like it had gotten dealt a bad hand from the West. It felt like the autocratic regimes supported by the West—Saudi Arabia, Kuwait, and whatnot—were illegitimate. So there was this pent-up rage and frustration; part of it was economic and part of it was social. Islam gave them a unifying connection, like soldiers in any war, 'Onward Christian Soldiers' in the Crusades. But I don't think that was what we were fighting, and I don't think it was why *they* were fighting."

Bush's redefinition did little to arrest the deterioration of his political power. The War on Terror saved Republicans in the midterm elections of 2002; the war in Iraq doomed them in 2006. Conservatives were the last to abandon their leader, but Bush's push for an immigration reform that would have legalized millions of undocumented immigrants alienated many. The president praised "the vast majority of illegal immigrants [as] decent people," and decried militarizing the southern border even as he and border state governors sent thousands of national guardsmen to it. "A few steps, including calling out the National Guard, significant though they may be, will not change the pervasive illegality of our current immigration system," lamented Sessions, who preferred increasing "short-term detention" and "expanding border fencing and barriers." The time had come to look past Bush, toward a new leader of the Long War. If even the Islam-is-peace president eventually, if tentatively, recognized the Islamic nature of the enemy, the next leader could do no less.

But the bleeding ulcer of Iraq was rapidly draining conservatives of the hold on power they thought the Long War would guarantee. They now faced the prospect that the liberals could control both the War on Terror and, as important, the wartime narrative.

CHAPTER THREE

LIBERAL COMPLICITY IN THE WAR ON TERROR

2001–2008

A s the FBI began rounding up Muslims and immigrants in the fall of 2001, a powerful Democrat worried that the government's domestic counterterrorism efforts were inefficient.

The organizational chart of security-adjacent functions displayed an incoherent patchwork of responsibilities. Airport security was the domain of the Department of Transportation. Confronting threats to and from shipping belonged to both Treasury Department customs inspectors and the Coast Guard. Bush brought Pennsylvania governor Tom Ridge into the White House to impose some degree of order, but the federal bureaucracy was too intractable, cabinet secretaries too powerful against a mere White House aide, and the stakes too high. "Governor Ridge obviously has the confidence of the president and our support," stated Connecticut senator Joe Lieberman, the Democrats' 2000 vice-presidential nominee. "I don't think he's been given all the tools he needs to get this job done."

Lieberman's concerns had nothing to say on behalf of the hundreds locked within the Metropolitan Detention Center. But he and his sober-minded colleagues in both parties could not abide the organizational chaos within domestic counterterrorism. Before 9/11 no one referred to American territory as the "homeland." The term, ironically, sounded foreign to American ears, uncomfortably echoing the claimed spiritual connection between a birthplace and its people, which was central to European nationalisms. Lieberman nevertheless introduced in October 2001 a Senate bill to create a Department of Homeland Security (DHS). Whatever its name, the concept had excellent technocratic credentials. The spring before the attacks, a bipartisan panel of two former centrist senators, Warren Rudman and Gary Hart, had recommended precisely this consolidation of domestic security functions. Characteristically, Lieberman worked alongside a centrist Republican, Arlen Specter, as serious people in Washington understood that bipartisanship was the way to change important things.

Bush wasn't convinced. Lieberman's proposed new cabinet department was itself unwieldy, as it cobbled together agencies with different missions and internal cultures into an entity with a $38 billion budget and the loosely defined mandate of preventing terrorist attacks. Lieberman persisted, calling for "bold organizational change." Bush, checkmated by his own War on Terror logic, finally acquiesced in June, bringing aboard congressional Republicans. Tom Daschle, the Senate Democratic leader, boasted that Democrats had supported creating the new department "before it was cool."

There was Democratic dissent over the Department of Homeland Security. Although Lieberman had reached the highest echelons of the party, he was distrusted by its progressive wing. House Democrats rejected DHS by wide margins. But only nine Senate Democrats voted against it. Senator Russ Feingold, who had resisted the PATRIOT Act, warned that the new department would weaken "protections against unwarranted government intrusion into the lives of ordinary Americans." Voices like his became peripheral within the party after 9/11, while voices like Lieberman's became central.

By the beginning of the twenty-first century, the Democratic Party believed the substantial and unequally distributed wealth created during Bill Clinton's presidency vindicated its decision to marginalize its left wing. Lacking firm ideological commitments after generations of loosening its ties to labor, increasingly divorced from the material conditions of the vast majority of Americans, and terrified of being on the wrong side of security issues, Democrats compensated with technocracy and institutionalism. No one, in an atmosphere of fear over the possibility of a radiological bomb being transported in a suitcase, could object to increasing port inspections of shipping containers. DHS also wasn't involved in foreign policy, and so would avoid provoking battles over war and peace that exposed divides in the Democratic Party. And DHS was unavoidably politically advantageous in a country rallying around Bush, even when the president stripped out union protections for the hundreds of thousands of federal workers within the new department, endangering a Democratic constituency.

All this rationality and opportunity concealed a radical shift that lay at the heart of the Department of Homeland Security. A massive government apparatus devoted to counterterrorism was now in control of immigration. During the twentieth century, the government had placed enforcement of its immigration policies within the departments of Treasury, Commerce, and then Justice, snapshots of how different generations understood the purpose of immigration. Those agencies variously withstood and reflected · severe immigration panics in American history, including a nativist ground-swell in the 1920s and a backlash to the relaxation of immigration restrictions in the 1960s. They reflected a consensus, however strained it often was, that immigration might be a contentious issue, but it was not a security threat. But Lieberman, his centrist Democratic and Republican colleagues, and the experts they consulted viewed immigration, a cornerstone of American identity, through the prism of terrorism.

To DHS's advocates, doing so was practical: the hijackers had exposed the fact that nineteen men without criminal records could easily enter the country, as would be inevitable in an open society. Republicans, taking an opportunity to exploit 9/11 for their preexisting antipathy to nonwhite immigration, portrayed American openness as a risk. Democrats, in that atmosphere, portrayed it as a challenge that sensible people could rationally address. "The real importance of this bill, which you should be commended for, is to tackle the problem of the border, which, as we've heard before, has been long ignored," the Brookings Institution's centrist governance studies expert Elaine Kamarck testified to Lieberman's committee in April 2002. "Let me point out that these problems of the border are not new, but until September 11 there was never the sense of urgency to overcome all the bureaucratic intransigence to this." Some among them understood the bill's potential implications. "We have five thousand unaccompanied alien children a year. Do they belong in a Department of Homeland Security? I don't think so," California senator Dianne Feinstein said that June, five months before voting to create the department.

The first DHS official in charge of what was called the Bureau of Immigration and Customs Enforcement (ICE) was a former New York federal prosecutor experienced in terrorism cases. Not only did Michael Garcia defend the post-9/11 Muslim immigrant roundups, he suggested baselessly that they prevented further terrorism. It was an "exercise in disruption," Garcia told Ted Kennedy, one of the few Senate Democrats to reject DHS. "It's hard to disprove a connection between a disruptive exercise and the fact that you did not have follow-up attacks."

The retooled Immigration and Customs Enforcement conducted a series of raids—not on suspected terror cells, but on businesses employing undocumented immigrants. In 2005, it raided thirteen hundred businesses. In 2006, it tripled its pace to forty-four hundred. That year, ICE began a years-long, nationwide roundup, Operation Return to Sender, which arrested twenty-three thousand people at work and even from their homes. Few of those seized had any criminal record. Under cover of homeland security, ICE "receiv[ed] millions [in] congressional funds to get dangerous criminals off the streets, but are using it for routine immigration enforcement," the executive director of the Arizona ACLU, Alessandra Soler Meetze, observed.

Before dawn on a Tuesday morning in March 2007, an ICE raid targeted a New Bedford, Massachusetts, textile factory where poorly paid workers made vests and backpacks for the military. Once the loudspeaker warned that immigration agents had arrived, chaos erupted on the floor as workers scrambled to hide. Some rushed the bathroom to jump from the window. ICE agents, some of them with their handguns drawn, arrested 361 people. While women in the factory screamed and cried, the agents sorted their quarry into groups, zip-tied their hands, and led them to detention on a nearby army base, where some remained for months before deportation. At a church that evening Luis Matias pleaded for help for the three-year-old girl and nine-month-old baby of his tenant, whom ICE had arrested. "It's inhumane to take a mother from her children. She's not a criminal," Matias said. Another of those arrested was the mother of eight-year-old Luis Gomez. Luis, unaware his parents had emigrated illegally, later remembered hiding for a week, missing school, out of fear he would be next. "Here I was," he recalled to a reporter, "suddenly in charge of my family."

Lieberman touted his role in creating DHS when he ran for president in 2004. It was part of a broader pitch: he was the Democrat who was going to take over the War on Terror from the hapless Bush. He argued that 9/11 exposed an "amorphous threat we face from fanatics who find justification for evil behavior in Islam," comparable to "fascism and communism." His 2003 definition of the enemy anticipated Bush's eventual description of a wellspring for terrorism existing within Islam itself. Lieberman wasn't so rabid as to describe most Muslims as radicals; "the vast majority" opposed the fanatics. Hearkening to a condescending liberal tradition two centuries old, one that justified brute military force, and one that gained extensive purchase in liberal intellectual circles for years after 9/11, Lieberman urged the United States to act in the name of such threatened Muslims, "who are being besieged by isolation and intolerance." The emerging quagmires in Iraq and Afghanistan, both of which the senator supported, were the result of Bush's botched execution, not any conceptual arrogance. Americans weren't doing enough "to adequately seed the garden to enable peace, pros-

perity and democracy to take root and to prevent terrorism from returning." But there could be no doubt that "forceful action" was necessary to
"drain the swamps that breed terrorism."

Anyone on the left looking for a champion against the wars did not find
a consistent, empowered Democratic voice. They certainly did not find one
who made opposition to the wars as central to his or her political persona
as Lieberman made his advocacy. Neither did those, such as Muslims and
immigrants, whom the War on Terror persecuted. With the Republican
Party increasingly rabid, millions of Americans seeking an alternative to
endless war had no choice but to hope the Democratic Party, perhaps belatedly, would hear them. Then, when the public mood turned against the
Iraq war, Democrats shifted with them, jettisoning their previous support.
The ultimate difference between Lieberman and the Democrats he once
helped lead was not that Lieberman was for the War on Terror and they
weren't. It was that Lieberman had conviction and they didn't.

LIBERALS EMERGED FROM THE COLD WAR divided, traumatized, and unsure of their principles. Anti-communist liberalism built the structures that
confronted the Soviet Union, but that did not spare it the demagoguery of
conservatives for whom liberalism was a stalking horse for communism.
Dean Acheson, a Cold War architect, sneered at this "attack of the primi-
tives." Cold War liberalism marched to its doom in Vietnam, but nothing
claimed its place within the Democratic Party. Progressives attempted
to harness the agony of Vietnam and the reactionary nature of domestic
anti-communism into a broader critique of militarism, but uncertain liberals, unwilling to part with American exceptionalism, kept the party from
moving too far in that direction. No sooner did liberals exhale at the fall of
the Berlin Wall than Democrats appeared to discredit themselves by voting
against the massively popular, successful Gulf War. The lesson Democrats
drew was that peace was a losing issue. The safest Democratic position on

military affairs was avoidance, followed by technocracy—often an attempt at aligning with what it saw as the responsible, pragmatic forces of the Security State—followed by attempts at marshaling American hegemony for liberal purposes. Rather than resolve the Democrats' foreign policy contradictions, Bill Clinton's presidency reflected them, bombing its way into an inchoate exceptionalist right to humanitarian-premised military intervention. Following in a liberal-imperial tradition they seemed not to recognize, the Clintonites tacitly premised their Balkans air strikes on enforcing standards of civilized behavior.

After 9/11, even the most left-wing Democratic legislators wanted no part in challenging the coalescing War on Terror. Bush vowed on September 20 to "rid the world of the evildoers." Afterward, California's Maxine Waters said the Democrats planned on resisting him "no time soon." She didn't want to send young people to war, she told CNN's Tucker Carlson, "but we're going to stand with the families who have been harmed. There is a lot of pain in this nation, and we are in mourning. We are trying to stay unified, and we don't want to create bickering and fighting at this time. There are questions to be asked. Now is not the time."

It was instead a time to exorcise the left and restore the reputation of the Cold War liberalism that had built an international order around American hegemony. An elite strain of liberalism reconciled with American power as a moral force during the Balkan wars in the 1990s, and came to view "humanitarian intervention" as a valorous legacy of Bill Clinton's. After 9/11, Democratic fear of opposition intersected with elite liberal enthusiasm for the opportunities the war generated. Outraged by Sontag and other "Blame America Firsters," with their "ignorant and dangerous appeasement of the terrorism of Sept. 11," *Newsweek*'s Jonathan Alter predicted that next terrorist attack would prompt "a big old-fashioned peace movement," something he considered contemptible. "Peace won't be with you, brother. It's kill or be killed." Alter, "like President Bush and the vast majority of the country," was in favor of a fantastical "targeted war that tries hard to avoid civilian casualties, Islamic blowback and other unintended consequences." In

June 2002 the liberal grassroots organization MoveOn issued a bulletin asking "Can Democracy Survive an Endless 'War'?" It quoted James Madison and Benjamin Franklin to decry the PATRIOT Act, and raised the plight of immigrants in detention. The editor of *The New Republic* later called it a travesty that reflected a "liberal base unwilling to redefine itself for the post–September 11 world" and its war against "totalitarian Islam."

As Bush shifted focus from al-Qaeda to Saddam Hussein in his 2002 "Axis of Evil" State of the Union address, the House Democratic leader, Dick Gephardt, acknowledged, "There has been no daylight between us in this war on terrorism. We have met almost every single week and built a bipartisan consensus that is helping America win this war." A few months later Daschle showed some daylight, remarking that the war "will have failed" if bin Laden remained at large. When DeLay called Daschle "disgusting" for that comment, Daschle's aides quickly clarified that their boss meant "no criticism of Bush or his campaign against terrorism."

Prominent Democrats also defended Bush as he filled Guantanamo Bay with men caught in a legally nebulous situation. A former Senate Judiciary chairman expressed confidence that "the president is right" to declare Taliban and al-Qaeda prisoners unlawful enemy combatants. Some detained Taliban "may very well" meet the criteria for prisoners of war, said Joe Biden, but it was an academic point, since "they all will be treated, though, in terms of humaneness, according to the requirements of the Geneva Conventions." Feinstein, one of Biden's colleagues on the Judiciary Committee, toured Camp X-Ray, the chicken-coop outdoor cages baking in the Cuban heat that served as Guantanamo's first terrorism jail. Given the choice of being imprisoned in San Quentin, Feinstein said, "I'd rather be in Guantanamo Bay."

Some were more straightforwardly bloodthirsty, as with Zell Miller's Senate-floor dismissal of civilian casualties. That sort of response made Democratic leaders wince, though rarely enough to condemn. Far more broadly shared among the center and the center-left was a respectable version of Miller's froth, one that accepted the violation of American Muslims' rights as a matter of grim necessity. Richard Ben-Veniste, a lawyer who had participated in the Watergate prosecutions, defended the FBI's right to infiltrate mosques. "We cannot allow an institution, a building, a mosque, to be specific, to be completely prohibited from any kind of intelligence activities, because that would provide sanctuary in an unrealistic way given the information we know," Ben-Veniste judged. Of course the FBI couldn't be allowed to penetrate mosques "willy nilly," which would be "grossly unfair to our loyal and patriotic Muslim population in this country." It was a hard problem, Ben-Veniste admitted, but "there's got to be a balance." Later Ben-Veniste would join the 9/11 Commission, which charted a technocratic, consensus course on the war that treated 9/11 as a Security State failure, absolving both Bush and American foreign policy more broadly.

With the Forever War fortified by liberal enlistment, leftist writers like Arundhati Roy saw early on where it would lead. The United States couldn't fight an enemy it didn't understand, she wrote in *The Guardian*, so "for the sake of the enraged folks back home, it will have to manufacture one. Once war begins, it will develop a momentum, a logic and a justification of its own, and we'll lose sight of why it's being fought in the first place."

Confident in their abilities to temper whatever excesses emanated from a president they considered oafish and arrogant, Democrats sought to make the War on Terror work more rationally, and helped construct the institutional architecture they thought would keep it that way. Whatever discomfort they felt with that effort did not develop into opposition. That would only come after scandal, disaster, or a groundswell of disgust from the Democratic electorate. Nowhere did these dynamics manifest more catastrophically than over the Iraq war.

THREE POLITICIANS PERSONIFIED the Democratic acquiescence to the Iraq war: Senators Hillary Clinton, John Kerry, and Joe Biden.

Over his decades in public life, Biden, by 2002 the chairman of the Senate Foreign Relations Committee, cultivated various images: yuppie liberal, Catholic working-class champion, global statesman. He and Kerry had voted against the 1991 Gulf War. Kerry's opposition emerged from his history. A twice-wounded combat veteran of Vietnam, navy lieutenant Kerry became one of the war's most famous protesters, testifying before Congress about the brutality of Vietnam and getting photographed with John Lennon. Clinton, a former first lady, was a committed feminist who had moved to New York in 2000 to launch an independent political career. The 9/11 attacks "marked me," she would tell WNYC, "and made me feel that [counterterrorism] was my number-one obligation as a senator." Aides would later say her hawkishness was not merely to forestall the inevitable objections to a woman's national-security leadership, but the result of "a textbook view of American exceptionalism." While conservatives merely heckled Kerry and Biden, they actively loathed Clinton for gendered reasons that they struggled to conceal.

Biden positioned himself as a War on Terror troubleshooter during and after the invasion of Afghanistan. His concern was that Bush was insufficiently committed to extending Hamid Karzai's writ throughout the country—"We are not talking about a task that is beyond our capability," Biden said in Kabul—which amateurishly showcased American weakness instead of strength. Biden hoped to strengthen the position of Colin Powell over Rumsfeld and the neoconservatives, whom Biden had long considered delusional. In the summer of 2002, as administration attention and resources flowed away from Afghanistan and toward a forthcoming invasion, Biden convened a two-day public tutorial in his committee on the merits and drawbacks of an unprovoked war, which he presented as a "national dialogue."

The hearings highlighted the dangers of occupation, such as the basic uncertainty around who and what would replace Saddam Hussein, and the bloody, long, and expensive commitment required to midwife a democratic Iraq. Like Biden himself, the hearings stopped far short of opposition to the war. The overwhelming focus of expert testimony concerned guessing at the extent of Saddam's weapons program, the pragmatic considerations of an invasion, and the diplomatic legwork required to justify an action whose justice—if not its wisdom—was presumed. Central questions about how the United States would handle the post-Saddam vacuum, supposedly the purpose of the hearing, received vague or vacuous answers. They included confident assurances from neoconservative professor Fouad Ajami that Iraqis would greet American soldiers with "kites and boom boxes." Rend Rahim Francke, a future Iraqi ambassador to Washington, insisted, "We will not have a civil war in Iraq." A retired army colonel boasted that the United States could "expect significant international involvement in any post-conflict situation."

While claiming the hearings were "not designed to prejudice any particular course of action," Biden signaled his own support for invading. "Even if the right response to his pursuit is not so crystal clear, one thing is clear: these weapons must be dislodged from Saddam Hussein, or Saddam Hussein must be dislodged from power."

Kerry, a member of the committee, was envisioning a presidential run. His concerns on Iraq were formalistic. "When and how, what is the process, what brings you to the point of pulling the trigger, what sort of makes you reach that point where you have made the decision that you have exhausted the doctrine of remedies, if you will, in the context of international law and of going to war?" he asked. Kerry wondered whether legitimizing a war required pressing for a more intrusive inspections regime than Saddam could tolerate. "Certainly, if he has the things that he does not want us to find, he will not live up to it, so those who want the justification to go in will get the justification," Kerry continued, "but in the absence of that, we do not have a chance of having exhausted that doctrine of remedies in a way that I think answers the question to mom and pop in America as to why their young child may come home in a body bag." Kerry, as it happened, outlined the exact course that Bush, at the behest of the similarly minded Powell, would pursue at the United Nations that coming fall.

The party's foreign policy luminaries made those process concerns central. Like Biden and Kerry, they sought not only to strengthen Powell but to portray an Iraq incursion less as an invasion than as a post-9/11 test of the relevance of the international institutions they selectively favored. "The path of inspections is all too familiar, but it is worth traveling one last time. If the Iraqis break their promise, the case for military action will be stronger," Clinton secretary of state Madeleine Albright testified to Biden's committee. Clinton's diplomatic hero of the Balkans, Richard Holbrooke, urged legislators to vote for the war. "This would help Secretary Powell in obtaining the best possible resolution at the Security Council by sending a signal of national unity to the Security Council's members," Holbrooke said, even as he stressed that UN approval was not "absolutely necessary" for a subsequent invasion, since Clinton hadn't obtained one for NATO's Balkan bombings.

Even as Kerry, Clinton, and Biden moved to embrace the war, other Democratic eminences showed what opposing it looked like in the wake of 9/11. Ted Kennedy and Al Gore—who had given his 2000 presidential rival pivotal post-9/11 support by calling Bush "my commander in chief"— both opposed invading Iraq, but on the grounds that it would imperil the War on Terror. Kennedy, noting the "open secret" of uniformed military discomfort with Rumsfeld's invasion plan, attempted to align opposition to the Iraq war with the interests of the Security State. Bill Clinton, by nature more equivocal, endorsed regime change on CNN two days before telling a Democratic fundraiser that bin Laden needed to be dealt with first.

On October 11, 2002, Hillary Clinton, Biden, and Kerry all voted for the Iraq war, each sounding different and characteristic notes about its merits. Clinton portrayed her preferred course—through the United Nations—as an alternative to Bush's unilateralism that granted greater "support and legitimacy" to the endeavor. She recognized that her vote "could lead to war" but expressed hope that a show of unity would "make success in the United Nations more likely and war less likely." She urged antiwar Democrats to vote for the war on that basis while presenting the trauma of her adopted state as a reason to launch an unrelated invasion. "In balancing the risks of action versus inaction," she said, "I think New Yorkers, who have gone through the fires of hell, may be more attuned to the risk of not acting. I know I am."

Biden echoed the sentiment that the vote was not "a rush to war. I believe it is a march to peace and security." That was effectively a key pro-war Democratic talking point—Gephardt used it in the corresponding House vote—but Biden added his own delusions. The wording of the resolution demanded Saddam's disarmament, not necessarily regime change, although Biden allowed that an invading army was likely to ensure Saddam's downfall. And it was wise to keep the regime-change objective euphemistic, lest the United States alienate "other countries who do not share that goal and whose support we need to disarm Iraq and possibly rebuild it." Attempting to bolster Powell, Biden praised the president for choosing a "course of moderation and deliberation," while in the next breath lamenting that the "imminence and inevitability" of the threat from Iraq "have been exaggerated."

If Clinton and Biden portrayed their votes for the war as a way to avoid it, Kerry covered his own motives in incoherent antiwar rhetoric. He praised the "tough questions" asked by the skeptical Republican statesmen Brent Scowcroft and James Baker. Protesting too much, Kerry castigated Bush for "casting about in an unfocused, undisciplined, overly public internal debate for a rationale for war" and "fail[ing] to prove any direct link" between Saddam and 9/11. But then Kerry asked if, in a post-9/11 world, "we can afford to ignore the possibility" of an alliance between Saddam and "some terrorist group."

Yes, Kerry, announced, he would vote for the war resolution, but that would not be the end of the story. "In giving the president this authority, I expect him to fulfill the commitments he has made to the American people in recent days" about creating a thorough UN inspections regime and building a large international military coalition "if we have to disarm Saddam Hussein by force. If he fails to do so," Kerry vowed, "I will be the first to speak out." Kerry insisted on removing "doubt or confusion" as to his position: "I will support a multilateral effort to disarm Iraq by force, if we have exhausted all other options. But I cannot, and will not, support a unilateral U.S. war against Iraq unless the threat is imminent and no multilateral effort is possible."

The anticipated invasion attracted some of the largest protest marches ever seen in cities across America and the globe. They registered not at all with the Democratic Party or elite liberal journalists. George Packer, a leading liberal invasion advocate, lamented in *The New York Times Magazine* that the protesters couldn't imagine that "the Iraqi people, while not welcoming the threat of bombs, might be realistic enough to accept a war as their only hope of liberation from tyranny." Leon Wieseltier, the driving intellectual force at *The New Republic* and a self-styled cultural policeman, asked, "How can any liberal, any individual who associates himself with the party of humanity, not count himself in this coalition of the willing?" Thomas Friedman, the *Times* foreign policy columnist, envisioned American forces "draining the swamps" of the Middle East. Defending America's open society, he said, required teaching millions of Middle Easterners to "suck on this." Bill Keller of *The New York Times* marveled that so many "unlikely" prominent liberal writers at "*The Washington Post*, the editors of *The New Yorker*, *The New Republic* and *Slate*, columnists in *Time* and *Newsweek*" agreed with him in supporting the war. He called it the "I-Can't-Believe-I'm-a-Hawk Club," demonstrating a stunning historical ignorance of the relationship between liberalism and empire for someone who would soon edit the paper.

As the 2004 election approached, Democratic leaders saw for the first time the anger of progressive voters who had watched in disgust as their leaders lined up behind Bush. Kerry, the front-runner for the nomination, saw the early Democratic enthusiasm go to the former Vermont governor Howard Dean, whose candidacy was predicated on opposing both the war and the Democratic acquiescence to it. Kerry played War on Terror politics against Dean in September 2003, calling him "dead wrong" for referring to Hamas militants as "soldiers." It was central to Kerry's argument for his candidacy: that he, a combat veteran turned protester turned statesman, was uniquely positioned to lead America in a time of danger.

But Kerry kept undermining his own appeal to competence. Everywhere he went, particularly as the Iraqi insurgency intensified, voters demanded to know why he'd voted for the war. When Bush asked the same Congress that approved the Iraq invasion to authorize $87 billion for "reconstruction," Kerry refused, and boasted of it to Democratic audiences, even as he declared himself for "winning the war." A *New York Times* reporter noted that it took Kerry "40 minutes to arrive at a somewhat simple formulation" of his position on the war: for it, but against how Bush pursued it.

In March 2004 Bush's strategists, acutely sensitive to Kerry's weakness, baited him with a West Virginia ad attacking him for voting against the reconstruction funding. Kerry, unable to refrain from addressing it, boasted that he sought to finance the reconstruction by repealing Bush's hated tax cuts—so, he explained, "I actually did vote for the $87 billion before I voted against it." Bush, a creature of certainty, assured voters that they would, at least, always know where he stood. Kerry, stung by the critique, insisted in August that even with the benefit of hindsight, he would have voted for the war.

Kerry clung to his military credentials, arriving at the Democratic convention via a ferry crossing Boston Harbor as if it were the Mekong. With a salute onstage, he declared himself "reporting for duty," and surrounded himself with fellow veterans. Yet Kerry's prominence in the antiwar movement a generation earlier aggravated those veterans who considered his war protest a betrayal. A conspiratorial lot of them, calling themselves Swift Boat Veterans for Truth, filmed TV commercials deceitfully accusing Kerry of faking the war wounds that yielded his Purple Hearts. Concocting that sort of fake news became known as Swiftboating. Its purpose was to *un-Troop* its targets, excluding them from the public veneration that the post-9/11 era afforded to military service.

With the election looming, Osama bin Laden observed the American landscape he had reshaped. His plan had "exceeded all expectations," he gloated, thanks to the indefinite, expanding war. "All that we have to do is to send two mujahideen to the furthest point east to raise a piece of cloth on which is written 'al-Qaeda,'" bin Laden marveled in a videotape he released October 30, "in order to make the generals race there to cause America to suffer human, economic, and political losses without their achieving for it anything of note other than some benefits for their private companies."

Bush was showing the Muslim world the America that bin Laden depicted: both a bloodthirsty oppresser and a vulnerable one. The United States looked like a rampaging tyrant, ruling through fear and coercion, yet one which Muslims in Iraq and Afghanistan were demonstrating could be defeated. Bin Laden explained his strategy as simply provoking America into being itself. Much as the Soviet Union had collapsed after the Afghanistan insurgency—which he neglected to mention had aligned him with the CIA—bin Laden said, "We are continuing this policy, in bleeding America to the point of bankruptcy." A strategically targeted, persistent resistance to the enemy would provoke a reaction the enemy could neither sustain nor end. And the enemy was every American, he reminded his audience, as he held all Americans collectively guilty for the violence U.S. policy inflicted upon Muslim countries. Their ability to "prevent another Manhattan" was in their own hands, "not in the hands of Kerry, nor Bush."

Kerry gave an interview to *The New York Times Magazine* a month before he lost the election. By then, it was an article of faith that the War on Terror would last perhaps a generation, a presumption that had removed any pressure on politicians to articulate the conditions for victory. For the first time, Kerry gestured at what he believed an acceptable outcome would be. "We have to get back to the place we were, where terrorists are not the focus of our lives, but they're a nuisance," he said, analogizing terrorism to prostitution, gambling, and organized crime. "It's something that you continue to fight," he continued, "but it's not threatening the fabric of your life."

It was not terrorism, however, that was threatening the fabric of American life, as bin Laden gleefully pointed out: *counterterrorism* was. Kerry had accommodated the politics that insisted that the terrorists ought to be the "focus of our lives." He was never able to reconcile the end of the war he sought with the politics propelling it, because they were irreconcilable. They would only get more people killed, traumatized, and robbed of their freedom.

AFTER THEIR LOSS IN 2004, Democrats, adrift and shut out of power, found a way to make Islamophobia work for them.

In fall 2005 a shipping conglomerate known as Dubai Ports World acquired a British company that operated several U.S. seaports. The changeover from one foreign firm to another caused little concern among U.S. regulators, particularly as Dubai Ports World was controlled by one of the monarchs of the United Arab Emirates. For years Democrats had gotten little political traction with issues of homeland security, but they now saw an opportunity to capitalize on Islamophobia and xenophobia. "Dubai has had a very strong nexus with terrorism," warned Chuck Schumer, a New York senator rising within the party leadership.

Schumer's claim was patently absurd. The port operations in question had long been privately managed. The current company doing so was foreign-owned—just by citizens of a European country. Dubai, an oligarchic playpen, had no substantive "nexus with terrorism." Schumer presented a fantastical theory that "the way terrorists would work is they would infiltrate an organization like Dubai Royal Ports." An Israeli shipping company executive, incredulous at the accusations, wrote Hillary Clinton, who had joined with Schumer, that Dubai Ports World "maintain[s] the highest security standards in all its terminals around the world." Bush's dismissal of the Dubai Ports World hysteria ensured Democratic intensity against the plan, and in March 2006 the now-embattled Republicans rejected the ports deal. The company promptly gave up and announced it would divest its American port operations, ultimately selling them to the insurance firm AIG, which would play a key role in 2008's global financial calamity.

Democratic demagoguery with respect to Arabs and Islam reinforced the degree to which Islamophobia was now part of American life. From at least July 2006 to February 2008, the FBI placed the executive director of CAIR, Nihad Awad, under surveillance, according to leaked documents. The leader of the largest American Muslim civil-rights groups was never charged with a crime. "The pressure, the stress—you don't see any relief coming," reflected Adham Hassoun, who by 2005 resided in the special housing unit of the Federal Detention Center in Miami, where he was charged with terrorism.

It was an unusual accusation. The Justice Department had not charged Hassoun with involvement in any act of violence. Nor had it accused him of plotting any support for terrorism against America. Instead, in a cascading series of indictments, it alleged that he was a cog in a "North American support cell" that raised money and recruits for overseas jihadist groups. The evidence the department cited came in the form of checks to jihad-adjacent refugee charities that Hassoun had written in the nineties, when doing so was legal. It also revealed that the FBI had already had him under surveillance, though he was never charged with any crime until well after 9/11. But Hassoun had a certain association. He was charged not only as a codefendant of Jose Padilla—who by now was functionally cleared of anything to do with the "dirty bomb" scare that had initially landed him in military detention—but also as having recruited Padilla for miscellaneous jihad.

"The second part of 2004, that's when the charitable stuff starts coming" up in his interrogations, Hassoun recalled. "Before that it was, 'Do you know any of these bad guys?' . . . They just wanted Padilla's head. I was collateral damage."

Bounced around a series of immigration lockups, county jails, and federal detention centers, Hassoun spent four years before his trial in solitary confinement. Miami guards took pity on him, urging him not to give up. ("You can't believe how nice they were," he said.) Every morning, following instructions, they would ransack his cell and confiscate his meager possessions; every evening the guards returned them. The "psychological warfare" of his solitude intensified as prosecutors pressed him to take a plea deal in exchange for testimony. "I get emotional sometimes. I have tears in my eyes," he remembered. "My belief as a Muslim helped me stay tough, because I know there's a day of judgment. I'll see them, one by one."

Although conservatives had derided a "law-enforcement approach" to terrorism after 9/11, the Bush administration prosecuted hundreds of people in federal courts for terror-related offenses. Liberals and civil libertarians typically highlighted those measures to argue that Bush's military tribunals and indefinite detentions were unnecessary, as if necessity was why Bush had opted for nonjudicial imprisonment. But cases like Hassoun's revealed that the post-9/11 criminal justice system had become uncomfortably similar to this supposedly exceptional apparatus. The typical posture for federal judges who heard terrorism-related cases, in criminal and particularly in constitutional contexts, was deference to the government's national security authorities. Judges tended to start from the perspective that they appropriately possessed minimal authority to review the executive's security claims in wartime. But now that this was an endless war, the state of emergency had become the new status quo, amounting to a separate justice system for Muslims.

In February 2005 federal prosecutors in Virginia charged Ahmed Omar Abu Ali, a twenty-three-year old from Falls Church, with plotting to assassinate Bush on behalf of al-Qaeda. They claimed he represented "one of the most dangerous terrorist threats that America faces in the perilous world after Sept. 11, 2001: an Al Qaeda operative born and raised in the United States, trained and committed to carry out deadly attacks on American soil." The entirety of the evidence in Abu Ali's case were his confessions during his twenty months in a Saudi prison. Judge Gerald Bruce Lee, a Clinton appointee, rejected Abu Ali's protests that his statements had been coerced through torture. Lee also permitted unnamed Saudi agents to deliver taped depositions assuring the court that the confessions were legitimate. There was no evidence, or much of a claim by prosecutors, that the plot was in any advanced stage. With Abu Ali's conviction never in doubt,

Lee sentenced him to thirty years. Perversely, he not only lost his sentencing appeal, but on remand he was sentenced to life imprisonment.

Hassoun considered his own trial a formality. Prosecutors were permitted to place an entire bin Laden CNN interview into evidence, because the FBI had wiretapped Hassoun mentioning to codefendant Kifah Jayyousi in 1997 that he planned on watching it, on the grounds that bin Laden "spoke to [Hassoun's] entire state of mind." The U.S. attorney, Alex Acosta, further contended that his discussions of aiding refugees of wars like Kosovo were "codewords for fighting violent jihad." In one conversation, predating the PATRIOT Act by five years, the FBI claimed that when Hassoun told someone "go and smell some fresh air," he actually meant "traveling to a jihad area." Hassoun was not permitted to introduce into evidence an account the government had of a man known as Uways, who was with Padilla at an Afghanistan training camp and said that someone named Abu Malki, not Hassoun, had sent Padilla there.

Regardless, American juries were not in the habit of acquitting Muslims in terrorism cases, and certainly not Muslims suspected of having set in motion a onetime enemy combatant who was said to want to detonate a radiological bomb. In such an environment, prosecutors were able to argue that Hassoun's refusal to talk to FBI agents in June 2002 "shows he remained committed to his program of religious extremism," even as the case centered on checks he wrote and conversations he had before material support carried the higher PATRIOT Act–imposed penalties. The aspect of the courtroom farce that surprised Hassoun the most was how tall his children had grown in the five years since his arrest. "I tried to hold my tears back," he said. "It's inhumane what they did to me. I expect it from Russia, from Lebanon, but from the United States? *What did I do?*"

Hassoun, Padilla, and Jayyousi were convicted on August 16, 2007. By now prosecutors were claiming that Hassoun "indoctrinated people and converted them to become al-Qaeda fighters," referring to Padilla. Hassoun was convicted on charges of abetting murder, maiming, and kidnapping, even though the government could not point to anyone to whom Hassoun had made financial contributions who was responsible for such crimes. At his sentencing, Judge Marcia Cooke rejected the Justice Department's recommendation for life imprisonment. The fact that the FBI had him under surveillance for years and "did nothing . . . does not support the government's argument that Mr. Hassoun poses such a danger to the community that he needs to be imprisoned for the rest of his life," Cooke said. She sentenced Hassoun to fifteen years.

"The FBI told me that I'm a 'casualty of war.' What war?" Hassoun said. "I'm sitting here in my house, in peace, in my community. Why are you bringing garbage from outside to throw it in my yard? '*Because we can.*'"

PATRIOTIC VENGEANCE FUELED the War on Terror. But the nightmare of the Iraqi civil war, combined with the jingoistic lies and denials that produced it, led to varieties of disillusionment. For the Security State, and the military in particular, failure was as unacceptable as it was inexplicable. For the right, it was explicable in terms of ungrateful Muslims who were unworthy of American sacrifice. Among liberals and leftists, it became a demand to be done with Iraq, one that the Democrats exploited to win control of Congress in 2006. But the Democratic agenda did not include withdrawal from Iraq, let alone abolition of the War on Terror.

Instead elites, in and out of uniform, recast the overall War on Terror not as Bush's theological crusade, but as a technocratic, salvageable struggle, guided by the hard-won rationality of its veterans and practitioners. The language of emergency persisted, and for the first time, it was acceptable to openly discuss failure—but the prospect of failure became an argument for rebooting the war through escalating it, not for abandoning its wreckage. Such technocratic attitudes were respectable among those who either loathed or regretted Bush, but they led to avoidance of a central contradiction. The longer the Forever War persisted, the more it fostered its nativist undercurrent, one that would never trust technocrats. However distrustful of the nativists the technocrats were, they would not accept that in a war fueled by outraged patriotism, their relationship to the nativists was symbiotic.

Reconciling the Democratic Party with those of its voters who had rejected Iraq turned out to be easy. The party simply acted as if it had not embraced the war, a path rendered politically safe after Representative Jack Murtha, a white working-class Vietnam veteran, called for withdrawal. But withdrawal was too controversial for the party as a whole. Biden proposed a compromise that flattered American exceptionalism: a soft partition of Iraq along its ethnic and religious fractures. It ironically united warring Arab Iraqis in opposition to Washington's latest imperialist fantasy.

Another option appeared in the northern Iraqi city of Tal Afar. Working through Iraqi forces and the city's political leadership, a cavalry regiment under the command of Colonel H. R. McMaster took the city from the insurgency and, through presence patrols, held it. It was a proof of concept for David Petraeus. Along with Jim Mattis, several like-minded officers with Iraq experience, and neoconservative think-tankers—all of whom had long believed a better war was possible—Petraeus contended that salvaging the situation depended on reversing the occupation's indifference to Iraqis. Iraqis' allegiances, to the U.S. or to the insurgents, would be decisive. That, they argued, required escalating the war, not scaling it back. Soldiers and marines would have to unite with Iraqi mentees to clear and hold territory, ostensibly on behalf of the besieged Iraqis, through everything from artillery strikes and patrols to diplomatic outreach to local leaders and simultaneous aid distribution. Bush, out of options and presented with an opportunity to reboot, appointed Petraeus his war commander. So began the "surge" of 2007–2008.

The surge was a compromise between the right and the Security State, with elements to entice liberals, particularly those Democrats rich enough to view the war as an abstraction, discomfited with both the status quo and withdrawal. The counterinsurgents were a network of cerebral officers who believed themselves to have been marginalized by an ignorant military establishment. They had won esteem in liberal publications for their willingness to forthrightly state that the United States was losing the war. It helped that however bellicose they were, they were not bloodthirsty. Petraeus, a professorial soldier attracted to "the paradoxes of counterinsurgency," advised that some of his forces' best weapons "do not shoot," tactical success "guarantees nothing," and a "high level of violence often benefits insurgents." In Baghdad he instructed his forces neither to torture captives nor to condone those who did. To the left, however, the surge offered nothing beyond a lifeline for a fundamentally immoral war. It empowered Iraqi police, often combatants in the civil war themselves, to crowd their jails with members of an opposing sect. "Just because they sympathize with a militia doesn't mean they can't do their job," said the U.S.-backed commander of police in Baghdad's Shiite neighborhood of Hurriyeh.

There were several conceptual lacunae at the heart of the surge. Petraeus's highly regarded counterinsurgency field manual did not substantively address the inflammatory relationship between foreign occupation and insurgency. It viewed local politics as the key to a sustainable outcome, but imposed unsustainable conditions by necessity. The contradictions were reconciled by, of all forces, al-Qaeda.

Al-Qaeda in Iraq's brutality proved the Americans weren't the only ones capable of catastrophic miscalculation. Abu Wail, the religious leader of an Iraqi jihadist group that once had sheltered Zarqawi, explained to a British special operator, "You're a force of occupation, and don't try to tell me differently." But while the United States was unwelcome, he continued, "we have come to the conclusion that you do not threaten our way of life, al-Qaeda does." That created an opening for Petraeus, who paid former Sunni insurgents from Anbar tribes to form the Sons of Iraq, an anti-al-Qaeda militia. The so-called Anbar Awakening bought Petraeus time, and he bought it in turn for Iraqi Prime Minister Nouri al-Maliki, whom Petraeus embraced. But Maliki, a sectarian Shia, considered the Sons a threat. Petraeus and the rest of the occupation forces decided that was a problem for another day.

That pointed to the biggest lacuna of all: whether success in the surge meant that the United States could finally withdraw afterward, or whether it meant it would have to stay, at lower force levels, in perpetuity. A senior military official involved reflected that the counterinsurgents' priority was to avert a disaster, which effectively meant remaining: "We weren't ready to throw in the towel." Perpetuity better suited American exceptionalism. When, in 2008, Maliki's government and the Bush administration reached a deal to withdraw forces by 2011, their "understanding" was that a follow-on accord would defer the departure. "Korea was cited," recalled Emma Sky, who advised Petraeus's deputy, Odierno. The surge would not end the war, only secure a long-term American outpost in the Mideast, akin to the one on the Korean peninsula.

A cult of Petraeus emerged. By the summer of 2007 Petraeus, whom journalists portrayed as supremely competent, produced data showing violence declining where before it had only accelerated. The fact that post-surge violence was still high—five hundred Iraqi civilians were being killed each month in the summer of 2008—was considered less important than the promise of Petraeus's trend, particularly since U.S. troop deaths had also dropped markedly. Like Bush, Petraeus could be dismissive of contrary intelligence. He clashed with CIA officials whose August 2007 assessment of Iraq—that the surge would bring only a "modest" drop in violence, but that no political reconciliation would follow to make it durable—he considered too pessimistic. Still, Petraeus was careful to avoid the word "victory," which he considered both overly simplistic and an overpromise that could come back to haunt him. To maintain political support Petraeus had to portray his strategy as advancing toward a goal that, asymptotically, it would never reach. It led him into absurdities, such as a quip to Congress that "at the end of the day, nothing succeeds like a little bit of significant progress."

Petraeus's approach compelled him to display a public respect for Iraqis that sat uncomfortably with the right's frequent contempt for them. He referred to the father of his chief Iraqi Shiite adversary as "the martyr Sadr."

His attitude conflicted with GOP legislators' insistence that, as one put it, "we're at war with Islamic jihadists," but since Petraeus was saving the Iraq war—and perhaps their political fortunes—they were disinclined to press the point. The cultural contradictions of counterinsurgency were less glaring than the central political fact that Petraeus had, for the first time, made support for the war seem rigorous and opposition to it fanatical. But they would reemerge in the presidential election, as a wave of resurgent progressivism empowered a symbol of unlikely antiwar hope whom the right would consider an abomination.

BY VIRTUE OF HIS BACKGROUND, Barack Obama had greater potential than any rival American politician to see the War on Terror through the eyes of those it terrorized. He had spent part of his childhood in Indonesia, where he became familiar with the exploitation of foreign and Islamic cultures by imperial powers. Through his father, a Kenyan economist, Obama could trace his lineage to a part of east Africa that became a U.S. battlefield when Bush backed a 2006 Ethiopian invasion to oust Somalia's jihadist Islamic Courts Union. As a professor of constitutional law and as a Black man in America, Obama had the legal scholarship and the personal experience to understand how 9/11 had inflamed white supremacy and how that anger would manifest. But also by virtue of who he was—prone to interpretive nuance, allergic to ideology, liberal—Obama was disinclined to take an abolitionist approach to the War on Terror.

The Iraq war was an insult to the public's intelligence, "a dumb war," Obama famously said as an Illinois state senator at an October 2002 antiwar rally. But being Obama, he challenged the rally's premise, contrasting dumb wars he couldn't support with necessary wars he accepted—conflicts waged "in the name of a larger freedom," like the Civil War and the Second World War. Into that category Obama placed the War on Terror. Beholding the horror of 9/11, he said, "I supported this administration's pledge to hunt down and root out those who would slaughter innocents in the name of intolerance," providing a clue to how he understood the ever-undefined enemy. He viewed Iraq, "a war based not on reason but on passion," as a distraction from the imperative of fighting terrorism. Attendees of an anti-war demonstration witnessed the unlikely spectacle of a politician demanding Bush "finish the fight with bin Laden and al-Qaeda," through "effective, coordinated intelligence" and a "homeland security program that involves more than color-coded warnings." Whatever his background, and whatever the presumptions white Americans held about it, Obama viewed the War on Terror in a manner that the right would deny he ever truly could: within the American exceptionalist consensus.

Asked years later why Obama didn't also consider the War on Terror to be a dumb war, his close adviser Ben Rhodes answered, "Because he thought a legitimate threat from al-Qaeda [had emerged], requiring a military response."

Torture repulsed Obama more than any other aspect of the war. He told Condoleezza Rice that the reason she resisted "defin[ing] torture too much" was so the Bush administration could have "a little bit of wiggle room" to brutalize people while claiming that they hadn't. On another occasion he warned that "a system in which we're tolerating torture or abuse or depriving anybody that we have detained [of] some basic rights" could come around on captured U.S. service members. By contrast, Hillary Clinton, in October 2006, said she could support a "very, very narrow exception" for torture under the law "within very, very limited circumstances." Obama voted against the 2006 law creating military tribunals for accused terrorists, citing "the innocent people we may have accidentally rounded up and mistaken for terrorists, people who may stay in prison for the rest of their lives."

He was otherwise flexible. When the *Times* revealed parts of STELLAR-WIND, Obama advocated not the end of dragnet surveillance but instead increased oversight through "some mechanism, the court, the Senate Intelligence Committee, that, in a secret way, is making sure the executive branch is not going off on tangents." During a November 2006 speech in Chicago, one of his first on foreign policy, Obama backed a "phased redeployment" out of Iraq and into Afghanistan, a war "backsliding into chaos." Swapping one war for the other was by now Democratic catechism, the result of politicians signaling that their opposition to Iraq was no omnibus reconsideration of U.S. bellicosity. Another of Obama's 2006 foreign policy speeches offered the mildest of rebukes to American exceptionalism: America needed to be "more modest" about its ability to impose "democracy" through military force.

Not only was Obama among the most popular politicians in America, he was so untainted by any association with the Iraq war that he could channel some of the anger progressives had at Democrats who backed it. In September 2007, as Obama challenged Clinton for her presumed Democratic presidential nomination, Petraeus arrived in Washington for dramatic marathon congressional testimony. Months before, Senate Democrats, Clinton and Obama among them, had come just short of passing a motion disapproving the surge; Lieberman helped Republicans thwart it. As Petraeus prepared an onslaught of statistics to portray the war effort as having turned around, the antiwar activist group MoveOn asked if he would "Betray Us" by injecting hope into a hopeless enterprise. Democrats lined up to dissociate themselves from an attack on a respected general. Petraeus was happy to frame the debate around the integrity of this or that statistic, since it made him look cerebral and his questioners petty.

Clinton, whose advisers were close to Petraeus, struggled to find a rationale beyond political necessity to oppose the surge, and so she treated Petraeus harshly. "A willing suspension of disbelief" was necessary to accept Petraeus's account of the war, she charged. It was a more refined version of MoveOn's point, and it stung Petraeus. His army mentor and an occasional Clinton adviser, Jack Keane, later said Clinton told him the following summer that the surge had worked. Obama was comparatively solicitous. The issue for him was that Iraq "continues to be a disastrous foreign policy mistake," compounded with the absurdity that the "modest improvement" that

Petraeus and his colleague Ambassador Ryan Crocker had made "is considered success." Obama clarified that his objection wasn't with "either of you gentlemen" but pointed instead to the reliance of the entire enterprise on a nonsectarian Iraqi government that simply did not exist. While Petraeus wouldn't gain Clinton's support because of expedience, for Obama it was never an option. But Obama's depersonalization of the issue made his differences with the general respectful, permitting each to find areas where their agendas might converge.

While Clinton campaigned on beginning a withdrawal within the first sixty days of her presidency, Obama proposed *completing* a withdrawal within sixteen months of his. "We will not have a permanent occupation and we will not have permanent bases," he vowed, rejecting the notion of a residual force that most politicians' withdrawal plans presumed. Then, reiterating a phrase he had tested in an earlier debate, Obama said he would not stop at ending the Iraq war, but at "end[ing] the mindset that got us into war in the first place."

It was an electric line—"We're having such a good time," Clinton groused—as it captured the bitter fact that the war continued with the complicity of liberals, who were supposed to know better, who *did* know better. His campaign harnessed an unapologetic antiwar boldness beyond what any other national Democrat, for six long years, had been willing to adopt. It made Obama seem like a decisive break from the past. But, in an ill omen, he did not define what his hated mindset was. His advisers provided an answer: the politics of fear. "For a long time we've not seen much creative thinking from Dems on national security, because, out of fear, we want to be a little different from the Republicans but not too different, out of fear of being labeled weak or indecisive," a senior member of his brain trust explained.

Years later, in his memoir *A Promised Land*, Obama mused on promising "a different kind of foreign policy than the sort we'd been practicing since 9/11," that being one he attributed to "a certain mindset." That mindset "saw threats around every corner, took a perverse pride in acting unilaterally, and considered military action as an almost routine means of addressing foreign policy challenges." Obama correctly diagnosed the unapologetic hysteria at the heart of post-9/11 America. But it was conspicuous that he defined the sort of foreign policy he wanted to change in terms of its habits, rather than its machinery, its authorities, or its material impact on human beings.

Obama was forthright that, in some form, the Forever War would continue. He spoke about escalating the Afghanistan war and pursuing bin Laden even to the point of unilaterally invading Pakistan. The idea of a war against a religion or a foreign culture appalled him. He spoke more specifically of al-Qaeda's broad network as the appropriate target, a disputable contention, but a significant shift away from Bush's metaphysical and ideological definitions. All that indicated that Obama saw the Forever War as somehow separable from the politics of fear that underlay it and that it in turn reinforced.

Aspects of Obama's coalescing war plans implied a large commitment. His campaign advisers spoke generically about "extremism" as a force they wished to confront by centering "dignity" in foreign policy. Not only would their "dignity promotion" alleviate poverty and respect foreigners' identities, particularly Islamic ones, it would deny bin Laden a receptive audience, perhaps even regaining the United States some Muslim allies the Forever War cost it. The Obama team sounded reminiscent of the Petraeus team, and they had a member in common. "He took many of the [counterinsurgency] principles—the paradoxes, like how sometimes you're less secure the more force is used—and looked at it from a more strategic perspective," observed Sarah Sewall, a Harvard human rights expert whom Petraeus and Mattis consulted for the counterinsurgency field manual. "His policies deal with root causes but do not misconstrue root causes as a simple fix. He recognizes that you need to pursue a parallel anti-terrorism [course] in its traditional form along with this transformed approach to foreign policy." The counterinsurgents' Washington think tank, the Center for a New American Security (CNAS), had figured it would be Clinton's defense team in exile, as it backed only a cautious drawdown in Iraq, but it came to reconcile with Obama.

Among Obama's counterterrorism advisers was John Brennan, one of George Tenet's senior deputies on 9/11 and a career CIA official with extensive Mideast experience. No one has yet been able to determine what role Brennan played during the establishment of the apparatus of torture, disappearance, and secret jails, but he was part of Tenet's leadership team during the creation. He instinctively bristled when the agency's use of torture was challenged. Brennan's CIA tribalism was part of the point, as it made him a bridge between Obama and the Security State, as CNAS was.

Obama's perspective on surveillance had changed during the course of the campaign season. He had pledged ending what he called the "illegal wiretapping of American citizens." But a month after he clinched the Democratic nomination from Clinton, the Senate voted to broaden the NSA's ability to intercept Americans' international communications. It was not the abolition of unconstitutionally broad surveillance, but legislative ratification of it, rationalized as an indispensable counterterrorism authority. Obama, surely thinking ahead to his own possible presidency, voted for it, calling the bill "improved but imperfect." Civil libertarian activists had pressed him to oppose what would become a crucial legal wellspring for a geometric expansion in the NSA's bulk digital collection programs. The vote marked the first time that Obama broke with a constituency.

In the summer of 2008, Obama traveled to Iraq and was photographed beside Petraeus in a helicopter overlooking Baghdad. Before the trip Obama belatedly rebuked MoveOn. "A general providing his best counsel on how to move forward in Iraq was accused of betrayal," he said, even comparing Petraeus to Iraq war opponents who were "tagged by some as unpatriotic." Maliki's government flexed its muscle as well. While Obama was in Baghdad, Maliki's spokesman endorsed a 2010 combat withdrawal deadline, a schedule that fit Obama's proposal, and undermined the Republican charges that such a timetable was irresponsible. At the end of their civil war, the Iraqis pinned the United States between its stated respect for a "sovereign" Iraq and the elite consensus behind remaining in Iraq. But for much of the right, there was a greater emergency at home.

AMID DISPLAYS OF FACTORY-FRESH TRACTORS and dairy machines, Rudy Giuliani entered an agriculture trade expo in California's Central Valley and reminisced about 9/11. "Most of the first hour was just reacting quickly," he remembered over breakfast with farmers and farm-equipment retailers. Giuliani admitted he didn't know much about farming, but warned those who did that a violent death loomed constantly: "This desire of these terrorists to come here and kill us is going to continue."

Giuliani supported the surge, but he had a sense of fatalism about Iraq. The former New York mayor, now running for president, instead proposed ramping up brutality in what he termed the Terrorists' War on Us: "If we succeed in Iraq, or if we fail in Iraq, the terrorists are still going to be at war with us." In such a war, anything America wanted to inflict on its enemies was justified, from waterboarding to "whatever method [interrogators] could think of." Giuliani's rival, the aristocratic Mitt Romney, had even less of a national-security background, and compensated by promising to "win the war on jihad" and to "double Guantanamo." When Ron Paul, the only antiwar contender among the Republican candidates, argued that the Terrorists' War on Us was sparked by American imperialism, Giuliani demanded that Paul retract his comment. Paul had a validator: Michael Scheuer, who had started the CIA's Usama bin Laden Unit. "Foreign policy is about protecting America," Scheuer said. "Our foreign policy is doing the opposite."

It was the Republicans' first post-Bush, post-9/11 election, and the Forever War was no longer the sure path to political power that Rove had forecast. The eventual nominee, though, framed perseverance in Iraq as a matter of national honor. John McCain was the premier war hero in American public life, owing to his endurance of five and a half years of torture in

Vietnamese captivity. From the start, McCain had backed the most aggressive of measures in the War on Terror, and through his endorsement gave the war a reflected valor. McCain was the War on Terror on horseback, a fantasy of the war that neocons and liberals wanted to believe might have been. His opposition to torture shamed and embittered its enthusiasts. McCain did not accept the concept of a war against Islam—although he accepted the endorsement of John Hagee, a Christian Zionist pastor who did. He instead pledged to bear any burden, boasting to "make it a hundred" years in Iraq if necessary. But that position was no longer enough to overcome nativist objections to McCain's permissive attitude toward immigration and other social positions. James Dobson of Focus on the Family, who warned of encroaching Islamic law and had been a fellow Iraq war enthusiast, refused to endorse McCain. In the Buchananite *American Conservative*, W. James Antle III observed the race and wondered, "Can the Iraq War rally the millions who entered politics to fight the Culture War?"

In Barack Obama, they saw how to square the circle.

The prospect of the first Black president erupted deep wells of white anxiety across the political spectrum. Biden "praised" Obama by calling him a "clean" Black candidate "like we've never had before." Hillary Clinton attracted supporters, like the ex-CIA officer Larry Johnson, who spread the lie that Obama somehow had faked his birth certificate to hide his lack of American citizenship. Clinton herself spoke of her following among "hardworking Americans, white Americans" and Obama's weakness among this *herrenvolk*.

An email began to appear in American inboxes calling attention to Obama's middle name, Hussein. "Obama takes great care to conceal the fact that he is a Muslim," it warned, inventing his attendance at an "Islamic school steeped in the radical teaching that is followed by the Muslim terrorists who are now waging Jihad against the western world." It signed off, "Let us all be on alert." *The Nation*'s Chris Hayes traced the spread of the secret-Muslim conspiracy through the popular conservative message board Free Republic and other online warrens before noting that "Barack Obama

Muslim" was the third-most-googled term regarding Obama. To motivate right-wing voters, the Islamophobic Clarion Fund distributed a free DVD called *Obsession: Radical Islam's War on the West* into critical states by the millions. Clarion received in 2008 an astonishing $17 million from Donors Capital Fund, one of the largest financiers of mainstream conservative causes. More visibly, a Fox News anchor asked if Obama giving his wife dap was a "terrorist fist jab."

Most importantly, McCain, behind in the polls and in need of rallying his base, chose the Alaska governor, Sarah Palin, for his vice president. As ignorant as she was rabid, Palin knew instinctively how to wield the War on Terror against Obama. She also knew why her white audience would embrace it. Exaggerating Obama's acquaintance with the former left-wing militant Bill Ayers, Palin told crowds that Obama "pals around with terrorists."

Many on the right began to believe that Obama was part of the same threat that arose on 9/11. Attendees of McCain and Palin's rallies acted accordingly. In Clearwater, Florida, when Palin invoked Ayers's ties to Obama, someone yelled, "Kill him!" The previous month, another yelled, "Off with his head!" Obama's willingness to negotiate with U.S. adversaries became, in Palin's telling, "his plans to meet unconditionally with terror state leaders like Mahmoud Ahmadinejad," as if they were calling on each other socially. Signs appeared with slogans like OBAMA, OSAMA. Rallygoers told McCain that they were afraid of an Obama presidency. A Florida sheriff, wearing his uniform, invoked "Barack Hussein Obama" at a Palin event, and defended himself as just "calling somebody by his middle name." At a Bethlehem, Pennsylvania, McCain–Palin rally, a woman demanded to know why Obama concealed his "Muslim heritage." Even the respectable *New Republic* ran a piece headlined JIHADISTS FOR OBAMA, which reported the existence of a "a strong Yes We Can contingent that seems to be firing their guns in the air this week." An appalled Colin Powell rebuked Republicans in October 2008, saying that even if Obama were Muslim, "Is there something wrong with being a Muslim in this country? The answer's no, that's not America."

In Minnesota weeks before the vote, McCain was booed when he told a crowd that it didn't have to fear an Obama presidency. An elderly white woman said she "had read about" Obama and couldn't trust him because "he's not—he's an Arab." McCain took her microphone and stumbled through an answer about how Obama was "a decent, family man, citizen." McCain meant to include Obama within the American fabric, but his formulation, however inadvert, excluded "Arabs," by which the woman meant *Muslims*, from it. Such exclusions were socially permissible in respectable discourse throughout the War on Terror, so McCain received praise for rebuking the woman. It appeared never to have occurred to McCain that the open-ended war he helped build, against an amorphous enemy, would lead her and other Americans to unleash racist fanaticism. Nor did he seem to realize that once such politics bestowed power, they would be wielded against those who came to take power away. By September 2008, when the global financial catastrophe erupted, it was clear that McCain and the Republican Party would suffer an electoral devastation.

An apparatus of death, surveillance, detention, and brutality, forged and implemented by the Bush administration and the security services, with the uncomfortable and occasionally regretful support of the liberal opposition, was now in the hands of Barack Obama. Antiwar enthusiasm helped bring Obama to this point, even as he cautioned that he did not thoroughly share it. An incensed portion of the country now felt itself disempowered by an ally of America's enemies—Muslim, Black, and foreign. Obama, opposed to dumb wars and committed to changing the mindset that ensnared America within them, now had to define how much of the War on Terror he would discard, and how much he would wield.

CHAPTER FOUR

OBAMA AND THE "SUSTAINABLE" WAR ON TERROR

2009–2013

F aheem had spent much of the long day on his feet, from Friday prayers to a food-shopping errand his mom ordered. One of his uncles had returned from a business trip in the United Arab Emirates, which meant he now had to listen to all the corny jokes and boring rants from the sidelines of the packed men's parlor. His mind wandered to the nearby playground, where the other Ziraki village kids were probably on the cricket pitch or the badminton courts. Then Faheem heard something that sounded like a plane taking off.

When the shock faded, he realized he had caught fire. Faheem ran frantically out of the ruined parlor and into the yard, grasping before him, as he couldn't see anything, hoping to douse his face with water from wherever he could find it.

The survivors of the blast found the thirteen-year-old unconscious and rushed him to the hospital, where he would not awaken for forty days. He had suffered burns so severe that the entire left side of his body required operations. The doctors had taken shrapnel from his stomach and used lasers to repair his right eye. They couldn't save his left.

Faheem's family kept the worst from him while he convalesced. The Hellfire antitank missile fired from the Predator drone above their home in Pakistan's North Waziristan province had killed two of his uncles and his twenty-one-year-old cousin, who was about to travel to the UAE for work. Fourteen of his cousins had lost their fathers. Once Faheem was released from the hospital, he would have to be one of the family's primary breadwinners. He'd have to abandon his ambitions to become a chemist and make his mangled body perform whatever work he could find.

The drone strike that forever marked Faheem Qureshi's life occurred on January 23, 2009, the third full day of Barack Obama's presidency. It was the inaugural act of an aerial bombardment campaign, conducted from remotely operated planes resembling giant gray mosquitoes, heralding a new era in institutionalized killing. Obama would intensify and proliferate these lethal attacks to the point where his name became synonymous with them.

Drone strikes were more than just the centerpiece of Obama's counterterrorism strategy. They represented how he saw the War on Terror: not as something to end, but something to reorient. The Iraq war proved the folly of a massive, ponderous ground invasion. Pakistan, like other countries the United States had turned into battlefields, had little interest in suppressing extremists in its own tribal areas on behalf of a deeply unpopular hegemon. Obama considered the drone strikes a responsible, calibrated use of lethal force, a weapon of *precision*, not one suited to indiscriminate killing. To guard against their excesses, Obama created a simulacrum of due process, which technocratic liberalism trusted to yield responsible outcomes, known as the disposition matrix. This framework empowered intelligence officials, who "nominated" someone for "disposition," and lawyers, who labored to impose consistency on this expanding enterprise. Obama and his officials found the term "War on Terror" as embarrassing as the Department of Homeland Security's color-coded ladder boxes that presumed to quantify justified fear—and jettisoned them both. They instead tended to refer to a "sustainable" approach to counterterrorism.

Although the United States was not at war with Pakistan, and no United Nations measure had ever sanctioned missile attacks on its territory, Obama's lawyers assured him that assaults on suspected members of al-Qaeda and its associated forces fell within the 2001 AUMF, now eight years old. Carrying cameras as well as missiles, the drones could follow and loiter above a target for half a day before receiving an order to fire. Because the guided missile fired by the Predator, a flimsy airframe, weighed only one hundred pounds, anyone close enough to the target to be injured or killed was likely be an intimate of the target. How innocent could *they* be? Better still, at a time when Obama attempted to reboot America's relationship with the Muslim world, the strikes were official secrets. Whatever disasters resulted from their deployment would never be officially acknowledged, leaving journalists, human rights groups, and survivors to sift through the wreckage to estimate how many died, why, and even who they were.

The drone strikes bound Obama and the Security State. As long as they did, there would never be any legal consequence for the CIA's torturers and jailers. As much as torture offended Obama, the man placed in charge of the drone campaign was Michael D'Andrea, the same CIA Counterterrorism Center director who had overseen the agency's black sites from 2006—the torture inflicted there continued until November 8, 2007—until Obama ordered them closed.

Because drone strikes could be an end result of the NSA's bulk surveillance, they also tied Obama to STELLARWIND and its successor programs. The drone strikes, as well as the video intelligence they accumulated, facilitated JSOC raids, the surge in Afghanistan, and the drawdown in Iraq. Through what CIA director Leon Panetta described as "the only game in town," the Security State learned it could do business with Obama. Just as fatefully, waging the Long War meant embracing many who designed, maintained, and carried it out, repudiating the civil libertarians who warned Obama that the horrors of the War on Terror would only continue if their architects faced no reprisal. Still, the relationship between Obama and the Security State was as wary as it was symbiotic, with both sides concerned the other's agenda would compromise its own. Obama's relationship with progressives was relatively expendable.

Panetta delivered his assessment around the time Faheem Qureshi finally left his hospital bed. Lawyers helped Faheem petition Islamabad for compensation. His family ultimately acquired official Pakistani documents that cited "nine civilians" killed in the strike on what they listed as Faheem's village. Journalistic accounts of the strike portray it failing to hit its intended target. But for years, when seeking justice, Faheem heard the same refusals—from the tribal liaison, from the U.S. embassy in Islamabad, and from the United Nations Human Rights Council. He could not even extract from the Americans or the Pakistani government the basic acknowledgment that his trauma had occurred at all.

Without such an admission, nothing prohibited the CIA from killing people as it liked. Sometimes derogatory information about specific individuals came from the CIA's paid Pashtun informants on both sides of the Afghanistan–Pakistan border, however reliable they might be. Usually the necessary data was sifted from voice, text, or email intercepts; or from the detritus captured in raids by Special Operations forces. Often the inception of the strikes was the result of information from several fragmentary sources that analysts would piece together, guessing at the identity and whereabouts of a potential target. Sometimes the CIA did not need a specific identity at all. Men as young as Faheem or as old as his grandfathers were classified as "military-aged males" by the agency and its allies. If the drones observed a threatening "pattern of life," such as military-aged males gathering or traveling while bearing the region's ubiquitous weaponry, and there weren't too many women and children around, the CIA could kill these men in what it called signature strikes.

The U.S. government held the power of the drones' narrative. Secret strikes required confirmation that only the CIA controlled. It provided reporters, off the record at all times, a narrative of uncanny technological precision. Obama's closest counterterrorism adviser, John Brennan, felt confident enough to insist that in one year, "There hasn't been a single collateral death" in the drone strikes. Obama's first director of national intelligence, Admiral Dennis Blair, explained to journalist Jeremy Scahill that the lethal program "plays well domestically, and is unpopular only in foreign countries."

An expanding war against an expanding collection of enemies came to include the deaths of anonymous people, deaths never acknowledged to relatives and survivors. At least sixty-six children were among those killed just in the tribal regions of Pakistan during Obama's presidency; more lay dead in Afghanistan, Iraq, Yemen, Somalia, and Libya. To shape how the public understood drone strikes, the CIA invented a euphemism to rival "enhanced interrogation." They called it targeted killing. Much as enhanced interrogation suggested a superior form of interrogation, "targeted killing" turned a missile strike into a stiletto. During Obama's second year in office, the drones fired missiles every third day, on average, on a portion of Pakistan roughly equivalent in size to New York City's surrounding tristate metropolitan area. It was easy to forget that all this had begun to avenge the only air strike that New York had ever suffered.

In March 2011 a tribal jirga council in Datta Khel, Pakistan, assembled to adjudicate an ownership dispute between clans over a chromite mine. The CIA considered the gathering consistent with terrorist patterns and killed forty people in a signature strike, sparking nationwide protest and a rare denunciation by the Pakistani military. A survivor, Ahmed Jan, his abdomen pierced by shrapnel, soon saw America kill his neighbors at bakeries, mosques, and even funerals. "They had to destroy every segment of our life," Jan said. Life "was miserable," remembered Kareem Khan, a journalist who compared living under the whine of the drone engines to besiegement by a swarm of bees. His brothers were killed in a December 2009 strike. "Anything evil," Khan said, "you always find America behind it."

By the time Faheem Qureshi was twenty-one, he looked forward to owning a business at some point. He had invested in two of his studious nephews the academic dreams he once cultivated for himself. "If there is a list of tyrants in the world, to me, Obama will be put on that list by his drone program," Faheem reflected.

EVEN AS OBAMA RULED OUT an abolitionist approach to the War on Terror, in his first year in office he introduced several significant restrictions. Some were definitional, symbolic, or cosmetic, like getting rid of DHS's color-coded terrorism chart. Others led to an estrangement with the Security State, prompting Obama to accommodate its objections. His most significant restraint concerned torture and detentions.

On his second day in office Obama formally abolished the CIA's post-9/11 torture apparatus. He overturned the legal decrees underpinning it, banned the agency from exceeding interrogation limits set by the army's field manual—whose Appendix M loophole nonetheless permits "separation" techniques like isolation and blindfolding—and closed the black site prisons for good. In practice Obama was moving the CIA out of the inter-rogation business. After a review period, he placed the FBI-led cadre in charge of interrogations of suspected high-ranking terrorists. That decision reflected an assumption that the fate of such a person in custody would now be their prosecution. Seeming to buttress that assumption was a complementary executive order that ordered the closure of Guantanamo Bay in a year, which Obama declared in "the interests of justice."

John Brennan remained Obama's most important security adviser. The rare analyst to have served as a chief of one of the CIA's foreign stations—Riyadh, where he was close with the Saudi regime—Brennan had thrown himself into the War on Terror. A fluent Arabic speaker with extensive Middle East experience, he had been elevated by George W. Bush from George Tenet's CIA team to the leadership of a new bureaucracy that would evolve into the National Counterterrorism Center, a nexus of threat information.

He defended what he called "enhanced interrogation" after leaving the government. Terrorists "don't play by Marquess of Queensberry rules," he told PBS in 2006. "Therefore, the U.S. in some areas has to take off the gloves. And I think that's entirely appropriate."

Brennan's defense of brutal interrogations had its limits. Waterboarding, for instance, fit "the classic definition of torture," he told CBS the following year. It was a noteworthy break from the continued advocates of the practice at Langley and made his entry into the anti-torture Obama camp viable. Doubt among progressives about Brennan's proximity to torture, most importantly from *Salon* commentator Glenn Greenwald, cost him the CIA directorship in Obama's first term. Yet Brennan emerged more powerful, as assistant to the president for counterterrorism and homeland security, which gave him unrestricted access to Obama.

But Brennan's objections to torture had limits, too. If waterboarding was deemed to be torture, he argued, then prosecutors were in the "very difficult position" of judging whether those "who authorized and actually used this type of procedure may be subject to some type of judicial action." With such sentiments, Brennan channeled an entire post-9/11 CIA generation unsure if Obama's election meant they would soon be the ones in cages. They had nothing to fear: the Sustainable War on Terror *needed* the CIA; an inconspicuous war could not occur without it. Obama didn't want "extraordinarily talented" CIA officials "to suddenly feel like they've got to spend all their time looking over their shoulders." Those at the CIA who "in good faith" relied on the Office of Legal Counsel's legal blessings for torture in 2002 and 2005 shouldn't be prosecuted, his chief of staff, Rahm Emanuel, told ABC News. Those "who devised the policy, [Obama] believes that they were—they should not be prosecuted either."

Everyone involved in CIA torture—Cheney, Tenet, Mitchell, Jessen, Yoo, on down to the interrogators—was absolved. A United Nations special rapporteur for torture believed forgoing consequences for such activities was not merely bewildering but a violation of American treaty obligations.

"The fact that you carried out an order doesn't relieve you of your responsibility," he told an Austrian newspaper. Obama's loyal attorney general, Eric Holder, ultimately opted to empanel a prosecutor, John Durham, to look into CIA torture that surpassed the minimal restrictions the Office of Legal Counsel emplaced. As expected, Durham brought no charges, not even for freezing Gul Rahman to death.

CIA officials intimately involved with the torture program not only escaped legal jeopardy but kept their jobs at the agency, even those in positions of responsibility. Gina Haspel remained, as did Counterterrorism Center analyst Alfreda Frances Bikowsky, who had an innocent man kidnapped for torture based on a mistaken identity and crafted the CIA's lies to Congress about the program's efficacy. It ruined the life of a man named Khaled el-Masri, whose sanity fractured in his adopted home of Germany. In one instance, Bikowsky misrepresented a report from the torture of Majid Khan to claim that al-Qaeda was interested in recruiting "any [Muslim] with U.S. status." A former colleague of hers told NBC News, "She should be put on trial and put in jail for what she has done." At a higher level was Michael D'Andrea. The profane, chain-smoking D'Andrea, who converted to Islam to marry his wife, captained the drone campaigns in Pakistan, Yemen, and beyond. *The Washington Post* identified him as the driving force behind signature strikes.

Obama had bet that he could conduct the War on Terror without the politics of fear. The bet failed decisively over Guantanamo. Then Obama made his failure worse by hollowing out the reason to close the jail at all.

By 2008 Guantanamo showed little sign of exciting the conservative imagination. John McCain was for shutting it down—paying no price on the right for that position—as was Bush. All that changed once the Black president made it an issue. In April 2009 Obama planned on resettling in northern Virginia two of seventeen Uighur detainees whom the Bush administration had concluded posed no threat beyond being Chinese separatists. Senate Republican leader Mitch McConnell said Obama was releasing "terrorist-trained detainees onto the streets of a U.S. community" without "a guarantee of safety for American citizens." Obama, reportedly guided by Emanuel, immediately backed down.

It was a downward spiral from there. McConnell called closing Guantanamo "dangerous." Obama had neglected to work with his congressional allies on a legislative strategy for the closure. If he expected Democrats to back him on the war as Republicans backed Bush, he misunderstood his party. The renewed smell of the politics of fear in the air made Democrats as timid as they were in the months after 9/11. "I'm not much interested in wasting my energy defending a theoretical program," the House Appropriations chairman, Democrat Dave Obey, said in early May after cutting $80 million in funding for the closure. The Senate, where Democrats had a supermajority, voted 90–9 to withhold money for closing Guantanamo. Bernie Sanders was among those 90.

There were three reasons that Guantanamo attracted global condemnation: the torture practiced there, the military trials Bush established there, and the indefinite detention without charge that applied to all its detainees who didn't go before a military tribunal. The 2005 Detainee Treatment Act had constrained the torture, and the Supreme Court's decision in *Boumediene v. Bush* had put an end to the tribunals. But in May 2009 Obama acquiesced to indefinite detention without charge. Portraying it as a difficult choice in a speech at the National Archives, the constitutional law professor lamented that some at Guantanamo "cannot be prosecuted"—perhaps evidence in their cases was tainted by torture, for instance—but also "pose a clear danger to the American people," without revealing the basis for an assessment that could not withstand the scrutiny of a courtroom. By the administration's closed-door accounting, there were dozens of these people, now known as forever prisoners, consigned to Guantanamo until an endless war concluded.

Ben Rhodes wrote that speech. "I had to defend this, so I was like, 'What are examples of people that are so dangerous that we can't release them even if we can't charge them?'" he recalled. "The best I got, and it's in the speech, is someone was a bomb maker, and somebody had [sworn] an oath to bin Laden. In retrospect, is that really a reason to hold people indefinitely? We released people from Bagram and Iraqi prisons, and the Bush administration released people far more dangerous."

Obama added that his administration's preference was to charge Guantanamo detainees in civilian courts on American soil wherever possible. But he undermined himself by deciding that the court's *Boumediene* decision would not be the final word on military tribunals. Obama accepted a congressional revision by McCain ally Lindsey Graham and Carl Levin, the Military Commissions Act of 2009, which revived the commissions to provide slightly more detainee rights than the 2006 version the court had struck down. In doing so, however, Obama invited confusion as to why his administration would even bother with criminal prosecutions when it was easier to secure convictions in a military venue. Already the distinctions between those prosecutions had blurred, as Adham Hassoun had learned over the previous four years. They blurred further when the Pentagon's top lawyer, Jeh Johnson, announced that even if a civilian jury acquitted someone of terrorism charges, "I think we have the authority to continue to detain." An effort predicated on bringing terrorism detentions in line with the law instead entrenched the wartime state of exception that Obama criticized Bush for creating.

Obama crafted a plan for an alternative to Guantanamo in Illinois. The government would purchase its decommissioned Thomson Correctional Center and move the 241 Guantanamo detainees there. Embittered civil libertarians, watching Obama undermine the rationales for closing Guantanamo, called Thomson "Gitmo North." Obama treated Guantanamo less as a venue for the state of exception than as "a symbol," he said, "that helped al-Qaeda recruit terrorists to its cause." He never explained why Thomson would not acquire that same symbolic value. McConnell adopted the Gitmo North label, arguing, with justification, that "the secure facility in Cuba" already did what Obama envisioned Thomson doing. In early 2010, *The New York Times'* Charlie Savage has revealed, Graham pursued with Emanuel a "grand bargain" over detentions that would have delivered the closure of Guantanamo in exchange for entrenching wartime indefinite detentions into a new law, even prioritizing them above criminal prosecutions. Its failure—a bureaucratic death by neglect rather than a decision—embittered Graham, who was already inclined to treat Obama with hostility over Iraq.

The politics of 9/11 were not Obama's only obstacle. The Security State, especially the military, was unwilling to relinquish Guantanamo. The Pentagon's head of detentions policy, retired marine colonel Bill Lietzau, had been a deputy of Jim Haynes, Rumsfeld's top lawyer during the establishment of the Guantanamo torture regime. He worked alongside commanders with operational concerns: If Guantanamo was not an option, what should they do with al-Qaeda captives? When JSOC caught an al-Qaeda suspect at sea between Yemen and Somalia, it ended up placing him for weeks incommunicado aboard the USS *Boxer,* which JSOC's commander, Admiral Bill McRaven, considered his best option. McRaven fired a shot across Obama's bow by telling the Senate that "it would be very helpful" to have somewhere to hold high-level terrorist targets the U.S. was not prepared to prosecute criminally. Conservatives argued, not incorrectly, that Obama perversely incentivized the military and the CIA to kill instead of capture.

As well, *Boumediene* granted Guantanamo detainees access to federal courts to challenge their detentions. But even as the Justice Department's formal position was that Guantanamo should be closed, its prosecutors made maximalist arguments that amounted to saying the detainees had the right to a court hearing and no more. Litigation over the habeas cases was tied up for years in the federal courts.

Then came a humiliation. To show he was serious about prosecuting accused terrorists, Holder indicted Khalid Shaikh Mohammed and four others for the 9/11 conspiracy. "It is fitting that 9/11 suspects face justice near the World Trade Center site where so many New Yorkers were murdered," applauded Mayor Mike Bloomberg. But NYPD commissioner Ray Kelly and downtown real estate interests vociferously opposed the trial as a security inconvenience and an economic headache. Bloomberg, an oligarch who saw New York as a "luxury product" rather than a grieving city in need of closure, reversed himself. KSM and his codefendants would be reindicted by the military in 2012. Their trial has yet to occur.

The detentions disaster convinced Ben Rhodes that the politics of fear were so entrenched and implacable in 2009 that any more robust Obama effort to roll back the War on Terror was doomed to failure. "Despite him being at his absolute high-water mark—control of the Senate, sixty votes, high approval ratings—there was something just so ingrained in the American psyche and the American political-media culture that he couldn't even move the Uighurs. The idea that he could've, in that environment, tried to end the War on Terror, I think, it would have just been politically impossible." Yet the argument Obama's most left-wing aides made for him in 2008 was that he saw, clearly, the need to challenge the politics of fear. Those politics would never change without the sort of confrontation that Obama typically sought to avoid. As commander in chief, the president could in January 2009 have ordered the military to relinquish or resettle any Guantanamo detainees they could not charge and made an affirmative case for why the restoration of the rule of law was worth any violent blowback. Instead Obama chose accommodation: accepting the forever prisoners, military tribunals, and indefinite military detention. His willingness to do so only made his opponents more intractable.

IN NOVEMBER 2009 an army major, Nidal Malik Hasan, murdered thirteen soldiers and wounded more than thirty at Fort Hood's Soldier Readiness Processing Center, shouting "Allahu akbar" before opening fire. On Christmas Day, Umar Farouk Abdulmuttalab, the son of a Nigerian banker, using explosives provided by al-Qaeda's Yemeni affiliate and packed into his underwear, attempted to detonate Northwest Airlines Flight 253 over Detroit. Abdulmutallab succeeded only in mutilating his genitals to the point of evoking his interrogators' pity. His cooperation after receiving assurances against both physical and legal abuse prompted Obama's DHS secretary, Janet Napolitano, to judge that "once the incident occurred, the system worked." She retracted her assessment after conservative outrage at the FBI's reading the terrorist his Miranda rights against self-incrimination.

Hasan and Abdulmutallab functionally halted Obama's Forever War restrictionism. The Sustainable War on Terror was about to cross a constitutional Rubicon.

Within weeks the FBI learned from Abdulmutallab that he had been in extensive contact with Anwar al-Awlaki, the former northern Virginia preacher radicalized by Ashcroft's 2002 crackdown. According to FBI summaries of his cooperation with his interrogators, which remained classified until 2017, Abdulmutallab was not merely inspired by Awlaki's jihadist preaching, but said that Awlaki had provided him with spiritual guidance during his breakneck terrorist training, sanctified his selection for martyrdom, and instructed him to wait until he was over U.S. airspace to detonate. Hasan had also emailed Awlaki seeking guidance, but Awlaki hadn't responded substantively. When Hasan freelanced his murder instead, Awlaki blogged that he was a hero.

Awlaki fled America for Yemen in 2002, but he remained a U.S. surveillance target. In 2005 he released a lecture series called "Constants on the Path of Jihad," which used religious texts and Islamic history to portray Islam and the West as irreconcilable. The West was "actually fighting Islam in the media and battlefield front," obliging Western Muslims to "fight them back with the sword" wherever possible. The series was enormously popular, particularly after the U.S. client regime in Yemen imprisoned Awlaki, lending him outlaw credibility. Although Awlaki was a U.S. citizen, the Obama administration and the Security State resolved not to indict him but to kill him.

Obama's Sustainable War on Terror presented itself as more lawful than Bush's. That presentation was important to the self-image of the lawyers, from Obama on down, shaping it. Many of them had criticized Bush as lawless and saw their own role as binding counterterrorism within a belt of law. But like Yoo and Ashcroft, the Justice Department under Obama delivered another contorted legal assessment meant to enable the outcome that Obama and the Security State sought. Awlaki's constitutional right to due process was not an obstacle to his execution.

Two Office of Legal Counsel attorneys, David Barron and Marty Lederman, relied in part on the Supreme Court's 2004 decision in *U.S. v. Hamdi*—ironically, a decision rejecting the indefinite detention of U.S. citizens at Guantanamo—to contend that a trial need not occur before killing a terrorist, citizen or not, who could not reasonably be captured. "'Due process' and 'judicial process' are not one and the same," Holder would later say, "particularly when it comes to national security." Neither Barron nor Lederman explained *why* capturing Awlaki was unfeasible. In fact, Abdulmutallab had told the FBI that it had taken him mere weeks from being a total stranger to becoming a guest sleeping on the second floor of Awlaki's row house, which he described in detail, down to its possessing "no guards and no surrounding exterior wall." Much as Abdulmutallab's testimony was all the proof necessary to consign Awlaki to death, the CIA's testimony was all the proof needed that Awlaki could not be apprehended, just as in 2002, when the agency represented to Yoo that "enhanced interrogation" was necessary. Charlie Savage of *The New York Times* reported that Barron and Lederman "did not see it as their role to independently reconsider the evidence." Like Yoo's torture-memo colleague Jay Bybee, Barron would later be rewarded with a federal judgeship.

Aided by the ACLU, Awlaki's father, Nasser, filed a request for an injunction against an impending execution. But the Justice Department, wary of setting a precedent inhibiting the Security State, fought the suit, even to the point of embracing absurd deceits. It argued that Nasser had no right to sue, since the apparatus of state secrecy prevented him from actually knowing the government was targeting Anwar. In keeping with the courts' typical Forever War posture, Judge John Bates proclaimed himself powerless, despite acknowledging that the "somewhat unsettling" result of his abdication would be to make potential executions of U.S. citizens "judicially unreviewable." Lamented ACLU attorney Jameel Jaffer, "It would be diffi-cult to conceive of a proposition more inconsistent with the Constitution or more dangerous to American liberty."

The drones came for Awlaki in September 2011, incinerating him and his convoy in the northern Yemeni desert when they stopped for break-fast. Another American citizen, Samir Khan, who published an English-language webzine about al-Qaeda's exhortations to DIY jihad, died with Awlaki. Two weeks later, another U.S. drone fired upon a Shabwah barbe-cue attended by Awlaki's sixteen-year-old son, Abdulrahman, and seventeen-year-old nephew, Ahmed. Obama later called it an accident. When their grandfather again sought justice, federal judge Rosemary Collyer—who, like Bates, was a FISA Court veteran—pronounced that holding Obama's subordinates accountable for "conducting war" was untenable. The Sus-tainable War on Terror presented itself as upholding the rule of law. Now it established the precedent that circumstances could permit the extrajudicial execution of American citizens. The loudest objection from anyone with power came not from any liberal but from the Republican senator Rand Paul, Ron's son, who in protest filibustered Brennan's elevation to CIA director.

THE SUSTAINABLE WAR ON TERROR departed from Bush's war in a funda-mental respect, but also undermined that departure. For the first time since 9/11, Obama focused the war on al-Qaeda—but with an important excep-tion. In 2011, for a military authorization bill, the administration wrote into law that the enemy would now include al-Qaeda's "associated forces." Those forces were never specified in public, permitting the administration to define al-Qaeda as it wished. Obama had intended the law to distinguish the enemy from anything resembling Islam, which he told a Cairo audience in 2009 that America would never be at war against. To the right, it was an alarming decision, one that made Obama's version of the enemy an even more dangerous euphemism than Bush's. To those on the receiving end of the war, it was a distinction without a difference. "I do not say drones have only killed civilians. They would have or might have killed some militants," said Faheem Qureshi. "But overall, they have killed mostly civilians who have nothing to do with what America is trying to do in Pakistan or Afghanistan or anywhere else in the world."

To Obama, abandoning a definition of the enemy as specifically Islamic was a matter of basic decency. But the machinery he retained was targeted at Muslims, something elected officials reflexively treated as the responsible thing to do. While Obama shut down the NSEERS Muslim registry that Ashcroft created, he didn't purge its highly sensitive records about tens of thousands of Muslims. A 2012 DHS inspector general report noted that the data was "transferred automatically to other DHS systems or captured initially in other systems." That indicated that the administration "condones and intends to continue policies that rely on discriminatory racial profiling," judged a Penn State Law report. In Cairo, Obama attempted to show that the United States respected the dignity of a religion with 1.8 billion believers. But in the same breath, he told the Muslim world to expect the continuation of the War on Terror, since al-Qaeda's expansion and agenda "are not opinions to be debated; [but] facts to be dealt with."

While Obama built his Sustainable War on Terror, he didn't like using the gauche phrase "War on Terror." Typically, when Obama described a military operation, he would name al-Qaeda or the Taliban or other specific adversaries. But when Obama spoke about the broader goals of counterterrorism, he used the term "violent extremists" as its targets. On one level, the nomenclature was another attempt to differentiate terrorism from Islam. But on another, its primary target remained Muslims, and specifically American Muslims.

Obama's approach, formalized in 2011, proposed "empower[ing] local partners" and "government-community partnerships" to identify and deradicalize at-risk youth. The American Muslim communities that the

Countering Violent Extremism (CVE) program was focused on resented both the euphemism and their treatment, by a progressive administration, as a threat. The primary administrators of these local "partnerships" were federal prosecutors, law enforcement, and homeland security, further alarming those communities. Despite its pledge of applicability to "all forms of violent extremism," CVE explicitly prioritized "preventing violent extremism and terrorism that is inspired by al-Qa'ida and its affiliates and adherents," the "preeminent security threats" the U.S. faced.

Early in the Obama administration, a Department of Homeland Security intelligence analyst learned that certain kinds of domestic terrorism would be functionally protected. Daryl Johnson, in 2009, warned that "rightwing extremist" groups could exploit the economic disaster and "election of the first African-American president" to swell the ranks of white supremacists. Although Johnson was the first to observe the catalytic effect Obama's presidency would have on white supremacist violence, his was not the first warning. The War on Terror's studious neglect of white terror had effectively provided networks like Grandpa Millar's with a reprieve. In 2006 the FBI both noted that white supremacists were infiltrating law enforcement and acknowledged the already existing presence of "law enforcement personnel sympathetic to white supremacist causes."

Johnson recognized that the combustible mixture of extant grievances over "appropriate immigration levels" and gun control, as well as the appeal of white supremacy to some Iraq and Afghanistan veterans, could result in outright terrorism. But his paper was broad and speculative. Its umbrella term "rightwing" implicated mainstream conservatism—or at least mainstream conservatism took it that way. Conservative media saw itself as the target and loudly objected. It did not take long for the Obama administration to repudiate Johnson's warning. Obama's DHS secretary, Janet Napolitano, quietly dismantled his analytical unit and pledged that DHS would "not ever . . . monitor ideology or political beliefs," a promise that would have surprised American Muslims. Some people's fanaticism was too powerful to name, let alone challenge.

Other people working in the Security State had accepted definitions of the enemy as Islamic, including defining it as Islam itself. Obama and his Security State allies moved to rid the agencies of them, an action that prompted right-wing backlash against both.

Obama kept Robert Mueller in charge of the FBI, which continued to infiltrate Muslim communities. The bureau taught its counterterrorism agents that the most sacred texts and traditions of Islam were drivers of terrorism. In March 2011 the FBI's Quantico training academy featured an elective course from a bureau intelligence analyst, William Gawthrop, that located terrorism within what his lecture slides called "mainstream" Islam. The courses purported to graph a relationship between Islam and violence in contrast to Christianity and Judaism, which Gawthrop asserted inspired peace within the more devout. His "Strategic Themes and Drivers in Islamic Law" lecture concluded, "There may not be a 'radical' threat as much as it is simply a normal assertion of the orthodox ideology . . . the strategic themes animating these Islamic values are not fringe; they are main stream [sic]." Another lecture taught agents to "identify the elements of verbal deception in Islam and their impacts on law enforcement." Gawthrop instructed that not only does Islam prompt Muslims to lie to unbelievers—a federal offense when committed against an FBI agent—but those lies included "shifting the focus away from the ideology" and onto concrete political grievances, like "the Palestinians [or] the perceived U.S.–Israeli axis." It was a little over a year after Napolitano swore that it was inappropriate for government counterterrorism to monitor ideology or political beliefs.

To the alarm of some bureau officials, the FBI library was filled with ignorant and Islamophobic books making similar points, including several by Robert Spencer. The FBI intranet, used to help agents research their casework, was filled with material that portrayed Islam as a civilization-ending threat. One posted item said that "Jihad in Action" progressed from "proselytizing" and the "belligerence" of "grievance fabrication" to massacres, persecution of non-Muslims with "Sharia Law [used] as a weapon," and even "genocide" before reaching "peace." Two months after offering his course, Gawthrop took his lecturing to an FBI partnership group in New York, where he declared focusing on al-Qaeda a "waste," since there would always be another jihadist group to take its place. Enduring and effective counterterrorism needed to discredit the fundamental texts of Islam, something Gawthrop rhapsodized would be like the moment Luke Skywalker's superhuman piloting destroyed the planet-killing Death Star in *Star Wars*.

Obama's horrified White House ordered an embarrassed FBI to get rid of the inflammatory material—it excised about 700 pages of training documents out of 160,000 reviewed—but its sentiments had already spread beyond the bureau. At the Joint Forces Staff College, a military institution educating senior officers from across the services, an army lieutenant colonel, Matthew Dooley, taught that "total war" would be necessary against the Islamic world. Dooley explicitly envisioned "taking war to a civilian population wherever necessary," including the destruction of the most holy cities in Islam, Mecca and Medina, in the style of "Dresden, Tokyo, Hiroshima [and] Nagasaki." Victory in this war could be achieved only when Islam "change[d]" or when the United States forced the "self-destruction" of a "barbaric ideology" that comprised the religious beliefs of well over a billion people. If just 10 percent of Muslims believed what their religion instructed, Dooley told the officers in his class, then they faced an army of at least 140 million. "Your oath as a professional soldier forces you to pick a side here," Dooley continued, encouraging colonels and navy captains to commit war crimes. Student officers gave the "thought-provoking" class a 90 percent approval rating, according to a spokesperson for the college.

The chairman of the Joint Chiefs of Staff, army general Martin Dempsey, canceled Dooley's class. Ordering a thorough review of what the military trained about Islam, Dempsey said the course was "totally objectionable, against our values and it wasn't academically sound." Unlike Gawthrop, who remained at the FBI, Dooley became unlikely to receive a promotion, the military's passive-aggressive way of ushering an officer out of the service. But like the FBI's, Dempsey's inquiry ultimately exonerated the military by generically declaring that its overall standards were both sound and, for the most part, adhered to. It did not explain the specific "institutional failures" that led to Dooley teaching the course in 2010, or whether the course itself had been offering similar instruction since its 2004 inception. There were possible preludes: reportedly, the head of the anti-Islam ACT for America organization told the college in a 2007 speech that a "practicing Muslim . . . cannot be a loyal citizen of the United States." In any event, Dempsey's review didn't recommend retraining any of the officers in attendance.

As the war persisted into its second decade, frustration within the security services created a fringe constituency for defining an undefeated enemy in conspiratorially broad terms. Some saw Obama's refusal to condemn Islam as proof of a betrayal, an attitude characteristic of liberals—and specifically of the first Black president, with his Muslim-sounding middle name. It occurred amid the backdrop of a war the Security State and Obama escalated but could neither win nor end.

FOR DAYS SERGEANT ROB'S* cavalry troop had fruitlessly hunted a Taliban weapons cache in the eastern Afghan province of Paktia. An informant's tip brought his platoon, the Hooligans, to a crumbling, sun-baked compound in a town called Spin Sarakalat in pursuit of a man named Dawood who, the informant said, was fencing stolen U.S. equipment. Under rules set by President Hamid Karzai, the Hooligans couldn't enter the *kalat* without Afghan escorts, so the local police were first through the door. They quickly brought out thirty-three-year-old Dawood Shadikhan, just three years older than Rob, who had been trying to disguise himself in a woman's flowing orange and red robes. A half dozen elderly women living in the small compound, their faces dotted with blue stipple tattoos arranged into diamonds, followed the soldiers outside, begging them to let Shadikhan go.

---

*I have obscured his name at the specific request of his family.

Rob had earlier quieted his soldiers when they complained about bringing along the unreliable Afghan police. A salty, stocky Kansan who liked riding out to Ram Jam's version of "Black Betty," Sergeant Rob—that was what his Hooligans called him—said they should suck it up, since unless the Afghans became better soldiers and police, "the mission won't end." But now an Afghan cop with a floppy pompadour dyed red was getting too into his job, grabbing a wooden pole and bashing Shadikhan between the shoulder blades. As Shadikhan crumpled to the ground, the women's wailing swelled. The officer swung around, arcing the pole dangerously close to them, and they sprung back. The eldest among them, tiny and dressed in black, lost her balance, took a nasty fall, and began to cry. The Americans shouted to the cop that it was enough.

As the Americans began to search Shadikhan and assured the women they meant no disrespect, the red-haired cop slipped into the compound and emerged with its maroon-colored motorcycle between his legs. Grinning at the Americans, he revved its engine.

The Hooligans' lieutenant, N. Blaine Cooper, was getting overwhelmed. He needed the Afghan police to take them to the weapons cache, which Shadikhan claimed the Taliban had moved, before nightfall. Technically, Cooper noted, if the women couldn't document ownership of the motorcycle, the police could impound it. Sergeant Rob quietly but firmly told Cooper that the police weren't impounding it; Rockabilly Cop was stealing it. "Look at the situation," Rob told the young officer.

Cooper, no longer equivocating, yelled to the police that the bike would stay with the women. They indignantly filed back into their trucks and drove off. With no Afghan escort to raid an Afghan home, the Hooligans, with Shadikhan in tow, called it a day. Watching the policemen ride away, Cooper muttered, "If they won't do it because we won't let them take a motorcycle . . ." before trailing off, unwilling to follow the implication through. Sergeant Rob had stopped a robbery and saved the women's motorcycle at the expense of his immediate mission and their relationship with the Afghan police. Alpha Cavalry Troop, 1-61 Cavalry would never get its weapons cache. This was what it meant to do the right thing in the Afghanistan war.

Counterinsurgency, ascendant after the Iraq surge, sometimes dictated that a soldier's priority was to protect civilians. At other times the priority was to mentor the local security forces, particularly to ward off corruption. At still other times it said a soldier's priority was to pursue an insurgent and his capabilities relentlessly. Sergeant Rob and the Hooligans found themselves in a circumstance where all three priorities conflicted. It was like that throughout Afghanistan, a Gordian knot of a war. A skeptical Obama, to his ultimate regret, followed the counterinsurgents' advice. Afghanistan chewed it up and spat it out.

Joe Biden, once Hamid Karzai's champion and now Obama's vice president, contended that the right course was to look past Afghanistan, as the Taliban weren't the issue; al-Qaeda was, and al-Qaeda's leadership was in Pakistan. Once they decided the Taliban was their problem, then so were the increasingly uncooperative Karzai and the weak Afghan state. Defining the Afghanistan mission narrowly—waging only as much counterterrorism as necessary while throwing money into building Karzai's forces—was the only way not to become entrenched more deeply into a destitute, unconquered, and unfamiliar country's problems, which were made even more intractable by U.S. involvement. At the dawn of 2009, with a Taliban insurgency increasingly effective, Biden informed Karzai that he would have to do more with less, starting with an end to his loud criticisms that the Americans were killing Afghan civilians. Pakistan was "fifty times more important" than Afghanistan, Biden told a seething Karzai.

With the exception of the CIA, the Security State and most of the Obama administration arrayed against Biden. There was a large appetite in the military, and particularly from Admiral Mike Mullen, Dempsey's predecessor as Joint Chiefs chairman, for recommitting to the Afghanistan war through some version of counterinsurgency. Petraeus, now at CENTCOM, considered Biden's war unviable, since a collapsing Afghanistan wouldn't tolerate an indifferent American military presence focused on its neighbor. Clinton, now secretary of state, backed Mullen and Petraeus. By March, Obama approved an extant request from the military command in Kabul for twenty-one thousand troops, in part to secure an upcoming presidential election, a move that could have satisfied his campaign pledge to escalate. While Obama said the mission was to "disrupt, dismantle and defeat al-Qaeda in Pakistan and Afghanistan," he described a meandering path to victory running through Afghanistan. It called for "promot[ing] a more capable and account-able Afghan government," a goal that required a "dramatic increase in our civilian effort," extending as far as enlisting agronomists. Michèle Flournoy, the CNAS cofounder who now ran the Pentagon's policy directorate, described the strategy as "very much a counterinsurgency approach" to a counterterrorism objective. It implied that nation building was necessary for durable counterterrorism, an expansive commitment.

That was not the sort of war that had been waged by the Joint Special Operations Command, the raiders of Zarqawi, but their commander, Stanley McChrystal, took it over in mid-2009. McChrystal's experience in Iraq sent him searching for an endgame in an endless war, something night raids would never deliver, and he accordingly became more Petraeus than Petraeus. His definition of victory—"a condition where the insurgency no longer threatens the viability of the state"—looked entirely past al-Qaeda. Backed by his fellow generals, McChrystal requested forty thousand more troops, even as the U.S. ambassador in Kabul, the former war commander Karl Eikenberry, called the entire strategy folly. But the Iraq surge established that losing a war only empowered those who wanted to escalate. Obama, granting thirty thousand more troops to generals he now distrusted, extracted from them a promise to deliver results within eighteen months. The discomfited officers, in no position to refuse without undermining confidence in their strategy, acquiesced. The stage was set for the Afghanistan surge: a campaign none of its factionalized architects fully embraced. In December Obama set "breaking the Taliban's momentum" as the objective, a purposefully subjective definition that would cover everything short of outright defeat.

It started coming apart from the start. In February, McChrystal picked his first major engagement, a town of eighty thousand in Helmand called Marja that the Taliban had occupied. He flooded it with fifteen thousand U.S., NATO, and Afghan forces. After only one day of fighting, McChrystal had to apologize for the deaths of civilians, the result of an errant artillery strike. He suspended the use of the artillery system and constrained air support. What McChrystal considered necessary to avoid alienating Afghans seemed to his infantrymen like disarmament before a resilient enemy. Anticipating victory in Marja within weeks, the first step in his plan to retake Helmand Province by occupying one river town after another, McChrystal boasted that he had brought "a government in a box, ready to roll in." But throughout the coming year, the Taliban continued to harry his forces in territory he had thought retaken, preventing him from turning security over to the Afghans as he had promised the local tribal leadership he would. Echoing Napoleon, he called Marja his "bleeding ulcer."

As the intractability persisted, the United States fought itself. McChrystal's relentless intelligence director from their JSOC days, Major General Michael Flynn, publicly accused the rest of the U.S. intelligence apparatus of not knowing anything about Afghanistan. His major complaint was that it was focused on the insurgency and not on the Afghans—who, counterinsurgency doctrine held, would determine the war's winners and losers—people, Flynn warned, who the U.S. still didn't understand. As McChrystal visited with his troops, he came under the opposite criticism. Soldiers at an outpost near Kandahar resented him after they were denied permission to destroy an abandoned, booby-trapped house where twenty-three-year-old Corporal Michael Ingram had been killed. "We aren't putting fear into the Taliban," one told McChrystal. "The more we pull back, the more we restrain ourselves, the stronger it's getting."

McChrystal lost his command after Michael Hastings reported in *Rolling Stone* his camp's disrespect for everyone else involved in Afghanistan except Clinton. Obama replaced him with Petraeus, who was effectively demoted from CENTCOM. With a year to go before the surge forces began coming home, Petraeus prioritized the kind of killing he had spent years arguing was counterproductive. His campaign plan was now reliant on overhead surveillance and Special Operations raids, as if he was commanding JSOC. He dismissed questions about the shift in tactics. "Targeted, intelligence-driven precision operations by those [Special Operations Forces] elements are absolutely part of a comprehensive, civil-military counterinsurgency campaign," Petraeus said soon after taking command.

Petraeus removed McChrystal's hated restrictions and air strikes returned in force. In October 2010 there were one thousand aerial weapons releases, the most since the invasion began. An extreme example occurred at a place called Tarek Kolache. Lieutenant Colonel David Flynn arrived in the heavy vegetation of the Arghandab River Valley, near Kandahar, to discover fields densely packed with IEDs. His task force suffered seven killed and eighty-three wounded in months spent fighting for control, mostly from the IEDs, which hindered efforts at clearing the local towns. After determining that the villages of Tarek Kolache, Khosrow Sofla, and Lower Babur were cleared of civilians—the Taliban having driven the people from their pomegranate trees, he claimed—Flynn informed the local leaders in exile that unless the villagers told the task force exactly where the IEDs were, he would have no choice but to blow up their homes. One journalist reported he framed it as a threat; Flynn denied it. But on October 6 Flynn dropped twenty-five tons of bombs and destroyed the villages to save them. He remembered telling the village elders, "I promise, I will rebuild the homes." Petraeus backed his officer. "We're being forced into these things," said his spokesman, Colonel Erik Gunhus. A *Washington Post* reporter visiting Tarek Kolache three years later found "a sandy ruin." The village elder, forty-seven-year-old Niaz Mohammed, asked, "What did we win in this war? We lost our homes. We lost our village." The Taliban, he said, were only fighting the Americans because the Americans were there.

To the northwest in Helmand Province was what one marine called a hell on earth. The marines had bled, twice, in taking Fallujah, sometimes one house at a time. But they had not yet experienced Sangin, where the

Taliban had kept the British at bay for four years. From September 2010 to April 2011, the one thousand marines of the Third Battalion, Fifth Regiment—the Darkhorse Battalion—entered a brown expanse of mud, vegetation, canals, and animal shit that the Taliban had turned into a killing field. Getting off their outpost involved dodging a maze of IEDs and small-arms fire. What awaited, as Flynn had encountered, were dense thickets of bombs. "You could not move outside of the district center without getting shot," the Darkhorse commander, Lieutenant Colonel Jason Morris, told NPR. The 3/5 marines suffered the highest casualty rate of the war: twenty-five dead, two hundred wounded, including dozens of men who underwent amputations and suffered other life-changing injuries. The military leadership responded as it had in Iraq: with delusional statements of assured victory. "We believe [the Taliban]'ll be returning to a significantly different environment than when they left last year," General David Rodriguez, the deputy commander, said.

One of the Sangin dead was a twenty-nine-year-old second lieutenant named Robert Kelly. A Fallujah veteran, Kelly stepped on an IED leading his men on a dismounted patrol. Marine general Joseph Dunford rang the Washington Navy Yard doorbell of marine lieutenant general John Kelly to tell his close friend that Kelly was now the most senior Gold Star parent of the war. Four days later, in St. Louis, Kelly gave a caustic speech accusing the nation of indifference to the unfathomable sacrifice of marines in faraway places. "We are in a life-and-death struggle, but not our whole country," said the anguished Kelly, who directed his venom not at those who ordered his son to Sangin to die for a marginal U.S. interest, but at those who opposed the war. Kelly claimed that combat veterans broadly "hold in disdain those who claim to support them but not the cause that takes their innocence, their limbs and even their lives." After this display of contempt, Gates made Kelly his senior military assistant, ensuring Kelly's ascent in the military and beyond.

None of the surge's architects bothered explaining how any of this knitted up into an acceptable outcome. No politician pressured them to. Some soldiers reacted with barbarism. A platoon from the Fifth Stryker Brigade formed a "kill team" to hunt and murder Afghan civilians, including children, whom they called "savages." Only low-ranking enlisted men were prosecuted for what a whistleblower described as an open secret within the company. In March 2011 Staff Sergeant Robert Bales snuck off his Panjwei base to methodically open fire on house after house until sixteen men, women, and children were dead, in the worst U.S. wartime atrocity since My Lai. The following year Clint Lorance, a lieutenant only days into his command, ordered his soldiers to open fire without provocation on three civilians. The platoon, many of whom suffered lasting scars from the experience, turned Lorance in. Yet the atrocities of Afghanistan barely registered with U.S. public opinion.

What passed for a theory of victory—pummeling the Taliban into suing for peace—was frustrated by the war's tangle of competing interests. Furtive and occasionally farcical diplomacy—the U.S. negotiated with an imposter at one point—had been official policy since September 2010. It sidestepped an outraged Karzai, prompting the Taliban to declare that further talks were off, thanks to the United States's "ever-changing position." The most the talks ever yielded was an exchange of five senior members of the Taliban at Guantanamo for army sergeant Bowe Bergdahl, an American deserter who would soon become widely loathed. The gesture had been intended as a confidence-building measure. All the Americans could do now, as the Taliban reconquered more of Afghanistan, was train Afghan soldiers in the hope they could take over the war. Some, in so-called Green-on-Blue attacks, fought the United States instead.

A year after the surge troops came home, Sergeant Rob returned to Afghanistan. Now thirty-five, he was beginning his second tour there, after an army career that began in 1996 when he was seventeen years old and had taken him to Bosnia and twice to Iraq. While on patrol in Pul-e-Alam on November 3, 2013, Rob's platoon came under small-arms and rocket-propelled-grenade attack. He had been scheduled for redeployment home to his wife and three daughters three weeks later. As Sergeant Rob died in eastern Afghanistan, his last words were said to be "Go get 'em, boys."

LATE ON SUNDAY, MAY 1, 2011, a SEAL team under McRaven's command helicoptered into a Pakistani town called Abbottabad, near the military academy it hosted and far from the tribal areas; raided a compound; and shot Osama bin Laden dead. At 11:00 P.M., Obama announced the end of the leader of al-Qaeda, the embodiment of the threat that for a decade had consumed America. Hundreds of college students ran into Lafayette Park, near the White House, and, unfurling American flags, partied. The cathartic, patriotic, vengeful joy struck *New Yorker* writer Peter Maass as uncomfortably reminiscent of "young Muslims on the other side of the world burning our flag and shouting 'Death to America!'"

Bin Laden's death suddenly brought into relief the fact that, even as John Kelly considered them strangers to the war, the young Americans celebrating in Lafayette Park had not known peace since they were children. "All my life has been defined by what Osama bin Laden did," said Ann Garcia, who had just begun high school on 9/11. Samantha McGowan, only ten years old on 9/11, who had run to the park in her pajamas, said: "This was more a celebration of conquering terrorism, an idea that has permeated our lives for ten years." Annabel Hogg, three years older, felt discomfited by the celebration but defended it. "I have and people of my generation have been profoundly affected by 9/11," she explained. Bin Laden "took away what the country had been before, one without terror alerts and men in caves who we are told want to kill us."

By defining the enemy so vaguely, Bush ensured that any declared end to the war would be a matter of political dispute. Different parties, factions, and interests would always be able to offer contending claims of who the enemy actually was and, accordingly, when the task at hand was actually completed. But with bin Laden dead, no alternative outcome in the War on Terror could more plausibly and universally be used to declare that the war was not only concluded but *won*. Instead, Obama squandered the best chance anyone could ever have to end the 9/11 era.

"His death does not mark the end of our effort," the president said in announcing the death. The following day Brennan called it merely the beginning of the end for al-Qaeda: a "strategic blow" necessary but insufficient to destroy it, "but we are determined to destroy it." (Brennan also claimed bin Laden was "engaged in a firefight" with the SEALs, which the White House later retracted, and he neglected to mention that the CIA had been gathering DNA information in Abbottabad by faking a vaccination drive, thereby putting at risk real, lifesaving public-health efforts.) Obama does not grapple with this decision in his memoir and treats it as self-evident. "[N]one of us believed the threat from al-Qaeda was over," he wrote in 2020, just that now it was "a step closer to strategic defeat," which he did not further define. Equivocally, he writes that bin Laden's death offered "a catharsis of sorts." At the time, his administration instead feared political exposure from overpromising what bin Laden's death meant. Few reporters even asked Brennan if the Forever War was now over, or could be over. It reflected a political consensus that would have punished Obama for declaring victory during the last, best chance for it that America would have.

"His read of political realities and public opinion is that he can't do that, and that part of being president is shaping public opinion and part of being president is understanding it," Rhodes offered. "He was president of a country where, let's say he did that, and dismantled our counterterrorism apparatus over that summer, and there's a terrorist attack and then the world ends."

The apparatus Obama built to constrain the War on Terror also generated the internal processes sustaining it. Unless it was disassembled, there would always be another target. And each subsequent target would be worse than the last, as tomorrow's enemy would react to the compounding outrages of torture, invasion, occupation, and everything else America inflicted. The resting state of the War on Terror was expansion, expansion of both action and enemies. Yet dismantling the War on Terror, rather than maintaining it, was considered irresponsible. What bin Laden began required a U.S. invasion to yield an al-Qaeda in Iraq. Awlaki was sympathetic to the Bosnian and Chechen jihads, but he only encouraged Western Muslims to attack in the West after Ashcroft's raids and what followed. A year before the bin Laden raid, a Pakistani American MBA named Faisal Shahzad attempted to detonate an SUV in Times Square. Pleading guilty, Shahzad explained that Americans should expect vengeance.

"I'm going to plead guilty a hundred times forward," he said, "because until the hour the U.S. pulls its forces from Iraq and Afghanistan and stops the drone strikes in Somalia and Yemen and in Pakistan and stops the occupation of Muslim lands and stops killing the Muslims and stops reporting the Muslims to its government, we will be attacking [the] U.S., and I plead guilty to that."

Shahzad blamed America, and America refused to listen, as doing so would contradict American exceptionalism's self-conception of innocence. That was another aspect of the War on Terror that Obama did not attempt to change. Ever since Sontag, elites from both parties and the Security State treated blowback explanations as calumny, no different than proclaiming that America *deserved* attack. The fact that any attack could take place ensured the maintenance of the apparatus of mass surveillance, detention, border security, and any other tool of the state of exception; the wars themselves were more controversial, taxing, and hence expendable. But even as America now had to face Hasans, Abdulmutallabs, Shahzads, Zarqawis, and Awlakis, none of them had the money, organization, or patience to execute a 9/11. Samir Khan's *Inspire* magazine encouraged American Muslims like himself to ram their cars onto crowded sidewalks; this generation of jihadists was not going to learn how to fly planes. None of that stopped substantial elements of the right from arguing that they faced an Islamic besiegement: certainly not the rarity of domestic U.S. deaths from terrorism, and least of all the fact that one of the street vendors in the square who alerted police to Shahzad's smoking car was a Senegalese Muslim immigrant named Alioune Niasse.

Yet having deprived the country of a chance at closure, Obama soon found himself in need of a plausible vision for how the War on Terror *would* come to an end. Part of how he got there was by conceding that a prime danger of the war was the spiraling American bloodthirst it had unleashed.

As terrorist attacks by self-starters, including Americans, persisted, Obama began speaking of "resilience" as a component of successful counterterrorism. He didn't only mean the resilience of counterterrorism institutions, focus, and funding. He meant the resilience of Americans against overreaction. It would be safer, certainly more sustainable, to respond to terrorist attacks through law enforcement and intelligence channels—left unsaid was how that ensured more Adham Hassouns and Faheem Qureshis—rather than by, say, invading foreign countries. It was a version of what John Kerry proposed in October 2004. It was also a combustible, politically dangerous position, especially for a Black president who millions continued to believe—despite the surge, despite bin Laden, despite the drones—palled around with terrorists. Obama did not go beyond an unfinished thought about how "a perpetual war would alter our country in troubling ways."

Shortly after reelection Obama considered strengthening the internal safeguards within the disposition matrix, his facsimile of due process. That prompted, the following May, the Presidential Policy Guidance. Holder and others had insisted that due process need not be a judicial process, and presented this as the alternative. Under its terms, any agency could nominate a "high-value target" for death or capture. Lawyers throughout the White House and the Security State would review a nomination, with the concurrence of a National Security Council attorney. The plan of action required specifying the counterterrorism "objectives to be achieved," how long the underlying authorities would have to last, and the commandos, drones, or surveillance assets required. The proponents of any action had to reach a "near certainty" that the attack would not kill or harm civilians, but the terms of the policy suggested that they did not necessarily require positive identification to kill or, more rarely, capture someone. A guideline required merely "employ[ing] all reasonably available resources to ascertain the identity of the target."

The interagency committee handling "nominations" to the matrix was called the Interagency Disposition Planning Group. Reviewing its work was the Restricted Counterterrorism Security Group, composed of representatives from the departments of State, Defense, Treasury, Justice, and Homeland Security; the CIA; the Joint Chiefs of Staff; the National Counterterrorism Center; and still-undisclosed others. The Security Group forwarded approved nominations to their departments' deputy secretaries and directors. This senior council, called simply "the Deputies" in official documentation, considered strategic questions, weighing the virtues of the strike against foreseeable consequences to "broader regional and international political interests of the United States." With a formal bias against the use of lethal force, the Deputies sent nominations up to the president—but not always to him. Obama's order states that "as appropriate," the life-or-death decision will be made by the president "or the nomination will be provided to the Principal of the appropriate operating agency for a decision, along with any views expressed by the President."

Obama unveiled the outline of these procedural changes in a speech at the National Defense University. He formally rejected the term "War on Terror," heralding instead a new phase of "persistent, targeted efforts to dismantle specific networks of violent extremists that threaten America." He recognized that the implications of expanding an easy method of killing people were profound, but insisted that the course was legal, as much as it required a thorough review of each case by a secret internal process. Here was what Obama considered a sensible path that took into account the intense pressures he and his successors were likely to encounter as the result of their now-unnamed War on Terror.

By then two years had passed since the death of Osama bin Laden. Having agonizingly outlined a lethal and carceral framework for a non–War on Terror, while obscuring the fact that mass surveillance was permanent,

Obama imagined the day it all could end. But without bin Laden to anchor an argument, he portrayed resilience against overreaction as victory itself. "Victory," he said, "will be measured in parents taking their kids to school; immigrants coming to our shores; fans taking in a ball game; a veteran starting a business; a bustling city street; a citizen shouting her concerns at a president." But all those things were already happening, and still the war ground on. Whatever profundity Obama aimed to invoke—the political courage in choosing normalcy over fear—collapsed under his cynical implication that ending the wartime footing that he had entrenched was the citizenry's responsibility and not his own.

After the killing of bin Laden, Ben Rhodes recalled, discussions began within the White House about envisioning an end to the War on Terror. Their guidepost was what Kerry said in 2004 about reducing terrorism to a nuisance. But those conversations came to a halt as the Arab Spring uprisings swelled in chaotic ways. "The Arab Spring hijacks everybody's attention after the bin Laden takedown and, in some ways, for the remainder of the presidency. It gets tangled up with the War on Terror in unhealthy ways. Just the generalized appearance of chaos in the Mideast plays into the Republican politics of fear," Rhodes said. Obama, however, chose to wage a war of regime change in support of one of those uprisings, resulting in state failure in Libya and, on the eleventh anniversary of 9/11, an hours-long assault on a CIA compound in Benghazi that led to the deaths of U.S. ambassador Christopher Stevens, foreign service officer Sean Smith, and CIA contractors Tyrone Woods and Glen Doherty.

"These sound like excuses. They are what they are. It's certainly how it felt at the time," Rhodes said. "You can break up the different pieces of this—drones, NSA, Gitmo—but to me, it's just the continued hyper-securitization of U.S. foreign policy with terrorism at its center that is the essential problem."

The positive case for the administration, Rhodes continued, was that during Obama's second term, "we are governing as an administration that *is* moving on. Obama's talking a hell of a lot less about terrorism. He's doing stuff like the Iran deal that is meant to signal a break from a certain mind-set. He's doing Paris and making climate change much more central to our foreign policy, the Cuba opening, we're obviously focused on Asia and talking about that all the time. So we're acting as if we're moving on, but you'd be right to point out that even as we're doing that, the [counterterrorism] apparatus is largely in place." Obama's second term did pursue a more progressive and ambitious agenda. But at the same time it led to a tendency among Obama's coterie to see the War on Terror as merely an asterisk to his foreign policy legacy. It would soon be the only aspect of Obama's foreign policy legacy to survive.

CHAPTER FIVE

THE RIGHT VS. OBAMA'S WAR ON TERROR

2009–2013

John Brennan's hatred of al-Qaeda was visceral. As he spoke about the terrorists to a Washington think tank in May 2010, Brennan insisted they were not warriors but criminals, and the religious legitimacy they claimed was fraudulent. The Obama administration would not "describe our enemy as Islamists or jihadists, because jihad is a holy struggle, a legitimate tenet of Islam," which he viewed in the context of striving to overcome imperfection. "There is nothing holy, or legitimate, or Islamic about murdering innocent men, women, and children," Brennan declared, his voice rising slightly.

Brennan, so instrumental to the Sustainable War on Terror, was making what he considered a point in its service. He had spent long enough in the Middle East to speak Arabic and thought he understood how most Muslims practiced and understood Islam. "Jihadi" could be a term of honor; there was a reason Zawahiri had titled his book *Knights Under the Prophet's Banner.* "Islamist" could, to one degree or another, describe the political beliefs of tens or even hundreds of millions of nonviolent people. Calling bin Laden a jihadi or an Islamist tacitly gave bin Laden the legitimacy Brennan saw him usurp. The lived belief of millions, however unfamiliar to non-Muslim Americans, was a weapon against bin Laden's drastically different interpretation of it. Brennan wanted to enlist that human experience in the Sustainable War on Terror.

Brennan was the center of gravity of Obama's War on Terror. But his views on Islam ensured the right would never view him as an ally. On Fox News, Charles Krauthammer called Brennan's perspective "insane," since "our enemy is describing itself in those terms and to deny [that] is unbelievable." *The Washington Times* editorialized that Brennan's "view of Islam as a universally benign force may lead him to dismiss some of al Qaeda's justifications for violence, which reveals willful ignorance." An anti-Islam activist called Brennan's remarks "the caliphate in the White House."

Obama had brought Brennan into his inner circle to benefit from Brennan's counterterrorism credibility. Once he did so, the right refused to acknowledge that Brennan possessed any. However congruent their agendas were, Brennan would forever after be a target of the right's contempt. Many respectable precincts of the right rejected Brennan's choice as false, adopting an anti-anti-anti-Islam posture. The less respectable didn't waste time pretending their civilizational contempt for Islam was anything else. Brennan, the CIA analyst, did not seem to recognize that the War on Terror, even Obama's sustainable version, provided the war on Islam with every weapon, process, opportunity, and justification it needed.

While Obama accommodated the War on Terror, conservatives saw him abolishing it, even surrendering. It was irrelevant that he did not prosecute torturers. What mattered was that the president persecuted the CIA with a Justice Department investigation premised on the "rights" of terrorists like Khalid Shaikh Mohammed. It was irrelevant that Obama retained indefinite military detention and military tribunals. He wanted Guantanamo Bay closed and to prosecute terrorists in courts as if they were common criminals. It was irrelevant that Obama deported millions of immigrants. What mattered was that he wanted their children to be citizens. It was irrelevant that Obama escalated in Afghanistan. He announced a date that that escalation would end. It was irrelevant that the drones he ordered killed Pakistanis, Yemenis, Somalis, Iraqis, Afghans, Libyans, and others. By doing so he was declining to interrogate them, thus preventing America from knowing what the terrorists were planning. Obama had praised Islam in Cairo and then went on a "humiliating" foreign "apology tour." The bottom line, Dick Cheney explained, was that "Barack Obama doesn't believe in an exceptional America."

Some of the right's criticisms had merit, as with Rand Paul's filibuster. Others emerged from honest and irreconcilable policy disputes, as with McCain's objection to the Iraq withdrawal. But only white supremacy can truly explain the depth of right-wing fury at Obama, given his innumerable symbolic and substantive reassurances to whites. It was not an accident that the principal conspiracy theory about him, birtherism, held that he was secretly a Muslim noncitizen. Literally and metaphorically, it not only denied the legitimacy of Obama's presidency but reframed it as an act of war against what Sarah Palin had called Real America.

Anti-Black racism, Islamophobia, and xenophobia were the rising forces on the right as the 2008 collapse brought on by neoliberal economics distributed precarity broadly and even upward. The condition of a permanent security emergency was all the opportunity necessary to fuse them. The War on Terror made birtherism urgent: a usurper, one of the enemy, held power. Nativist fervor, present and powerful throughout American history, first achieved its current twenty-first-century critical mass in Europe. But its American champions would quickly point to the "invasion" of Europe by Muslims. They warned that America was next to lose its culture.

What Palin sparked, Donald Trump stoked. Trump had long been familiar with the power that the media held to manufacture reality. By the time Obama became president, Trump hosted a popular reality TV show in which he portrayed a leader. Contestants clashed ruthlessly to demonstrate their value to him. Now, before the army of reporters he could easily summon, Trump insisted the president was hiding his birth certificate—a document that Obama had in fact produced three years before—and claimed his "investigators" were combing Hawaii to find it. "He may have one, but there is something on that birth certificate—maybe religion, maybe it says he's a Muslim, I don't know." He portrayed himself as the only one brave enough to stand up for the law: "You are not allowed to be a president if you're not born in this country."

Trump's celebrity legitimized the white backlash. New Yorkers were well aware that he had played this role before. In 1989, Trump called for the execution of five Black teenagers the police had coerced into falsely confessing to a brutal rape. "Bring Back the Death Penalty, Bring Back Our Police," read an ad Trump placed in the New York papers. "I want to hate these muggers and murderers. They should be forced to suffer and, when they kill, they should be executed for their crimes." Yusef Salaam recalled to *The Guardian* what he felt as a fifteen-year-old defendant reading those words: "I knew that this famous person calling for us to die was very serious." When the five, who grew up in prison, were freed and won a $41 million settlement with the state, Trump refused to concede their innocence.

He did so knowing that the force of his persona would intimidate establishment journalists, who were already disinclined to label something "racist." "Even respected liberal commentators have given Trump something of a pass for the racial tension animating Birtherism," observed journalist Ari Melber. All this made Trump, flirting with a presidential run, a tribune of the rising nativist tide. Mitt Romney, the Republicans' eventual nominee, pursued and won Trump's endorsement. "You know, I don't agree with all the people who support me," Romney said when questioned about Trump's racism.

Obama's illegitimacy was, as Brennan was the first to learn, a powerful tool to discredit obstacles to a right-wing agenda, even those that patriotism typically rendered sacred. What began with the Bush-era right denouncing the State Department and CIA over Iraq became something more existential. David Petraeus was not exempt from such treatment, as he learned when he attempted to dissuade a Florida pastor from burning the

THE RIGHT VS. OBAMA'S WAR ON TERROR

Koran. Frank Gaffney, the head of an Islamophobic think tank, said Petraeus performed "a kind of submission" to Islamic sharia law. Mueller's FBI was another target, for removing the anti-Islam counterterrorism training. Through insufficient fealty to a civilizational war, demonstrated through proximity to an illegitimate president, a Security State could become a deep state. But there could also still be heroes in uniform—those who guarded the border, who hunted illegals, who gave terrorists what they deserved—who could be trusted to save America.

Reacting to Obama, conservatism took specific intellectual and institutional steps toward the nationalism that would soon consume it. Far from Washington, in states like Tennessee and Oklahoma, right-wing legislators introduced bills to stop the nonexistent prospect of sharia achieving legal parity with civil law; twelve such "anti-sharia" laws passed statehouses during Obama's presidency. In Washington conservative lawmakers held hearings on the loyalty of American Muslims. A funding network pumped tens of millions of dollars into right-wing political channels to fund "education" about the threat from Islam, through organizations like the Clarion Fund, ACT for America, and Gaffney's Center for Security Policy. A new media infrastructure, shaped by Andrew Breitbart's red-faced racist anger at Obama, peddled endless accounts of the immigrant and Muslim threats alongside verticals about "Black crime."

All this white anxiety existed in extreme disproportion to the actual existence of Islamic terrorism in America. In 2010 Brian Michael Jenkins of the RAND Corporation found that a decade after 9/11, Americans did not remotely suffer the levels of terrorist violence that they had in the 1970s, which saw "a level of terrorist activity 15 to 20 times that seen in most of the years since 9/11, even counting foiled [post-9/11] plots as incidents." Jenkins delicately concluded, "A mistrust of American Muslims by other Americans seems misplaced." But by now the point was not anything Muslims did. It was everything Muslims were. And not only them.

The ascending right-wing coalition considered Obama's "violent extremism" euphemism far more offensive than Bush's "terrorism" label. It

proved he was not only out to conceal his complicity with America's enemies but that he would dare to equate them with white people. "Radical
Islam" or "Radical Islamic Terrorism," their preferred definition of the enemy, and its more respectable variants had had just enough deniability—a
step shy of calling Islam itself terrorism, but only one step. They sought to
charge the gates of respectability and reclaim power. Their first mission of
redemption was fought on the soil that 9/11 had sanctified with blood.

IN THE OLD SPANISH CITY OF CÓRDOBA, Islam had built a European plural-
ism that anticipated cherished American values. Faisal Abdul Rauf considered it a place America would embrace. The lessons of an ancient city, the
New York imam thought, could help resolve the post-9/11 crisis afflicting
both America and Islam.

Founded in the eighth century, Córdoba was the intellectual center of
Europe, a haven of tolerance, education, and achievement. The wealthy
city, centerpiece of a breakaway Umayyad emirate, attracted and nurtured
Christian, Jewish, and Islamic scholars and cosmopolitans. Founding ruler
Abdel Rahman I, who had fled the dominant Abbasid caliphate, wrote
wistful poetry about being a refugee. A citywide midsummer festival celebrated John the Baptist.

But over centuries, under the stresses of internal political fracture and
external war, Córdoba's multiculturalism broke down. In his 2004 book,
What's Right with Islam Is What's Right with America, Rauf hailed native son
Moses Maimonides, the titan of Jewish philosophy and theology. Maimonides, however, fled Córdoba when the conquering Almohad dynasty re-
voked protections for dhimmi—Jewish and Christian minorities—and
persecuted Spanish Jewry, even separating children from their parents.

Rauf considered American history a narrative of progressive triumph
over such prejudices. After Pakistani jihadis murdered the *Wall Street Journal* reporter Daniel Pearl for being Jewish, Rauf delivered a moving address

to the Upper West Side's B'nai Jeshurun congregation. He told Pearl's griev-ing father, Judea, "Today I am a Jew. I have always been one, Mr. Pearl."

"We strive for a 'new Córdoba,'" Rauf wrote, "a time when Jews, Chris-tians, Muslims and all other faith traditions will live together in peace, enjoying a renewed vision of what the good society can look like."

Rauf had been preaching twelve blocks from the World Trade Center since 1985. He located his new Córdoba there. At 45 Park Place was a mid-nineteenth-century building left vacant after undercarriage debris from the doomed planes cratered several floors of what had been a Burlington Coat Factory. Aided by Sharif El-Gamal, a real estate developer and self-described "shark," Rauf and his wife, Daisy Khan, purchased the property for $4.85 million in July 2009. They planned to restore it as the thirteen-story Cor-doba House, which would feature a community center, pool, restaurant, performance space, mosque, and culinary school. Rauf conceptualized it as a Muslim version of the 92nd Street Y, a Jewish space on the Upper East Side that plays a cherished role in the intellectual life of New York City. The site of the new Córdoba struck Rauf as poetic, even sublime. It was a chance, he said, to send "the opposite statement to what happened on 9/11."

But to Rauf's horror, several in New York's 9/11 survivor community did not believe the project was sending a different statement at all. When Khan unveiled Cordoba House to a Manhattan community board's fi-nance committee early in May 2010, Rosemary Cain, mother of fallen 9/11 firefighter George Cain, said it was "atrocious that anyone would even con-sider allowing them to build a mosque near the World Trade Center." Khan, shaken, explained to the committee that she and her husband felt "an obli-gation as Muslims and Americans to be part of the rebuilding of downtown Manhattan."

Fanning the flames was Pamela Geller, who blogged that a "monster mosque" was coming to Ground Zero, an "insulting and humiliating . . . victory lap" celebrating terrorism. A veteran of the business side of ruling-class broadsheet *The New York Observer*, Geller was radicalized by 9/11. She told *New York Jewish Week* that she was embarrassed not to have known who it was that attacked America, so she turned to authors and journalists who revealed that the culprit was Islam. Geller was also a birther, though not one tied to any particular theory of Obama's origin; she once published a reader's theory positing that his real father was Malcolm X. Her ally against Cordoba was Robert Spencer, whose books lined the FBI library at Quantico. Spencer claimed Rauf was erecting a "victory mosque." Together, they created a pressure group called Stop Islamization of America. Asked by *The Washington Post* if he was being deliberately provocative, Spencer replied, "Why not? It's fun."

Soon the *New York Post* ran columns about "mosque madness" generating anger from "fed-up New Yorkers." Fox News crusaded against it. By the end of May protesters holding signs reading SHOW RESPECT FOR 9/11. NO MOSQUE! packed a four-hour-long public hearing on Cordoba House. "This is humiliating that you would build a shrine to the very ideology that inspired the attacks of 9/11!" Geller lectured. Rauf, who had the support of New York's power structure, was left pleading that they had "condemned terrorism in the most unequivocal terms." El-Gamal described the anger at the meeting as "the scariest thing I've ever seen in my life."

By now the right-wing media, setting the tone for their mainstream counterparts, didn't call Rauf's project Cordoba House at all. They called it the Ground Zero Mosque. The demonization of Rauf followed. Rudy Giuliani told a radio host that Rauf had "a record of support for causes that were sympathetic with terrorism," which was a complete fabrication. A Republican candidate for governor in New York, Rick Lazio, called Rauf a "terrorist sympathizer." Trump, meanwhile, portrayed himself as saving the city from the Islamist menace while operating as a shakedown artist. He wrote one of Rauf's investors, "As a resident of New York and a citizen of the United States," with an offer to buy out his share at a 25 percent markup. Rauf would have to move to an admittedly worse location, Trump said, "because it will end a very serious, inflammatory, and highly divisive situation that is destined, in my opinion, to only get worse."

The protests began that summer. Demonstrators carried signs reading

SHARIA in a dripping blood-red font and spoke of a "hijacked Constitution." A puppet dressed like a jihadi hung over a mock missile, advertising, OBAMA, YOUR MIDDLE NAME IS HUSSAIN, WE UNDERSTAND. BLOOMBERG, WHAT'S YOUR EXCUSE. The twenty-five-year-old nephew of a fireman who died at the World Trade Center seethed at the "level of defiance" he considered Muslims to be showing. "They're saying, 'We're doing this whether you like it or not,'" he told the *Times*. At the end of August a cabbie named Ahmed Sharif, a Bangladeshi immigrant and a father of four children, picked up a blond film student named Michael Enright. Enright, drunk and wielding a Leatherman knife, asked if Sharif was Muslim. "'This is the checkpoint, I have to take you down,'" Sharif recalled Enright saying as he slashed and stabbed, "talking like he was a soldier."

As thousands filled the streets on the ninth anniversary of 9/11 to denounce the Ground Zero Mosque, local Muslims rode out a terrifying moment. Geller led a protest at the site featuring signs objecting to "Obama's Mosque." One of the speakers was Geert Wilders, a Dutch legislator and Islam's premier persecutor in Europe, whom Geller introduced as a "modern-day Churchill." He urged the protesters to "draw the line" against Rauf, "so that New York, rooted in Dutch values, will never become New Mecca." Another speaker, by teleconference, was Bush's U.N. ambassador, John Bolton, who, Geller enthused, spoke "bluntly and unequivocally" about the "affront to American values" the "mosque" represented. One protester told *Time* that it was "the first stage of Saudi Wahhabist takeover of the United States." He might have been more extreme than most, but by then, a CBS poll recorded 71 percent of Americans objecting to the "mosque."

Rauf had few allies. Obama gave a statement of support for religious freedom, but several national Democrats reverted to their Dubai Ports World posture. The Democratic Senate leader, Harry Reid of Nevada, said the "mosque" ought to be "built someplace else." Three Democratic congressmen from New York declared their opposition. Michael Arcuri, a Utica centrist, argued that the project, rather than the mob opposing it, "will continue to fracture the faiths and the citizens of our city and this country."

New York's Jewish community, which Rauf had supported, either kept silent or joined in the denunciation. As the High Holidays approached, B'nai Jeshurun's Rabbi Rolando Matalon chose a sermon dwelling on "the tremendous polarization in our society" rather than the persecution unfolding downtown. Judea Pearl said Rauf's project reflected "anti-American ideologies of victimhood, anger and entitlement" within American Islam and should relocate.

Rauf tried accommodation. He apologized for calling American policy "an accessory" to 9/11, conceding it was "insensitive" of him to suggest as much. Had Rauf known the outrage that Cordoba House, now rebranded as "Park51," would generate, he wouldn't have chosen the same location. But if he moved, he explained, "the story will be that the radicals have taken over the discourse."

It turned out capital was his biggest enemy. "I'm not a humanitarian, I'm a capitalist," said Rauf's partner, El-Gamal, who had not expected to become a pariah. He ousted Rauf from what would now never be Cordoba. By January, Rauf was marginalized. He remained a member of Park51's board but no longer served as a spokesperson for the project. El-Gamal deemphasized and ultimately abandoned the community center aspect of the property in favor of, eventually, luxury condos. The protests dissipated.

Rauf continued expressing hope for reviving the sentiments animating Cordoba, but hope was all he had left. Rauf had discovered an invisible border marking the hard limit of American acceptance. America would not permit a new Córdoba, not even in the city Rauf already thought of as one. The transformation of Cordoba House into the Ground Zero Mosque marked the moment a presidency like Trump's became inevitable.

"There are individuals who are working very hard to promote fear and antagonism towards Islam and Muslims in this country. It's fueled, in part, by the first African-American president that we have," Rauf said in 2012. "Obama's father was a Muslim and people have used this to arouse hostility against him. A kind of racism still exists in the United States, and Islamophobia is a more convenient way to express that sentiment."

A THEORY OF CIVILIZATIONAL replacement took hold on the right. Islam was not in America because Muslims sought a better, freer, more prosperous life. It was here to wage "civilization jihad." It aimed to replace the Constitution with sharia law. This had nothing to do with stopping terrorism. Islam itself, as Gawthrop instructed at the FBI, was the real problem. Accepting its role in civic life was "accommodating sharia," Spencer said. An infrastructure developed to besiege American Islam—with public pressure, law, and, if necessary, violence.

Nashville had seen a growth in its Muslim population since the city became a gateway for resettling refugees who fled the carnage America unleashed in Iraq. Forty miles southeast, the thirty-year-old Islamic Center of Murfreesboro became so crowded that worshippers had to pray outside. In the summer of 2010 it planned an expansion onto a fifteen-acre plot of fallow land. Fox News began to report on anxiety among local non-Muslims that the construction of the center and others like it "went far beyond their need." Prayer vigils accompanied hearings at the county commission, at which residents argued that the expansion was part of a plot against the Constitution. "I don't want them here," a vigil attendee named Evy Summers told local news. "Go start their own country overseas somewhere. This is a Christian country. It was based on Christianity." In late August unknown assailants poured gas on the construction equipment at the expansion site and set it aflame. The very next day, as CNN filmed a segment about the arson, gunshots rang out.

Four residents sought an injunction, claiming they were suffering harm from "the risk of terrorism generated by proselytizing for Islam and inciting the practices of sharia law." Those practices, they said, included child abuse, misogynistic and homophobic violence, "Constitution-free zones, and total world dominion." They were horrified to see the Justice Department intercede on behalf of the center. Islam, the residents contended, was not a religion, but rather a political agenda, entitled to no religious protection under the Constitution. To bolster their case they brought in the Center for Security Policy's Frank Gaffney, who averred from the witness stand, "I am not an expert on sharia, but I have talked a lot about it as a threat."

When the judge ruled in favor of the center, a new cycle of resistance crested. Construction faced numerous delays as contractors and subcontractors refused to take on the project, something opponents had urged at the county commission hearings. With the arsonist still free, the center's answering service filled up with anonymous threats demanding its members leave the country or heralding the coming destruction of Islam. In early September 2011 one of those calls informed the mosque that it would receive a bomb on the tenth anniversary of 9/11. The bomb never manifested, and a twenty-four-year-old Texan was later indicted for the threat. For Muslims in the town of barely a hundred thousand people, menace came from powerful figures as well. "You mark my words," warned Pat Robertson, "if they start bringing thousands and thousands of Muslims into that relatively rural area the next thing you know they're going to be taking over the city council." Sally Wall, an influential real estate broker who helped fund the suit against the center, added, "Here is this enormous building which is going to be occupied by people who are of the same religion that the people are who we're fighting in Afghanistan, who we have been fighting in Iraq." Litigation continued until the Supreme Court declined to hear the case in 2014. The Islamic Center of Murfreesboro remained the target of suspicion and vandalism for years afterward.

As the Murfreesboro clash unfolded, Tennessee's legislature passed the "American and Tennessee Laws for Tennessee Courts" bill. Its purpose was to forbid "foreign law," a euphemism for sharia, from influencing American jurisprudence. Within two years anti-sharia bills were introduced in twenty other state legislatures. Rarely did they attempt to explain how something like a religious consultation in a divorce proceeding would infringe on any non-Muslim's freedom, but to the believers in replacement theory, no explanation was necessary. The following year a Tennessee Republican lawmaker introduced an unsuccessful follow-up bill declaring that "knowing adherence to sharia and to foreign sharia authorities is prima facie evidence of an act in support of the overthrow of the United States government—with the aim of imposing sharia on the people of this state."

One reason for the proliferation of the attempted legislation was Gaffney. His think tank, the Center for Security Policy, developed templates for anti-sharia legislation pluggable into any state legislature. A subsequent investigation documented how once Gaffney's "American Laws for American Courts" initiative received statehouse sponsorship, Brigitte Gabriel's ACT for America would urge its membership to flood representatives' offices with statements of support. Gaffney, Gabriel, and allies like Spencer and Geller believed that the Muslim Brotherhood—the foreign Islamist association whose insufficient radicalism had prompted Ayman al-Zawahiri to found al-Qaeda with bin Laden—was executing a broad infiltration of the United States. They tended to locate their Muslim Brotherhood "operatives" among the civil-rights advocates and attorneys of the American Muslim community. Even where their bills failed, they reduced civic space for Muslims.

Like Geller, Gaffney was a birther. An infamous 2008 *Washington Times* column of his railed against Obama's "dalliance with jihadists"; claimed the goal of the Muslim Brotherhood in America was to establish a "fifth column" of American Muslims to attack the United States; and lied that "there is evidence Mr. Obama was born in Kenya." In 2010, the same year Gaffney testified about not being a sharia expert, his Center for Security Policy published a book, *Sharia: The Threat to America*. It accused the Muslim Brotherhood of advancing a "civilization jihad" of what amounted to public acceptance of Islam. The Brotherhood "seeks to supplant our Constitution" and had a "very deliberate plan to manipulate the nation into piecemeal submission" to Islamic law. "Its ambitions transcend what American law recognizes as the sacrosanct realm of private conscience and belief," wrote Gaffney's "Team B," a name meant to invoke an intelligence reassessment of the Soviets that neoconservatives regarded as a truth suppressed by a timid Security State. It was imperative that the government "cease their outreach to Muslim communities through Muslim Brotherhood fronts," by which they meant government cooperation with American Muslim leaders and institutions. Denunciation of sharia ought to be made a requirement for government and military service. Outright sharia advocates—that is, imams, if not every practicing Muslim—should be instructed "they will not be immune from prosecution" for advocating "sedition." It referenced Muslim "compounds and communities" as actual or potential "no-go zones for law enforcement," a wholly invented phenomenon, and urged an end to "immigration of those who adhere to sharia."

The Muslim Brotherhood held totemic force. Affiliation of any sort with it or its members was enough to spark demonization of Muslim teachers, attorneys, activists, politicians, charities, and civil rights groups. A central piece of the case against the Brotherhood was a 1991 document entered into evidence in a federal terrorism money-laundering case against the Holy Land Foundation, a Muslim charity. Penned by Brotherhood member Mohammed Akram Adlouni for discussion at a council meeting, it proposed a "civilization jihad" through "eliminating and destroying Western civilization from within and 'sabotaging' its miserable house." The Adlouni memo appeared to be an Islamophobic fever dream vindicated: black-and-white proof of a replacement conspiracy by a powerful Muslim group—and entered into evidence in a prosecution that treated Muslim civil-rights group CAIR as an unindicted co-conspirator. But as researchers for Georgetown University's Bridge Initiative found, other documents revealed that the outlandish idea was not entertained in any official capacity by the conference. At one point, Adlouni's memo implored readers "not [to] rush to throw these papers away," acknowledging that the Brothers might recoil at this "strange" proposal "without an antecedent."

Significantly, the Center for Security Policy attracted a number of veterans of the Security State, usually malcontents and hard-liners who felt their truths had been suppressed by their ignorant superiors. One of the leading figures guiding the Center's sharia book was Jerry Boykin, the Pentagon intelligence official during Rumsfeld's tenure who had declared "my God

[is] bigger" than Islam's. Others included the former CIA officer Clare Lopez, the former Defense Intelligence Agency director Harry Soyster, Rumsfeld-era Pentagon inspector general Joseph Schmitz, and the former CIA director Jim Woolsey. Woolsey had been allied with the neoconservatives, and his presence on Gaffney's Team B heralded that, through Islamophobia, neocons could join the nationalist coalition.

One of Gaffney's particular villains was Robert Mueller. Although the FBI director constructed and presided over an apparatus of domestic infiltration of Muslim communities throughout the country, that was irrelevant. Mueller had scrapped the Islamophobic FBI training. "Now we have the Muslim Brotherhood telling us what we can know, what we can train to, who we can use as trainers," Gaffney complained.

However distant from respectability the Center for Security Policy and its allies were, their financing came through many respectable right-wing funding channels. By 2011 these groups had received $40 million over the course of a decade from fixtures of the GOP firmament like the Donors Capital Fund, which bankrolled climate denial; Richard Mellon Scaife's network, benefactor of the major conservative think tanks; and the Lynde and Harry Bradley Foundation, a major right-wing donor network with the funding power of the Scaifes and the plutocratic Koch brothers.

Internal Bradley grant documents outline the money trail into the anti-Muslim networks. By 2013 a Center for Security Policy grant request for $120,000 to cover "general operations" was pro forma, though Bradley staff recommended only a $50,000 grant that year. Since 1988 Bradley had given Gaffney's small group $1.3 million, slightly less than the $1.5 million financiers had doled out to the mainstream defense group the Center for Strategic and Budgetary Assessment since 1995. The vast majority of the Bradleys' largesse, $905,000, was distributed after 9/11. The 2013 grant request scarcely and only euphemistically mentioned Gaffney's work against Islam, referring to it simply as "monitor[ing] Islamist political movements active in U.S. borders." It contained no mention of the anti-sharia bill campaign. More important was the center's "coalition" work connecting "policy experts" with congressional staff, "state law enforcement and legislatures." The Bradleys hardly accounted for the lion's share of the Center for Security Policy's funding. Tax records indicate that the center took in nearly $4.5 million in 2011, a year the Bradleys contributed $70,000, representing 1.5 percent of its funding. But while even Fox News would rarely book Gaffney, the conservative financial infrastructure was willing to bankroll him. The Scaife foundations underwrote the Center for Security Policy to a much larger degree, doling out $2.9 million between 2001 and 2009.

Inevitably the sharia panic reached Capitol Hill Republicans, though only on the fringes at first. In 2011 an obscure Florida group, Citizens for National Security, gathered supporters into the Rayburn House Office Building basement. It had called a press conference to announce that thousands of Americans were secret Muslim Brotherhood sleeper agents, "a fifth column movement," according to founder Peter Leitner, working to "eventually erode [America's] institutions, policies, and sense of self." Leitner claimed to have compiled his list from "open source" internet searches connecting anyone in America in whatever way to the Muslim Brotherhood, which was not a banned organization in the United States. A protesting student from American University, Udit Thakur, wondered, "How do I know my Facebook page won't be an 'open source' of information for them?"

To release the names of the alleged six thousand individuals and two hundred organizations would be "irresponsible," Leitner said. He acknowledged that being charged with a crime was not a prerequisite for inclusion. A graphic he provided to reporters to illustrate the network of subversion looked, he conceded, "like a plate of spaghetti," but he insisted on his analytical rigor.

It was not a well-attended event, and its placement in the basement was testimony to its social position. Its shepherd was Florida's new Republican congressman, Allen West. The nativist right adored West for his willingness to fire a gun near the head of an Iraqi man he was interrogating and then for enduring martyrdom at the hands of the politically correct army.

They also liked that he was a rare Black Republican who thought as they did. Leitner's warning against the Islamization of America, West agreed, "is about the protection of each and every American citizen." It was a statement about whose citizenship was guaranteed and whose was conditional.

AS DISTINCT AS THE RIGHT'S hostility to Islam was, it fit neatly within a long-standing hostility to immigration that was boiling over. The Southern Poverty Law Center reported in 2010 that 136 new "furious anti-immigrant vigilante groups" had arisen since Obama's inauguration. That April, Arizona, led by Tea Party favorite Governor Jan Brewer, enacted what became known as the Show Me Your Papers law, permitting police to hunt undocumented immigrants. Even as Holder's Justice Department took Arizona to court, the law's author, Russell Pearce, with Brewer's support, mused about legislating against what he called "anchor babies." The term derided the citizenship, guaranteed under the Fourteenth Amendment, of people born in the United States to immigrant parents. "This is an orchestrated effort by them to come here and have children to gain access to the great welfare state we've created," the state legislator explained.

Coming to Arizona's defense was Texan Tea Party representative Louie Gohmert. On the House floor Gohmert attacked birthright citizenship as a weapon in the hands of al-Qaeda. He claimed he was told by an FBI agent (whom he would never identify) that al-Qaeda wives would travel to the United States to give birth, take the new American citizen back home for indoctrination and training, "and then one day, twenty, thirty years down the road, they can be sent in to help destroy our way of life." Gohmert was eviscerated on CNN, but that was less a deterrent than a badge of honor to the nativist right. The following year the Center for Immigration Studies, one of its institutions, attacked birthright citizenship through panicking over "fertility rates" of "non-immigrant" women in the United States on visas. Anwar al-Awlaki, the center claimed, was "a product of our current lax birthright citizenship rules."

The Department of Homeland Security had aligned immigration enforcement with counterterrorism. Border crackdowns were now just as sprawling as any other part of the war effort. In 2010 *The New York Times* reported that Customs and Border Protection (CBP) agents had begun boarding Amtrak trains running from Chicago to New York City at western New York state stations and then moving car to car looking for non-whites, demanding they prove their legal citizenship. Their jurisdiction was as expansive as their authorities. Although the trains did not run near any border crossings, federal regulations granted CBP the authority to operate within one hundred miles of an "external boundary." Nonwhites who could not show their papers—and who were not informed that cooperation with CBP in such a circumstance was voluntary—entered a maze of immigration jails. When a twenty-one-year-old New York woman originally from Guatemala couldn't produce proof of her legal entry, CBP detained her for three weeks before releasing her in Texas. A CBP official in charge of the de facto border checkpoint explained, "Our mission is to defend the homeland, primarily against terrorists and terrorist weapons. We still do our traditional mission, which is to enforce the nation's immigration laws." Corruption within CBP was so routine that a 2009 message from its deputy chief warned agents that they would "find no safe haven among fellow criminals."

Obama had voted for Bush's failed immigration reform plan as a senator in 2007. As president, and despite a campaign promise, he shelved pursuing another. Obama had a theory of how he would convince congressional Republicans to, at the least, tone down their opposition to immigration. With a policy that was as accommodationist as the Sustainable War on Terror, Obama would try deporting his way to consensus.

By September 2011 Obama had overseen over 1 million deportations, putting him on pace to exceed in his first term the 1.5 million deportations Bush had conducted over the course of eight years. For much of his first term, most of Obama's deportations occurred within the interior of the country, until deportations at the border overtook them in fiscal 2012—though CBP's rides along the Chicago–New York Amtrak line showed how DHS could blur the distinction. He formally prioritized focusing on people with criminal records, but in practice DHS considered misdemeanor offenses—crossing the border without authorization was a misdemeanor—within Obama's mandate. During the fiscal year beginning October 2010, DHS conducted a record 397,000 deportations. According to Reuters, by the end of that fiscal year, only half the deportees were actually criminals. The accelerated enforcement coincided with a lull in illegal border crossings.

The deportations devastated families and communities. When First Lady Michelle Obama visited a Maryland school in May 2010, a little girl asked if the president was going to deport her undocumented mother. An immigration judge in San Francisco permitted a woman to stay in the country to raise her daughter after her husband was deported. Separating the family would be "unconscionable," the judge said, warning ICE that its lawyers had "worn out your welcome" by so frequently trying to overturn judicial rulings against deportation. During the first six months of 2011, DHS deported approximately forty-six thousand parents whose citizen children had only ever lived in America. *Colorlines* found that parents were growing as a percentage of all people deported. It estimated that fifty-one hundred children languished in foster care as a result.

DHS could deport with expanding efficiency. A congressionally approved program known as Secure Communities, which began during Bush's final year, provided DHS with fingerprint records of people whom local police arrested and booked, the same information that the FBI received for its nationwide databases. Access to these records supercharged ICE's identifications of the undocumented. A DHS task force in 2011 found that "in most cases" an ICE agent was not interested in apprehending immigrants for the reasons police had arrested them, but instead "because he or she entered the country without inspection or overstayed a visa."

Secure Communities met with a vociferous public reaction. Ahead of a planned nationwide expansion set for 2013, the task force held a series of public meetings and "by a very significant margin" heard objections to its implementation. "Many speakers commented that the program is resulting in deportation of persons arrested only for minor offenses as well as victims of crime, that such deportations split families apart, and that Secure Communities makes people afraid to call their local police when they are victims of or witnesses to crime," the task force reported. Obama's home state of Illinois was the first to revoke its optional participation in Secure Communities in May 2011.

Obama thought that spiking deportations would purchase him credibility with the right for a larger compromise on immigration. He badly misunderstood their agenda. The conservative response was to pocket the deportations, call them insufficient, and reject any legislation conferring citizenship upon the undocumented. Not even focusing on morally blameless people could diminish the opposition. In late December, during the final days of the Democratic Congress, Obama watched as five Democratic senators doomed a bill granting a path to citizenship to people brought into the United States as children. Granting them citizenship would only be, at its "fundamental core," a "reward for illegal activity," said Alabama's Jeff Sessions. Except when Obama's deportations record was convenient to throw in the faces of angered progressives, the right portrayed Obama as leaving the border unguarded. "Comprehensive immigration reform" was no more than "amnesty and a few other new laws," said Kris Kobach, the architect of Ashcroft's immigration crackdown. "What we need is for the executive branch to enforce the laws that we already have."

With Congress under Republican control, Obama could do little more than vent his exasperation. He traveled to El Paso in May 2011 to defend the centrality of immigration to American life while boasting of his deportation record and of continuing the Bush-era expansion of a border patrol force that had reached twenty thousand officers. "I actually saw some of them on horseback, who look pretty tough," Obama quipped. He placed the nativist mood in a historical context of "fear and resentment at newcomers," though his observation that "what it means to be an American" generates "strong emotions" was as close as he came to shaming it. He sought instead to reason with it. "We have gone above and beyond what was requested by the very Republicans who said they supported broader reform as long as we got serious about enforcement. All the stuff they asked for, we've done," he said, joking, "they'll want a higher fence. Maybe they'll need a moat. Maybe they'll want alligators in the moat." Tea Party congressman Joe Walsh, who frequently called the president a Muslim, commented that perhaps the alligators "will do the job Obama seems so reluctant to do." But Obama would not back off his accelerated deportations and other immigration measures that had not yet reached the limits of their draconian potential. "Being a nation of laws goes hand in hand with being a nation of immigrants," he said.

Maintaining the War on Terror permitted the nativists to cite an ongoing state of emergency. In a 2010 hearing, Representative Peter King of New York pressed for collecting biometric identifiers from visa holders, arguing that the absence of such a system "has and will continue to be exploited by terrorists." Texas Representative Lamar Smith, the senior Republican on the House Judiciary Committee, warned Holder that "amnesty" for the undocumented "could legalize many would-be terrorists who are already in the U.S. and give them cover to plot attacks against innocent Americans." One New Mexico man told CNN his state ought to be tougher on undocumented people "considering the threat, you know, terrorism."

EVOLVING THE WAR ON TERROR into a civilizational counterjihad was valuable to conservatives. Like the Iraq surge, it was a chance at a reboot. It distanced conservatism from the wreckage of Bush's legacy. It offered an explanation for the lack of victory in the War on Terror, the one that nativists had warned about since Bush called Islam a religion of peace. And it aligned conservative politicians with a rising nativist movement that distrusted elected Republicans.

In March 2011 the chairman of the House Homeland Security Committee held hearings on his longtime preoccupation: the loyalty of American Muslims. Peter King, a sour Long Islander, had fretted in 2007 that America hosted "too many mosques." Inside 80 percent of those mosques, he later baselessly declared, "radical imams" held sway. On Frank Gaffney's radio show, King said that Muslims, unlike earlier immigrant groups during wartime, weren't "cooperat[ing] anywhere near to the extent that [they] should" in the War on Terror. He claimed law enforcement was "constantly telling me how little cooperation they get from Muslim leaders."

Muslim civil rights groups initially rejected and denounced King's hearings as collective government persecution. When King persisted, they shifted tactics. If King, whom they compared to Joe McCarthy, was intent on holding hearings on domestic radicalization, he should examine it "in all its forms," fifty Muslim groups and their allies wrote to congressional leaders. They explicitly referenced the rise in hate crimes against Muslims during 2010, the year of the Ground Zero and Murfreesboro panics. King, disgusted, rejected their argument as "political correctness at its worst," since "we'd be sending the false signal that we think there's a security threat equivalency between Al Qaeda and the neo-Nazi movement, or Al Qaeda and gun groups. There is none."

King began his hearings in a martyrdom pose. "Special interest groups and the media" treated his endeavor at measuring the loyalty of a minority with "disbelief to paroxysms of rage and hysteria." But were King to surrender, it would be an "abdication" of the committee's responsibility "to protect America from a terrorist attack." There was nothing "radical or un-American" about investigating American Muslim loyalties; it was "the logical response" to homegrown radicalization. One way "responsible Muslim-American leaders" could demonstrate their moderation, he continued, was by "reject[ing] CAIR," which he insisted was not a "legitimate" organization.

The most vehement objections to King from within his committee came from African American Democrats, who reminded the crowd of the still-active lineage of white supremacist terrorism. Mississippi's Bennie Thompson, the senior Democrat, noted that a member of the white supremacist National Alliance, Kevin William Harpham, had recently placed a bomb in a backpack to explode at a Spokane celebration of Martin Luther King Jr.'s birthday. Texas's Sheila Jackson Lee cited the case of a white man, Andrew Joseph Stack, whose belief that the tax code served plutocracy led him to crash a small plane into an Austin building full of tax preparers. No one was more passionate than Minnesota's Keith Ellison, who in 2006 became the first Muslim ever elected to Congress, a distinction earning him relentless right-wing scrutiny. Ellison's voice broke and he shed tears inveighing against the injustice inherent in defining a minority as a threat. "Demanding a community response, as the title of the hearing suggests, asserts that the entire community bears responsibility for the violent acts of individuals," he said. There was no one demanding that whites account for Stack, let alone Harpham. Yet King refused to "dilute" his hearings by discussing "neo-Nazis, environmental extremists and other isolated madmen."

More mainstream Republican Party figures had the burden of figuring out exactly what they believed. It was easy enough to oppose Obama; McConnell had done so on Guantanamo and won. Others, particularly McCain, kept the old faith. They knew the Security State was closer to their position on Iraq than to Obama's desire to withdraw. Both warned of a disaster when, in 2011, Obama followed through once the Iraqi parliament would not authorize a continued U.S. troop presence. ("We should be staying there to strengthen that democracy," argued surge architect Jack Keane, conveniently eliding the expressed wishes of the actually existing Iraqi democracy.) But there was far more appetite to cast Obama as re-losing a war the surge had saved than there was to challenge the pullout. By 2011 Iraq was a settled issue.

That left neoconservatives with a problem. To stoke outrage over Obama's deviations from the War on Terror catechism that Dick Cheney had created called attention to the carnage of their wars. One solution came in the form of a group called Keep America Safe, founded by Cheney's daughter Liz along with neocon impresario Bill Kristol. Another of Keep America Safe's cofounders was 9/11 widow and prominent Ground Zero Mosque opponent Debra Burlingame. Burlingame said in 2010 she "ascribe[d] to the clash of civilization theory," which she believed required "enlisting the Muslims who have already bought into the American program and not adjusting" to them. With Liz Cheney in the vanguard, it turned out neoconservatism could pivot neatly into nationalism.

Keep America Safe ran an ad implying that seven Justice Department–appointed lawyers had the same missions as the Guantanamo detainees they had represented. "Whose values do they share?" the ad asked as a pixelated Osama bin Laden waved in the background. The attorneys were called the "al-Qaeda Seven." Cheney explained her rejection of Obama as a disgust with his imagined persecution of CIA interrogators, something that spoke to her father's legacy. "Threatening to prosecute CIA officials was indefensible," Liz Cheney said. "It was just so far beyond what you could stay silent and watch."

That pointed to how the right responded to a politically agonizing moment: the bin Laden killing. It was out of the question to credit Obama, who, after authorizing the raid, had delighted in mocking Donald Trump to his face at the White House Correspondents' Dinner. In one of the more generous Republican reactions, Eric Cantor, the House GOP majority leader, "commend[ed] Obama," but for "follow[ing] the vigilance of President Bush in bringing bin Laden to justice." A more convenient narrative, promoted by Liz Cheney and others, offered that *torture* made killing bin Laden possible. Obama could still be portrayed as disarming America.

This was the explanation that the CIA wanted the public to accept, particularly about torture producing the identity of a key bin Laden courier. Its chief proponent was Jose Rodriguez, the CIA Counterterrorism Center chief who for years ran the torture program before he and his deputy Gina Haspel destroyed the videotapes of Abu Zubaydah and Nashiri's waterboardings. The evidence disproving their assertion about the value of torture in this instance was at that point widely known: surveillance was most important in uncovering the trail leading to bin Laden. The CIA already had the courier's name before the particular instance of torture. But the evidence showing it remained hidden in agency files that a Senate intelligence committee staffer named Daniel Jones was quietly excavating. McCain produced a comment from then-CIA-director Panetta contradicting former attorney general Michael Mukasey's assertion that waterboarding produced the identity of the courier. Yet at the CIA, with White House and Pentagon support, negotiations quickly began with filmmakers Mark Boal and Kathryn Bigelow on a Hollywood depiction of the bin Laden killing that presented CIA torture as paving a straight path to Abbottabad.

Reaction to a Middle Eastern upheaval underscored the influence that the nativist coalition had achieved within the right. The Arab Spring uprisings beginning in 2011 beguiled GOP foreign policy as much as they did Obama. Despite initial elite rapture over mass demonstrations for democracy, the nativists' critique took hold: it was a disastrous triumph of the Muslim Brotherhood.

Obama didn't know what position to take. The protests were not merely destabilizing American quasi-adversaries such as Moammar Qaddafi and Bashar al-Assad but also clients like Yemen's Ali Abdullah Saleh and allies like Egypt's Hosni Mubarak. For thirty years Mubarak had guaranteed the cold but real peace with Israel that his predecessor died to forge. With Cairo's Tahrir Square holding the world's attention, Obama equivocated. While Biden said Mubarak was not a dictator, Obama finally called for the Egyptian president to gradually relinquish power. McConnell and GOP House Speaker John Boehner backed Obama. Mitt Romney, discomfited by ushering a longtime ally from power, ultimately agreed that Mubarak's time was up. Newt Gingrich, by contrast, heralded where the energy on the right was heading. "I think there are a lot of differences between the Muslim Brotherhood and the rest of us," he said.

When Mohamed Morsi, the Muslim Brotherhood candidate and an

erratic man, became Egypt's first elected president, gone were any vestiges on the right of Bush-era faith in democracy to render Mideast politics convivial to American hegemony. Sean Hannity, whom Imam Rauf granted an interview, was stunned when Rauf would not call the Brotherhood terrorists. As Rauf praised the vote, however "messy" the new democratic politics were, Hannity cried, "They're voting for a radical Islamist."

With Egypt under Muslim Brotherhood influence, the Arab Spring began to seem on the right like a civilizational calamity. Speaking at a South Carolina fundraiser for his presidential campaign, Gingrich said it was shaping up "more like an anti-Christian spring." A conspiracy theory began to spread that a classified White House study on political reform in the Arab world was an accord with the Brotherhood on regime change in Egypt. "Listen, President Obama was negotiating with the Muslim Brotherhood and saying that they are moderates," ACT for America's Brigitte Gabriel asserted as fact on Hannity's show.

At the Western Conservative Summit the following year, Gaffney portrayed Obama as colluding with the Muslim Brotherhood to weaken a historic bulwark against Islamization. After awkwardly joking that the audience would want "cyanide" after his lecture, an indignant Gaffney showed a photograph of Morsi, "a radical Islamist, a Muslim Brother, a man who seeks to impose sharia on his own people," before lamenting "we have helped him come to power." Gaffney explained the whole calamity by claiming the Brotherhood had infiltrated Obama's government. Proof of the conspiracy was Adlouni's memo, which Gaffney called "the strategic plan, the mission statement" of the Brotherhood in America. As for the Brotherhood's agents in government, Gaffney deceitfully cited Huma Abedin, a senior aide to Hillary Clinton and a Jordanian American whose combination of Muslim background and proximity to the hated Clinton ensured her harassment by racists. Abedin was just one of several identifiably nonwhite or Muslim officials or advisers he flashed on the screen under the header THE BROTHERHOOD'S PENETRATION OF TEAM OBAMA.

Obama's Libya war fed this new mode of right-wing critique. To prevent

Moammar Qaddafi from carrying out a threat to raze the city of Benghazi, Obama joined a British-and-French-led coalition to bomb the Libyan leader into submission. There was not much enthusiasm on the right for war with Qaddafi. But Obama's choice to keep America a junior partner in a British–French coalition fighting by air and sea offended the right's American exceptionalist honor.

The minimal congressional appetite for a war in Libya prompted Obama to commit a flagrant violation of the war powers the Constitution vests in Congress. As broad as the 2001 AUMF was, there was no arguing that Qaddafi or Libya were part of it. Obama instead bypassed Congress entirely, armed with dubious justification from the Office of Legal Counsel about why he wasn't breaking the 1973 War Powers Resolution. All pretense of a non-war vanished with the death of Qaddafi. Hillary Clinton, visiting Tripoli, spoke like Caesar: "We came, we saw, he died."

Thinking he was applying the lessons of Iraq, Obama, determined to keep U.S. troops off Libyan soil, forswore any involvement to rectify the vacuum he helped create. What followed Qaddafi was chaos, state failure, and a desperate, politically incendiary refugee flow across the Mediterranean and into Geert Wilders's narrative of Islamic conquest. For years afterward the United States attacked Libyan jihadist targets from the air and accepted little responsibility for a nation it had destabilized. Among the debacles of the invasion was the jihadist assault on Benghazi that killed Ambassador Stevens. Now the right saw a humiliation for America owing to forces Obama encouraged. Helpfully, Benghazi seemed like a checkmate on Hillary Clinton's presidential ambitions. It became an obsession on the right—but in the process, Benghazi itself became the debacle, not the Libya war.

Libya vexed Mitt Romney, who was running for president. In an echo of John Kerry, he initially supported the war "and the mission," while indulging conservatives by calling Obama "weak" and denigrating the United Nations and the French. At a New Hampshire campaign stop in July 2011, Romney asked the only relevant question about the war—"Who's going to own Libya if we get rid of the government there?"—but never called for its end. He was left talking in the abstract about Obama's insufficient faith in "America [as] an exceptional nation."

Romney's inauthenticity had already been on display during his unsuccessful 2008 campaign. With an explosion in white petty-bourgeois mobilization on the right, the patrician Romney would only find himself in ever more painful contortions. The moderate Massachusetts governor who had enacted a precursor to Obama's health care expansion was now, Romney said in February 2012, a "severely conservative" man. While Gingrich embraced Gaffney's "stealth jihad" conspiracy, Romney found himself caught between his ambition and his decency. "We're not going to have sharia law applied in U.S. courts. That's never going to happen," he said in a 2011 debate, but, acknowledging the subtext, he added, "People of all faiths are welcome in this country." Accurately reading the regnant politics on the right, Romney gave no such quarter on immigration. He would support the DREAM Act only if it made military service a condition of citizenship. The furthest he would moderate his position was to pledge not to "round people up," but migrants would have to reapply for U.S. citizenship back in their "home" countries. Asked to reconcile those positions in January 2012, he said that an estimated 12 million people would have to "self-deport." By April, the Arizona state legislator who wrote the Show Me Your Papers law said Romney's immigration policy was "identical to mine."

One of Romney's delusions was the opposite of Obama's: Romney wanted to deemphasize the Forever War yet intensify the politics of fear. He did not advocate any rollback of the War on Terror but submerged it in broader symbolic themes. He stressed the need for unapologetic American global leadership and other traditional Republican defense themes, like confronting a resurgent Russia or enlarging the navy. That satisfied American exceptionalism while straddling the respectable balance between sounding like a businessman's Reagan at some times and, at others, the opponent of sharia whom Donald Trump endorsed in Vegas.

Romney, agonizingly, could not find a critique of Benghazi to indict

Obama. His first statement in the aftermath of the attack drew overwhelming criticism for its accusation, now pedigreed on the nativist right, that Obama "sympathiz[ed] with those who waged the attacks." A fallback attack he settled on could not survive scrutiny. Romney said Obama could not bring himself to call Benghazi a terrorist attack because doing so would undermine his claim of decimating al-Qaeda. Yet Obama had called Benghazi an "act of terror" that very day. When Romney made the claim in a presidential debate, moderator Candy Crowley pointed out that it was false.

The Benghazi-centric right was so certain that the attack was a dream opportunity to discredit both Obama and Clinton that it was incredulous when Romney lost. One of Romney's advisers, Gabriel Schoenfeld—a neoconservative *Commentary* writer who in 2006 demanded the prosecution of the *New York Times* reporters who exposed STELLARWIND—blamed the defeat on the candidate's inability to capitalize on Benghazi. It was an unpersuasive explanation, but it spoke to a certain political shock, a decade after 9/11, that a terrorist attack might not benefit the right.

It also spoke to a predicament Romney shared with other establishment Republicans. Socially and economically distant from the nativists of the Tea Party, they had lost the ability to convince the enraged nativists that they were ultimately aligned culturally and politically. The Tea Party had no patience for Republican politicians they saw as accommodating Obama. Obama's reelection, occurring in the context of Benghazi, where the United States looked helpless before vengeful Muslims, reinforced the calamity. The nationalists on the right, having already endured McCain's rebukes and Romney's haplessness, were disinclined to listen to the establishment Republicans telling them they needed to moderate even further in defeat. True to form, the mainstream members of the party believed that Romney's embrace of immigration restrictionism had doomed him, and urged fellow Republicans to "embrace and champion comprehensive immigration reform" lest they become a party of their "core constituencies," meaning whites.

"That loss was really catastrophic," Donald Trump reflected the following year. Trump had no need to convince the nativists that he, so socially and economically distant as well, was aligned with them culturally and politically. Accordingly, he had a contrary diagnosis of the party's loss. It was the GOP's election to win, but Romney was just so inauthentic. "It looked so false," Trump continued. "Somebody was giving him just horrible advice."

AT MIDMORNING ON AUGUST 5, 2012, Wade Michael Page entered the Sikh temple in the Oak Creek suburb of Milwaukee holding a nine-millimeter pistol. Temple staff were preparing lunch for the coming services. As Page opened fire, congregants grabbed children and ran for the nearest room to hide. Satwant Singh Kaleka, the sixty-five-year-old temple president, was hit with two shots near his hip. Bleeding, he grabbed a butter knife and charged to his end. The first police officer to arrive, Brian Murphy, was shot twelve times—three other bullets lodged in his body armor—while trying to get Kaleka's congregation to safety. Page killed five others and wounded four more before another policeman shot him in the stomach. He turned his gun on himself rather than be captured.

Page left behind no manifesto. But he was a white supremacist and army veteran executing a deliberate terrorist plan, exactly the type of potentially violent personality the DHS analyst Daryl Johnson had warned about three years earlier. Page had the fourteen-word white supremacist credo tattooed on him and played in a white-power band called End Apathy. The accepted explanation, based on a rise in post-9/11 hate crimes against Sikhs and a general lack of white supremacist interest in targeting them, was that Page likely thought he was killing Muslims. A criminology professor in Omaha who had known Page recalled him talking about "towel heads" and "sand niggers." Johnson, disgusted, said Wade's rampage showed that "DHS is scoffing at the mission of doing domestic counterterrorism, as is Congress."

Mark Potok of the Southern Poverty Law Center called Page "the American Anders Breivik."

Breivik was a Norwegian in his thirties who believed what his favorite "counterjihadist" blogs and web fora—Gates of the West, Robert Spencer's Jihad Watch, the American neo-Nazis' Stormfront—told him about the Islamization of Europe. Living with his mother, selling fake diplomas online, and playing World of Warcraft in what he called his "fart room," Breivik nurtured his grievances until they became a worldview. He wrote about reimposing patriarchy on the insufficiently docile women around him. His enemies, after the Muslims and the women, were the progressive, respectable "cultural Marxists" who dominated Norwegian politics, and he divided them into categories of traitors to be executed or spared. It made no sense to him that the bloggers who had so insightfully diagnosed the horror of the white man's condition stopped short of endorsing the mass Muslim deportation that was so clearly necessary. Like Grandpa Millar of Elohim City, what Breivik sought was, functionally, a white man's caliphate.

On a rented farm, Breivik, now calling himself the Judicious Knight Commander of a new Knights Templar, put together a plan. Whatever his feelings about Muslims, al-Qaeda had left helpful bomb-making tips on the internet. He marveled at how easy it was to acquire the chemicals to make a bomb "unless you're called Abdullah Rashid Muhammed." On July 22, 2011, he bombed the Oslo parliament house before driving an hour to embark for the island of Utoya where, dressed as a policeman, he slaughtered teenagers attending the Labour Party's youth retreat. After killing seventy-seven people, most of them children, he told the police, "That's what they call terror, isn't it?"

Breivik left behind a manifesto he called *2083: A European Declaration of Independence.* Its citations included the leading figures of the American and European counterjihadist right, including Pamela Geller and Frank Gaffney, as well as work done by the neoconservative-originated Foundation for the Defense of Democracies. None of them made as big a mark on

Breivik as Robert Spencer. The manifesto quoted Spencer 64 times and referenced Spencer's work 162 times. Spencer disclaimed any responsibility, taking umbrage at the "blame game . . . as if killing a lot of children aids the defense against the global jihad and Islamic supremacism, or has anything remotely to do with anything we have ever advocated." For her part, Geller railed against "a sinister attempt to tar all anti-jihadists with responsibility for this man's heinous actions."

Beyond the outraged self-defense lay the sort of apologia that the counterjihadists typically accused Muslims of engaging in. Bruce Bawer, author of a book called *Surrender: Appeasing Islam, Sacrificing Freedom* and another writer cited by Breivik, lamented in *The Wall Street Journal* that Breivik had "a legitimate concern about genuine problems," namely "the Islamization of Europe," and now their shared cause would suffer. "If anyone incited him to violence," Geller judged, "it was Islamic supremacists."

More than a decade of socially acceptable depictions of Muslims as a threat to America and Europe yielded a substantial cohort who believed Islam threatened Western civilization. At Oak Creek, Islamophobia crossed an undefended border. It was by no means the first time Sikhs had suffered because of post-9/11 white supremacist ignorance. But Oak Creek made unignorable the reality that Islamophobia did not only imperil Muslims. Wade Michael Page was merely the first to decide the times called for an American Breivik.

CHAPTER SIX

THE LEFT VS. OBAMA'S
WAR ON TERROR

2009–2014

I n Democratic politics and much self-identifying liberal journalism, there remained a fundamental allergy to leftist critiques of the War on Terror. The largest mass protests in human history—including a 12-to-14-million-person demonstration in eight hundred cities on February 15, 2003, the largest single-day protest recorded thus far—had as little influence on the senior Democratic leadership as it did on Bush. Few reporters attended a cathartic 2008 evening in Washington, D.C., emceed by antiwar journalist Jeremy Scahill, at which a service-member panel convened by Iraq Veterans Against the War discussed what they considered the horrors they had committed or witnessed. It attested to a marginalization of the left that seemed, in retrospect, foreordained the moment the planes hit the Twin Towers.

Obama, the locus of much antiwar hope, entrenched the War on Terror, something excruciating to progressives. Brennan, whom journalist Glenn Greenwald and allies had blocked from becoming Obama's first CIA director, became his third. Some of Obama's transgressions the left hadn't yet learned of, such as the prolonged NSA bulk surveillance or administration-supported efforts by the CIA to thwart congressional investigation of torture. Advisers to the president, meanwhile, lectured the left on what was realistic to protect national security. At his National Defense University speech on drone strikes, Obama grew testy at the disruptive Code Pink protester Medea Benjamin before congratulating himself for hearing her out.

By the dawn of Obama's second term, a cohort that included activists, attorneys, journalists, and concerned citizens who considered themselves leftists—along with some liberals—found themselves embittered by his presidency. It was conspicuous to them that the right, unlike the left, expanded its ambitions all throughout the 9/11 era. The left wing of the Democratic Party started to become more assertive, initially through warning about the institutionalization of Bush-era offenses like the PATRIOT Act, and then on to calling out Obama-era offenses like drone strikes. In the Senate Bernie Sanders voted against the inevitable PATRIOT Act renewal. But while his seminal 2010 filibuster against austerity described the coalescing war against the working class, Sanders did not draw it into a broader critique of a Forever War that redistributed to the military and the defense industry the wealth needed to address the growing precarity of working-class and even middle-class life.

The Bush-era coalition of advocates for civil liberties, privacy rights, human rights, civil rights, transparency, immigrants, and refugees would now see Obama in court. They were respectable professionals, and they knew Sontag had been right all along. By culture as much as by interest, their vision of America came into conflict with the one the War on Terror presented. For many it felt uncomfortable to fight Obama—it had been righteous, *patriotic*, to oppose Bush—but he had made the Forever War truly *forever*. There were too few degrees of professional distance from the lawyer-heavy administration for the break with them to ever be total, so the breaks came to each of them as a matter of degree. Some were expressed on Twitter or on the legal national-security *Lawfare* blog, which was highly critical of the human rights lobby and wrote as the tribune of the Security State. It had that in common with the right, which considered the human rights coalition an adversary to defeat. Asserting that people like Khalid Shaikh Mohammed were entitled to legal redress prompted Keep America Safe's vicious "al-Qaeda Seven" ad campaign. The right, as always, considered Obama a result of the left–libertarian coalition rather than an obstacle to it.

Conflict between all these forces would have an impact on hundreds of millions of people worldwide. The venues for that conflict were fundamentally elite institutions: newspapers, courtrooms, legislatures. Activism from outside these circles opposing the war was rarely afforded respect by those within. Few news outlets considered Code Pink more than an annoyance during congressional hearings.

The most impactful activism against the War on Terror came from within the Security State itself. It was not the result of the campaign that Comey waged against Bush White House counsel Alberto Gonzales at John Ashcroft's hospital bed over whose legal argument more convincingly sanctioned bulk surveillance. It would come instead from low-ranking soldiers and intelligence contractors whose exposure to the war prompted them to expose it to the world.

For violating a Security State oath of secrecy, they became public enemies. They would be made to suffer in prison, or face a choice of prison or exile. Their rare advocates in legal, political, and journalistic circles risked denunciation for taking them seriously. Hillary Clinton's State Department spokesman, P. J. Crowley, resigned from his untenable position two days after denouncing the military's cruel captivity of Private Chelsea Manning. Obama accepted the army's assurances that Manning's pretrial treatment— she was stripped nude at night and held in isolation for eleven months— was humane. The United Nations called it "at a minimum cruel, inhuman and degrading treatment in violation of article 16 of the convention against torture." Even veterans who had turned against the wars often expressed disgust at Manning or NSA contractor Edward Snowden for acting dishonorably. Manning and Snowden were un-Trooped. Their service did not invest their whistleblowing with greater public respect. Instead, their whistleblowing cost them the post-9/11 public reverence accorded to military or intelligence service.

Not all dissent from within the Security State took the form of whistleblowing. A former FBI counterterrorism analyst working for Senate Democrats spent six years in a windowless room, growing radicalized by what he discovered about the CIA. He was one of few people outside the agency to learn even a fraction of what Langley had done to at least 119 people at the black sites. Daniel Jones kept those secrets to himself while he documented bluntly and rigorously how the agency had committed brutality far worse than previously understood, and how the CIA lied to cover it up. He demolished the false narrative on torture the CIA had sold the public. For that, the CIA requested that the Justice Department prosecute Jones to distract from the espionage it had, in fact, committed against him.

Manning, Jones, Snowden, and similar rejectionists from the Security State acted primarily out of an outrage at the War on Terror. They issued no manifestos. While their ideological affiliations might have been idiosyncratic, and divergent from one another's, it was the left that embraced and championed them, not liberals, with the exception of Jones. Their revelations did more than any previous activism to usher in an era of exhaustion with the War on Terror. In that manner they reinvigorated the moral imagination of a left that would demand a politics of abolition.

THERE WAS MUCH SPECULATION about what Obama's grassroots supporters would do once he was in office. One theory among young Washington-area progressive activists in the first months of his administration concerned the antiwar movement. The swell of antiwar anger—mostly focused on Iraq, rather than the entire War on Terror—that had risen since Bush's reelection helped make Obama's presidency possible. Under Obama, it fell apart.

Obama's election had settled the debate on the viability of the Iraq war. But liberal circles in 2009 accepted the justice of the Afghanistan war, which limited elite debate on its wisdom. Thanks to the trust Obama had among much of the progressive infrastructure, to say nothing of the distaste elite circles generally have for antiwar activists, those activists committed to the end of the War on Terror were always going to struggle. As Obama prepared to escalate in Afghanistan, Ilyse Hogue of MoveOn told the *Times*, "there is not the passion around Afghanistan that we saw around Iraq." Obama would soon feel no meaningful constraint coming from an antiwar movement. At times, as in the National Defense University speech, he showed irritation with what remained of it.

The progressive legal apparatus that had opposed Bush initially gave Obama a wide berth, while keeping its same focus. But Obama provided no end of disappointment. Almost immediately upon taking office, his administration contested habeas cases from Bagram and Guantanamo, undercutting what was supposed to be a pathway toward the goal of closing both detention facilities. Holder's Justice Department retained the Bush-era opposition to a lawsuit brought by torture victims against aviation firm Jeppesen Dataplan, a Boeing subsidiary that the CIA used as a renditions ferry. It used the same argument as its predecessor: discussing the case publicly would be too damaging to national security. Soon after, it refused to release a classified trove of Bush-era wartime detention photography on the grounds that what it recorded was so brutal that the resulting outrage could endanger deployed troops.

Human rights attorneys wielding the Freedom of Information Act and discovery motions had already compelled government disclosures of torture. What they wanted was a reckoning modeled on South Africa's post-apartheid Truth and Reconciliation Commission. Disclosure and accountability—a version preferred by Senator Patrick Leahy targeted all the Forever War's detention and surveillance activities—would be the only way to ensure the United States would not return to torture. Obama made it unambiguous that no such thing would happen.

In summer 2009 Obama disclosed Bush-era legal opinions on torture that he had repudiated. That would constitute the entirety of the time he spent looking backward instead of forward. Holder, his conscience troubled by torture, expanded the mandate of a special prosecutor he inherited, U.S. Attorney John Durham, who was examining the CIA's destruction of torture videotapes. Now Durham would examine the brutality itself—but only to see if the CIA's torturers surpassed the expansive permissions that the Justice Department provided in 2002. That approach treated illegal torture as a deviation, rather than a policy.

It also aimed entirely at the practitioners of torture instead of those who ordered them to torture people. Politics preordained such a focus. Whatever crimes an administration may have committed, its successor would face a backlash for prosecuting them, something journalists considered the criminalization of political disagreement. The distinction didn't matter to congressional Republicans, who warned of a witch hunt against the valiant interrogators of the CIA, or for Obama's chief of staff Rahm Emanuel, who considered it political malpractice. "You only want to look back at a previous administration if you feel you really have to," Holder ambivalently told an interviewer.

Human rights groups that expected an ally in the White House were left asserting first principles against Obama. "So-called 'enhanced interrogation techniques' like mock executions and threatening prisoners with guns and power drills are not only reprehensible but illegal," Anthony Romero, the ACLU's executive director, said about Durham's probe. Unsurprisingly, Durham ended his investigation in 2012 without bringing any charges. The Center for Constitutional Rights denounced how "once again, the United States has shown it is committed to absolving itself of any responsibility for its crimes over the past decade." The center no longer saw a need to distinguish the agendas of Bush and Obama in the War on Terror. Obama complained in a 2009 meeting with civil libertarians that he found such rhetoric unhelpful. "Do we just release [Guantanamo detainees] and take the chance they blow you up? There's only so much a democracy can bear," he said. The Sustainable War on Terror had to undermine democracy in order to save it.

The civil libertarians had hoped Obama would finally make the War on Terror respect the law. They watched in disbelief as Obama continued to make the law respect the War on Terror. Now a different form of resistance would bypass the courts entirely.

A UNITED STATES-BACKED IRAQ ARMY UNIT in Tal Afar, the town McMaster had pacified three years earlier as the surge's proof of concept, took a handcuffed detainee into the street and shot him. It was an obscure atrocity that twenty-one-year-old Chelsea Manning watched from her classified-network terminal in Iraq in 2009. And it was one of innumerable "SigActs," or significant activities, created by the war's bureaucracy—records of notable, granular developments in both ground wars, as well as much other material. In her role as an intelligence analyst, it was Manning's job to make sense of SigActs for the slice of eastern Baghdad where her unit operated. Back at Fort Drum, she had seen many others—"war porn," she later called them—such as one recounting U.S. troops opening fire on a bus in Afghanistan and hitting fifteen people.

Manning came to learn that there was no place for her in the War on Terror. She had enlisted two years before, a nineteen-year-old hoping for "real world experience" and for the promise of money for college. In an army where service by openly LGBTQ people was formally banned, she was understood to be a man named Bradley and bullied by a homophobic roommate. Over several months in 2009, with the wars weighing on her mind, she realized the images the SigActs contained "could spark a domestic debate on the role of the military and our foreign policy in general." As the blank CD-Rs littering her secured workstation filled up with backups of SigAct records, she resolved to be the spark.

Years later, after experiencing deliberately cruel military detention,

REIGN OF TERROR

Manning, in dress uniform, evenly recounted the events that followed. During her leave from Iraq at her aunt's house in Maryland, she labored unsuccessfully to contact *The Washington Post*, *The New York Times*, and *Politico*. She then decided to trust a group she knew only through IRC and Jabber chats, where she felt like a valued part of a community: the anti-secrecy group WikiLeaks.

Billing itself as an "uncensorable Wikipedia for untraceable mass document leaking and analysis," WikiLeaks framed exposure as an ideological act, not just a journalistic one. Every powerful institution was a target to expose. Often they released government, corporate, and military secrets, even material digitally smuggled out of the Church of Scientology. Directing its media releases was the Australian Julian Assange, who was equal parts libertarian and authoritarian. As a young hacker, he chose the handle "Mendax," a reference to Horace: someone who lies for noble reasons. Assange partnered with news outlets to promote WikiLeaks' disclosures but deeply distrusted journalists, whom he believed layered narrative—subjective and often ignorant narrative—over events.

Hovering over the WikiLeaks submissions form during a blizzard in January 2010, Manning composed a message about the tens of thousands of SigActs she was about to upload: "This is possibly one of the more significant documents of our time removing the fog of war and revealing the true nature of twenty-first century asymmetric warfare. Have a good day." When she sent it to WikiLeaks, she recalled, she felt a burden lift from her conscience.

Manning's resolve heightened after she returned to Baghdad. Her access to classified military networks extended to a State Department server that contained huge numbers of diplomatic cables. It was a real-time hidden history of U.S. foreign relations, kept secret despite many cables being marked unclassified, and one that recorded what Manning saw as a superpower imposing its will. Over 250,000 of the cables went to WikiLeaks. She also sent the group a video of a helicopter crew killing two Reuters employees in 2007 while speaking of them in dehumanizing terms. "I wanted the American public to know that not everyone in Iraq and Afghanistan are targets that needed to be neutralized, but rather people who were struggling to live in the pressure cooker environment of what we call asymmetric warfare," she later explained. It became a breakthrough video for WikiLeaks, which released it in April under the title "Collateral Murder." Troves about Afghanistan, Iraq, and U.S. diplomacy were still to come.

Manning would not be free to see their release. While chatting from Baghdad with a prominent hacker, Adrian Lamo, Manning revealed that she was WikiLeaks' source for "Collateral Murder" and many forthcoming items. Although Lamo had donated to WikiLeaks, he quickly contacted the army. "I wouldn't have done this if lives weren't in danger," he told journalists Kim Zetter and Kevin Poulsen. The army's Criminal Investigation Division arrested Manning that month and held her in Kuwait.

Assange gave *The New York Times, Der Spiegel,* and *The Guardian* an advance look at the ninety-two-thousand-document trove on the Afghanistan war ahead of his publication in July 2010, at the height of the Afghanistan surge. Incidents where U.S. forces fired upon civilians, known as "blue on white" events, were documented 144 times in the leaked material. Manning, now incarcerated and awaiting a military tribunal, had expected the SigActs leak to spark a debate over the war. She was wrong.

While *The Guardian,* an explicitly progressive news outlet writing primarily for a non-American audience, presented the logs as documenting dehumanization, the dominant American reception to accounts of civilian deaths and other atrocities was indifference. In a typical comment, Gian Gentile, a retired army colonel and insightful counterinsurgency critic, predicted, "these wikileaks [*sic*] on Afghanistan will be front page for a day or two then swept into the dustbin of history where the only folks interested will be wonks, experts, historians doing current history, and military bloggers." Rarely did anyone shrugging off the revelations grapple with the implication that brutality committed by Americans and their proxies was unremarkable. Such reactions set the template for the quick American dismissal of a far larger and even more horrifying trove of SigActs from the Iraq war, such as the campaign of torture by U.S.-sponsored Iraqi security forces. *The New York Times*'s description of the 392,000-document trove was so anodyne—undermining its own coverage by assuring readers the documents "provide no earthshaking revelations"—that a blogger for *BoingBoing*, Rob Beschizza, coded what he called a *New York Times* Torture Euphemism Generator to shame the paper.

WikiLeaks began to fracture as it racked up its greatest achievements. The organization did not take sufficient care to fully redact names of Afghan informants in the first batch of documents, and human rights groups from Amnesty International to the Open Society Foundations warned the group that it had imperiled vulnerable people. By September, with Assange vowing to press on with Manning's Iraq disclosures the next month, WikiLeaks staffers revolted, fearful of compounding an error that horrified them. German tech activist Daniel Domscheit-Berg quit after big-picture disagreements with Assange over WikiLeaks' future. Accompanying him was an important programmer known as The Architect, whose departure took WikiLeaks' submission system offline. "Children shouldn't play with guns," Domscheit-Berg explained in a memoir. An increasingly dictatorial Assange, who faced a rape accusation in Sweden, took the resignations as disloyalty. "I am the heart and soul of this organization, its founder, philosopher, spokesperson, original coder, organizer, financier and all the rest. If you have a problem with me, piss off," he told one disaffected staffer.

The Obama administration went after WikiLeaks as quickly as it dismissed the Iraq and Afghanistan revelations as old news. Admiral Mike Mullen, in a typical comment, said WikiLeaks "might already have on their hands the blood of some young soldier." When WikiLeaks asked for the administration's help with redactions, the State Department's Harold Koh demanded instead that Assange return the Manning files and purge its website of all the materials she provided. Joe Biden called Assange, someone who had never committed political violence, a "high-tech terrorist."

A federal grand jury began considering espionage charges against

WikiLeaks, an investigation that risked criminalizing national security journalism. The administration's primary imperative was to deter anyone else within the Security State from becoming another Manning. The Pentagon expanded its monitoring of its employees' network usage and contracted for algorithmic analysis to determine who might pose what it called an "insider threat." Protecting the apparatus of secrecy was a higher priority than dealing with the ugly truths that secrecy concealed.

Manning's treatment in pretrial captivity bore disturbing similarities to the torture techniques that the CIA and military had gotten away with using. Guards bringing food to her Kuwait cell told her she would be sent to Guantanamo Bay. She contemplated castrating herself, later writing of the toll of "living as and being treated as a male," and attempted to choke herself with her blanket. At the Marine Corps brig at Quantico, she was stripped nude at night, frequently in view of her captors and despite the coldness in her cell. When she was permitted to exercise, she would be shackled. Her isolation from all but the guards, under conditions of twenty-three-hour surveillance, lasted nine months atop the two she had already endured in Kuwait. The pretext for this cruelty was to prevent her from hurting herself.

It was the first time in the War on Terror that such treatment was visited on a white person. One difference was relative transparency. Manning's treatment was public enough to prompt State Department spokesman Crowley to call it "ridiculous and counterproductive and stupid" before a small MIT audience. It marked how deeply Manning was vilified that Crowley had to resign for that comment. Reporters were not present, and the public learned about his remark because Philippa Thomas, a BBC journalist on a fellowship at Harvard, blogged what she had heard at the discussion. "Nonetheless [Chelsea] Manning is in the right place," Thomas also quoted Crowley as saying.

Not long after Crowley's resignation, Obama insisted that Manning's treatment inside the brig was humane. "I have actually asked the Pentagon whether or not the procedures that have been taken in terms of his confinement are appropriate and are meeting our basic standards," he said, and the Pentagon assured him they were. The following month, when Obama stopped by the St. Regis hotel in San Francisco for a morning fundraiser, a group of singers interrupted him with a song about Manning "alone in a six-by-twelve cell." This time, Obama lectured the protesters, insisting, "[Manning] broke the law." Since Manning was then in pretrial military detention and Obama was still her commander in chief, his remarks improperly presumed her guilt.

While Bill O'Reilly called Manning a "traitor" who should be "executed or put in prison for life," a growing body of people considered her a hero who had acted in the noble tradition of uniformed war resistance. Even more simply did not want Manning treated with cruelty. They found themselves arrayed against Obama.

A secret Pentagon study that concluded that the damage from Manning's leaks was marginal was later obtained and published by Jason Leopold of *BuzzFeed*. The Pentagon's WikiLeaks Task Force found in 2011 that twenty-three soldiers in Afghanistan had their full names and Social Security numbers exposed, and that "risks" to local informants and U.S. intelligence capabilities did result. But it could not connect Manning's disclosures to anyone who suffered physical harm. The task force further reported that the helicopter crew from "Collateral Murder" had been found to have followed the rules of engagement "to a satisfactory degree" and overall concluded that "there is not any significant 'strategic' impact to the release of this information." Meanwhile, a UN special rapporteur found that Manning's treatment in Kuwait and at the brig, defended by Obama, "could constitute torture."

In 2013, after almost three years of detention, Manning appeared in a military courtroom to plead guilty to ten of twenty-two charges, guaranteeing her twenty years of what was ultimately a thirty-five-year sentence. She continued to plead not guilty to the most serious charges against her, principally aiding the enemy. Reporters streamed into an overflow room at Fort Meade to hear Manning speak for the first time since the leaks began.

Years of rumors about her collapsed mental health were undone by the eloquent statement she read, uninterrupted, for over an hour. Manning took "full responsibility" for the leaks, denied that WikiLeaks solicited them— a critical statement, legally, since it undermined an espionage accusation against the group—and warned of the dangers of counterterrorism operations divorced from "their effect on people."

The only time her voice caught came when she spoke about the relief she felt when she communicated with WikiLeaks. On WikiLeaks' IRC channel, she was free from the alienation she felt from her fellow soldiers, "free of any concerns about social labeling in real life." She recalled the friendship she felt with someone she understood was likely Assange, whose name she mispronounced in court, whom she had called "Nathaniel," after the author Nathaniel Frank. They spoke almost daily, particularly after she had uploaded the "Collateral Murder" video. "In retrospect," Manning told the court, she realized that "these dynamics were artificial and were valued more by myself than Nathaniel."

THE 2008 FISA AMENDMENTS ACT gave new license to perhaps the most portentious endeavor of the entire War on Terror. Previewing Obama's "sustainable" war, it transformed bulk surveillance from an emergency activity, executed in secrecy from Congress and most of the FISA Court, to a core function. Much of the coverage of the time focused on the retroactive legal immunity the new law afforded the telecommunications firms. But the broader tectonic shift, a milestone in what Shoshana Zuboff calls "surveillance capitalism," rendered those traditional phone companies and internet service providers less relevant than the emergent giants of a maturing internet.

Social media companies, search giants, and web hosts were repositories of unfathomable amounts of data—data they monetized before their users grasped that their online activity was commodifiable. Any person's status update contained a bounty of surveillance-relevant information, as it indicated what they were doing or feeling at a discrete point in time and space. But hundreds of millions of people's accounts, posts, and interactions created an entire infrastructure of data. Expanding like the universe after the Big Bang, it waited to be analyzed for patterns and exploited, revealing untold stories about human behavior depending on how it was mined. The infrastructure of surveillance capitalism involved accounts given away free to users who were unaware of the economic model at work. It was the cost of entry to the social and economic conditions of the twenty-first century. Not only was this economic structure built to exploit users, it was agnostic as to whether an advertiser, an analytics firm, or the NSA exploited them.

A company like Google or Amazon, two of the most important surveillance capitalism pioneers, was classified as a "U.S. person" under the Foreign Intelligence Surveillance Act, and as such was entitled to certain privacy rights. But thanks to the 2008 FISA Amendments Act, now known as Section 702 of FISA, the NSA could conduct what internal documents described as "legally-compelled collection" from the servers—the exact form of access remains unknown—of these giants. NSA received access to Microsoft servers in September 2007; to Google in January 2009; to Facebook that June; to Google's YouTube the following year; and to Apple in October 2012. While the debate over the 2008 law was focused on terrorism, the NSA's collection was not. Intelligence reporting emerging from the data collection during a single week in February 2013 concerned Mexican internal security, Egyptian politics, Palestinian finances, Iraqi oil, Israeli cyberplanning, Japanese trade, Venezuelan military procurement, and, for good measure, al-Qaeda. The suite of surveillance on the data empires of these Silicon Valley giants was codenamed PRISM.

That kind of surveillance was not always sufficient. But 702 provided contingencies. The NSA, citing 702, digitally siphoned data as it transited the internet between servers, a process known as UPSTREAM collection. Sometimes the agency intercepted data coming from or headed to Google or Yahoo servers overseas. Section 702 permitted the NSA to presume the overseas clientele of "U.S. person" data giants were foreigners. Internal descriptions from the NSA's in-house wiki referred to "full take" operations from those servers. These operations were known by the codename MUSCULAR, a partnership with the UK's GCHQ.

While the NSA was collecting Americans' communications data wholesale—PRISM, UPSTREAM, MUSCULAR, and other programs were supplemented by the mass collection of Americans' phone call records— the Justice Department erected a wall of secrecy around it. That wall came into view over a case called *Jewel v. NSA*, a lawsuit filed in 2008 by the Electronic Frontier Foundation after AT&T technician Mark Klein discovered the company was routing its internet traffic to the NSA. Holder's Justice Department moved to dismiss the case, as its central allegation was a state secret. Such secrecy, federal prosecutors contended, prevented any plaintiff from being able to claim their particular communications had been collected or analyzed by the NSA or its partners. In criminal cases, individuals like Fazliddin Kurbanov found themselves prosecuted for material support for terrorism without knowing that they had come to the government's attention through a warrantless and legally inadmissable search. By 2011, FISA Court judge Bates, the same judge who dismissed the lawsuit to save Anwar al-Awlaki's life, paused NSA's 702 internet collection, citing repeated "substantial misrepresentation" by the government about how the surveillance worked. Bates, concerned about the lawlessness of UPSTREAM, found that 702 surveillance had grown to accumulate hundreds of millions of internet communications annually, the overwhelming majority from PRISM. Yet the growing corpus of surveillance and secrecy also generated its own antibody.

Edward Snowden, born in 1983, was a child of the internet. He was raised in the Maryland middle-class environment of service members, federal employees, and government contractors. Snowden remembered his early experiences with the internet as an idyll filled with human potential. It was the community-forging frontier that John Perry Barlow envisioned "without privilege or prejudice accorded by race, economic power, military force, or station or birth."

But Snowden was also a child of 9/11. That September morning, under what he recalled was a "Microsoft-blue sky," Snowden drove to Fort Meade, where he did web design in the on-base house of a woman he had a crush on, and watched anguished NSA officials speed out of their black-glass headquarters once Hayden gave the evacuation order. On what he would later describe as a quest "to be a part of something," Snowden enlisted in the army but washed out. Unwilling to quit, he applied for a security clearance, realizing his digital fluency would be more valuable to the government than his body. Over the next seven years, working for the CIA and then the NSA through contractor cutouts, Snowden became part of a generation of spies for whom "it was less about clandestine meetings and dead drops [than] about data." He would later call his "reflexive, unquestioning" support for the War on Terror "the greatest regret of my life."

Snowden's devotion to the America that was advertised in the aftermath of 9/11—the freedom-sworn place where resolute people stuck Dixie Cups through chain-link fences to spell UNITED WE STAND on highway overpasses— was visible in his disgust with what the country had him do. Snowden was an accomplice to wholesale surveillance on Americans and most of the world. It was bitterly ironic that Snowden was present to witness and facilitate the NSA's exploitation of his beloved internet. Had he not known the internet so thoroughly—with a system administrator's facility for its endless pathways and all the identifying markers that traveling down them created— Snowden might not have been radicalized. Working for the NSA for the first time in Japan, sysadmin Snowden suddenly had access to the constellation of digital surveillance operations, and he immediately understood its implications. Snowden's admin credentials even made him privy to the secret NSA history of STELLARWIND. He recalled a vertiginous feeling after realizing the devices guiding him around Tokyo meant that the NSA could know where he was going even if he didn't.

Like Manning, Snowden reached a crisis point. But he didn't turn to WikiLeaks. Snowden wanted journalists—not himself, not Assange—to sift through them and determine what was and wasn't in the public's interest to know. He loaded NSA drives with documents detailing the architecture of mass surveillance and in May 2013 arranged to meet with the prominent civil-libertarian columnist Glenn Greenwald and filmmaker Laura Poitras in Hong Kong; Ewen MacAskill of *The Guardian* accompanied them. Snowden also gave a copy of the trove to Barton Gellman, an investigative reporter who worked with *The Washington Post*. One of the handles he used to communicate with Poitras was "Verax," or truth-teller, a deliberate contrast to Julian "Mendax" Assange. Snowden, unlike Manning, wanted the public to know the source of the documents. Days after *The Guardian* and the *Post* began their revelations—bulk collection of all domestic phone data, PRISM, an indexing tool called Boundless Informant—he announced his identity and explained why he had executed the greatest data breach in NSA history. "This is something that's not our place to decide. The public needs to decide whether these programs and policies are right or wrong," he said in a conversation with Greenwald that Poitras filmed. His greatest fear about his disclosures, Snowden continued, "is that nothing will change."

Snowden's revelations created a legitimacy crisis at the NSA. Authorities that the agency understood as having been settled by Congress in 2008 and functionally ratified by Obama not long afterward were now in question. The intelligence apparatus helmed by Director of National Intelligence James Clapper needed to know that its congressional allies and the White House would support Fort Meade.

The NSA could rely on the bipartisan congressional leadership and leaders of the intelligence committees, the so-called Gang of Eight. Dianne Feinstein, the Democratic chair of the Senate intelligence panel, immediately said Snowden had engaged in an "act of treason." Michigan Republican Mike Rogers and Maryland Democrat Dutch Ruppersberger made the crucial House Intelligence Committee safe terrain for NSA and allied officials to contend that it was Snowden, and not surveillance, that was the outrage. But discomfort, particularly over the bulk collection of Americans' phone data, ran beyond the expected precincts of the Tea Party–adjacent House Freedom Caucus and congressional progressives. A month after the disclosures, the Freedom Caucus's Justin Amash came only twelve votes short of putting a ban on the domestic collection in a sure-to-pass defense bill. Nancy Pelosi and John Boehner voted with Rogers against it, as Rogers asked if his colleagues had forgotten 9/11.

By any measure the NSA could also rely on the White House, but the Security State continued to grade Obama on a curve. "Even Obama didn't know the extent of what the NSA was doing in 2009," Ben Rhodes avers. But he retained NSA's mass surveillance despite its making three "substantial misrepresentation[s]" to the FISA Court between 2009 and 2011. In an August press conference Obama said Snowden was "not a patriot," unlike "the men and women of our intelligence community." He offered a characteristic response to bulk surveillance: it could continue, but under "additional safeguards," like greater congressional and FISA Court oversight. Yet those restrictions applied only to the phone records surveillance. He proposed no substantive limitations on any of the surveillance under Section 702, which was far more important to the agency as collectable digital communications expanded. The NSA seethed nevertheless. "There has been no support for the agency from the President or his staff or senior administration officials, and this has not gone unnoticed by both senior officials and the rank and file at the Fort," its former inspector general said in October.

Clapper and the uptight, occasionally hapless NSA director, General Keith Alexander, attempted to reframe NSA surveillance. Clapper, officious and impatient with the many he considered fools, came to the task weakened. Snowden's disclosures revealed that Clapper had lied during a Senate appearance in March at which he said in response to Oregon Democrat Ron Wyden that the NSA did "not wittingly" collect what Wyden had characterized as "any type of data at all on millions or hundreds of millions of Americans." Clapper first explained his response as the "least untruthful" answer he could publicly provide; later, in an apology, he insisted he had forgotten about the phone records surveillance. With that out of the way, Clapper denounced Snowden's revelations as "one of the most egregious violations of trust I've seen in more than 50 years in intelligence."

But the NSA made headway in Congress by arguing that it wasn't actually listening in on Americans' calls. It fell to civil libertarians like Wyden to warn his colleagues that the metadata was all the NSA needed to construct a "human relations database on millions of Americans." That was a harder point to grasp than the balm that Clapper and Alexander had offered. When the balm didn't work, Alexander showed the steel, claiming that PRISM had disrupted more than fifty terrorist plots—though only ten were domestic terror incidents, and at least two weren't incidents at all, but rather financial support to terror groups. (Alexander later defined it down as disrupting "terror-related activities," rather than attempted *attacks*.) He suggested, untruthfully, that the phone records surveillance had prevented any terrorism at all.

Another argument from the NSA's defenders was more profound. "Bulk collection" was not surveillance, contended Alexander, Clapper, and their allies. Surveillance occurred not when someone's search history, Fitbit records, or webcam imagery made their way into the NSA's data troves, but only when one of the intelligence agencies actually searched through them for patterns. It was the same distinction Mike Hayden had attempted at the dawn of STELLARWIND, now hardened into NSA dogma. Even more euphemistically, the NSA described the purely domestic internet communications its surveillance captured as "incidental," a term suggesting that such collection was inadvertent, rather than a cost of doing business. Bates secretly found in 2011 that "tens of thousands of wholly domestic communications" made their way into UPSTREAM collection by what an intelligence official later told reporters was an unavoidable result of the way the surveillance was architected.

Lurking within the redefinition was the seed of an honest statement about twenty-first-century digital surveillance. Clapper and his allies insisted that actual U.S. surveillance, particularly under Section 702, was still a targeted process. NSA and its partner agencies mined their massive data sets for specific patterns, specific activities, specific connections to specific people. But those searches required assembling those massive data sets. "It's like finding a needle in a haystack. If you have to—the terrorist being the needle," insisted Ruppersberger. "And if you need to find those terrorists throughout the world, you have to have the haystack." Indeed, replied Alexander's deputy, Chris Inglis, "It needs to be the whole haystack. As you comprise this and you put it together, it needs to be such that when you make a query, you come away confident that you have the whole answer."

Intelligence officials resisted congressional oversight even as they publicly cited it as one of the reasons why their surveillance was less alarming than it appeared. From their perspective, they had stayed within the framework Congress set with Section 702; and since May 2006, the domestic phone records collection had received FISA Court approval. All the democratic consent they needed came through the congressional intelligence committees or, when necessary for the most sensitive surveillance endeavors, the congressional leadership council known as the Gang of Eight. A significant portion of the public, horrified by the Snowden revelations, considered the arrangement a self-serving simulacrum of consent. That summer Alexander was heckled at a Las Vegas hacker conference by someone yelling "Freedom!" The general was left to insist, "Exactly, we stand for freedom," as shouts of "Bullshit!" erupted. During Alexander's retirement send-off the following spring, Clapper called the crowd "Eddie Snowden supporters."

Manning's disclosures inflicted a flesh wound to the Security State. Snowden's induced a coronary. The NSA, which styled itself the master of the internet, had somehow neglected the reality that, as Snowden wrote in his memoir, "the computer guy knows everything, or rather can know everything." Constructing a digital panopticon required, as a matter of technical necessity and economic interest, outside contractors like Snowden. Making the system work better required giving the Snowdens of the apparatus expansive administrator privileges. Security-state tribalism would prevent the emergence of very many Snowdens (and Mannings); fidelity to their mission did as well. But one Snowden had been catastrophic, and despite the rise of so-called "insider threat" detection efforts, there could be no way to screen out every potential Snowden if the surveillance apparatus was to continue to exist. For all these reasons, the Security State needed Edward Snowden in custody and made a far more fearsome example of him than it had of Manning. It also needed to assert and explain that he was motivated by something more sinister than freedom.

It had its narrative handed to it by circumstance. With the help of the WikiLeaks staffer Sarah Harrison—WikiLeaks was aligned with Snowden over the NSA documents, whatever Snowden's discomfort with Assange—Snowden attempted to fly to Ecuador in pursuit of asylum. He never made it out of a layover in Moscow. The United States, after vainly sending an extradition order to the Hong Kong authorities, canceled his passport, leaving him stranded—as it turned out, in the last place Washington wanted him. As his stay extended for six weeks in Sheremetyevo Airport, where he explained to an FSB officer that he was not going to cooperate with Russian intelligence, the United States and its allies went to extremes. They forced Bolivian President Evo Morales's plane to reroute on the false suspicion he was smuggling Snowden to asylum. Russian president Vladimir Putin, handed a delicious opportunity by his hapless American adversaries, granted asylum to Snowden instead.

Snowden had insisted consistently that he took no NSA documents out of Hong Kong, so they could not have fallen into Russian intelligence's possession. It made no difference. The fact that he was in Russia, even if he was there despite his intentions, was enough to portray him as a Russian asset. John Schindler, a conservative NSA veteran who became a chief Snowdenista antagonist on Twitter, explained that by definition, Snowden's flight into Moscow ought to be understood as a defection. It reflected the the Security State's inability to comprehend what Snowden had done outside of a framework of espionage. The fallback response was to mock Snowden, of all people, for his naïve understanding of the internet. On this theory every internet user knew or ought to have known that they consigned themselves to corporate and government surveillance, and made this bargain knowingly, and weren't just clicking ACCEPT on a terms-of-service agreement they didn't bother to read.

It was hard to square the argument with the other one they needed to make against Snowden, which was that the surveillance wasn't *that* intrusive. Some liberals preferred to imply Snowden was a "paranoid libertarian" crypto-rightist, as Princeton's Sean Wilentz did in *The New Republic*. To their left, even allies like Wyden kept Snowden at arm's length while attempting to legislate against the abuses Snowden exposed. "When there is a criminal charge—and here you're talking about espionage—I don't get into making comments," Wyden said about Snowden. An exception was Bernie Sanders. While there was "no question that he committed a crime," Sanders told CNN, Snowden "has gone a very long way in educating the people of our country and the people of the world about the power of private agency in terms of their surveillance over people of this country, over foreign leaders, and what they are doing." Sanders was a rare voice calling for "some form of clemency" for Snowden.

The NSA would retain far more than it lost. Two years after Snowden's leaks, a watered-down compromise between Obama, the NSA, and the Hill resulted in a ban on the bulk collection of domestic phone records, though the new measure still gave the NSA access to what would turn out to be extraordinary amounts of call records held by the telecoms. The tech giants disclaimed responsibility for PRISM—"the government blew it," Mark Zuckerberg insisted, whatever that meant. A strained relationship with Silicon Valley could not derail the NSA's bulk internet surveillance, since Section 702 made it compulsory pending the FISA Court's approval of the NSA's methodology. Meanwhile, surveillance capitalism in Silicon Valley and far beyond, so symbiotic with bulk surveillance, continued unimpeded. But the NSA no longer looked invulnerable. Exposed from within, it appeared fearful.

A great number of Americans would never be persuaded that Snowden's revelations were anything other than a hostile foreign machination. But that perspective conspicuously failed to recognize how dramatically Snowden's odyssey encapsulated that of much of the 9/11 generation. Snowden started out wanting to help his country win the war. Exposure to it only convinced him that its most important weapon had to be disarmed if his country was to remain the country he recognized. It turned out not to be Edward Snowden's country after all.

IN DECEMBER 2014 CLAPPER warned the Senate intelligence committee of imminent violence from outraged Muslims. Uprisings, fueled by dire accounts of American brutality, were likely, the Office of the Director of National Intelligence (ODNI) assessed, as was damage to crucial intelligence partnerships worldwide. It was a familiar prediction after thirteen years of Forever War. Committee members often made it themselves, especially when, as with Snowden or Manning, information inconvenient to the war emerged. This time they were its target.

The committee did not expect to find itself in this position. Six years earlier the panel had begun investigating CIA torture and found that the agency had lied about it so relentlessly as to create an alternate reality. Committee Democrats, though inclined to support the intelligence agencies, were preparing to expose the CIA's false narrative. For this the CIA and its allies had treated their congressional overseers like the enemy: not only spying on them but making the counteraccusation that *they*, in their mendacity, had spied on *it*, down to making a frivolous demand that the Justice Department prosecute the committee's lead investigator. It was a desperate lie to protect an edifice of even more desperate lies. Now, to top it off, the intelligence agencies delivered a threat: if the Senate declassified its torture report, it could have blood on its hands.

It wasn't only the Security State claiming this. The Obama White House backed the CIA over the Senate. Kerry, now secretary of state, told his old Senate colleagues that releasing their report could fracture the renewed war against jihadists in Iraq. But Clapper undercut whatever credibility Kerry's message carried. The breathlessness of ODNI's warnings made the CIA's mischaracterizations of the sixty-seven-hundred-page report conspicuous, as when it falsely said the committee identified the countries that hosted CIA black sites. "It was a poorly done intelligence product with clear factual errors and it inaccurately described the study we were about to release," remembered West Virginia's Jay Rockefeller. When the lead Senate torture investigator, Daniel Jones, pointed out the assessment's falseness, he remembered his ODNI interlocutor replying: "It doesn't matter what's in the report. It matters what people think is."

Jones was accustomed to such behavior by now. In a basement CIA satellite office in northern Virginia, sifting through the torture program's internal documentation, he came to understand that the agency had constructed a Big Lie, one that didn't have to be consistent. Under the pro-torture Bush, the CIA asserted that torture worked. For the anti-torture Obama, the agency modified its position to argue that no one could know for certain that torture *didn't* work. Fundamentally it was an American exceptionalist fable about valiant Americans who did messy things to dangerous people—or people who *could* have been dangerous—in order keep their countrymen safe, the premise of *24*. Conservative and centrist politicians embraced the fable, making martyrs of torturers along the way, and progressive politicians had to weigh the political costs of challenging it. But the rigor of Jones's investigation, along with the brazen overreach of the intelligence agencies, put Senate Democrats in the uncomfortable position of refuting the Big Lie.

Like Manning and Snowden, Jones started out as a member of the Security State. His patriotic post-9/11 journey led him to the FBI, where he worked as a counterterrorism analyst for four years before joining the Intelligence Committee staff. By then the committee had learned from *The New York Times*—not CIA director Hayden or his predecessor Goss—that back in 2005, senior CIA officials Jose Rodriguez and Gina Haspel had destroyed over ninety videotapes documenting the torture of Abu Zubaydah and Abdul Rahman al-Nashiri. The committee assigned Jones to investigate Hayden's claim that the agency's voluminous record-keeping ensured that Rodriguez and Haspel hadn't destroyed evidence of a crime. Poring through accounts from the Bangkok black site, the one Gina Haspel briefly ran, Jones discovered the reality concealed by the CIA's "enhanced interrogation" euphemism. Nothing that had already leaked to the press about torture was as graphic as the cables describing Abu Zubaydah's becoming catatonic from waterboarding to the point that bubbles formed from the water still in his open mouth, being locked in a coffin for 266 hours, or obeying his torturers like a dog when they snapped their fingers. All of it had been concealed even from the classified offices of the Senate overseers. "Everything that we were told was basically the opposite of what happened," he remembered. Jones, an institutionalist compared to Snowden and Manning, never considered slipping his findings to reporters, let alone WikiLeaks.

In March 2009 the committee nearly unanimously expanded Jones's investigation to the entire CIA torture program. With Leahy's truth and reconciliation commission proposal dead, the panel was now the sole venue for looking back. But the cost of GOP support was to exclude the Bush administration from Jones's purview. What Langley did would be viewed outside the context of what Cheney, Addington, Yoo, and others had demanded and facilitated. But as Jones began his broader work, Holder inadvertently complicated it. Durham's criminal investigation meant the CIA would not grant Jones interviews with key personnel, since they might incriminate themselves. It cost the investigation Republican support and planted the seeds of a CIA counterattack: *Senate Democrats didn't even bother talking to the CIA officials they railroaded.*

Chair Dianne Feinstein reached a deal with a nervous CIA director Panetta that spring. The CIA would provide the committee with a large cache of torture-relevant documents over a shared network drive in the classified CIA-controlled outpost. Only the agency's IT people would have access to the committee's digital work product. But as Jones pieced together the torture program, hundreds of documents the CIA placed on the Senate side of the drive would mysteriously disappear. Feinstein enlisted White House mediation, but still the documents went missing. That would remain in the back of Jones's mind when he discovered on the network a pivotal document.

The CIA had secretly compiled for Panetta a one-thousand-page narrative history of the torture program. It came to many of the same conclusions that Jones's team had. Not only was the brutality worse than anyone outside Langley was aware of, not only was it useless for developing intelligence, but the uselessness and the brutality locked the agency into lying about it. "It has thirteen findings. And one is, basically, they provided inaccurate information to support the use of EITs [torture]," Jones said.

But by spring 2013 Brennan was finally running the CIA, the institution to which he had devoted his life, and Brennan rejected Jones's findings. In particular, it was "flawed" for Jones to conclude that torture hadn't produced "unique intelligence" and that the CIA "deliberately misrepresented" the program. The CIA's official response flatly contradicted what the committee called the Panetta Review. Jones had noticed early on that senators were looking past the Big Lie. "I thought that's what people would be taken with—holy shit, we've been sold a bill of goods. But what they were really taken with was the brutality." Jones remembered the documents vanishing from his supposedly firewalled network, as well as the fact that his inquiry only existed because Rodriguez and Haspel had ordered the torture footage destroyed. One summer night, Jones snuck printed portions of the Panetta Review into his bag and, in violation of the Senate's agreement with the CIA, left the outpost. He drove to the Senate and locked the Panetta Review in a committee safe.

It remains a mystery, even to Jones, how the Panetta Review got placed on the shared network—whether it was the work of a sympathetic CIA officer or simply a mistake. Investigators would not have known to ask for the review. Although by then she already had the copy Jones had ferreted out, Feinstein formally requested the document from the CIA around Thanksgiving 2013. But Brennan grew alarmed when her colleague Mark Udall referred to it publicly. Brennan hadn't authorized its release, and negotiations over Jones's conclusions had grown heated. It led the CIA to a fateful decision. With Brennan's knowledge and approval to "use whatever means necessary" to determine how the Senate got the document, the agency surreptitiously bypassed the firewall to access Jones's work. Breaking its deal with the Senate, the CIA spied on its overseers. A forensic unit called the Cyber Blue Team reconstructed the investigators' emails. Spying on a Senate oversight committee, a fateful move under any condition, prompted an inspector-general investigation. After Obama backed the CIA, Feinstein revealed the spying on the Senate floor and accused the CIA of creating a constitutional crisis. "CIA hacking into, you know, Senate computers, nothing could be further from the truth," Brennan said in response. "I mean we wouldn't do that." A CIA attorney implicated in the torture program, Robert Eatinger, formally requested that the Justice Department open a case against Jones for espionage.

It was an absurd attempt at intimidation—Jones was incapable of hacking the CIA—and it demonstrated panic at the agency. But the CIA effort backfired. The inspector general vindicated the Senate, even on the Jones accusation, and excoriated the agency's "lack of candor." Still, the White House continued to back Brennan on the central point: declassifying the torture report. Behind closed doors, it helped the CIA keep much of the narrative heavily blacked out. "We tortured some folks," Obama acknowledged in August, but "it's important for us not to feel too sanctimonious in retrospect."

The Senate released the report in December. The story the CIA had helped tell about torture paving the path to bin Laden, as with the agency-aided Hollywood thriller *Zero Dark Thirty*, was revealed to be a lie. One of Jones's footnotes cited a 2011 document, "The Public Roll-Out," indicating "the CIA sought to publicly attribute the UBL operation to detainee reporting months prior to the execution of the operation." An entire annex rebutted a flurry of lies that Hayden had told the Senate during testimony on a single day in 2007.

But the CIA's resistance intensified. Brennan began a rebuttal press conference by narrating the 9/11 attacks for five minutes. After placing torture in the context of patriotic trauma, Brennan argued it was "unknowable" whether torture worked, meaning it was slanderous to call the CIA liars. Agency veterans, including Rodriguez and Hayden, went further in a book called *Rebuttal*. Senate Democrats were "almost street-like in their simplistic language and conclusions," Hayden insisted. Brennan even convened a panel, led by ex–Indiana Democratic senator Evan Bayh, to undermine the inspector general's conclusions about spying on the Senate. Brennan's deputy, Avril Haines, who tended to advocate maximum constraint in the Sustainable War on Terror, accepted Bayh's exonerating narrative.

It was a tribal response. Brennan and these alumni, known as "Formers," spoke for a generation of CIA officers implicated in torturing at least 119 people. Many of them, including Alfreda Bikowsky, Michael D'Andrea, and Haspel, remained at the agency; during Brennan's clash with the Senate, he quietly promoted someone over Haspel to run the clandestine service. Having won the fight over criminal liability for torture, the CIA would accept no political liability, and neither the truth nor the constitutional oversight of the Senate would be an obstacle. Glenn Carle, who interrogated a man he came to believe was innocent at an Afghanistan black site, explained the agency's paranoia: "We're always the ones left holding the bag after we're asked to mine the harbors or overthrow the government." But the CIA's response to the Senate was "intellectually shoddy, simple-minded, unnecessarily defensive, circle-the-wagons reactive and wrong and harmful." And to spy on the Senate "is flat criminal activity."

Asked years later if it was appropriate for ODNI to have told the Senate violence would result from the release of the report, a spokesman, Timothy Barrett, said the office stood by its warning, explaining that "lack of violence does not reflect a lack of threats."

EVEN IF MANNING, Snowden, and Jones were not recognizable leftists, it was, in the main, leftists who championed them, centrists and conservatives who disdained them, and liberals who weren't sure about them. Their actions were understood as resistance to the War on Terror, and so the only place for them would be on the left, however uncomfortably. Snowden had committed a radical act but was himself no radical. In 2019, he described "the major ideological conflict of my time" as "between the authoritarian and the liberal democratic."

Left-wing movement politics during the Obama years were not fueled by antiwar activism. The primary issues at that time concerned the increasing precarity of everyday life, such as the Occupy protests against a stillborn economic future. But antiwar perspectives and values were infused throughout the left. Both the Dreamers' fight for citizenship and the hostility it aroused spoke to the post-9/11 conception of immigration as a terrorism threat. Another social movement put on display what the War on Terror had brought back home, and whom it could be aimed against.

On August 9, 2014, in a largely Black suburb of St. Louis, police officer Darren Wilson fatally shot eighteen-year-old Michael Brown six times, twice in the head. Wilson, driving, chanced across Brown and a friend, who enraged him by crossing the street too close to his SUV. Wilson ordered them out of the road, an altercation followed, and Wilson chased the unarmed teenager. Brown's body lay in the baking heat of Ferguson, Missouri, for four hours. Six days of growing protests followed before Ferguson officials identified Wilson as the killer.

The stonewalling reflected the impunity the police had long held over majority-Black Ferguson. The Justice Department would later find that the cops looted residents by treating policework as an opportunity for "revenue generation." Wilson claimed he had been charged by Brown and feared for his life. A grand jury declined to indict the officer in November. A chorus of white justification across the political and journalistic spectrum warned against rushing to judge Wilson. Pushing against it were the activists of a movement on the rise called Black Lives Matter (BLM). A decentralized challenge to white supremacy, BLM had been born the previous year when cofounder Alicia Garza coined the phrase on Facebook in grief after a jury acquitted George Zimmerman of murdering seventeen-year-old Trayvon Martin. Now it mobilized.

Beginning in August, Fergusonites were reinforced by hundreds of mostly Black out-of-towners for enraged protests. Demonstrators threw rocks and batteries—the police would claim there were gunshots, though no officer was hit—burned police cars, looted stores, and burned buildings. Against that was a police response fit for an occupying army. The *St. Louis Post-Dispatch* reported that Ferguson's police "look far more like soldiers deployed to Iraq or Afghanistan than the police of decades ago." They sported ballistic helmets with night-vision mounts, body armor, pixelated camouflage fatigues, Ka-Bar-style knives favored by marines, wraparound sunglasses or goggles, desert boots, and sniper rifles. They drove giant black BearCat armored vehicles—the Ferguson police even had Humvees—mounted with satellite-dish sonic weapons known as long-range acoustic devices, which pummel eardrums. Officers leveled their M4 carbines at protesters and fired .60-caliber rubber bullets. One hit a pastor, Renita Lamkin, as she mediated between police and protesters demanding the release of local alderman Antonio French. Others hit reporters, including *The Intercept*'s Ryan Devereaux and *Bild*'s Lukas Hermsmeier, both of whom were arrested for "failing to disperse." Nighttime curfews and "keep walking" rules became licenses for police to arrest demonstrators and journalists such as *Washington Post* reporter Wesley Lowery and *HuffPost*'s Ryan J. Reilly. Police threw flash-bang grenades, obscured identifiers including their name tags, and intimidated protesters with dogs and doused them in tear gas.

The deliberately disproportionate, militarized response to basic demands for racial justice brought international condemnation, including from the UN commissioner for human rights. Palestinians tweeted advice for Ferguson protesters to defeat tear gas clouds by running against the wind. In a rare move, Amnesty International sent human rights observers to an American city. One of them was thirty-four-year-old Mandy Simon. Simon had spent much of the 2000s fighting against the War on Terror. "For years, I had worked with colleagues at ACLU and Amnesty as we warned about the dangers of militarizing the police, and now we were watching a small midwestern police department with military-grade weapons roll up against its citizens," said Simon. "To see those warnings manifest so clearly in front of our eyes was surreal and absolutely terrifying."

The Ferguson and St. Louis County police got their arsenal from the Defense Department. Since the 1990s the Pentagon had operated a program known as 1033, which transferred surplus military equipment to police departments. Journalist Radley Balko described a 1033 program newsletter from 2011, a year when the military distributed a record $500 million worth of hardware, bearing the tagline "From Warfighter to Crimefighter." It revealed that not only military equipment but military culture—or a facsimile of it—flowed down to police, validating their certainty that they manned the thin line between civilization and savagery. But even more valuable to police than the 1033 program were the counterterrorism grants distributed to cash-strapped precincts from the Department of Homeland Security. In fiscal 2014 DHS told Congress it planned to disburse $1.6 billion of such funding, which enabled purchases of BearCats by police from such unlikely terror targets as Fargo, North Dakota; Syracuse, New York; and Manchester, New Hampshire. Thanks to a 2007 law tacitly nodding at the reality that terrorism was rare, cops only had to spend "not less than 25 percent" of the money on "law enforcement terrorism prevention activities."

Helping police make their quota was a cottage industry marketing anti-Islam training to them. Seminars offered by a former FBI agent, John Guandolo, reportedly instructed that mosques enjoyed no constitutional rights, as such Islamic centers were "potential military compounds," and encouraged investigations into local ties to the Muslim Brotherhood. In February 2012 Guondolo's Strategic Engagement Group delivered a three-day-long instruction to Nashville-area police in such topics, just as the Murfreesboro Islamic Center expansion was proceeding. The course taught that under sharia, "non-Muslims must ultimately convert or submit to Islam or be killed." NYPD commissioner Ray Kelly cooperated with a movie called

The Third Jihad that accused Muslims of planning to "infiltrate and dominate" America. Kelly said he regretted his participation, two years after the department screened it for more than fourteen hundred officers.

Supplying military equipment and counterterrorism training to police followed the economic logic of permanent war. With the ground wars in Iraq and Afghanistan persisting, innovative hardware for them would remain in development; with both reduced in manpower, priority, and budgeting, defense contractors sought new markets. The Department of Homeland Security was a consumer as well as a distributor. Customs and Border Protection flew unarmed versions of the Predator over the southern border. Those flights were pioneers of the homeward migration of the war's technological innovations, particularly after the military's drone budget plateaued around 2012. That year DHS took control of a military camera suite called the Kestrel. Mounting the 360-degree-capable device on tethered aerostats like the ones that once floated above U.S. bases in Afghanistan, DHS suddenly saw "miles [of border] with a single image frame," an official enthused. A year earlier the Miami-Dade police bought a T-Hawk drone from the military contractor Honeywell after receiving the first FAA certification of any police department to operate one.

Drones were hardly the only Forever War technology acquired by police. Several bought a device called a Stingray, which spoofed cell towers, enabling it to siphon location and communicant data from connecting phones. It had previously been the sort of surveillance tool reserved for the NSA or the FBI. Journalist George Joseph soon found that police departments in Baltimore, Milwaukee, and Tallahassee "overwhelmingly" used Stingrays in "nonwhite and low-income communities."

By the time Black Lives Matter galvanized people beyond Ferguson, a white backlash, much of it uniformed, knew how to characterize the movement. The sheriff of Georgia's Gwinnett County, Butch Conway, said Ferguson protesters ignited a "firestorm" that "dehumanized police." Speaking as if cops were at greater risk to suffer a "slaughter" than inflict one, Conway called the protesters "domestic terrorists with an agenda." *Fox & Friends* interviewed a North Carolina police chief forced into retirement after calling Black Lives Matter activists terrorists. "It is a terrorist group, if you can march down the streets and you can call for the death of police officers and a race of people," the ex-chief said. In Minneapolis the police union chief, Bob Kroll, denounced Black Lives Matter as a "terrorist organization" and not "a voice for the black community in Minneapolis." Patrisse Khan-Cullors, a cofounder of Black Lives Matter, titled her memoir *When They Call You a Terrorist.*

Black people had indeed experienced terrorism—from the planter aristocracy, from agents of the state, from white vigilantes—for the entirety of their existence in the United States, and for the supremacist reasons cited by Grandpa Millar at Elohim City. Now, after they had stood in the streets against BearCats and sniper rifles, a nativist–police alliance portrayed Black liberation as terrorism. To combat it, they had the same prescriptions for police as for the rest of the Security State during the War on Terror: brutality and impunity. They bristled as Obama's Justice Department chipped away at that impunity through civil rights investigations of police departments, much as the CIA had resented the meager torture investigations. Their grievances channeled the politics of the War on Terror toward a new destination, a place more viscerally satisfying than the foreign wars, which had proven agonizing, humiliating, and disillusioning. There was an expanding set of enemies at home, and now there were new tools to confront them.

In Hong Kong, Snowden had warned that the architecture of mass surveillance was outpacing any hope of democratic control. Policy had already trumped law; STELLARWIND proved it. It would only be a matter of time before a malefactor took control of the White House and saw the possibilities that mass surveillance offered.

"A new leader will be elected. They'll flip the switch, say that because of the 'crisis,' because of the dangers we face in the world, some new and unpredicted threat," Snowden said, "we need more authority. We need more power. And there will be nothing the people can do at that point to oppose it. And it'll be turn-key tyranny."

CHAPTER SEVEN

THE DECADENT PHASE OF THE WAR ON TERROR AND THE RISE OF TRUMP

2013–2016

A t the dawn of Obama's second term, the War on Terror, for all its supposed sustainability, reached a point of destabilization. The source of the instability was the war's central feature: its endlessness. Protracted war gave rise to a successor organization to al-Qaeda that was more ambitious and more psychopathic. The Security State fought to preserve its authorities while it dealt with the legitimacy crisis prompted by Manning's, Snowden's, and Jones's disclosures, and to keep the war itself on a path of equilibrium. It was aligned with Obama in deemphasizing the war, preferring other geopolitical priorities like climate change or great-power competition, even as both acquiesced to its escalatory pressures. Meanwhile, an embittered right increasingly came to view the war more as a civilizational struggle than as a series of specific battlefield campaigns. All of this rendered the War on Terror something elites no longer enjoyed engaging with but couldn't imagine abandoning. What resulted was an exhausted, decadent phase of the conflict. It began with an attempt by desperate men to force their own end to the conflict.

Men who had been locked inside Guantanamo Bay for years, some having endured physical torture, nearly all enduring the mental torture of indefinite detention without charge, recognized there was no way out for them. Obama had pledged to close Guantanamo—never mind the fine print about Gitmo North and his acceptance of indefinite detention—but four years later, there they remained. The absence of hope became resolution. They decided to refuse food. Their deaths would testify to the injustice of their captivity.

The final straw came in February 2013, when guards took their Korans for "searches." One detainee, Obaidullah, explained, "Eleven years of my life have been taken from me and now, by the latest actions of the authorities, they have also taken my dignity and disrespected my religion." By June, at least 106 of the remaining 166 detainees were refusing food. Guantanamo was no longer a synecdoche for terrorism, torture, impunity, or broken promises. It was the scene of real human suffering, and the world once again paid attention.

Both the strike and the renewed focus on Guantanamo Bay caught the jailers off guard. Bill Lietzau, the Rumsfeld Pentagon holdover whom Obama had put in charge of detention policy, insisted the Koran searches were necessary to expose "improvised weapons" that had somehow been hidden within the pages. The solution that the military's Joint Task Force–Guantanamo employed combined brutality with humiliation. Guards in riot gear seized skeletal detainees and bound them to infirmary beds with wrist and ankle restraints. Medical staff passed a feeding tube up detainees' noses—sometimes lubricated with olive oil, creating a risk of inflammatory pneumonia—and down through their throats. A Yemeni striker, Samir Naji al Hasan Moqbel, described "agony in my chest, throat and stomach." The medical staff even inserted a catheter into Moqbel's penis. As long as Obama was commander in chief, he felt obliged to defend the procedure. "I don't want these individuals to die," he said in April.

The measures the Joint Task Force took reflected their architect. John Kelly's venomous comments about civilians were overshadowed by respect for his son's death in Afghanistan, and after Bob Gates chose Kelly for his military assistant, his fourth star was assured. Within a year, Obama made Kelly head of the military's Southern Command, responsible for delicate security and political relationships from Guatemala to Chile. But while the president rhetorically looked forward to the end of the War on Terror, Kelly vocally advocated fighting for as long as it took. Speaking in 2013 at the dedication of a marine regiment's Afghanistan war memorial, Kelly predicted America would be at war "for years, if not decades to come," something he said "may be inconvenient to some." Kelly was not without insight about the nature of the war. After Fallujah and Sangin, he had no illusion of victory, only a determination to fight what he interpreted as a war of national survival. "It is not in our power to end it, but simply to fight it, until our murderous enemy, who hates us with a visceral disgust for everything we stand for, either gives up or we kill him," Kelly said.

Few by now paid attention to Kelly's invective. Anyone discomfited by it gave him a wide berth, since he was the only four-star Gold Star parent. The result was that Kelly was in command of a wartime prison that Obama sought to close. He set to work breaking the hunger strike.

Kelly's tactics became a debacle one predawn morning in April. A senior defense official recalled that Kelly had notified the Pentagon that an extraction was about to take place. Lietzau warned Kelly it would become a fiasco. Hunger strikers who had blocked surveillance cameras nevertheless awoke to find guards demanding they separate from their communal housing—a privilege for compliant detainees—and into individual cells. Told to lie on the ground, detainees instead threw water bottles at the guards. They grabbed broomsticks to keep the guards at bay and struck them when the opportunity presented. The Joint Task Force responded by firing rubber bullets in the enclosed space of a barracks, but the detainees managed, remarkably, to fend them off for hours.

When that failed to stop the protest, Kelly realized he could break the strike by denying the outside world information about it. By September he ordered an end to updating reporters on how many detainees were striking, simultaneously claiming that most had begun eating again. Kelly's spokesperson explained the blackout as an effort to end a "self-perpetuating story." Even calling the strike a "hunger strike" offended Kelly, who insisted on the absurd euphemism "Long-Term Non-Religious Fasting." The detainees could not maintain public attention, their only asset, if Kelly cut off access to them. It turned out to be a far more successful tactic than brutality. Neglect favored the Guantanamo status quo, and over time Kelly expanded the press blackout throughout the wartime prison.

As unsubtle as Kelly was about his opposition to closing Guantanamo, Obama had put himself in a position in which he would pay a high price for firing the general. Opposing Kelly wasn't worth it to Obama. He could truthfully argue that the episode made it even more urgent that he repatriate most of the 166 detainees present during the strike. But he conceded that emptying Guantanamo would mean circumnavigating Kelly, and that ensured that Obama would leave office with 41 people still in Guantanamo. The right had triumphed in a battle it hadn't prioritized before Obama's election. While Kelly might have been more caustic than most Security Staters, he kept Obama in check on Guantanamo, which suited their purposes.

The fight over Guantanamo Bay revealed a certain exhaustion with the War on Terror. Inertia played a bigger role in keeping Guantanamo open than passion did. The right was fighting against Obama more than it was fighting for Guantanamo. Whatever partial victory Obama might claim, he had to grind it out, and it would be nothing satisfactory to anyone concerned with justice. The exhaustion extended beyond Guantanamo, too. In 2015 a respected consortium of pro-peace physicians, International Physicians for the Prevention of Nuclear War (IPPNW), translated into English a War on Terror "body count" from Iraq, Afghanistan, and Pakistan. Its findings were staggering, far higher than competing epidemiological studies. The wars, "directly or indirectly," had led to the deaths of 1 million Iraqis, 220,000 Afghans, and 80,000 Pakistanis in the first twelve years after 9/11. IPPNW explained that lower estimates had been the result of poor available data and political timidity in establishing casualty models. Its goal in presenting these figures was not merely accuracy but to force accountability. Yet American media largely ignored IPPNW's conclusions. By 2015 the various difficulties in determining death tolls—from a lack of official data to political controversies over calculating it—had functionally obliterated the truth about the lethality of the U.S. wars. Accepting any of the various estimates, like accepting definitions of the enemy, was effectively a political act.

Exhaustion also had the perverse effect of substituting an attribution of collective guilt for a pursuit of war. That showed itself in Boston. In April 2013, during the Boston Marathon, the brothers Dzhokhar and Tamerlan Tsarnaev, children of a Chechen-Kyrgyz asylee, detonated two bombs they rigged from pressure cookers. Three people were killed and 264 were injured in a long-predicted terror attack at a civic sporting event. Obama praised Boston's resilience—symbolized by the Red Sox's David Ortiz's "this is our fuckin' city" speech—in his National Defense University speech, as a path to argue that the U.S. didn't need to respond with further repressive measures. James Clapper, at an intelligence sector breakfast in northern Virginia, expressed irritation with the suggestion that Boston was an intelligence failure. Anyone who expected the intelligence agencies to have anticipated and found two young immigrant men before they committed such an atrocity was really calling for a more intrusive Security State, Clapper said, weeks before Snowden proved how intrusive that Security State truly was.

Since the Tsarnaevs acted on their own, any politician inclined to treat Boston as another 9/11 didn't have a country or an organization to bomb or invade in retaliation. But once Obama and the Security State aligned on a subdued reaction to Boston, the right interpreted it as another surrender. They found unlikely allies in Russia, which had notified the FBI before the bombings that the Tsarnaevs were potentially dangerous. A congressional fact-finding delegation to Moscow (bizarrely featuring the actor Steven Seagal) resulted in a statement of purpose from its right-wing members. "If Americans and Russia can conquer space together, we can defeat radical Islam together," said Representative Steve King of Iowa. Robert Spencer blamed the "see-no-jihad, hear-no-jihad FBI" for purging the Islamophobic training material. In Washington, Lindsey Graham and others reminded Clapper and the Security State that "we're at war with radical Islamists and we need to up our game." But now the Ground Zero Mosque generation was in Congress, and it made Graham look timid.

A Kansan Tea Partier, West Pointer, and businessman animated by a political Christianity, Mike Pompeo had been a reliable demagogue through-out his brief congressional career. He had made the Benghazi crusade his own. Returning from a trip to Guantanamo during the hunger strike, Pom-peo quipped, "They look to me like a lot of them have put on weight." But in June, responding to the marathon attack, Pompeo took to the House floor for a career-defining speech.

He accused "Islamic leaders across America" not only of silence after the Tsarnaevs' attack but of being, through their silence, "potentially complicit in these acts, and, more importantly still, in those that may well follow." It was beside the point that Islamic leaders across America had condemned the bombings. The head of the California chapter of the maligned CAIR had said that anyone "who claims an Islamic basis for such a heinous crime is no more faithful to the teachings of Islam than a KKK member who claims a biblical basis in committing bigoted crimes." Pompeo's point was to dictate what those Islamic leaders "must say." And by 2013 it was par for the course on the right to view Obama as a step removed from terror itself. "Is the Bos-ton killer eligible for Obama Care to bring him back to health?" tweeted Donald Trump.

That was too uncouth for a Security State that wanted to avoid involve-ment in a culture war it knew was a destabilizing force. Even as the GOP moved further in that direction, the Security State looked instead to the reliability of its Republican allies in positions of power, like Mike Rogers at the House Intelligence Committee, who laced into Snowden. Richard Burr, Rogers's counterpart in the Senate, was another bulwark. Once the 2014 election gave the Republicans Senate control, Burr, now the Intelligence Committee chair, ensured the suppression of Feinstein's CIA torture report. Feinstein had sent the unseen classified version of the full report to the security agencies as a measure to prevent them from ever again embracing torture. Burr demanded the copies back, ensuring no one could ever obtain and release the report through the Freedom of Information Act, from which Congress is exempt. Obama rejected Burr's request, but the agencies refused to even take the torture report out of its packaging. The Justice Department used Burr's request to thwart FOIA lawsuits for the report. Burr was not merely undermining his colleagues; he was assuring Brennan and the CIA that they no longer had to worry about their overseers imposing an end to impunity.

There was another obstacle to the Security State's quest for stability. Much as Obama rewarded Kelly with SOUTHCOM, in 2012, he made one of McChrystal's and Petraeus's key deputies head of the Defense Intelligence Agency (DIA), a military intelligence backwater. Mike Flynn had transformed the Joint Special Operations Command into an intelligence heavyweight and wanted to do the same for the DIA. Yet his erratic personality and questionable hold on reality—his staff used to label his misstatements "Flynn facts"—alarmed his subordinates and his superiors. Improbably, he traveled to Moscow. The same month King's delegation visited to learn about the Tsarnaevs, the GRU, Russia's military intelligence giant, gave Flynn an unprecedented welcome to its headquarters. It was a "great trip" to talk "a lot about the way the world's unfolding," Flynn would remember.

Flynn was ousted by April 2014, but there would be no stability dividend for the Security State. A catastrophe was on the horizon, one that ought to have demonstrated conclusively the futility of the war and the danger of waging it.

THE SECURITY STATE WAS NOT alone in longing for stability in the War on Terror. Abu Muhammad al-Maqdisi had once been in the elite tier of theologians who justified violence. He had called the Saudi royal family un-Islamic when bin Laden was still pledging them his service. For his part, bin Laden thought Maqdisi went too far. Maqdisi was al-Qaeda through and through, but had mentored Zarqawi in a Jordanian prison. For three decades, Maqdisi had been a legend in jihadist circles. Then, suddenly, he became a relic.

Like the rest of al-Qaeda, Maqdisi set his own obsolescence into motion. His legacy was Zarqawi, creator of the most nihilistic, most relevant, and least controllable al-Qaeda franchise. Al-Qaeda in Iraq rebranded as an even more extreme outfit but found its real opportunity for rebirth once it entered the Syrian jihad under its third commander, the hardened fighter Abu Bakr al-Baghdadi. Baghdadi had been a prisoner of the U.S. occupation. Camp Bucca's commanding officer recalled that Baghdadi had told him, "I'll see you guys in New York." For chief theologian, Baghdadi chose another Maqdisi protege, Turki al-Binali. These religious extremists were more hard-line than orthodox. The Iraqis who joined them were often former Baathists, religious novices mostly interested in sanctification for their revenge fantasies. Their theology was heavy on declaring other Muslims to be un-Islamic and therefore permissible to kill or dominate.

Baghdadi's growing army, a confederation of factions, provided al-Qaeda with most of its strength in Syria. But he bristled at the Pakistan-based command's persistent disrespect. In 2013, after Zawahiri ruled against him in a power struggle, Baghdadi did the unthinkable: he not only split from al-Qaeda but his forces fought it, eventually ousting al-Qaeda's Nusra Front from five hundred crucial miles of border crossing into Turkey. Then, in a historic turn, Baghdadi marched his estimated six to ten thousand soldiers back into his native Iraq. As his army entered Mosul in June 2014, the U.S.-built Iraqi army, central to every American exit strategy, fled.

Baghdadi used Iraq's second city to declare the fulfillment of a jihadist fantasy: the caliphate had returned, reborn as what Baghdadi now called the Islamic State, or ISIS. As its bulldozers erased the border barriers between Iraq and Syria, the so-called Islamic State portrayed itself as an avenger of Islam against the imperialist Sykes–Picot Agreement that had shaped the modern Middle East after World War I. "All Muslims," in turn, had to obey Baghdadi. "The legality of all emirates, groups, states, and organizations, becomes null by the expansion of the khalifah's authority and arrival of its troops to their areas," declared spokesman Abu Muhammad al-Adnani.

Maqdisi had devoted his life to the restoration of the caliphate. But with its fetishized violence, especially gendered violence, and punitive theocracy, this was a perversion of how even he understood it—however familiar the ISIS Caliphate would have been to Grandpa Millar of Elohim City. It was obvious, even to the apologists for 9/11, that the Islamic State was not Islamic. ISIS were "deviants," declared Maqdisi as he waged a flame war against Binali. Committed jihadis were apoplectic that a cynical thug had crowned himself leader of global Islam. "The gangs of al-Baghdadi are living in a fantasy world," said a member of a rival Syrian jihadist militia. "You cannot establish a state through looting, sabotage and bombing." Maqdisi's friend and fellow al-Qaeda luminary, Abu Qatada, explained that Salafist theologians were there to spark the revolution that more qualified men would inherit: "We cannot run governments. We can't even run a nursery school, let alone a caliphate." Like bin Laden, Maqdisi and Abu Qatada believed global Islam wasn't ready to establish a caliphate, least of all one created by "thugs and gangsters [who] have no religious credentials."

ISIS didn't disagree. "If you think people will accept the Islamic project [voluntarily], you're wrong," one militant stated. "They have to be forced at first. The other groups think that they can convince people and win them over but they're wrong." Yet ISIS recognized the dilemma posed by declaring a caliphate that lacked religious legitimacy in the eyes of even the most hardcore jihadists. Binali first tried to bribe Maqdisi and Abu Qatada into supporting ISIS. When that didn't work, ISIS denounced them as "stooges" of the West and "misleading scholars." Out of necessity, it adopted the absurd critique that eminent jihadist theologians were no more than tools of apostate regimes. Abu Ali al-Anbari, a high-ranking cleric in ISIS, lectured extensively on what the author Hassan Hassan described as "the illegitimacy of institutions in Muslim countries, including mosques and courts." When Maqdisi gestured at reconciliation, ISIS texted him a file whose password was "Maqdisi the pimp, the sole of the tyrant's shoe, son of the English whore."

Al-Qaeda, like the Marquis de Lafayette, lost control of its revolution. At its height it commanded dozens of adherents with Western passports; Baghdadi attracted thousands of such individuals. The 9/11 hijackers included men with advanced degrees. ISIS's recruits included people for whom, as a relative told journalist Mike Giglio, it was the only way to afford a family. Like many an eclipsed radical, Maqdisi was rattled to the point of disillusionment. Al-Qaeda had birthed a jihad "of spite," he reflected to *The Guardian*. Now that the revolution was in the hands of the thugs of ISIS, even 9/11 seemed discredited. "The actions in New York and Washington, no matter how great they appeared to be—the bottom line is they were spiteful."

If al-Qaeda was ISIS's spurned father, the War on Terror was its mother. Washington's compounding post-9/11 errors gave ISIS life and then opportunity. Zarqawi could not have created al-Qaeda in Iraq (AQI) had the Bush administration not invaded. The occupation gave Zarqawi the chance to recruit followers who were hardened through fighting U.S. soldiers and marines. Baghdadi's fury had grown in the U.S. prison at Camp Bucca. The surge empowered Nouri al-Maliki, who erased the gains of the Anbar Awakening by suppressing Sunni Iraqis, giving AQI its new lease on life. The American withdrawal from Iraq, however inevitable and prompted by the Iraqis, left behind a force that was no match for Baghdadi. The War on Terror led directly to an enemy that was more powerful and more nihilistic than the earlier generation of jihadis, and it was out for vengeance. ISIS dressed the Westerners it kidnapped and beheaded in orange jumpsuits like those worn by Guantanamo detainees. Others it placed in stress positions or waterboarded, in homage to the CIA. After more than a decade of occupation, bombing, surveillance, detention, and torture, it was ISIS, not the Security State, that threatened al-Qaeda's existence. ISIS drove off from Mosul in twenty-three hundred U.S.-made Humvees, encapsulating the War on Terror's legacy.

Charles Lister of the Brookings Institution spoke for many when he called Baghdadi's declaration of the Caliphate "likely the most significant development in international jihadism since 9/11." But the response established during the surge held. The Security State's reaction to the fall of Mosul was to return to war in Iraq, not to consider that the rise of the Caliphate resulted from nearly fifteen years of conflict. Obama, who had months earlier suggested ISIS was a "jayvee squad [in] Lakers uniforms," conceded, "There will be some short-term, immediate things that need to be done militarily." The pattern for the remainder of the Obama administration involved compelling the president to ratchet up participation in the war, which came as a bitter heartbreak to him. McCain and Graham argued that the calamity of the Caliphate was the result of Obama's withdrawal, not the unprovoked invasion they championed in 2003. Fox News, in the wake of Benghazi, settled on this narrative.

There was little liberal resistance. No one wished to defend a withdrawal that indisputably failed to secure Iraq from the Caliphate. Some pointed out that the Iraqis had insisted on the U.S. departure, but it made little difference. While conservatives found it easier to blame Obama personally, the president only exposed the untenability of the American position in Iraq. He had made boastful statements about "moving forward from a position of strength" when anticipating withdrawal in 2010. Now ISIS was marching south on Baghdad while besieging a Yazidi minority that fled up Mount Sinjar with their elders, children, and the infirm rather than be raped and owned by ISIS. With the entire enterprise in Iraq facing a Saigon moment, Obama united with the Security State to prevent it.

There was consensus, in the Security State and on the right, that a 2003-style reinvasion was unthinkable. That left fighting a war on Sustainable terms. The United States would raid as necessary, detain minimally, surveil maximally, and use as a tentpole air strikes and "advisory" military missions that foregrounded local "partner" forces. It also reached a tacit accommodation to permit militias controlled by Iran external-security chief Qassem Soleimani to attack ISIS on the ground as U.S. warplanes harassed it above. To render the situation even more Sustainable, Obama leveraged two figures of Security State continuity, General John Allen and the longtime diplomat Brett McGurk, to coordinate a global coalition of nations that considered the Caliphate a disaster. The thin end of the wedge, the one that gave the emerging war a humanitarian cast, was stopping the agony atop Mount Sinjar. U.S. bombs began falling on Iraq again in August. The alignment of the ISIS era was born. Designed by General Martin Dempsey and known as By, With, and Through, it was a strategy of persistence and inconspicuousness. Put another way, an exhausted United States wanted the Iraqi military it had smashed, rebuilt, and bankrolled to fight its war for it.

But Washington found the bill from its earlier mistakes had come due. There would be no Anbar Awakening–style Sunni tribal revolt, not after Maliki, with the aid of Joe Biden, had remained in power to persecute the Sunnis, not even after the U.S. pushed Maliki aside for Haider al-Abadi, who knew how to cultivate both Iran and America. In Syria, where the CIA could not find the absurdly named "moderate rebels" it wanted to support, a U.S. effort at building a Sunni force against ISIS failed spectacularly. CENTCOM's General Lloyd Austin testified in September 2015 that he could count its membership on his hand after a year and $500 million. But once again, failure did not mean *finality*. It meant *escalation*.

Saving Baghdad was nonnegotiable for the military and the intelligence agencies. But by now, doing so exposed a conspicuous weakness: The

Security State's actions to avert disaster kept the War on Terror perpetually on the precipice of disaster. The Security State escalated to *maintain*, a position that kept it from achieving any finality, let alone one that could pass for victory. It failed to appreciate two factors. First, maintenance of the Forever War incubated even worse enemies than the ones the war sought to destroy. Second, maintenance strengthened the audacity of those who considered the Security State and liberals the crucial obstacle to attaining victory. Flynn would soon recast his humiliation at Clapper's hands as martyrdom for "the stand I took on radical Islamism and the expansion of al Qaeda and its associated movements."

Conservatives, unwilling to propose outright reinvasion, reached instead for a framework for understanding ISIS that would double as an indictment of Obama for being too weak to fight it. The civilizational subtext of the War on Terror now became explicit. To conservatives, ISIS's unspeakable brutality confirmed the barbarism of Islam that liberals refused to admit. In fact, ISIS itself had so few Islamic credentials that it tried to buy Maqdisi's and Abu Qatada's support. Yet a rising portion of the American right became convinced that the ISIS Caliphate proved they had been right all along in warning that Islam licensed terrorism. Hawkishness was now no longer something the right advocated against people overseas, but against a perceived foreign invader at home. It helped that Obama called ISIS "not Islamic," thereby demonstrating to conservatives what position they had to adopt in response. "As we sit here this morning, in the face of radical Islam," Petraeus's army mentor and surge architect Jack Keane testified in January 2015, "U.S. policymakers refuse to accurately name the movement as radical Islam." Leaders of the Security State avoided the argument over "Radical Islamic Terror." They considered arguments over apportioning blame to Islam both vulgar and outside their mandate—a domestic political question, one that the Constitution kept outside the purview of generals and intelligence chieftains. Functionally, that meant dismissing the vulnerability of American Muslims to a toxic and dangerous atmosphere as someone else's problem, no matter how much the war they waged and protected was jeopardizing the lives and freedom of their Muslim neighbors.

Early in the evening of February 10, 2015, Deah Barakat, a twenty-three-year-old University of North Carolina dental student, answered his door to a neighbor in their condominium complex, Craig Hicks. Hicks raised his .357 and murdered Barakat with multiple shots. He entered the Barakat home to then kill Yusor Abu-Salha, Barakat's wife, and Yusor's sister Razan. Hicks, who turned himself in, claimed he snapped after seeing a car parked in his spot. At their funeral Yusor and Razan's father, Mohammad, stated, "We have no doubt why they died." A professor of Islamic studies who taught Barakat at N.C. State told *The New Yorker*, "Muslim Americans have [a systematic feeling of insecurity] vis à vis a certain sector of the society that is becoming more vocal and increasingly comfortable expressing not just its dislike for Islam but its profound distrust."

The year of the North Carolina slayings would see a 67 percent rise in hate crimes against Muslims. Yet when the Security State interacted with American Muslim communities, it was not for their protection. The Department of Homeland Security's Countering Violent Extremism program was a "community-based" initiative of Obama's designed to be a showcase for humane, vigilant, Sustainable domestic counterterrorism. Its name was deliberately agnostic as to *whose* violent extremism was the issue, but its overwhelming focus was on U.S. Muslim communities. American Muslims seethed at the euphemisms of the War on Terror, but from the opposite position of the right's, since those euphemisms obscured the precariousness of their lives. Federal prosecutors, FBI liaisons, and Homeland Security officials swore their community empowerment meetings weren't actually the intelligence-gathering enterprises that internal FBI documents called opportunities to "strengthen our investigative, intelligence gathering and collaborative abilities to be proactive in countering violent extremism." Through CVE, the Sustainable War on Terror didn't need to label anyone as a Radical Islamist Terrorist to justify treating them that way. When Obama held a scheduled CVE summit at the White House days after the slayings, an administration official assured *The Guardian*, "This is not an intelligence-gathering summit." Meanwhile, denunciations of ISIS by American Muslim leaders were so fervent that a September 2014 press conference condemning what one called the "Anti-Islamic State" actually featured a prominent appearance from the Department of Homeland Security's CVE chief.

The Security State continued to fear blame for missing the next attack, and it noted with great alarm that ISIS's appeal to disaffected Muslim youth in the United States far surpassed anything al-Qaeda had been able to manage. Its influence was especially conspicuous online. Through Twitter, Skype, and Telegram, Americans, especially alienated youths, found themselves in conversations with ISIS members or supporters who, as one radicalization manual instructed, shared their joys and sadnesses. Like fascists and cultists everywhere, ISIS justified violence by stoking feelings of cultural and religious besiegement by outsiders. They dissuaded new followers from exposing themselves to mainstream Islam. The community ISIS offered could feel profound. "I [now] actually have brothers and sisters. I'm crying," a woman in her early twenties from rural Washington State tweeted after her ISIS friends convinced her to convert. Radicalization over the internet was something the FBI knew how to leverage and exploit. Its agents and informants infiltrated platforms popular with ISIS, built relationships, and through them facilitated arrestable offenses by their new screen pals. "We're not going to wait for the person to mobilize on his own timeline," explained the bureau's counterterrorism chief, Michael B. Steinbach.

The FBI was by now in the hands of James Comey, nominated by Obama for his Republican pedigree and his reputation for integrity after the 2004 surveillance-law showdown at John Ashcroft's bedside. Snowden revealed that Comey and his allies had *not* stopped the domestic internet surveillance that, for years, they implied they had obstructed; they were now only lawyering it better. Comey displayed no interest in learning what might compel a young American to kill for ISIS. He compared ISIS's social-media presence to a "devil sitting on the shoulder saying, 'Kill, kill, kill, kill' all day long."

For all Comey's dedication to surveillance, he had no answer for psychopaths like Omar Mateen, who swore vengeance for the slain Muslims of the War on Terror and murdered forty-nine people at Orlando's Pulse LGBT nightclub in 2016. When Comey could not solve his security problems, he exploited them. In an age of mass surveillance he knew intimately, he had the audacity to claim that cell phone encryption created an unreasonable "darkness" for the FBI and called on the tech firms to build him a back door. When technologists informed him that creating one would jeopardize everyone's digital security, Comey replied that with that attitude, Americans wouldn't have gotten to the moon. He found an opportunity through a locked iPhone belonging to an ISIS-loyal married couple who killed fourteen in a mass shooting in San Bernardino in December 2014. Comey took a shocked Apple to court to compel them to jailbreak not just the couple's phone, but effectively everyone's. Before a judge could rule, the FBI admitted that it was able to purchase a commercially available software exploit that unlocked the phone, a feat Comey had earlier insisted was impossible.

European nativists used ISIS to spark panic over Islam. Millions of refugees from Syria, Libya, and elsewhere were desperately fleeing ISIS. Syria, Jordan, and Lebanon had already taken in millions of Iraqis. Now people sought to cross the Mediterranean for Europe. Geert Wilders and Anders Breivik had already provided a framework for understanding the exodus: those fleeing ISIS were no different from ISIS themselves, conquering Europe through the civilization jihad. The potency of their critique in a time of widening wealth inequality and political exhaustion made liberal governments across the continent buckle.

Exposing the impotence of the established order was a specialty of ISIS. On November 13, 2015, it atypically launched an al-Qaeda-style multi-location attack on six targets across Paris. It was an unspeakable atrocity, involving at least five suicide bombers, that slaughtered 130 and wounded

494 at, among other places, an Eagles of Death Metal show at the Bataclan, where ISIS took hostages. Authorities immediately described one ISIS killer who had accompanied migrants from Syria. Another was from south of Paris, which only strengthened the vitriol of those on the right who saw their Islamic minorities as a public menace. But the reality of the migration crisis was the anguish of the father of young Alan Kurdi, a three-year-old boy who drowned in the Mediterranean as his family fled ISIS.

Again, the American right looked to Europe as a harbinger. With ISIS overwhelming the continent, by gun and by refugee, Islam was on the attack again, enabled by useful-idiot liberals and their treasonous, neutered, useless security barons. For the American right it was the second front in a civilizational war; Obama's allegedly open borders were the first front, through which migrants from Mexico and Central America entered at will. By 2015 the nationalist news site *Breitbart* was pronouncing it to be one big war. Citing unnamed private security contractors, it reported on a "Muslim prayer rug" (which looked like nothing so much as a torn red-and-white checked Adidas shirt) supposedly found on the southern border. The sheer absurdity of the claim was less important than what it revealed about a white nativist appetite for a narrative of besiegement, replacement, abandonment, and betrayal. Jeff Sessions and his immigration adviser, the Duke University anti–"radical Islam" activist Stephen Miller, went to find proof. Along with the Texan provocateur Senator Ted Cruz, they demanded the administration disclose the "immigration histories" of anyone tied to the now-frequent ISIS shootings. The overwhelming majority of people accused of ISIS-era terrorism were either U.S. citizens or in the country legally. Around this time, according to emails later obtained by the Southern Poverty Law Center, Miller was recommending that *Breitbart* journalists "point out the parallels" in the immigration debate that he thought vindicated the French white supremacist novel *The Camp of the Saints*. Cruz, soon to run for president, would later declare, "The front line with ISIS isn't just in Iraq and Syria, it's in Kennedy Airport and the Rio Grande."

Whatever bulwark Security State grandees thought their institutions offered against such demagoguery, John Kelly, in his marine uniform, made the same points. He opined frequently on the security of the southern border, even though NORTHCOM, not SOUTHCOM, is the military command with border jurisdiction. In 2014, as the right sought to capitalize on fears around an Ebola outbreak in western Africa, Kelly warned that immigrants could bring the virus up through the United States–Mexico border. An outbreak would mean a "mass migration of Central Americans into the United States." The following March he speculated in Senate testimony that Central American criminal networks could "unwittingly, or even wittingly" help move "terrorist operatives or weapons of mass destruction toward our borders." Kelly quickly added that there was no evidence of any of this happening but warned that migrants from "Somalia, Bangladesh, Lebanon and Pakistan" were entering the United States from the south, and that Iran was building its influence in Central America.

Everything Obama did with regard to ISIS followed a grim pattern. He showed much deference to the Security State—he was in no position not to; they had wanted a residual force in Iraq—but acted more slowly than they wanted. For convenience, he jettisoned core principles. At the National Defense University in 2013, the president said he looked forward to the expiration of the 2001 AUMF. Not a year later he was relying on it for the most frictionless path into the ISIS war—and after launching an air war without congressional authorization. By treating ISIS as indistinct from al-Qaeda, he erased the most salient fact about ISIS. The absurdity reminded one of the CIA's Zarqawi targeters, Nada Bakos, of the "same distinction we had to make prior to the Iraq war" when the Cheneyites rendered al-Qaeda indistinguishable from Saddam. Few congressional Democrats objected, and even fewer Republicans. Bernie Sanders was "very strongly opposed to sending combat troops back into Iraq or to Syria" but noted correctly that Obama had the authority he needed for air strikes. Sanders called for a vote on any return to war. It never happened. Once again the AUMF's power proved irresistible. A fallback legal justification for the return to war in Iraq was, of all things, the unrepealed 2002 authorization to oust Saddam.

By, With, and Through, a supposedly Sustainable approach to ISIS, kept the Security State and Obama aligned. Austin was replaced at CENTCOM with the JSOC veteran Joe Votel. Votel and his various theater commanders directed a war heavy on air strikes, reconstituting the Iraqi army, Special Operations raids, and other indicators of a reluctant undertaking. Unlike the 2003–2011 Iraq occupation, northeastern Syria became a central battlefield for a small contingent of U.S. forces. McGurk and Allen styled themselves coordinators and special envoys, not occupation administrators. But a core aspect of the war was deeply un-Sustainable. Without a U.S.-trained Syrian force, America had to sponsor an existing one—in this case a determined military from the Kurdish region of Rojava, in northeast Syria. To the alarm of neighboring NATO ally Turkey, the United States committed itself to a separatist force.

A geopolitical complication arose. Obama's unheeded position that Syrian leader Bashar al-Assad had to step down became untenable in the fall of 2015, when Vladimir Putin intervened militarily on Assad's behalf. Obama, only half-committed to Syria, was disinclined to risk U.S.–Russian air combat. Putin and Obama had irrevocably fallen out in 2014 after the Russian client in Ukraine, Viktor Yanukovych, lost power to a NATO-backed regime in Kiev. Soon afterward Russian military intelligence sent a handful of young Russians to explore the United States, and particularly its political and media cultures. It already had an ideologically protean English-language state news channel, RT, that postured as a venue for outsider voices marginalized in the American press. Now Moscow launched its first military campaign outside its traditional sphere of influence since Afghanistan in the 1980s—to checkmate Washington. Since 9/11 the Security State had often pined for the imagined simplicity and honor of great power competition while lamenting the messiness of counterinsurgency and counterterrorism. In Syria those paths converged, on Moscow's terms.

The Security State also aligned with Obama in working to alleviate the enormous migration burden ISIS had sparked. European allies would tell McGurk and Allen that they needed the United States to admit its share of refugees, something it had never done during the Iraq occupation. In 2015 Obama agreed to accept 85,000 refugees, up from 70,000 the previous year, and the next year's admissions included 12,500 Syrians. It was largely the work of Brennan's deputy Avril Haines, who, returning to the White House from the CIA, framed it as a counterterrorism measure "contradicting [extremists'] message." There was no objection from the Security State, but it was out of touch with an empowered nativism. By late 2015, thirty-one state governors, all but one Republicans, refused to resettle Syrians. "Texas will not accept any Syrian refugees & I demand the U.S. act similarly," tweeted Texas governor Greg Abbott. This accelerating trend was about to find its champion.

EVERY REPUBLICAN NATIONAL LEADER since 9/11 had backed the harshest possible prosecution of the War on Terror. Even Mitt Romney pledged to double Guantanamo. Those relatively few prominent Republicans who did object to the war, like senators Rand Paul and Mike Lee, did so on the respectable grounds that it was costing America freedom and wealth. They were openly disdained by the ascendant McCains of the party. Rand Paul's father, Ron, sought the presidency on an antiwar platform, but he was even more marginal, despite an enthusiastic following on the far right.

Handling the party's nativists was a more delicate proposition for GOP leaders. Romney and McCain, uncomfortable fits in nativist circles, compensated by advocating "self-deportation" for undocumented immigrants or releasing "complete the danged fence" ads, to say nothing of proposing that the nativist Sarah Palin should be a heartbeat from the presidency. No Republican since 9/11 had been able to combine nativism with antipathy to the futility of the War on Terror and seize control of the party. It occurred to few to try. Then, in June 2015, Donald Trump descended his escalator at Trump Tower.

In his infamous announcement speech, the one claiming Mexicans were rapists and criminals invading a supine America, Trump demonstrated just how effortlessly 9/11 politics amplified nativism. His great insight was that the jingoistic politics of the War on Terror did not have to be tied to the War on Terror itself. That enabled him to tell a tale of lost greatness: "We don't win anymore." Trump was able to safely voice the reality of the war by articulating what about it most offended right-wing exceptionalists: humiliation.

It was a heretical sentiment to hear from someone seeking the GOP nomination. Every major Republican figure had spent the past fifteen years explaining away the failures of the war or insisting that it was a noble endeavor. Trump called it dumb. His America was suffering unacceptable civilizational insults. "We have *nothing*" to show for the war, he said, and certainly not the spoils of war that Trump believed were due America. "Islamic terrorism" had seized "the oil that, when we left Iraq, I said we should have taken." The war was a glitch in the matrix of American exceptionalism, and Trump offered a reboot.

But except for the Afghanistan war, which he considered particularly stupid, Trump was no abolitionist. "I want to have the strongest military we've ever had, and we need it now more than ever," he stated. He threatened to sink Iranian boat swarms, even as Iran was aligned with the United States against ISIS in Iraq, engaged in the ground combat Obama desperately sought to avoid. Then there was ISIS, at home as well as abroad. Trump pointed specifically to ISIS's spoils: the twenty-three hundred Humvees they drove out of Mosul. "The enemy took them," he complained, pledging that "nobody would be tougher on ISIS than Donald Trump." His latest position on Iraq was that it was dumb to get in, dumb to get out, and now the United States *had* to win, whatever that ultimately meant.

Trump's incoherence was less important than what it revealed: a disgust at waging the war on its familiar terms, along with an enthusiasm for voicing its civilizational subtext. The same weakness that made the War on Terror a no-win situation had also yielded the current wave of Central American migration. Trump promised to crash the wave against a giant wall on the southern border for which he would make Mexico pay. The socialist writer and critic Daniel Denvir observed that Trump's pledge to extort Mexico's wealth for the wall was effectively a demand for imperial tribute. The analysis applies equally to his claim on Iraq's oil.

Trump would tolerate no more nonsense about a "war of ideas." Brutality would be defeated by greater brutality. The euphemism of the War on Terror had been an attempt to conceal such disreputable behavior, but Trump brought it unapologetically into the open. He lied that "thousands and thousands" of Muslims in Jersey City had cheered the fall of the Twin Towers. As vengeance, Trump would "bomb the shit out of ISIS" and stop fighting "a politically correct war," by which he meant one that distinguished between guerrillas and civilians. "You have to take out their families," he told Fox. Torture "absolutely" works, Trump asserted, showing faith in the CIA's fifteen-year-old narrative. He pledged to bring back "a hell of a lot worse than waterboarding" and stock Guantanamo Bay full of "bad dudes." ISIS's assault on Paris meant there was "no choice" but to close mosques within the United States. Before 2015 had ended, Trump delivered his ultimate response to ISIS: calling for a ban on all Muslim immigration. "We can't take a chance," he said, denying that ISIS fighters were meaningfully distinct from the Muslim civilians they raped, terrorized, and turned into refugees. It was Cheney's one-percent doctrine applied civilizationally. Stephen Miller was so excited by these promises that the following month he joined Trump's campaign. His old boss, Jeff Sessions, the first senator to endorse Trump, helmed the candidate's foreign policy and national security working group.

Trump's instinct for violence extended from his rallies, where he offered to post bail for anyone arrested for beating up protesters, to Moscow, where he praised Vladimir Putin as a strong leader. The path blazed by the white supremacist Steve King was still too far for most Cold War–forged Republicans. Trump ambled down it. "[Putin's] running his country and at least he's a leader, unlike what we have in this country," he said in December 2015. Even Bill O'Reilly was discomfited, and when he asked Trump about

Putin's assassinating his enemies, Trump responded, "What, do you think our country's so innocent?" After all, he continued, Russia fights "Islamic terrorism all over the world, that's a good thing." Where others, liberal and conservative alike, flinched at or denied the brutality that built America, Trump was proud of it. It made America great.

There were legions who had been waiting for such a champion. At a March 2016 Trump rally at the Kentucky International Convention Center, a twenty-five-year-old man in Trump's signature Make America Great Again (MAGA) hat physically pushed out protester Kashiya Nwanguma, whom he called "leftist scum." The man, Matthew Heimbach, pleaded guilty to a misdemeanor but was proud of his actions, which he justified by claiming that Nwanguma was a member of Black Lives Matter. "White Americans," he wrote, "are getting fed up and they're learning that they must either push back or be pushed down." Heimbach was a neo-Nazi, leader of the fascist Traditionalist Worker Party. A more bourgeois but no less fascist Trump supporter was Richard Spencer, who through the "alt-right" united white nationalists and internet-addicted provocateurs. The alt-right was a bridge between Trump support and open fascism, possessed of just enough deniability. "This is a movement of consciousness and identity for European people in the twenty-first century," Spencer explained to NPR. The Southern Poverty Law Center later concluded that through Trump, "the radical right suddenly felt a connection to mainstream politics and a realistic hope of gaining political power, which drew more adherents—and a wider variety of adherents—to the movement."

Fifteen years of brutality as background noise made it easy for many to misinterpret Trump's position on the War on Terror. Journalists listened to his invective against it and called him antiwar, as if he had not been promising to "bomb the shit" out of millions of people. "Donald the Dove," Maureen Dowd of *The New York Times* wrote, "in most cases . . . would rather do the art of the deal than shock and awe." Such attitudes revealed what elites chose to believe about Trump and what they opted to consider merely an act for the rubes. What they overlooked by focusing on Trump's criticisms of the ground wars was that he wanted to expand the War on Terror to frontiers it had yet to reach. Most important, they heard Trump describe the enemy as Radical Islamic Terror. For fifteen years, nativists, stoked by Fox News, had considered such a definition a prerequisite for winning the war. Elites had never understood why the right was so spun up about the phrase. Trump knew that "Radical Islamic Terror" extracted the precious nativist metal from the husk of the Forever War.

None of this was tolerable to the Security State and its allies. Sean Mac-Farland, a Petraeus-favored officer during the Iraq occupation who now commanded the war against ISIS, rejected indiscriminate bombing as "what the Russians have been accused of doing in parts of northwest Syria." Dozens of Republican-aligned security luminaries signed open letters refusing to serve in a Trump administration, birthing the Never Trump Beltway movement. But the architects, contractors, and validators of the War on Terror were placed in awkward positions. One of the letters decried Trump's "expansive" embrace of torture, since their own embrace of "enhanced interrogation" foreclosed on a more categorical rejection. Mike Hayden, who had lied so extensively about torture that the Senate compiled his falsehoods into a separate annex of the torture report, who secretly constructed a surveillance dragnet around the United States while imploring Congress to set the balance between liberty and security, characterized Trump as "unwilling or unable to separate truth from falsehood." Nor was there any self-reflection from signatories like Iraq occupation chief Bob Blackwill, who took over as Bush's personal envoy after Bremer, and who had asserted against "the professional pessimists within parts of the U.S. intelligence community" that "2005 will be a good year in Iraq for President Bush." None of them seemed to understand that they had created the context for Trump. He was about to show them.

Trump relished his critics' revulsion. He presented it to his crowds as validation: the people who had gotten America into an unwinnable war hated him. Why listen to them? After a suicide bombing in Afghanistan, Trump lamented, "When will our leaders get tough and smart?" He thanked the Never Trump signatories for stepping forward, "so everyone in the country knows who deserves the blame for making the world such a dangerous place." There was no credentialism capable of stopping Trump, not even from the military. His uniformed detractors weren't *truly* reflective of the military, as they had been "reduced to rubble" by Obama. He insisted he had a secret plan to defeat ISIS that the generals would either love or, in disliking it, reveal their incompetence. It was a dominance politics rarely played against the military. To make it work, Trump, a Vietnam draft dodger, had to show he was unintimidated by attacking even the most venerated. McCain, who could not abide Trump, was no genuine war hero because, as Trump boasted, "I like people who weren't captured."

Because the Security State couldn't win the War on Terror it was waging, Trump had a permanent cudgel against it. Why accept the expertise of the architects of a quagmire? He championed the explanation that these so-called intelligence experts, political generals, amoral attorneys, and other liberals had misunderstood that this was a war of survival against Radical Islamic Terror. All of them had condescended to the nativist right since 9/11, and they had marched America into humiliation. Wrapped in a redemptive flag, the nativists were not afraid to challenge the authority of the military. The Cheneyites hadn't been, either, though neither side tended to see the continuity.

Trump and his nativist followers, the coalition known as MAGA, did not quite offer a *Dolchstosslegende*. They didn't claim the Security State had deliberately lost the War on Terror, but rather that it had flinched at confronting a civilizational assault. The offer Trump made to the Security State was an alibi. He would "unleash" the military, which meant, as John Rambo had said, that the military had not been allowed to win. It was easier for the MAGA crowd to accept that than to accept that their American exceptionalism had marched America into ruin.

The sense of civilizational besiegement that the Forever War inspired was central to MAGA. With *Breitbart* providing a voice, and social media providing networking and amplification, the alt-right was able to rebrand white nationalism and even outright neo-Nazism. Its members spoke in terms of civilizational "replacement," by which they meant the loss of a racial caste hierarchy with whites at the top, a status conferring though never guaranteeing substantial material benefits. (Demagogues and bosses had long divided the working class by blaming any unfulfilled white expectation of material comfort on nonwhites.) Fluent in online sarcasm and provocation, members of the alt-right half joked that they were "meme war veterans," by which they meant propagandists out to radicalize conservatives, and not merely the "101st Fighting Keyboardists" whom progressives had mocked as chicken-hawks when they typed their vituperative defenses of the Iraq war. In the style of fascists everywhere, the alt-right reveled in its transgressions and its apocalyptic fantasies of crushing its opponents. Such transgressions extended into classical anti-Semitism, previously taboo among conservatives, such as using "(((globalists)))" as a term for Jews to evade internet-platform censorship. Nonwhites had a place in the movement, provided they espoused the superiority of "Western civilization."

The alt-right understood what could fuel their appeal to so-called "normies." In July 2016 the troll site 4Chan began a petition to call Black Lives Matter a terrorist organization "due to its actions in Ferguson, Baltimore, and even at a Bernie Sanders rally." It garnered over 120,000 signatures in a week. BLM cofounder Patrisse Khan-Cullors wrote, "The accusation of being a terrorist is devastating, and I allow myself space to cry quietly as I lie in bed on a Sunday morning listening to a red-face, hysterical Rudolph Giuliani spit lies about us."

For his entire career, manipulating reality had redounded to Trump's benefit. Two generations earlier he had aggressively courted New York reporters to ensure frequent publicity. He planted anonymous quotes, sometimes using the fake name John Barron. When he told his crowds that the lying news media used anonymity to cover for what he called fake sources, he spoke from experience. He pledged to Alex Jones, who had matriculated from calling 9/11 an inside job to becoming an all-purpose right-wing conspiracy broadcaster, "I will never let you down." He surrounded himself with criminals like his fixer, Michael Cohen, who would threaten reporters when necessary. Trump specialized in areas that often function as cash laundries: real estate, casinos, licensing. He covered repeated business failures with debt while portraying himself in entertainment and news media as the embodiment of capitalist brilliance and sexual potency. His campaign rallies played "Real American," the theme music of professional wrestler Hulk Hogan.

His defining features—gilded apartments, ridiculous hair, media thirst, transparent lies—occasioned contempt from the sophisticated. As did Trump's unsubtle bigotry; they preferred theirs structural instead of flagrant. Trump, like a good con man, harnessed that contempt. It drew him closer to his constituency, who hated all the people who laughed at Trump. After all, the ones laughing loudest were the liberals from the upper middle class, who preferred Hillary Clinton.

IT WAS FINALLY HER TIME. There would be no Iraq war vote to derail her. She had endured endless Republican questioning over Benghazi—much of it from Mike Pompeo—with her hand contemptuously holding her chin, returning theater in kind. When she was secretary of state, she was the most popular public figure in America. Her marathon Benghazi session, lasting an entire workday across two committees, left her with an astronomical 67 percent approval rating. She left the Obama administration as Obama's designated successor.

The fact that Hillary Clinton was to Obama's right gave much of the Security State a reassurance it appreciated. There was not a single policy decision in Obama's first term where Clinton had deviated from the Security State's preferences. She displayed none of what they considered Obama's indecision, and they trusted her judgment better than his. Clinton had favored deeper involvement to oust Assad. While Obama was in their view too solicitous of Moscow, Clinton infuriated Putin in December 2011 by calling for an Organization for Security and Co-operation in Europe investigation into Russian election fraud. It was a moment of vulnerability for Putin—his party had triumphed in the parliamentary vote, but by a lower than typical margin—and Clinton chose to press the U.S. advantage. Among much of the Security State—but hardly all, as this was still a right-leaning conglomerate by default—she was considered not only strong but supremely competent. Petraeus in particular respected her.

Clinton's challenge within the Democratic Party came from the political faction the Security State took least seriously. The only politician drawing rallies of Trump's size was Bernie Sanders. Sanders rejected most of Clinton's agenda as irrelevant or harmful to the wave of economic precarity soaking most Americans. His defense of working-class interests alternately inspired, scandalized, and divided the Democratic Party. Bernie made it clear that he did not share Clinton's bellicosity, but he did not make rejecting it part of his revolution. It is surely an issue on which Bernie's supporters were more strident than he was. In November 2015, Sanders presented his vision of democratic socialism in the most ambitiously left-wing speech a presidential candidate had given in generations. Tacked at the end of it he discussed the "global threat of terror." With his emphasis on multilateral solutions, Sanders suddenly sounded like John Kerry in 2004. He complained that Saudi Arabia wasn't paying its fair share for fighting ISIS. His challenge to Clinton was as potent as it was urgent, but not because of his opposition to the War on Terror.

Clinton did not seem to mind being pitted against Sanders. It was indisputable that she was ready to lead a global hegemon, having already shaped and conducted its foreign and domestic policy. For this presidential run, she swung to the right of her 2008 geopolitics. After Russian warplanes entered Syrian airspace, Clinton proposed that the air force establish a no-fly zone over a U.S.-policed safe area for refugees from Assad and ISIS. This would entrench the United States in the Syrian civil war, risk escalatory dogfights with Russian warplanes, and spare America and Europe from accepting Muslim refugees. Despite Benghazi, Clinton did not acknowledge that Libya, the war of choice she had championed, was a disaster. She now proposed the most aggressive American intervention in the Mideast since the Iraq invasion. Clinton simultaneously lambasted Trump's Islamophobia while practicing its condescending liberal variant, causing American Muslims to wince as she referred to them as the "front lines" of the War on Terror and implored them to be "part of our homeland security." Her brain trust felt she had found her moment. "There's no doubt that Hillary Clinton's more muscular brand of American foreign policy is better matched to 2016 than it was to 2008," key aide Jake Sullivan told *The New York Times*.

She was also the most demonized individual in American public life. At bottom, the Benghazi accusations were an attempt to demonstrate that "Killary" could not be trusted to fight Radical Islamic Terror—even while Trump, losing the plot, decried her for pursuing ever more hopeless Mideast wars. Alongside the attacks against her was a vicious lie. Clinton's longtime aide Huma Abedin, claimed Congresswoman Michele Bachmann and much of Fox News, was tied to the Muslim Brotherhood. It was pure nativism, and John McCain denounced it on the Senate floor.

But decades of demonization from the right, by now a habit, succeeded in keeping a cloud of suspicion over Clinton. In that political context, it emerged that Clinton maintained a private email server over which she conducted public business.

Use of the server meant Clinton was hoarding public records, though her aides denied any such intent, and Clinton herself had no better explanation than its being a matter of convenience. The State Department had a policy explicitly prohibiting use of personal communications for department business. As was inevitable, she had deleted thousands of emails from the server, something that became the subject of an FBI investigation. With the Benghazi circus fruitless, the right lunged for Clinton's emails as another magic weapon to vanquish her. At Trump rallies she was "Crooked Hillary"; the crowds chanted "Lock her up!" Conservatives made the server a national security issue: Who knew *what* foreign power had exploited her communications? Trump, at a press conference, lost the plot again. "Russia, if you're listening," he said in late July, "I hope you're able to find the thirty thousand emails that are missing." Within hours, email accounts controlled by Russian intelligence sent messages containing malicious links to fifteen accounts associated with Clinton's private office.

By then Trump had ample reason to expect that Russia would do him a favor. The previous fall, fixer Cohen had pursued a deal, with Trump's signed approval, to license a Trump Tower in Moscow. Cohen's partner on the project, Felix Sater, emailed him, "Buddy our boy can become President of the USA and we can engineer it. I will get all of Putin's team to buy in on this." Cohen made contact with Kremlin spokesman Dmitry Peskov's office in January to apprise the Russian government of the ultimately futile hotel scheme. Cohen's initiative continued, fruitlessly, through the spring of 2016—at which time a different effort coalesced. In April, George Papadopoulos, a Trump campaign foreign policy aide who had proposed that the candidate meet with Putin, learned from a London-based contact that the Russians had "thousands of emails" worth of "dirt" on Clinton. Papadopoulos urged Stephen Miller, campaign chairman Paul Manafort—who had consulted for the Russian-backed Ukrainian regime ousted in 2014—and others to redouble efforts to bring about a Trump–Putin meeting. Manafort, for his part, kept an open channel to a long-time contact and Russian intelligence officer named Konstantin Kilimnik, feeding Kilimnik internal information about the campaign for purposes that a Republican-led Senate committee investigation was unable to determine. (The panel judged that Manafort posed "a grave counterintelligence threat.") On June 9, Manafort attended a meeting at Trump Tower with Donald Trump Jr. and Trump's son-in-law, Jared Kushner, predicated on getting dirt on Clinton from a different vendor: Kremlin-connected attorney Natalia Veselnitskaya. An associate of Don Jr. had mentioned that a Russian senior prosecutor could provide damning information, "part of Russia and its government's support for Mr. Trump." The younger Trump replied, "If it's what you say I love it." But while Veselnitskaya claimed dirty money flowed from Russia to Clinton, she couldn't document any instance of it, and urged the Trump representatives to lift corruption sanctions on Moscow.

The following week the Democratic National Committee announced that Russian hackers had penetrated its servers. Infiltration had begun months earlier, after elements of the Russian GRU had stolen DNC user credentials, entered the party's network, and exfiltrated tens of thousands of emails and other documents, including opposition research on Trump. The following day a GRU creation calling itself Guccifer 2.0 claimed it was a "lone hacker" responsible for the theft. Using its Guccifer 2.0 persona and another called DCLeaks, Russian intelligence gave purloined documents to WikiLeaks, which began releasing them on July 22, shortly before the Democratic National Convention. Assange wanted the material to deepen division between supporters of Sanders and Clinton, whom he called a "sociopath." Awkwardly, Guccifer 2.0 boasted of providing WikiLeaks with the DNC material shortly after cybersecurity specialists identified it as Russian. Assange denied it to the point of alleging falsely that a DNC employee who had recently been killed in a random robbery, Seth Rich, was the leaker and that his murder was a reprisal.

While the NSA preferred to exfiltrate user data from American social-media networks, Russian intelligence opted to post. On Facebook, You-Tube, Instagram, Tumblr, and Twitter, Russians used poorly translated handles like Being Patriotic and Secured Borders to impersonate Americans and build pro-Trump, anti-Clinton audiences. They convinced Americans in at least seventeen cities to turn out for rallies. Knowing their audience well, the operators of the Russian accounts powered their grievance machine with white racism. A rally that Secured Borders attempted in Idaho urged that "We must stop taking in Muslim refugees!" Being Patriotic advocated executing Black Lives Matter protesters. They impersonated an American Muslim group and boosted Clinton, in an effort to associate her with Muslims. Tens of millions of American accounts interacted with content created by the Internet Research Agency, a St. Petersburg entity that brought shitposting into the annals of intelligence history.

Trump denied that the DNC hack came from Russia. While it was possible, he acknowledged, he suggested that China might have been responsible, or "someone sitting on their bed that weighs 400 pounds." His consigliere Roger Stone insisted that Guccifer 2.0, with whom he was later in contact, had hacked the DNC, not the Russians, which was also GRU's cover story. Trump then committed another GOP heresy by proclaiming his love for WikiLeaks.

But Papadopoulos blundered. In London the Trump campaign aide discussed the Russian dirt offer over drinks with the Australian high commissioner to the UK, Alexander Downer. Downer reported the conversation to his government, which in July 2016 informed the Obama administration. For the first time in its history, the FBI investigated two presidential rivals at once. Comey managed to blunder worse than Papadopoulos.

None of the Security State's institutions was politically monolithic, but the cleavages in the FBI over Clinton and Trump were extreme. They provided grist for both camps that the powerful law enforcement agency was out to get them. Senior bureau counterintelligence officials were horrified by Trump. Peter Strzok, who worked on both the Clinton and Trump probes, sent an ominous text in August to FBI attorney Lisa Page, with whom he was having an affair. When Page wondered if Trump was really going to be elected, Strzok replied, "No. He won't. We'll stop it." But at lower levels there was enough MAGA enthusiasm, particularly from the overwhelmingly white special agents in the bureau, for one FBI official to remark in the fall of 2016, "The FBI is Trumpland." The division was particularly acute in the New York field office, which was widely considered to be the source of the FBI's longtime ally Rudy Giuliani's cryptic televised remarks suggesting that Clinton was soon to fall under the FBI hammer. The New York office investigated the Clinton Foundation largely because of accusations made by a dubious right-wing book. A veteran of the office explained, "There are lots of people who don't think Trump is qualified, but also believe Clinton is corrupt."

Comey's instinct, going back to his youth, had been to insert himself into complicated situations where he believed honor demanded it. That instinct had compelled the clash over surveillance authorities at John Ashcroft's bedside, as it had his futile showdown with Apple. Comey rarely drew the obvious conclusion that his interventions often made things worse. That insight might have prevented him from declaring, in July, that Clinton ought not to face criminal charges for her email server. As a former U.S. attorney, he was well aware that charging decisions are for prosecutors to make, not FBI directors. He added, in a transparent attempt at mollifying Republicans, that Clinton had been "extremely careless" with the server and that it was "possible" that foreign actors might have accessed it. Even as he cleared Clinton criminally, Comey placed a new cloud over her, particularly considering there was no evidence of any foreign compromise—and that evidence of such compromise exclusively centered on the Trump campaign, about which Comey was silent.

Then, in late October, in violation of Justice Department policies on noninterference in an election, Comey suddenly revealed that the FBI was reviewing new information from Clinton's server that it had unexpectedly acquired through a sex crimes probe of Abedin's estranged husband, Anthony Weiner. Trump, who had lambasted the FBI for closing the probe, now said Comey showed "a lot of guts." Two days before the vote, Comey announced that the Weiner material did not change the conclusion against charging Clinton. Comey loudly drove federal law enforcement into the center of an election against Clinton while remaining silent about a counterintelligence probe into Trump associates, each step of the way insisting he had done only what probity demanded.

As the Comey drama unfolded, Obama attempted to enlist Republican congressional leaders in a statement of unity against Russian election interference. They were uninterested. McConnell, the Senate Republican leader, expressed skepticism that the Russians were the culprits, which Democrats and intelligence officials understood as an effort to protect Trump. He signed on to a much weaker statement warning state election officials to be diligent in their digital hygiene. Clapper and DHS secretary Jeh

Johnson issued a stronger warning that fall attributing the intrusion to Russia, as did Feinstein and her House Intelligence Committee counterpart, Adam Schiff.

While the Security State leadership had come to view Trump as an adjunct of Russian power, he gained his most important Security State ally from one of their embittered ex-colleagues. Mike Flynn presented himself as a martyr of Obama's War on Terror, the warrior sacrificed so liberalism could deny the threat of Islam. One of the premier special operators of the 9/11 era became a Fox News guest commentator. He accepted a stipend from the Russian English-language state news channel to sit at Putin's table during its tenth-anniversary gala. As his profile grew, he took $530,000 on behalf of Turkish interests without registering as a foreign agent with the Justice Department. He saw no contradiction in operating on behalf of an Islamist government while denouncing Islam as a cancer. "Islam is a political ideology" that "hides behind this notion of being a religion," Flynn told Brigitte Gabriel's ACT for America convention in August. Flynn was the ideal validator for Trump. More than nearly anyone else on earth, Flynn had waged the War on Terror, and the lessons he took from it were the ones Trump was selling. All the Security State mandarins lining up against Trump were people Flynn hated so much as to portray them as what was wrong with wartime America. He stood on stage at the Republican convention to lead a chant of "Lock her up" after warning that America's "very existence is threatened." It was as if the id of the War on Terror endorsed Trump even as its superego opposed him.

That superego manifested as Mike Morell. The acting CIA director between Petraeus and Brennan, Morell was, like Flynn, a representative of the 9/11 generation at Langley. He had been Bush's briefer, had led the bin Laden hunt, and had defended CIA torture against the Senate report. Clinton had shown her strength to Morell, he wrote in *The New York Times*, not least when she was an "early advocate" of the bin Laden raid "in opposition to some of her most important colleagues on the National Security Council," a swipe at Biden. He suggested that had Obama heeded Clinton on a "more aggressive" approach in Syria there might have been no ISIS Caliphate. By contrast, Morell called Trump dangerous—even an "unwitting agent" of a hostile foreign power. Someone who had excused torture wrote that Trump "plays into the hands of the jihadist narrative that our fight against terrorism is a war between religions." Morell stated proudly that a Muslim at the agency was the man "most responsible for keeping America safe since the Sept. 11 attacks." He was referring to Michael D'Andrea, who took the Counterterrorism Center from the final phase of the black sites into the era of drone strikes. Morell did not pause to reflect on how his open-ended era of patriotic brutality aimed at Muslims might have produced leaders, and constituencies, who embraced a narrative of war between religions.

The widespread opposition to Trump by Security State eminences reflected the certainty among elites, and apparently Trump himself at the time, that Clinton was certain to win. Every poll demonstrated it. Assange DM'd Guccifer 2.0, "trump has only a 25% chance of winning against hillary." Obama, calling back to his 2011 White House Correspondents' Dinner roast of Trump on the eve of the bin Laden raid, mocked Trump to TV host Jimmy Kimmel as an inevitable loser.

To an intellectual named Michael Anton, a Trump loss would be nothing less than the existential threat to America that Flynn had warned of on the convention stage. Clinton's taking power was "Russian Roulette with a semi-auto." Conservatives had correctly itemized the civilizational rot befalling America, he thought, starting with "illegitimacy" and proceeding to an "inability to win wars against tribal, sub-Third World foes." But Anton was after something more profound: "virtue, morality, religious faith, stability, character." On that front conservatives were losing, and because conservatives were right and their causes important, "our liberal-left present reality and future direction is incompatible with human nature and must undermine society."

Apart from dutiful nods to the realities of "lower wages, outsourcing, de-industrialization, trade giveaways," Anton was unconcerned with material issues. That permitted him to see Clinton not as the obstacle to socialism that she was, but instead as someone who was "pedal-to-the-metal on the entire Progressive-left agenda." As if the record deportations of the Obama years never happened, Anton said the Democrats' open borders policy was nothing less than replacement. The mask slipped from his politics of *virtù*. Clinton augured the "ceaseless importation of Third World foreigners with no tradition of, taste for, or experience in liberty." Once enough nonwhites had arrived to vote Democratic, the party that made Barack Obama president would feel no more need to "respect democratic and constitutional niceties." The end of America—white America, great America—was nigh.

The purpose of this Wagnerian conception of politics was to give Anton permission to seek Valhalla. Only in Trump resided any hope of preserving virtue, morality, religious faith, stability, and character. So it was that Anton decreed 2016 "the Flight 93 Election." He urged the right to rise up with him, like those American heroes on 9/11 above Pennsylvania, and storm the cockpit occupied by Hillary.

Anyone who would compare an election loss to the agony aboard Flight 93 revealed that to them 9/11 was never more than a jingoistic opportunity. But that was not the real obscenity of Anton's racist fugue state. The real obscenity of the Flight 93 Election and its adherents was that, as much as they imagined themselves as Todd Beamer saying "Let's roll!," they were fantasizing about a suicide mission. Within months, Anton was the spokesman for Donald Trump's National Security Council.

CHAPTER EIGHT

MAKING THE WAR ON TERROR GREAT AGAIN

2017–2020

With time served, Adham Hassoun prepared to finish his fifteen-year sentence under the PATRIOT Act in October 2017. It was his first chance at freedom since June 2002. But there was a complication.

Hassoun, a Palestinian who grew up in Lebanon, was not a U.S. citizen. He knew that he would be deported. Imprisoned at Marion, Illinois, he expected that he'd be sent back to immigration, likely in nearby Chicago, for a few weeks while the Lebanese completed the bureaucratic process of repatriating him. Instead he learned that no country would take him.

On October 10, Hassoun said goodbye to his fellow inmates and left Marion. He was greeted, he remembers, by "a platoon of armed men, twenty or something," standing by a fleet of SUVs. For a moment he thought he'd be shot. "No, no, they're escorts," he remembered being told; "you're going to immigration." When they drove him to the airport, Hassoun figured he was in for a short flight to Chicago. The plane instead landed in western

New York, where he was placed in the custody of Immigration and Customs Enforcement. Hassoun became a Forever War trailblazer yet again: its first *post-conviction* detainee.

He had spent most of his pre- and post-conviction detention in segregated units, even spending a month in solitary. There was Krone in Miami, the Palm Beach County Jail, Terre Haute, even the infamous Supermax in Florence, Colorado. His favorite was, paradoxically, the *"real* prison" he experienced his second time at Marion, when he was "stepped down" into the general population. He made friends inside Marion, and liked cooking for the whole unit. Andy Stepanian was imprisoned with Hassoun during Hassoun's first time there. He credited Hassoun with helping "pull me out of my institutional behavior" to reclaim himself from who prison was making him. "Adham changed my life," Stepanian recalled. "There were individuals there who were true threats. He was not. He talks to the guards all the time. That's because he's not a criminal."

When Hassoun walked into the ICE prison at Batavia, near Buffalo, he saw his picture displayed, "our convicted terrorist." He noticed a man whose uniform bore the fearsome letters SHU—segregated housing unit—and panicked. Desperate not to relive another stint in solitary, he pleaded that he didn't need the "protection" they were offering. They agreed to give him a cell without a bunkie, but Hassoun was struck by the conditions in in Batavia's general population. "We're locked in eighteen hours a day," he recalled. "It's extremely creepy because it affects your psychological situation. My ordeal started all over again."

Hassoun had begun his imprisonment in an immigration detention center at the dawn of the Bush administration. When he returned to one, at the dawn of the Trump administration, the cages had swollen. Filled with nonwhites treated like criminals for committing no more than a civil misdemeanor, they were the signature of the Trump immigration era. Trump may have promoted the Wall, but it was never truly built, nor did he deport the multitudes Obama had. The real nativist innovation of Trump was to lock up the migrants who were already in America. He empowered

ICE as never before. In Fairfax County, Virginia, ICE agents waited to arrest people leaving a church hypothermia shelter. By March 2019 ICE's prisons, many of which were for-profit, held a record fifty thousand people.

While those prisons, and the adjuncts run by Customs and Border Protection, were instantly understood to herald the Trump era of immigration, it was relatively rare to hear them discussed as a mark of the Trump era of the War on Terror. Trump never fulfilled his promise to load up Guantanamo, nor was he known to have reopened the CIA black sites. The up-close cruelties practiced within them, the ones that Trump championed, the ones that a generation of right-wing politicians and media figures excused or applauded, were practiced closer to home: on immigrants.

There is no record tracing what James Schlesinger called the "migration" of torture techniques into the immigration intake centers, jails, and camps. Yet it was nevertheless conspicuous that variants of CIA and military torture techniques occurred within the immigration detention system. CBP intake cells known as *hieleras* kept people in frigid conditions, "iceboxes" reminiscent of the Salt Pit in Afghanistan where Gul Rahman froze to death in 2002. People spent up to three days there, sleeping on floors, wrapped in Mylar blankets. A woman named Victoria told Human Rights Watch that as CBP piled people into a small room with her in February 2017, "They turned up the air conditioning. . . . We slept on the floor with the kids in the middle, trying to keep them covered up as much as possible." After spending three days inside a CBP hielera, nineteen-month-old Mariee Juarez and her mother were transferred to ICE-contracted custody in Dilley, Texas, where sickness spread easily around a detention complex built to hold a massive twenty-four hundred people. The toddler developed a respiratory infection. Two months after she left the for-profit detention center, Mariee was dead.

Lights in CBP cells were kept on all night, much as CIA and Rumsfeld-era military detention used sensory bombardment as a mechanism for sleep deprivation. Guards would wake sleeping detainees to question them, like their Guantanamo counterparts, except now there could be no pretext of extracting urgent information from them. Dignity violations were a feature of immigration detention, as they had been for CIA and military detention. ICE detainees, many penned inside chain-link fences, wore orange jumpsuits reminiscent of those worn by Guantanamo prisoners. Guards were reported to have called them dogs. One who died in ICE custody in Florida was listed on his death report as having "vomited feces." A senior ICE official in Maryland, Dorothy Herrera-Niles, emailed "a thought" to her colleagues in May 2018: "I think we should send all new border apprehensions to GITMO and detail judges and asylum officers down there. Maybe they can be removed directly from GITMO to El Salvador, etc. . . ."

Women, men, and children were subject to rape and other sexual abuse. Gay and transgender detainees endured sexual and physical violence from other detainees. One ICE prison in Pennsylvania told a court it could not be held responsible for "consensual" sexual activity between detainees and its guards. As ICE guards in Florida restrained a female detainee who had fought with another, one straddled and rubbed his erection on her. They filmed her as she showered off Mace. During Trump's first year in office there were 237 reports of sexual abuse in immigration detention, among 1,448 such allegations filed against ICE between 2012 and March 2018, according to the ACLU. A doctor known as the "uterus collector" allegedly performed hysterectomies on women detained at ICE's privately operated prison in Irwin County, Georgia, according to a nurse turned whistleblower named Dawn Wooten.

Richard Zuley, the Chicago police interrogator and navy reservist, was a forerunner in demonstrating how easily the abuses he visited on Black Chicagoans could be exported to Guantanamo. There was by now a considerable constituency for his methods. Whether at Guantanamo, the black sites, the border, the prisons of ICE, or the streets of Staten Island where the NYPD's Daniel Pantaleo choked Eric Garner to death, Trump's allies, validators, and many of his voters typically saw themselves in the guards, interrogators, or officers, not in their typically nonwhite victims. The brutality was easier to justify when viewed as necessary, as National Security Council

spokesman Michael Anton had contended, against the two-front civilizational emergency represented by Radical Islam and Latin American migration. Trump portrayed the people fleeing the violence of the Salvadoran
MS-13 gang as indistinct from MS-13 itself, much as he portrayed the people fleeing the violence of ISIS as indistinct from ISIS. Both flights for
refuge were, in material ways, downstream effects of earlier destabilizing
American military operations and deportation decisions.

For years CBP had been detaining children who crossed the border
without their parents—many fleeing violence in Central America—in
what an *Arizona Republic* reporter called, during Obama's presidency, "a
juvenile prison camp." John Kelly, retired from the marines and now
Trump's secretary of homeland security, went far further. He might have to
take people's children away, he told CNN barely a month after assuming
his new position, "in order to deter movement along this terribly dangerous
network." The children would be fine, argued the man who once ran Guantanamo, as years of experience had ensured the government did "a very, very
good job" of finding relatives in the United States—or placing the children
in foster care.

It would be another year before Attorney General Jeff Sessions and Kelly's successor, Kirstjen Nielsen, unveiled Zero Tolerance, the official name
for their policy of kidnapping. But the practice began under Kelly, whose
functionaries thought seizing children and threatening their parents with
prosecution "would have a substantial deterrent effect." At least fifty-five
hundred children, twice the number the Justice Department claimed in a
court filing in 2018, were swallowed by a system that, despite Kelly's assurances, made not the slightest effort at reuniting families. An inspector general's report found instead that the system was unprepared to address the
overwhelming trauma exhibited by ever-younger children who had no way
of knowing if they would ever see their parents again. Children unfamiliar
with the concept of anxiety attacks reported suffering chest pains that they
described as feeling as if their hearts were hurting. They were penned into
places like a converted Texas Walmart that housed fourteen hundred. A

care worker who visited in July 2018 called it "very clearly a prison for children." Fox News's Laura Ingraham called it "essentially a summer camp."

Public revulsion at this policy, which had deep American roots in chattel slavery and native genocide, prompted the Trump administration to react with the closest thing to shame that it displayed in its four years in power. While the administration usually took pride in its cruelty, it denied that anything resembling child separation was taking place. "We've never had a policy for family separation," Nielsen testified to the Senate in a lie soon disproved by internal documents. Protesters drove her out of a Mexican restaurant in Washington, prompting a wave of indignation on the right about the incivility of the left. The administration made a show of ending Zero Tolerance in June 2018, barely three months after its launch. DHS still took more than a thousand children from their parents after that.

Asked in 2018 if the policy was cruel, Kelly replied that "the big point" was to disincentivize those mothers who "elected to come illegally into the United States, and this is a technique that no one hopes will be used extensively or for very long." Their children would be placed in "foster care, or whatever." By the end of Trump's presidency, at least 545 children did not know where their parents were.

The blitheness Kelly exhibited toward the fate of thousands of families was no obstacle to his reputation as one of the "Adults" around Trump. Centrists, liberals, marginalized anti-Trump conservatives, and others horrified by Trump hoped that the Adults would stop him from turning his nativist instincts into policy. They were inclined to view these retired military officers, all distinguished figures from the Forever War, as their allies within, surely opposed to Trump and offended by him. It was much the way Joe Biden had seen Colin Powell during the Bush administration: a check on the worst instincts of the president and an assurance behind policies that had their assent. James Mattis even received special dispensation from the Senate to become Trump's defense secretary despite not having been out of uniform long enough. Flynn lasted less than a month as national security adviser—he was a general, of course, but was never respected by those who respected the Adults—and Trump replaced him with H. R. McMaster, the counterinsurgency hero.

Many of their moves did constrain Trump's impulses. McMaster banished the phrase "Radical Islamic Terror" from the National Security Council and fought a yearlong rearguard battle to push out Flynn's residual staff. They included McMaster's surgenik colleague Derek Harvey, a Defense Intelligence Agency Mideast analyst and a conduit to Harvey's once and future boss, House Intelligence Committee chairman Devin Nunes. McMaster and Mattis used their influence inside the administration to maneuver the Forever War toward equilibrium—only with the violence intensified to a level that MAGA, whatever its supposed antipathy to the war, respected. Mattis called it "lethality," as if the War on Terror had not been lethal for hundreds of thousands of people, and made it his mantra at the Pentagon.

The outraged liberal #Resistance, as it came to be known in the increasingly online political environment, blurred, as ever, the distinction between resistance and complicity. The very Democrats who called Trump a unique threat to the republic were willing to grant him the same extensive surveillance powers they had allowed Bush and Obama. They saw themselves granting these authorities to the Security State, as if Trump himself were irrelevant. They voted for his astronomical military budgets and denounced his deviations from the national security norm that had mired the United States in unwinnable, agonizing conflicts, which bred frustrations that Trump harnessed. Six Senate Democrats followed the lead of Brennan and Clapper in approving the CIA torturer Gina Haspel to become Trump's second CIA director. The #Resistance was the next phase of liberal complicity in the War on Terror. It was determined not to miss an opportunity to align with the Security State now that Trump and the Security State clashed.

On Mattis's first day at the Pentagon, Trump visited to sign one of his first executive orders, banning entry to the United States to people from seven Muslim-majority countries. It was his first attempt at building a wall, and it trapped relatives on either side. Not even those who had served

America during the Forever War were exempt. An Iraqi named Haydar, who had translated for the U.S. occupation behind Ray-Bans and a ski mask during the surge, had spent four years trying to obtain a visa from the American embassy when Trump slammed the door shut. "I know that executive order [is] just racist," he said from Baghdad, days before he learned he would not be permitted to board his flight out. The cerebral Mattis, who had spent so long in the Middle East fighting alongside Muslim allies, grinned and applauded as the president signed the Muslim ban.

But if Mattis, McMaster, Kelly, or any other Adult sought to constrain the Trump agenda, their service in the Forever War guaranteed them no more consideration than Haydar's did. McMaster, owing to an insubstantial connection to George Soros's Open Society Foundations, became the target of anti-Semitic accusations in *Breitbart* that he was doing Soros's bidding. A more shocking excommunication came when MAGA renounced McMaster's replacement, John Bolton, a bellicose Bush veteran who had constituencies in neoconservatism and the Islamophobic wing of MAGA. After Bolton emerged as an obstacle to what he called a "drug deal" in which Trump sought to extort the Ukrainian president for a public accusation of corruption against Joe Biden, Lou Dobbs excoriated Bolton as "a tool of the left."

Trump's institutional impediments in the Security State were, to MAGA, manifestations of a "Deep State." Service in the wars could now be seen on the right as suspicious. It was an intensification of the same anger the neoconservatives had directed at the State Department and CIA for, in their estimation, obstructing the momentum of the invasion of Iraq. Worst of all were the corrupt intelligence barons, who MAGA believed had launched a "coup" to overturn Trump's election by inventing the fake narrative of #Russiagate. For military validation, they had the example of the martyred General Flynn, whom they refused to believe Trump had wanted to fire. They saved their greatest disdain, however, for the FBI—Comey, Mueller, and their cronies—which had dared investigate Trump. It mattered not at all that many who were vituperating against the Deep State were people like Flynn, an intelligence chief; Blackwater founder Erik Prince, a Navy SEAL who made a fortune from the War on Terror; Harvey, an army colonel and intelligence analyst; Michael Scheuer, the founder of the CIA's Usama bin Ladin Unit; and Nunes, who was privy to the government's most sensitive intelligence. MAGA defined itself in opposition to the usurper Deep State. The course of the War on Terror was now determined by the conflict between these two forces.

Since 9/11, the coalition now uniting under the MAGA banner had applauded the heaviest police, prosecutorial, and intelligence measures against Muslims, immigrants, and Black people. But now that Trump's criminality had attracted the scrutiny of the Security State, MAGA claimed that invoking obscure laws or leveraging perjury to compel cooperation showed deep corruption within law enforcement. That was the key to the passion play of Mike Flynn, prosecuted for lying to the FBI about conversations with the Russian ambassador that made him a subornable national security adviser. As with all nationalist movements, the license for impunity stopped where uncertain loyalty to the leader began. For men like Adham Hassoun, there would only be another cage, or worse. It would be the most coherent characteristic of the War on Terror in the Trump era, a time when the War on Terror became its most authentic self.

OBAMA BUILT THE DISPOSITION matrix to guide his successor's lethal decision-making as much as his own. Since his lodestar had been "a smart strategy that can be sustained," as he put it in his final counterterrorism speech, the inheritance of the disposition matrix mattered. If the next president discarded it, then Obama's Sustainable War on Terror would prove to have never in fact been sustainable, revealing Obama to have misread the political consensus. Obama made no move to restrict drone strikes or surveillance at scale as he prepared to hand power to a man who considered him a secret Kenyan Muslim usurping the White House.

Trump, characteristically, had little interest in what he understood as idiotic bureaucratic constraints. Within days of taking office he approved a JSOC raid against an al-Qaeda target in Yemen that Obama had resisted. The raid's mission, CENTCOM said, was to seize and exploit al-Qaeda in the Arabian Peninsula (AQAP) documents. But the commandos' tilt-rotor Osprey malfunctioned during the predawn incursion in the southern village of Yakla, and they emerged from a hard landing to incoming fire from panicked residents. The result was a dead SEAL, Chief Petty Officer William "Ryan" Owens, and an estimated twenty-five Yemeni civilian casualties, including an eight-year-old girl, Nawar—the daughter of Anwar al-Awlaki. Her grandfather Nasser, who had already buried his son and grandson, did not believe the Americans had intentionally killed Nawar. Trump immediately denied any responsibility for the disaster. "They lost Ryan," he said of the generals who brought the raid to him for his approval.

In his first year in office Trump declared much of Yemen and Somalia areas of "active hostilities," a decision sought by the military, thereby placing them under battlefield rules instead of disposition-matrix restrictions. He delegated authority for lethal air strikes, drone or piloted, downward to regional and local commanders. Obama veterans comforted themselves that Trump retained their language regarding the need for a "near certainty" that strikes wouldn't kill civilians. But the commanders, across multiple battlefields, knew what Trump wanted to see. In April 2017 a mountain near Jalalabad believed to contain a tunnel complex used by Afghanistan's ISIS franchise buckled under the impact of the largest non-nuclear bomb ever used by the U.S. military. The GBU-43 "Mother of All Bombs" left a mile-wide blast radius and vaporized an estimated thirty-six people suspected of being ISIS militants. The previous month, air force statistics showed, U.S. warplanes released more ordnance on Iraq and Syria than at any time since the war resumed in 2014. An air war that gave meaning to "bombing the shit out of them" had begun.

Trump hoped that this effort would unite him with the Security State. But days before his inauguration, Clapper, Brennan, Comey, and Alexander's

successor at NSA, Admiral Mike Rogers, issued an intelligence assessment
stating that Russia had interfered in the election to aid Trump. Trump exploded, comparing the intelligence agencies to Nazis, but showed up at
Langley the day after his inauguration with an olive branch. He did it
his way, standing at the agency's memorial wall to falsely boast about
his inauguration crowd size, which unsettled several in attendance. But
those listening to Trump more dispassionately heard a promise to stop the
CIA from being "restrained" in the War on Terror. "You're going to say,
'Please don't give us so much backing,'" Trump claimed. "Radical Islamic
terrorism—and I said it yesterday—has to be eradicated, just off the face of
the earth."

To head the CIA, Trump appointed Mike Pompeo, whom a White
House official described to *The New Yorker* as "sycophantic and obsequious" when it came to Trump. ACT for America beamed that Pompeo had
always been a "stalwart ally," just months after giving him its highest award.
For his deputy, Pompeo made an inspired choice: Gina Haspel, the avatar
of the CIA's 9/11 generation, whom Brennan had stopped from running the
clandestine service. In a signal of where Trump intended to move the war,
Pompeo put Michael D'Andrea, who had run the CIA's drone strikes *and*
its black sites, in charge of planning operations against Iran. Pompeo
showed that Trump was serious about unleashing the CIA, no matter how
hysterically he tweeted against its former leaders. Nor was Pompeo shy
about editing Trump. The president might have welcomed WikiLeaks'
campaign season alignment, but Pompeo, who had himself cited those
leaks to chastise Clinton, declared WikiLeaks a hostile intelligence service,
foreshadowing the Justice Department's long-awaited indictment of Assange. Trump's expansive support for CIA counterterrorism could unnerve
Langley. Once, as Trump reviewed footage recorded by a drone, he watched
an agency target walking away from his home and family before the tar-
geter opened fire. "Why'd you wait?" he asked.

By November 2018, and to almost entirely no notice, Trump had
launched at least 238 strikes, far exceeding the 186 drone strikes Obama

ordered in his own first two years, the most intense bombing period for the drones before Trump's own. There was even less transparency around the attacks than during Obama's term, a stance codified in 2019 by executive order. Among the details it concealed was the effect of declaring Somalia a zone of active hostilities. With commanders needing less certainty to order a strike on a target, "that automatically opens up the aperture," recalled the senior Special Operations commander in Africa at the time, army brigadier general Donald Bolduc. U.S. commanders in Somalia launched 35 drone strikes in 2017, two more than during Obama's entire presidency, and followed up with 47 more in 2018. Bolduc observed that none of it—not the raids, not the drone strikes—made any real difference. "The big problem with this," he said in 2018, "is that there's no long-term success with this."

It was often said that Afghanistan was the forgotten war. Somalia could never earn that distinction, since no one in the United States had ever paid any attention to it. When Trump took office, the U.S. had been at war in Somalia, indirectly or directly, for a decade—McChrystal, who led the first JSOC wave into that country, called targeting al-Qaeda there "sensitive, difficult business"—yet the House Armed Services Committee had made no study of any of it. There was no longer anything unusual about a decade-long war.

With the tactical possibilities expanded and oversight practically nonexistent, atrocities mounted. In August 2017 U.S. special operators in command of their Somali protégés raided the farming village of Bariire and killed ten civilians, including a child, whom the U.S.-backed government falsely labeled as members of al-Shabaab. Witnesses said the Americans instructed the Somali soldiers to plant AK-47s on the corpses—sloppily; most of the shell cases found on the scene by a reporter were NATO-issue 5.56 mm—which outraged villagers kept unburied until Somali leaders recanted the al-Shabaab accusation. The following May, U.S.-supported Somali soldiers tore through another Lower Shabelle village, Ma'alinka, and killed five locals either directly or through stray fire in a shootout. The drone strikes, rising to 63 in 2019, were similarly devastating. In February

2020 a disabled eighteen-year-old woman, Nurto Kusow Omar Abukar, had just sat down to dinner with her family when a missile tore through their house and killed her instantly. AFRICOM reported that the strike "killed one terrorist." By then, Amnesty International found, the command was regularly listing absurdly low estimates of civilian casualties. AFRICOM knew it would face no pressure from anyone in power to admit a realistic death toll.

Bolduc's observation that U.S. violence in Somalia yielded nothing durable applied equally to the war sprawling across northern, western, and eastern Africa. The CIA turned an air base at Dirkou, in northeastern Niger, into a staging ground for drone strikes in southern Libya, even though the air force had already spent three years and an absurd $110 million to establish its own Nigerien drone base, at Agadez, from which it aided the French war against Islamist guerrillas in Mali. Mali and Niger represented additional fronts in a continental war that expanded by drift, a development concealed by virtue of its principal combatants being Special Operations Forces. One of the officers the U.S. special operators trained to fight West African jihadists, Colonel Assimi Goita, led a coup in August 2020 that ousted Malian president Ibrahim Boubacar Keïta.

In Niger, where some eight hundred U.S. troops now operated, eleven Army Special Forces troops, backed by thirty Nigerien mentees, drove an unarmored and unarmed SUV through the southwest into a devastating October 2017 ambush. A Pentagon investigation found that the team of mostly Green Berets was scheduled to meet with local leaders, but had to change their mission after a drone spotted an Islamic State potentate. Their captain, the target of blame from a Pentagon report that the soldiers' relatives denounced as a whitewash, expressly warned his superior officer that the unit was neither equipped nor informed enough to execute the raid. More than a hundred militants opened fire on Operational Detachment-Alpha Team 3212. Air support and evacuation did not arrive for four hours, by which time Sergeant First Class Jeremiah W. Johnson, Staff Sergeant Bryan C. Black, and Staff Sergeant Dustin M. Wright were dead. Sergeant

La David Johnson was missing, and his body would not be recovered for two days.

Less than two weeks later Trump called Johnson's grieving widow. Myeshia Johnson was with her mother and a family friend, Miami congresswoman Frederica Wilson, who paraphrased Trump as saying that Johnson—whose name Trump evidently didn't remember—must have known what he had signed up for. Trump immediately called Wilson a liar. But it sounded like a garbled version of how Kelly, now Trump's White House chief of staff, had eulogized two fallen marines in his caustic St. Louis speech in 2010: "they were in exactly the place they wanted to be: among the best men and women America produces." Kelly, in an extraordinary press conference, assured that Trump had said nothing different from what his friend Joe Dunford told him when informing him of his son's death.

Myeshia, pregnant with their third child, tearfully recounted how Trump's disrespectful call had increased her anguish. "And it made me cry 'cause I was very angry at the tone of his voice and how he said he couldn't remember my husband's name," she told *Good Morning America*. "If my husband is out here fighting for our country and he risked his life for our country, why can't you remember his name?"

Kelly had bitterly valorized Forever War sacrifice by placing it on a higher plane of citizenship. Now he protected Trump against his fellow Gold Star family. Unrestrained, Kelly also falsely accused Wilson, whom he called an "empty barrel," of inflating her role in the opening of an FBI office in Florida. Wilson, who is Black, received nooses in the mail. Anyone shocked by now at Kelly's ruthlessness had condescended to him by ignoring his patterns of behavior. "General Kelly needs counseling from a pastor or someone who can help him ask for forgiveness from the nation for all of his insults, not just to me but to the Dreamers who he said were lazy," Wilson later said.

Far more disruptive was Mike Flynn. Flynn and his aides, several of whom were his favorites from the DIA, entered an administration full of like-minded people who believed that the vast security bureaucracy they now helmed was implacably hostile. They aligned themselves instead with the nativist wing of the Trump presidency, a particularly strong faction within the White House. Career officials who had been billeted to the National Security Council (NSC) to work on refugee admissions suddenly saw Stephen Miller, who was not a member of the NSC, begin to dominate their agenda. Steve Bannon, the *Breitbart* nationalist impresario turned White House chief political strategist, even acquired a spot on the NSC. Wandering without portfolio was the theatrical Islamophobic blowhard Sebastian Gorka. A strategist from the surveillance-capitalist billionaire Peter Thiel's orbit, Kevin Harrington, joined Flynn's NSC staff and soon proposed withdrawing forces from the Baltics as a gesture of detente to Russia.

Flynn's agenda alarmed the Security State. At a meandering White House press conference early on in Trump's presidency, he notified Iran that it was "on notice." Islamophobia, along with catechistic right-wing contempt for Iran, offered Bannon and the nationalists a way to reconcile their antiwar postures with their alliance with Flynn. Another Flynn initiative attracted alarm, particularly from Mattis. The national security adviser wanted to expand a U.S.–Russian military communications channel, intended to prevent midair collisions or confrontations in Syria, into an avenue to explore greater detente.

That wing of the Trump coalition, if not necessarily Flynn himself, was hostile to the war in Afghanistan. *Breitbart* had considered it a stupid, wasteful conflict, defined by its humiliations, like the Bowe Bergdahl swap. Alarming the military in particular was the influence of Erik Prince, the Blackwater founder. Aligned with Bannon despite doing business with MAGA bête noir China and with the UAE, which cultivated close ties with Jared Kushner, Prince publicly proposed a way out of Afghanistan for Trump: leasing him the war. In interviews, Prince analogized his venture to the British East India Company, sounding like the MAGA version of Max Boot's 2001 enthusiasm for self-confident Englishmen in jodphurs and pith helmets. Prince neglected the part where Britain nationalized the collapsing enterprise to quell India's 1857 uprising, but his pitch was less about history than about making money redressing the martial humiliations of white civilization. The Taliban could be beaten by a force made up of soldiers from countries "with a good rugby team," Prince quipped. Neither Mattis nor McMaster was keen on Prince's venture.

Prince and his cohort were dealt a substantial setback less than a month into the administration when Flynn found himself out of a job and in serious legal trouble. Beginning in summer 2016, the FBI had opened a counterintelligence probe, known as Crossfire Hurricane, into the apparent connections between Trump's campaign and Russia. It was bound to investigate Flynn, a disgruntled intelligence chief who had sat beside Vladimir Putin at a gala for Russian state TV, which paid him for a speech. By the election, some within the FBI felt their concerns about Flynn were resolved. But after Flynn became President-elect Trump's national security adviser designate, the FBI intercepted what they considered alarming conversations between Flynn and the Russian ambassador, Sergey Kislyak. As the Obama administration expelled various Russian diplomatic and intelligence personnel, Flynn cautioned Kislyak not to escalate a sanctions battle—signalling that Trump did not intend reprisal measures over election interference that had benefited him—lest it jeopardize Flynn's long-desired U.S.–Russian counterjihadist alliance. "We will not achieve stability in the Middle East without working with each other against this radical Islamist crowd," he explained to Kislyak on December 23. Kislyak replied to Flynn that he considered the sanctions aimed "not only against Russia, but also against the president elect." Within days the Security State also discovered that Flynn had lied to the Trump administration and to journalists about the sanctions discussion. Mike Pence, soon to be the vice president, said Flynn had assured him the pair did not discuss the sanctions issue.

The holdover attorney general, Sally Yates, feared that Flynn's lies had created a point of Russian leverage, and she hastened to inform the White House counsel. Yet Comey and his deputy, Andrew McCabe, moved forward unilaterally with an interview of Flynn on January 24. Notes later released show Crossfire Hurricane officials who would soon become MAGA villains, FBI attorney Lisa Page and counterintelligence agent Peter Strzok—Strzok was also a leading figure in the Clinton email investigation—fretting over the delicacy the Flynn interview required, including when they might need to inform the national security adviser that lying to them was a felony. As a matter of law they were under no such obligation, which was something a man in Flynn's position was expected to know. Flynn sealed his fate by lying to the FBI about the Kislyak call, as if a man who had headed an intelligence agency could be unaware that the Security State intercepted Kislyak's communications. With news stories now emerging about the conversations, Trump accepted Flynn's resignation less than a month after his appointment, a stunning humiliation only weeks after the general's redemption.

It got worse for Flynn. Soon after his firing, Flynn belatedly registered as an agent of a foreign power for his undeclared half million dollars' worth of lobbying on behalf of Turkey. Both the lies to the FBI and the unreported foreign lobbying were points of leverage for his subsequent prosecution. Flynn pleaded guilty for lying to the FBI in exchange for leniency and cooperation. In a rarity for the Trump coterie, the president did not treat Flynn as disloyal, but instead found political value in portraying Flynn as a martyr to a Deep State gone mad.

Into the national security void at the White House stepped McMaster, a three-star general then in an army training command position. McMaster neither wanted the job nor had a history with Trump: he was given the national security adviser appointment after a JSOC veteran, retired vice admiral Robert Harward, passed on it. McMaster ousted Bannon from the NSC and over the next several months oversaw an exodus of Flynn's staff from key positions. An island of Flynn loyalism remained in Devin Nunes's Capitol Hill office, where NSC Mideast chief Derek Harvey landed, while McMaster kept Michael Anton as his spokesman. On the whole, McMaster treated the position as a redoubt against the nativists, and opted to reinterpret Trump's positions as consistent with traditional

Republican internationalism. That meant, among other things, escalation in Afghanistan.

Although Trump had railed for years against the futility of the Afghanistan war, he yielded to McMaster, Mattis, and the military in nearly doubling the size of the deployment. In an echo of Obama's 2009 Afghanistan review, senior officers got the time and resources they wanted but had to contend with the president's distrust that their plan would work. Hours before Trump announced the escalation in August 2017, Security Staters worried he would change his mind. McMaster threaded the needle by portraying a strategy commensurate with the status quo as a departure from Obama: no timetables this time. But Trump's "clear definition" of victory was less an outcome than a process of "attacking our enemies, obliterating ISIS, crushing al Qaeda, preventing the Taliban from taking over Afghanistan, and stopping mass terror attacks against America before they emerge." Trump gestured at a "political settlement"—a negotiated accord with the Taliban—but undercut it by musing that "nobody knows if or when that will ever happen."

Few in the military paused to reflect that the unlikelihood of the Taliban's suing for peace discredited McMaster's strategy of suppressing them until the elusive day when they would. Faith in such a disproven strategy had held strong throughout the Security State for over a decade. Two very different presidents had now acquiesced to it. By November 2017 the eighty-four hundred troops Obama had left in Afghanistan had risen to fifteen thousand. Yet by the following year the Taliban was, predictably, potent enough to infiltrate a meeting of U.S. and Afghan leaders in Kandahar. General Abdul Raziq, Kandahar's police chief—a title that understated his local influence—was shot dead within sight of the commanding U.S. general, Scott Miller, a JSOC alum and favorite of McChrystal. Seeking a way out of the morass, a former U.S. ambassador to Pakistan, Robin Raphel, and Chris Kolenda, a retired army colonel who had been part of the stillborn Obama-era effort to negotiate with the Taliban, shuttled to Doha to discuss the prospects for a settlement to the war with Taliban figures.

Kolenda briefed the Pentagon on what he had learned. Trump's antipathy to the war meant diplomacy to end it was no longer politically toxic.

There was even more continuity on the other major front of the war. Trump boasted about a secret plan to end ISIS. But in reality, the plan was just the extant By, With, and Through strategy, which was closing in on its endgame for the Caliphate. Trump inherited Brett McGurk as the lead diplomat holding the coalition against ISIS together—as well as Iraqi militias, operating at a remove from their Iranian paymasters, as an auxiliary ground force.

At the end of the Obama administration, U.S., Iraqi government, and Iranian-backed Iraqi forces began retaking Mosul through intense, block-by-block fighting unseen since the darkest days of the occupation. The U.S. commander, Lieutenant General Stephen Townsend, called the recapture of Mosul "the most constant heavy combat that we have [seen] probably since before Vietnam." An encirclement, siege, and advance on the city met determined ISIS resistance that held out for nine months, until July 2017, three times longer than the initial forecasts. The battle devastated the city—credible unofficial estimates reported by the Associated Press put the civilian death toll as high as eleven thousand, more than ten times official tallies—and displaced an estimated nearly 1 million people. ISIS detonated the al-Nuri Mosque, an eight-hundred-year-old treasure and the spot where Baghdadi had declared the Caliphate, rather than let the Iraqi flag fly over it. Writing in *Military Review*, two army officers drily noted that Mosul's civilians "did comparatively little to enhance coalition operations." That left Raqqa as the final capital of the Caliphate, which held out until October. As Raqqa fell to the U.S.-backed Kurds, McGurk gloated, "Once purported as fierce, now pathetic and a lost cause." It was remarkable confidence from someone with experience watching American advances in the War on Terror evaporate.

If, as was commonly assumed in Washington, Mattis and McMaster had entered the administration to prevent Trump from foreign policy departures—and particularly from disengagement—then by early 2018 their success looked formidable. But their apparent success revealed what they were willing to tolerate in order to keep the Forever War going.

The War on Terror had made Mattis into a widely respected figure internationally. His role in the administration was to reassure traditional allies that the United States was not really going to act in the manner that Trump's tweets suggested. Mattis's most public success came when Trump said that "Mad Dog" assured him that returning to a torture policy wouldn't be necessary. That invested centrists and some liberals in believing that Mattis was broadly opposed to Trump.

In 2017 Trump unexpectedly tweeted that military service by transgender people was banned, reversing a tentative Obama initiative. There was no pretext to cite; Mattis would later testify that the military had no cases of transgender service members causing any disruptions. Trump simply took an opportunity to show a minority group who disgusted his constituents that they could not presume to possess equal citizenship. Mattis, who had opposed repealing the ban on open LGBT military service, acceded to it, while letting journalists know it hadn't been his idea. After pausing implementation for a study—interpreted by liberals as welcome bureaucratic subterfuge—Mattis left an "exception" for trans service members to serve in their "biological sex"—that is, in a closet. Multiple lawsuits did not dissuade Mattis from this act of cruelty.

Mattis had stood beside the president when Trump unveiled the Muslim ban and showed no sign of concern for the Muslim service members separated from their relatives abroad. It wasn't long before the nativism of the Trump administration targeted undocumented troops. Since 9/11, an estimated 130,000 people had become citizens through their U.S. military service. But post-9/11 nativism was now stronger than post-9/11 jingoism, and Mattis's Pentagon's policies reflected it.

Within months of Mattis taking office, the Pentagon froze an already-stalled program, begun under Bush, that expedited citizenship in exchange for enlistment and specialization in short-handed areas like foreign languages. Memos seen by NPR in July 2017 cited ten thousand enlistees who would be caught in the pipeline, unable to complete the program, leaving one thousand of them subject to deportation. Addressing the rising anxiety in the ranks, Mattis promised in February 2018 that undocumented service members would "not be subject to any kind of deportation," a pledge he said came with Nielsen's concurrence.

But a month later ICE deported Miguel Perez Jr., who had come to the United States legally as an eight-year-old and enlisted in the army months before 9/11. His two tours in Afghanistan left him with PTSD and the substance abuse problem that led him to pass a laptop case full of cocaine to an undercover officer, which ICE used to justify the deportation. The following month ICE prepared to deport Xilong Zhu, an honorably discharged and undocumented soldier who enrolled in a university surreptitiously established by ICE as a visa-fraud trap. If Mattis had been sincere in his pledge, he did not vigorously enforce it, nor did it outlast his tenure. A Government Accountability Office study in 2019 found that ICE was deporting veterans at a rate that made it difficult to calculate just how many had been removed. Whatever Mattis's promises against deportation, they did not extend to retention. Dozens of undocumented recruits in the expedited-citizenship program ended up purged from the military under Mattis. By the following year, after Mattis's departure, the military began to deny enlistments for what *The Washington Post* called "existing as foreigners."

Shortly before the 2018 midterm elections, the administration manufactured a crisis along the southern border, where illegal crossings had hit a historic low. Trump and Fox News endlessly focused on a migrant caravan heading northward to the border. The men, women, and children within it were not described as what they were—people fleeing poverty and violence—but instead as an "invasion" force, against which military action would be justified. Trump also lied that there were "Middle Easterners" in the caravan. Mattis acquiesced to a fifty-eight-hundred-troop deployment to backstop CBP, and denied to reporters that it was at all a political stunt. In Texas, where he traveled with Nielsen to observe the nebulous mission—

one that would continue into 2020—Mattis defended it as falling in the tradition of the 1916 Punitive Expedition against Pancho Villa.

It was part of a pattern of compromise for both Mattis and McMaster. McMaster had debased himself by defending Trump's sharing Israeli intelligence on ISIS with Russia as "wholly appropriate." None of it was enough to save them. Trump, after taking McMaster's advice on Afghanistan—and adopting McMaster's security strategy, beloved by the defense commentariat, for "great power competition" against Russia and China—fired him and prompted the end of his army career.

A critical disagreement between Trump and McMaster concerned Syria. After the fall of the ISIS Caliphate, McMaster advocated remaining indefinitely in northeastern Syria, a place where the United States had no legal mandate to wage war, but where state failure left no force to oust it. The Americans effectively guaranteed an autonomous statelet for the Syrian Kurds, who had done most of the fighting to oust ISIS. Less than a week after firing McMaster, and six months after the fall of Raqqa, Trump promised at a rally that he was getting out of Syria "like very soon." But he had picked the wrong national security adviser for that. McMaster's replacement, John Bolton, instead redefined the war to accommodate his hostility to Iran. By September 2018, not only were two thousand U.S. troops still in Syria, but Bolton promised to remain "as long as Iranian troops are outside Iranian borders, and that includes Iranian proxies and militias." The following spring Mike Pompeo hinted at expanding the War on Terror to Iran outright. In a manner reminiscent of 2002, Pompeo declared, "There is no doubt there is a connection between the Islamic Republic of Iran and al-Qaeda. Period. Full stop."

Neither Mattis nor the military was interested in redirecting the war away from ISIS, but Bolton's advocacy of an open-ended presence suited their interests. Bolton, however, had entirely overreached. Turkish president Recep Tayyip Erdogan, eager to assault the Kurds, and a strongman who Trump admired, goaded Trump toward the exits by threatening to invade northeast Syria. Erdogan turned out to be startled at how precipitously Trump was prepared to pull out. Shortly before Christmas 2018 the president issued a declaration that no president had made since Bush announced MISSION ACCOMPLISHED on the aircraft carrier: the assertion of victory that his base desperately wanted to hear. "We have won against ISIS," he said in a video he tweeted, so the troops were "all coming back, and they're coming back now." The military was able to roll the order back, but not before both McGurk and Mattis resigned in disgust. Mattis had declared in his highly public resignation letter that he would stay until February, but Trump told him not to bother. The people lamenting Mattis's departure the most were Security Staters like Jim Clapper, who lionized Mattis's resignation as a "classic" document of patriotic integrity.

Mattis left the same month as an exasperated Kelly. With them ended the era of the Adults—but not the illusion that they had waged an internal resistance. When Mattis reemerged in 2019, it was to promote a memoir that was hostile to Obama and Biden but silent on Trump. That silence affected Mattis's reputation as a sage not a bit, just as it had remained unsullied after the trans ban, the border deployment, and the troop deportations. In May 2019 Mattis's deputy and interim successor, the former Boeing executive Patrick Shanahan, approved a request from DHS to make military bases available for "temporary facilities to house and care for a minimum of 7,500 total single adult male and female aliens" in the custody of ICE. Mattis had slow-walked creating the camps after Trump had instructed him to do so in a June 2018 executive order. Pentagon officials would explain the delay by claiming that they had never received a formal request from DHS. But Mattis had not refused the order. He certainly did not offer his resignation over what Paul Yingling, who had been a senior officer on McMaster's staff at Tal Afar, called "participation in hostage-taking."

By suborning three lions of the War on Terror, Trump prolonged the situation he so often lamented. Even after the U.S.'s near pullout, Trump's envoy for Syria, apparently believing Trump had been contained by the Security State, told the Kurds not to bother seeking a separate peace with

Assad, which might have forestalled a Turkish invasion. The U.S. military encouraged the Kurds to destroy their defensive fortifications. Kurdish commander Mazloum Abdi was led to believe that "Turkey would never attack us so long as the U.S. government was true to its word with us." In October 2019, Trump ordered an abrupt abandonment of Syrian Kurdish positions to permit Erdogan his assault on the U.S.'s allies. Yet even as Rojava's citizens pelted departing U.S. Humvees with rotten fruit, Trump would not fully withdraw. He boasted instead of plunder, redeploying to eastern Syria's oil fields on the promise of taking the resources he had called America's rightfully due spoils. It was as if enabling the slaughter of those who had bled to retake the Caliphate was fulfilling a campaign promise. Trump had no time for any outrage about staining the national honor. He blamed the Kurds for "releasing" ISIS prisoners from positions they abandoned to flee Erdogan's forces. Two years after gloating that ISIS was a spent force, McGurk told an Abu Dhabi conference in the wake of the Turkish rampage, "I think we are likely to see a significant comeback by ISIS."

In the midst of the pullback, the end of the month brought a revealing moment: a redux of the bin Laden raid. Backstopped by the CIA, Delta Force commandos landed in late October in a village in western Syria called Barisha, far from the former Caliphate, where they killed ISIS leader Abu Bakr al-Baghdadi. Trump gloated that Baghdadi died "whimpering and crying and screaming," pursued by Special Operations dogs. Yet like Obama in 2011, he did not use the raid as an opportunity to claim victory in the war. He had already declared it, and had ordered a withdrawal predicated on it, but instead he spoke as if the mission would continue. America's "reach is long" against "these savage monsters," he said, who "will never escape justice." Despite the Pentagon assurances that no harm came to civilians, thirty-year-old Syrian farmer Barakat Ahmad Barakat told reporters that he had lost an arm to U.S. helicopter fire that killed his two companions. Barakat would forever remember an episode that America forgot within days. Trump, committing the same mistake as his hated predecessor, provided Americans no reason to view Baghdadi as anything more than the latest dead terrorist.

He devoted far more emphasis, two weeks later, to granting clemency to three service members who were facing consequences for Forever War atrocities. Army lieutenant Clint Lorance had been serving a sentence at Leavenworth for ordering his soldiers to open fire on Afghan civilians in 2010. Mathew Golsteyn had been stripped of his Special Forces tab and was awaiting trial for murder. Then there was Navy SEAL Eddie Gallagher. Gallagher had become a Fox News cause célèbre. His fellow SEALs had turned him in, calling him "toxic" and even "evil." They told investigators that in Iraq, Gallagher had shot civilians with relish—"burkas were flying," they quoted him saying—and used a hunting knife to slit the throat of an ISIS captive. Gallagher was acquitted of the most serious charges, but even after the White House clemency, Trump intervened to ensure that Navy Special Warfare Command did not oust Gallagher from the SEALs, a decision that cost Trump his navy secretary. The president was redeeming not only Gallagher, Golsteyn, and Lorance, but the exceptionalist strain on the right that held that American troops, by virtue of being Americans, could not commit atrocities, especially not against so frustrating and subhuman an enemy. To Trump, their service was honorable *because* of their brutality, and those opposed to it, even if they were in uniform, showed their dishonor. "I stuck up for three great warriors," Trump told a MAGA rally in Florida, "against the Deep State."

To his constituents, whom he had promised victory, none of Trump's Forever War contradictions mattered, if they noticed them at all. Trump successfully positioned himself as an opponent of the War on Terror simply through his derision of the status quo. None of his escalations, at home or abroad, undermined that narrative in the eyes of either elite media or his supporters. MAGA was less interested in ending the war than in wresting control of it from the Security State. Nowhere did that struggle manifest more heatedly than where the fissure between the Security State and the right first emerged after 9/11: the intelligence agencies.

AMONG TRUMP'S GOVERNMENT APPOINTEES, Islamophobia was practically de rigueur. Shortly before arriving at the White House, budget chief Russell Vought wrote that Muslims stood "condemned" for rejecting Jesus. Trump's pick for the International Organization on Migration, Ken Isaacs, withdrew from contention after his social-media habits of blaming Islam for terrorism emerged. A Health and Human Services official, Ximena Barreto, had called Islam a "cult" with no place in America, something she had in common with the USAID religious freedom adviser Mark Kevin Lloyd. Pete Hoekstra, the buffoonish House Intelligence Committee chief who suggested that al-Qaeda had penetrated the CIA, became Trump's ambassador to the Netherlands. He apologized after causing an international incident over 2015 remarks that Muslims had turned imaginary parts of Holland into "no-go zones." A Flynn appointee on the NSC, Rich Higgins, was fired after Mc-Master learned he had penned a memo portraying Trump as under attack from a "cultural Marxist" cabal that united "the Deep State," "Islamists," Black Lives Matter, and others ("ANTIFA working with Muslim Brotherhood doing business as MSA [Muslim Students' Association] and CAIR").

For its part the broader MAGA movement built up an intense fury aimed at a bloc of four progressive Democrats elected to Congress in the 2018 election. The Squad was an alliance of four nonwhite women who championed the multiracial working class. Two of them, Rashida Tlaib of Michigan and Ilhan Omar of Minnesota, were Muslims; Omar became the first U.S. representative to wear a hijab. She and Massachusetts's Ayanna Pressley were Black. Alexandria Ocasio-Cortez was a democratic socialist from the Bronx who terrified the Democratic power structure in New York, and many on the left cheered her willingness to do the same to the Democratic power structure in Washington.

MAGA forgot its pretenses to working-class politics by mocking Ocasio-Cortez for having worked as a bartender. But the fury it directed at Omar was distinct. Having come to the U.S. as a child refugee from Somalia, Omar represented a diverse Minneapolis, politically and metaphysically, that anti-Islam nativists had been warning for thirty years was white replacement in progress. Smear campaigns circulated, particularly on Facebook, attempting to depict her as an incest practitioner and, inevitably, a terrorist. At a rally in North Carolina in July 2019, Trump said Omar blamed America for terrorism. Months later she asked a judge to show compassion to a New York man convicted of threatening to put a bullet in her skull. If MAGA recognized the Squad as a threat to nationalism, in Omar it saw a threat to national security.

Trump, however, had the same recommendation for all of them, which he tweeted that July: "Why don't they go back and help fix the totally broken and crime-infested places from which they came?" In case there was any doubt that he was informing them that they were not truly American, he clarified that the Squad "originally came from countries whose governments are a complete and total catastrophe." These congresswomen had the temerity, he continued, to "loudly and viciously" tell "the people of the United States" how to run their affairs. Trump's crowd at a North Carolina rally days later singled out Omar and chanted, "Send her back!"

Open cheering for civilizational brutality was a spark dropped onto the tinder of white terrorist violence, whose adherents prepared to mete out the vigilante justice they considered the state too fearful to execute. Before and during Trump's first months in office, the various militant factions aligned with the emboldened alt-right clashed in street skirmishes with left-wing counterprotesters. They told themselves white genocide was at hand, that BLM was destroying their cultural patrimony, and that they were broadly under attack from a censorious liberal culture and specifically from left-wing anti-fascist warriors. Some styled themselves militants, a fetishized posture adopted from over fifteen years of war; some of them, as Daryl Johnson had warned, had actual military experience. Ten people were injured in a summer 2016 melee in Sacramento, where 30 white supremacists, including some from Matthew Heimbach's Traditionalist Worker Party, were outnumbered by 350 anti-fascists. In New Orleans the following May, white nationalists wearing makeshift armor from sporting-goods stores took the measure of anti-racist demonstrators calling for the removal of Robert E. Lee's statue during a tense but ultimately nonviolent confrontation.

In mid-August a white supremacist convocation called Unite the Right planned to march on Charlottesville, Virginia. The night before the event, white supremacists wearing polo shirts and carrying tiki torches chanted "Jews will not replace us" and "white lives matter" as they marched to confront demonstrators at another statue of Lee. Trump said there were "very fine people, on both sides" of the fascist versus anti-fascist fracas. The following day was uglier. Hundreds of white supremacists paraded through Charlottesville, attacking anti-racist counterprotesters in a show of force. One of them, an active-duty marine, bragged about "crack[ing] three skulls open." A group of six, including a man wearing a tactical helmet, mobbed anti-racist protester DeAndre Harris in a parking garage, breaking his wrist and tearing open his scalp—but it was Harris, not his assailants, who was served with a misdemeanor assault charge. (Harris hit with a Maglite a man who had attacked his friend with a flagpole.) Not far away, twenty-year-old James Fields drove his Dodge Challenger through the anti-racist lines, much as al-Qaeda's *Inspire* magazine had recommended, killing thirty-two-year-old Heather Heyer.

The subsequent law-enforcement scrutiny, media frenzy, and infighting ended up fracturing the alt-right as a force. But Charlottesville was more of a harbinger than a Waterloo for white supremacist violence. Armed militias like the Atomwaffen Division, which trained for a race war and whose members glorified McVeigh, and the Base—literally a translation of "al-Qaeda"—augured a resurgence of American fascist militancy. The leader of the Base, Rinaldo Nazzaro, worked for the Department of Homeland Security from 2004 to 2006, and appears to have spent time in Iraq. The newest wave of white-nationalist militancy fed accelerationist propaganda to extremely online white youth the same way ISIS did to extremely online Muslim youth. Surveillance capitalism was formally agnostic on that point, except that the surveillance capitalists themselves were far quicker to ban jihadists from their platforms than fascists. Less organized forms of terrorism gathered force as well. The worst incident of anti-Semitic violence in American history unfolded in October 2018 in Pittsburgh, when Robert Bowers entered the Tree of Life Synagogue and shot eleven people to death to show that he, the latest American Breivik, would not be replaced. A day earlier police in Florida arrested a Trump superfan, fifty-six-year-old Cesar Sayoc, for mailing pipe bombs to Trump enemies George Soros, Hillary Clinton, and CNN. The following year a deliberate anti-Latino massacre erupted when Patrick Crusius shot dead twenty-two people in a Walmart in El Paso. Like Breivik, Crusius left a manifesto; his vowed to avert a "Hispanic invasion of Texas."

Beginning on chan sites and expanding rapidly through Facebook, Twitter, and YouTube, an amorphous Trumpist revenge fantasy called QAnon soon took form. A supposed member of the Security State, Q, claimed Trump was on the cusp of secretly sending a group of pedophilic Trump enemies in Democratic politics and the Deep State to Guantanamo Bay. An accumulation of contrary evidence did not stop its astonishing growth. By summer 2020 QAnon groups on Facebook had at least 1 million members. Among them was Michael Scheuer, who had been part of the CIA's Renditions Group and its first chief of the Usama bin Laden Unit. Scheuer called Jews "agitators" for "a covert and overt war that is meant to destroy the legitimately elected Trump administration, as well as the American republic and its Constitution." (In a different post, he confessed, "I am not an admirer of the democratic system as it has evolved in the United States since the Founding.") Scheuer knew the Security State as well as anyone and wanted its brutality aimed at "gallows-headed traitors," including Brennan, Obama, Clapper, and, in a separate post, "Nazi-like terrorist groups, such as ANTIFA [and] Black Lives Matter."

That particular fusionist perspective, which saw Islamists in collaboration with the Security State, spoke to something else that had snapped on the right. There was nothing new about conspiratorialist thinking among nativists, nor resentment against the Security State. The neoconservative assault on the supposed institutional obstacles to the Iraq war, while far more respectable, had demonstrated that the right exempted itself from the post-9/11 deference it wanted the left to accord the security institutions. But those earlier manifestations of right-wing resistance to the Security State were in pursuit of particular objectives. MAGA viewed its own war with the Deep State as an existential struggle: either they or the Security State would dominate. But as Trump's empowerment of ICE and CBP showed, fealty to Trump was, in MAGA world, the true difference between heroes of the security services and a Deep State. From the start Trump had decried "Nazis" in the intelligence agencies, aligned with Democrats and journalists, determined to go to criminal lengths to undo his election.

Liberals watched in horror as Trump turned on the intelligence community and law enforcement. Horror became identification. What became known as the #Resistance on Twitter was a mockably earnest expression of, most often, white bourgeois outrage at Trump. Its adherents tended to surgically separate their hatred of Trump from any examination of the America that produced him. That exceptionalist position inclined the #Resistance to favorably view the FBI no longer as Hillary Clinton's irresponsible persecutor but as the swift blade of justice dangling above Trump's criminal reign. The FBI, the CIA, the NSA, and the Justice Department were the foundations of the rule of law, not manipulators, torturers, serial violators of fundamental constitutional liberties, and justifiers. To the #Resistance, which heeded figures like the NSA and CIA's Hayden, Iraq warmonger Bill Kristol, and Clapper, Trump's clash with the Security State testified to the virtues of the Security State.

Accordingly, liberals overinterpreted Russia's election interference and Trump's unadulterated solicitousness toward Putin. An obsession with the baroque, fragmentary details of what became #Russiagate inclined the

#Resistance toward a Cold War liberalism. Many #Resistance validators, like *Lawfare*, had primarily seen Snowden as a Russian dupe or operative, so the narrative of a renewed geopolitical rivalry had deep roots among Democrats. But believing Russia had suborned Trump avoided reckoning with how deeply American Trump and his movement actually were. The #Resistance tended to condemn Trump's threats to pull troops out of Afghanistan or Syria without bothering to argue the merits of the Forever theaters. After the Yemen raid that killed Ryan Owens and young Nawar al-Awlaki, columnist Ramzy Baroud noted how "Yemeni lives suddenly matter" now that the man taking them was Trump. "There is hardly a single bad deed that Trump has or intends to carry out that does not have roots in policies championed by prior administrations," he wrote. The #Resistance cheered on the "Adults In The Room" without considering that an earlier set of adults, the adults they esteemed, had already prepared the room.

The terms of the culture war drawn, the conflict took an unexpected early casualty: Jeff Sessions. Trump's election had been the triumph of Sessions's politics. Running the Justice Department had been beyond his wildest expectations, and he set to work abandoning the department's oversight of brutal, criminal police; misrepresenting terrorism data to portray it as immigrant violence; and championing Zero Tolerance. Yet when Sessions inherited control over the FBI's investigation into a campaign whose foreign policy team Sessions had led, the former prosecutor recused himself. It was fatal to his relationship with Trump. Sessions had not understood that Trump valued him according to his ability to protect Trump from legal trouble. Trump would humiliate Sessions on the way to firing him.

Within weeks of Sessions's recusal, Trump, aware that the FBI was investigating his campaign, fired Comey. The president had tried to get the FBI director—who kept as quiet about Crossfire Hurricane as he had been loud about the Clinton probe—to drop the case against Flynn and publicly state that Trump himself wasn't under investigation. The head of the Russia probe, Sessions's deputy Rod Rosenstein, helped draft a boldfaced pretext for why firing Comey was proper. Rosenstein then himself immediately earned the ire of Trump and his loyalists for appointing the FBI's post-9/11 director, Robert Mueller, as a special prosecutor. Comey leaked his accounts of his conversations with the president, infuriating Trump, who admitted to firing Comey because of "this Russia thing"—an admission of obstruction of justice—before later lying that he had said no such thing.

The Mueller investigation immediately became the chief political threat to Trump. Charateristically, his response was to craft a counternarrative. In March he declared without evidence that Obama had ordered his "wires tapped" at Trump Tower. Trump called Mueller's investigation a "witch hunt," distracting from the real crime committed by the Black president, the Deep State, and their deceitful media cronies. Trump's allies strained to make the fabrication real. Nunes claimed to have received word from an intelligence whistleblower validating a version of the claim—that Trump and his associates, who had conversations with people under surveillance, had their identities improperly unmasked and leaked to hostile media. It soon emerged that the chairman of the House Intelligence Committee had concocted the narrative right after Flynn allies provided it to him at the White House. Still, it would become an article of faith on the right that the craven Security State had put Trump under surveillance in order to effectively overturn the 2016 election. The #Russiagate narrative and the Mueller investigation were a means to a soft coup. Rosenstein had appointed Mueller, Bush's FBI director, to make the inquiry unquestionably legitimate. He failed to realize that to MAGA there could be no such thing. That spring, Nunes took an astonishing step for an Intelligence Committee chairman: he suggested that the Republican Congress might kill Section 702, the wellspring of the NSA's PRISM and UPSTREAM data collection, in retaliation.

At that moment the House Intelligence Committee web page that Nunes controlled had a pull-down explainer about the need to reauthorize "FISA 702." Nunes was stumbling into an anti-surveillance position that no House Intelligence chair had suggested since 9/11. "FISA abuse" would soon become an article of faith among elected Republicans, especially in the House. Yet this accusation against the Security State came in startling contrast to their silence over how much surveillance the Trump administration was actually carrying out.

At the dawn of Trump's presidency, the NSA did away with so-called "about" collection, whereby it collected communications data from people merely discussing a targeted person. The following year, the only post-Snowden collection reform collapsed. The 2015 USA FREEDOM Act tasked the telecoms with providing the massive graphs of association requested by the NSA and providing the results to Fort Meade for analysis. But the novelty of the tasking resulted in such a stunning amount of "overcollection"—that is, automatic surveillance on hundreds of millions of Americans' phone records—that NSA opted to purge its entire USA FREEDOM database and abandon the program. Its cancellation did not stem from any Trumpist crusade of principle against a surveillance apparatus run amok; the NSA continued to violate guidelines set by the FISA Court and Congress to restrain suspicionless digital surveillance on Americans at scale.

The NSA hardly closed its dragnets. FISA surveillance orders on stateside targets spiked to a high of 1,833 before falling sharply in 2019, to slightly over 1,000 targets. But thanks to Section 702, collection on Americans' outward-bound internet communications and records was much easier than obtaining a FISA order. Under Trump, Section 702 orders continued to skyrocket. In 2018 they reached 164,770 targets—a total that vastly underestimates the amount of surveillance conducted on those whom the targets contacted and so on. By 2019, 702 orders reached a high of 204,968 targets. Once the data reached the 702 databases, the FBI could sift through it without a warrant, the so-called "backdoor search" that Senator Ron Wyden railed against. In 2018 a FISA Court judge found that the FBI's backdoor searches were "inconsistent with statutory minimization requirements and the requirements of the Fourth Amendment," a ruling that would not become public for another year.

The schizophrenia reached its peak in January 2018. As the House was set to vote on 702, Trump tweeted his opposition to it. A furor erupted as it looked as if Republicans might actually vote down the intelligence community's highest priority for fear of crossing the president. Trump instead reversed himself, and the bill passed, uniting Nunes and his hated Democratic counterpart, Adam Schiff. The outcome reflected the state of the surveillance coalition. The Republicans deplored surveillance against Trump while having no reservations about the surveillance dragnets expanding ever further over untold millions of others, at home and abroad. The Democrats, despite proclaiming Trump a unique threat to the Constitution, kept handing him surveillance authorities. Their identification with the Security State inclined them to take increasing ownership of Forever War architecture in the name of rescuing it from the Trumpists. But it needed no saving. Even as Trump's crusade against the FBI for its "witch hunt" intensified, a Justice Department official told *The New York Times* that there was no "fear of using the FISA tool."

But Mueller's "witch hunt" soon indicted key Trump allies, including Flynn, and established, at minimum, receptivity at senior levels to suggestions of Russian election interference. Trump countered with a typical alternative narrative: the whole thing was the result of corrupt Democrat cops. Text messages emerged showing Strzok and Page discussing Trump as a humiliating, treasonous clown. Nunes, aided by the former Flynn ally Harvey, constructed a narrative about Deep State persecution of Trump out of, principally, an unfairly adverse surveillance warrant re-up before the FISA Court against Carter Page, a Trump campaign foreign policy aide whom an earlier FBI case had established was proximate to Russian intelligence operatives in New York. ("You get the documents from him and tell him to go fuck himself," was how one of them, Victor Podobnyy, explained how to deal with Page on an intercepted call.) If all this wasn't enough for Trump and his allies to adopt a narrative of a shadow coup by the Democrat-aligned Security State, it was conspicuous that a Democrat like Schiff, a former California prosecutor, raised his profile considerably through the constant investigations. There was a #Resistance trade in cringeworthy anti-Trump merchandise like Robert Mueller votive candles. Schiff and other congressional Democrats signaled that they were there to help the Security State and the Adults restrain a threat to the republic.

Before the reckoning there was an abrupt detente. Ultimately desirous of a good relationship with the CIA, Trump nominated Gina Haspel to become the agency's director. It was a brilliant move, elevating one of the leading figures of the 9/11 generation of the CIA to be its first woman leader. Nothing could have felt more like a vindication. Not four years after the Senate torture report, Haspel prepared humanizing autobiographical testimony for the panel that had once sent Dan Jones through her affairs. Clapper and Brennan took a break from assailing Trump as a threat to the republic to hail her. "She is capable. She has integrity," Mike Morell vouched in a quote circulated by the White House.

The CIA's push for Haspel was gratuitous in a manner that suggested Langley took her ascension as a matter of honor. The agency refused to release any but the vaguest of details about her torture tenure. Revisionism was its strategy for the rest. The CIA general counsel who clashed with Rodriguez and Haspel when they destroyed the torture tapes, John Rizzo, wrote in his memoir that the then-pseudonymous Haspel "ran the interrogation program." Now that his account unexpectedly threatened Haspel, Rizzo insisted that he must have gotten it wrong, even though the CIA had never requested a correction in the four years since the book's publication. Haspel was confirmed with the aid of six Senate Democrats, including Mark Warner, the senior Intelligence Committee Democrat who oversaw the Senate version of the Russia "witch hunt."

But by the time Mueller delivered his report, in spring 2019, Trump had finally found what he was looking for in an attorney general. Bill Barr, along with a younger Mueller, had created a predecessor to STELLAR-WIND at the Drug Enforcement Administration during the George H. W. Bush administration by building a bulk phone-data interception system for Americans' international calls. He was Verizon's senior lawyer during the actual STELLARWIND and pressed Congress for the telecom immunity delivered by the law establishing Section 702. Among the legal wing of the #Resistance, which at blogs like *Lawfare* had defended the Security State's prerogatives throughout the Forever War, Barr was a familiar quantity. "A very decent outcome," tweeted *Lawfare's* Ben Wittes, since Barr "knows and values the department's traditions." He responded by rubbing their faces in his shamelessness.

Ahead of the public release of Mueller's report, Barr released a deceitful summary claiming it exonerated Trump. Mueller, after a crucial silence, objected to Barr's characterization. He detailed the Russian influence and espionage operations, as well as Trump's resistance to the investigation, explicitly stating that his report "does not exonerate" Trump. But Mueller said he lacked definitive evidence to prove what in nonlegal shorthand was known as "collusion" with Russia, and he stopped short of saying conclusively that Trump had obstructed his attempts at acquiring that evidence. In any event, by the Office of Legal Counsel's non-judicial precedent, one concocted during Richard Nixon's presidency, a sitting president cannot be indicted. After two years of investigation, Mueller said Congress was the proper venue for adjudicating Trump's perfidy. But months later, in congressional testimony, Mueller declined to meaningfully characterize what his report implied about Trump's threat to the Constitution. The president, once again free from consequences, boasted of his "Complete and Total EXONERATION."

The day after Mueller's testimony Trump had a conversation with the newly elected president of Ukraine, Volodymyr Zelensky. Zelensky needed a substantial shipment of weapons to repulse a Russian military and proxy advance, along with assurances of continued American support. "I would like you to do us a favor, though," Trump replied. Having already pursued seemingly unsuccessful efforts to acquire Russian dirt on Hillary Clinton, Trump wanted Zelensky to provide Ukrainian dirt on Joe Biden, who had recently declared for president. The plan was hatched by an increasingly unstable Rudy Giuliani. Giuliani, by now Trump's personal attorney but with a penchant to crumble under non–Fox News questioning, had pursued Ukrainian contacts to establish that Biden had ousted the senior Ukrainian prosecutor in order to spare Burisma, a natural gas company on whose board Biden's son Hunter served, from investigation. In truth, the prosecutor was widely considered to have been corrupt, and the corruption demonstrated by Burisma in granting a board seat to the son of the U.S. vice president was the sort practiced by respectable elites worldwide.

With Trump's assent and the knowledge of Secretary of State Pompeo, Giuliani put together an effort to subordinate Ukraine policy to his scheme for Trump's reelection. Giuliani worked along and through a loyalist clique known as "the three amigos": Energy Secretary Rick Perry; State Department Ukraine envoy Kurt Volker; and EU ambassador Gordon Sondland, a hotelier who had donated $1 million to Trump's inaugural. Their antics prompted alarm from career diplomats, military officers, and the NSC's Russia desk—and, surprisingly, the opposition of John Bolton, who said he wanted no part of Giuliani's "drug deal." In a move that could not remain secret for long, the administration withheld $400 million in aid and a White House visit for Zelensky in what Sondland later testified was a "quid pro quo" for Zelensky announcing an investigation into Burisma.

Before Zelensky could announce anything, a CIA detailee to the NSC informed Michael Atkinson, the inspector general of the intelligence agencies, of the drug deal. Atkinson did as he was legally obligated and reported it to the congressional intelligence committees. Pelosi, Schiff, and the House Democratic leadership announced the impeachment hearings they had long dreaded holding.

Trump and MAGA erupted. So soon after they had done away with Mueller, here was Deep State Witch Hunt Part 2. "The time and necessity for vengeance is upon us," Scheuer blogged. Nunes and key Republican legislators defended Trump by telling the story in reverse. The plot was nothing more than Trump's selfless concern for eradicating corruption from Ukraine. The real story was the collusion among Deep State bureaucrats from the CIA and elsewhere with the Democrats to protect Biden's corrupt son. John Ratcliffe, a Texas Republican, made theatrically baseless defenses of Trump, such as his insistence that the Trump–Zelensky conversation was merely "a congratulatory phone call where there are no crimes alleged." Harvey began to leak a name supposedly belonging to the CIA whistleblower, which would soon make appearances in right-wing media and on Twitter for both retaliation and to deter future whistleblowers. Army lieutenant colonel Alexander Vindman, who came to America as a young Soviet Jewish refugee and was injured by an IED in Iraq, was un-Trooped when he testified against Trump from his vantage on the NSC. Allies of the president, including John Yoo and Rudy Giuliani, questioned Vindman's loyalty. Schiff implored in vain for Republicans in the House to finally oust this threat to the republic, but not one voted to impeach. In the Senate, Mitt Romney, who had once boasted of Trump's endorsement, was the only Republican vote to convict.

Once again it was time for retribution. Just as he had cleared the FBI of Comey, McCabe, Strzok, Page, and other Crossfire Hurricane officials, Trump now purged people connected to impeachment, including Sondland and Vindman, who was humiliatingly escorted out of the White House on his way to losing his army career. A long-sought target of this latest purge was the intelligence agencies. The housecleaning went far beyond what Bush did in placing Goss atop a distrusted CIA in 2004. Atkinson, the inspector general who reported the Ukraine whistleblower account to Congress, was out. So, too, was his boss, Acting Director of National Intelligence Joseph Maguire, along with deputy Andrew Hallman, after an intelligence official gave an election briefing asserting continued Russian election interference for Trump's benefit. Trump learned about the briefing from Nunes. He exploded at Maguire at an Oval Office meeting for what he saw as disloyalty. Brennan called the "virtual decapitation" of the intelligence leadership a "full-blown national security crisis."

Trump replaced Maguire with a former Bolton aide and Twitter troll, the pugilistic ambassador to Germany, Richard Grenell. Grenell used his appointment—an interim one that the Senate was never going to confirm—to leak information suggesting the Obama administration had inappropriately exposed Mike Flynn's identity after intercepting Kislyak's calls with him, a charge that a prosecutor would later invalidate. Grenell's obvious cronyism was also a lever for Trump to get Senate Republicans to vote to replace him with an even bigger loyalist with less intelligence experience: John Ratcliffe. Ratcliffe acted quickly to declassify documents seeming to exonerate Trump, like an annex from the 2017 intelligence assessment saying the intelligence agencies had "limited corroboration" for a salacious dossier prepared by the former MI6 officer Christopher Steele, which was peripheral to the assessment. The impulse to please Trump with intelligence spread beyond ODNI. At the Department of Homeland Security, a whistleblower in the intelligence directorate said Trump appointees deemphasized threat assessments about violent white supremacists in favor of making false equivalences to left-wing groups. "The bottom line from the White House," explained Miles Taylor, DHS chief of staff under Nielsen, "was they didn't want us to talk about domestic terrorism because they worried that if we talked about right-wing extremism, we would alienate many of the president's supporters."

Ever since Bush first clashed with the CIA over the Iraq war, elements within the right had seen the intelligence agencies as a hindrance to their ambitions. It was a position that required ignoring their stewardship of the surveillance, rendition, torture, and assassination missions of the War on Terror. That tension eased when the right aimed its hostility not at intelligence operatives but at analysts and senior leadership, who tended to act, as a matter of professional pride, without the personal loyalty Trump demanded. With MAGA seeing the stakes of political conflict to be as existential as the Flight 93 Election thesis implied, the intelligence chiefs' pretense at independence seemed to them like hostile Deep State intransigence. Trump had accommodated institutions fearful of him by installing the graybeard GOP senator Dan Coats as director of national intelligence. That had resulted in #Russiagate and impeachment. Installing Grenell and Ratcliffe as directors of national intelligence was more than an attack on the independence of the intelligence agencies. It was an attack on the idea that intelligence *ought* to be independent. Trump's career-long achievement had been to manipulate reality to his benefit. He wanted from intelligence the sort of thing that Giuliani was doing with his Ukraine drug deal, or from the "investigators" he claimed to send to Hawaii for Obama's birth certificate: material to invent the crimes of his rivals and explain away his own. Trump, to the acclaim of much of the Republican Party, was not fighting a Deep State. He was building one.

As the man House Democrats had impeached attempted to suborn the intelligence agencies, they again raced to preserve his surveillance power. Impeachment prevented congressional Republicans from easily renewing the main surveillance provisions of the PATRIOT Act. Even though those provisions had nothing to do with Crossfire Hurricane, it was politically untenable to give MAGA's FBI enemies what they wanted. Longtime GOP surveillance reformers took the opportunity to kill not only the Call Detail Records program—uncontroversial after NSA's suspension—but also PATRIOT Section 215's warrantless business records collection, which had been how NSA and the Justice Department laundered bulk domestic phone records collection. For the first time since 2001, a key PATRIOT authority expired for an extended period.

Schiff, backed by Pelosi, worked unsuccessfully to revive it. In exchange he allowed his Republican colleague Jim Jordan to add a provision permitting the attorney general to disapprove surveillance on an elected official. Then, over the howls of civil libertarians in both parties and more strident ones outside, Schiff weakened protections against the FBI's warrantlessly collecting Americans' browser and search histories on a scale just short of bulk. "He dishonestly mischaracterized both the Daines-Wyden and Lofgren-Davidson [reform] Amendments and successfully stalled FISA reform," said one of those civil libertarians, Ohio Republican Warren Davidson.

Democrats, aligned with the besieged intelligence agencies, mumbled through their acceptance of a Justice Department inspector general report that MAGA trumpeted. Although the inspector general, Michael Horowitz, found that there was none of the deliberate bias in Crossfire Hurricane that MAGA claimed, he established that the FBI had provided the FISA Court with misleading justifications to continue the surveillance on Carter Page. But neither MAGA nor the #Resistance paid commensurate attention to a follow-up report from Horowitz that attempted to explain the failings of Crossfire Hurricane. After taking a sample of twenty-nine FBI submissions to the secret court, he found an average of twenty errors in each of them. "[I]t appears that the FBI is not consistently re-verifying the original statements of fact within renewal applications," Horowitz said, describing a process error that risked guaranteeing an investigative perpetual-motion machine.

In the twenty years since 9/11, FBI submissions to the FISA Court had exploded—the eight field offices from which Horowitz gathered his sample had submitted seven hundred such surveillance applications over five years—and the FBI was, at a minimum and with frequency, stretching the evidence necessary to put Americans under national security surveillance. And this was for the most legally rigorous of the FBI's menu of options for such surveillance. Horowitz's report indicated that the problems with Crossfire Hurricane emerged from a process that the bureau had routinized and used against anonymous Americans, most of them Muslim, for an entire generation. His findings impacted American politics not at all.

A DIFFERENT PATRIOT ACT PROVISION than the ones Schiff tried to save turned Adham Hassoun into a Forever War pioneer yet again.

In January 2019 a judge ruled that the predicament Hassoun's statelessness presented during his ICE detention was perverse enough to permit him to be temporarily released into his sister's custody back in Florida. But the Justice Department cited a post-9/11 immigration regulation to keep him at Batavia as a potential security risk. He was now a man in his fifties, in poor health, who had committed no act of violence. The administration had to find a jailhouse snitch in order to portray Hassoun as dangerous.

The untested regulation sparked the interest of the ACLU in defeating it. Backstopping local attorneys, it filed a habeas corpus case to free Hassoun. Rather than back down, the administration escalated its efforts. In November, as filings in the case moved toward an evidentiary hearing before a federal judge to determine the danger he posed, the Justice Department and the Department of Homeland Security fired a Chekhov's gun of the War on Terror.

Buried deep within the PATRIOT Act was a lost artifact: Section 412. The subject of great civil-libertarian fear shortly after passage but never exercised, it explicitly provided for the indefinite detention, renewable every six months, of undeportable noncitizens deemed terrorism risks. The PATRIOT Act had criminalized Hassoun. Now, after he had served his time, after he was taken into a completely different cage, the PATRIOT Act could keep Hassoun in such cages forever.

"This is the USA. It's not like a Third World country," he marveled. "You can't do this to people—this country, they say they cherish freedom." Soon, in an adjoining building of the ICE prison where he lived, came a virus that threatened to speed his release in a different sense.

CHAPTER NINE

THE INVISIBLE ENEMY

2020-2021

On the last day of 2019, an inflamed procession of Iraqis passed unchallenged into the Green Zone and set fire to a way station outside the U.S. embassy. During the tensest days of the occupation, attacks on the embassy had been a matter of rockets and mortars fired from a distance. Now, long after most Americans had forgotten that U.S. troops even remained in Iraq, Baghdadis fought at close range, using metal poles as battering rams to bash the bulletproof glass from security-guard stations. No one was hurt—this was no Benghazi—as the point of the violence was to remind the United States that it was not the dominant power in Iraq. Its adversary, Iran, was.

The war against ISIS on Iraqi soil had been a war of an unspoken coalition. Oversimplified, the United States provided air cover for Iraqi Shiite militias—sixty thousand fighters incorporated into the defense apparatus in a face-saving gesture as "Popular Mobilization Forces"—many of which were under the ultimate command of Qassem Soleimani. As he boasted to David Petraeus during the surge, Soleimani was the architect of an expansionist Iranian strategy that exploited every mistake the United States had made in the Middle East since 9/11. He was pragmatic enough to cooperate with Washington when it suited Iranian interests, as destroying the Caliphate did, and was prepared to clash with Washington when it suited Iranian interests, as with Soleimani's backstopping of Syria's Bashar al-Assad or, earlier, with IED modifications that killed hundreds of U.S. troops and maimed more. Soleimani's impunity infuriated the Security State and the right. His success stung.

Following the July 2017 defeat of ISIS in Mosul, Trump's withdrawal from Obama's Iran nuclear deal the following year and his adoption of a "maximum pressure" policy of economic strangulation restored the familiar U.S.–Iranian posture of antagonism. Although there were fewer U.S. soldiers on patrol, Iranian roadside bombs reappeared on Iraqi highways, as did militia assaults on Iraqi military bases that collectively hosted more than five thousand U.S. troops. Throughout 2019 the United States quietly escalated Mideast force levels by fourteen thousand to counter Iran, even as Trump promised withdrawal. The escalations led to the Iraqi militia Kata'ib Hezbollah rocketing a base in Kirkuk on December 27, 2019, killing Nawres Hamid, a thirty-three-year-old contract linguist and naturalized American citizen who had fled Iraq in 2011. Trump ordered strikes on five Kata'ib Hezbollah positions in Iraq and Syria that killed at least twenty-five people. Those strikes prompted the riot at the Baghdad embassy.

It was a humiliation that capped, in the eyes of many on the right, a generation of humiliations at the hands of Iran. Some senior military officers considered themselves straitjacketed by the traditional reluctance to risk open war with Iran—a war that, compounding their frustrations, they recognized would eclipse the horrors of Iraq and Afghanistan. Trump decided instead to fulfill the eighteen-year-old right-wing desire to bring the War on Terror to Iran. He boasted to guests at his Mar-a-Lago resort that they should expect "big" action.

On January 2, as Soleimani drove from the Baghdad airport after collecting the Iraqi official in charge of the militias, Abu Mahdi al-Muhandis, a drone strike killed them both. The military had presented Trump with the strike option insincerely, through its typical Forever War practice of presenting presidents with an array of otherwise absurd options to convince them to choose its preferred approach. Trump instead sealed Soleimani's fate. Gina Haspel, who the Security State mandarins insisted would restrain Trump, reportedly emphasized the dangers of *not* killing Soleimani. The War on Terror's ever-expanding target list now included the leader of a foreign country's external security.

Fury and fear swept the region. Even the Saudis, sworn enemies of Iran, urged de-escalation. Iraq's prime minister, installed largely by the Americans, said Soleimani had been in Baghdad on a mission to reduce tensions when he was killed. Tired of having their country being used as a proxy battlefield, an Iraqi parliament created by the United States voted to evict the American forces it had invited back to fight ISIS. In Iran, crowds estimated in the hundreds of thousands turned out to mourn Soleimani and demand revenge. It came, days later, in the form of a ballistic missile strike on the Ain al-Asad base, resulting in no deaths but over a hundred cases of mild traumatic brain injury for U.S. troops there. The lack of carnage was considered Iranian restraint.

When it became clear Iran was not going to let the assassination go unanswered, Trump and his administration reached for the 9/11 template. First they described their escalation as de-escalation, a move to "stop a war, not start one," much as Bush had framed the invasion of Iraq as the prevention of a worse conflict. Then, despite the fact that the intelligence revealed continuity with the past months' pattern of low-level Iranian proxy violence, Trump and Pompeo, an enthusiastic advocate of killing Soleimani, insisted they had foiled an "imminent" attack. Trump invented a plot against four U.S. embassies that his latest defense secretary, Mark Esper, could not substantiate. Sometimes "dozens" of Americans were at risk in the phantom plot, while at other times the administration insisted it was "hundreds." Pompeo, pressed by reporters, dissembled that the question of imminence didn't ultimately matter. Seeing the narrative escaping, Pence recycled a long-debunked insistence that Iran had been in on the 9/11 attacks, even managing to mistake the number of hijackers in the process. While insisting that he had restored "deterrence" against Iran, Trump simultaneously tweeted that he stood ready to bomb its cultural treasures, an unambiguous war crime and signal that killing Soleimani was truly about civilizational retribution. Above all, Trump portrayed Soleimani not as an official of a sovereign country, but as a mere terrorist whose life was forfeit.

There was no strategy behind Trump's response. He had called Iraq a stupid war and told his MAGA followers that the end of endless wars was nigh. But his American exceptionalism meant he would never tolerate Iraqis forcing U.S. troops out. In response he threatened to sanction Iraq, whose brittle economy had prompted massive protests months before, which caused the Iraqis to back down. When outgoing prime minister Adil Abdul Mahdi urged the United States to negotiate a withdrawal, the State Department replied that "any delegation sent to Iraq would be dedicated to discussing how to best recommit to our strategic partnership—not to discuss troop withdrawal, but our right, appropriate force posture in the Middle East." Trump had no interest in leaving Iraq if it meant America had to respect Iraqi sovereignty, so more than five thousand U.S. troops would remain there despite the poisoned relationship. Two of them would die at Camp Taji when, two months after the administration had insisted its deterrent was restored, Iranian-aligned militias again rocketed the base. Rocket attacks continued, against Taji and the Green Zone, through June. At the end of his presidency, Trump left twenty-five hundred troops in Iraq.

If 2013 began the decadent phase of the War on Terror, and 2016 showed an eruption of right-wing frustration with it, then 2020 began with the culture of the war—its offended pride, its civilizational contempt—consuming America. The nation's post-9/11 moral exhaustion, on display through Trump's presidency, meant that he would be the latest leader to achieve neither peace nor victory, only prolonged violence. He was in no position to triumph against the literally invisible enemy that was about to overwhelm the country. But he was perfectly poised to aim the War on

Terror at his domestic opponents when they marched in their millions against the system that produced him.

EIGHTY THOUSAND PEOPLE HAD DIED in two months. Consigned to a year of sustained anxiety, Americans—tens of millions of whom simultaneously experienced an agonizing slide into poverty—wondered if their neighbors, staring out at them from behind a mask at a distance, would infect them. In New York City sirens punctuated a deathlike public silence no New Yorker alive had ever known. The sirens were a reminder of the closeness of death, just as the awful, lingering smell from the burning World Trade Center had been. The novel coronavirus pandemic revealed that America's entrenched socioeconomic reality made life an agonizing choice between health and economic survival. Beyond a twelve-hundred-dollar stimulus check and six-hundred-dollar weekly unemployment checks that ceased in July, Congress was not interested in paying people to stay home. There could be no Bush-like call for fearful citizens to go shopping. "Essential" workers, the working class that kept the deliveries coming to the middle and upper classes, alongside health-care workers who were also treated as marginal, were neither paid commensurately nor properly equipped with safety gear. Like the firefighters breathing in the toxic fumes of the World Trade Center before them, they were instead dubbed "heroes."

The White House responded with waves of denial that right-wing politicians and media amplified. White people brandishing guns and signs reading I WANT A HAIRCUT protested what they perceived to be the tyranny of quarantine. Meeting no resistance from local police, a demonstration of white anger at a public-health lockdown swelled until the Michigan legislature, fearful of men with AR-15s roaming its hallways, canceled its session. The protesters were a small minority—polls showed that by margins of almost 80 percent, people in all communities favored the quarantines—but they were politically expedient to Donald Trump.

And so on May 11 Trump proclaimed victory over the coronavirus. He announced, baselessly, that America led the world in testing. Two months of quarantine, and the economic collapse that Trump had long feared as the only true threat to his presidency, resulted in a rejection of the new reality among Trump's constituencies so pronounced that reopening prematurely began in Georgia. "We have met the moment and we have prevailed," Trump said in the Rose Garden. "Americans do whatever it takes to find solutions, pioneer breakthroughs, and harness the energies we need to achieve a total victory." It was the pandemic equivalent of Bush on the USS *Abraham Lincoln*, announcing major combat operations against COVID-19 had ended. At least 260,000 more Americans would die from coronavirus in 2020.

Narratively Trump had come full circle. His first public response to the outbreak had been to deny the novel coronavirus was anything more than a flu. "We've never closed down the country for the flu," he told Fox as late as March 24, less than a week after he privately told Bob Woodward, "I always wanted to play it down," since the coronavirus was "deadly stuff." Fox News whipsawed from framing the coronavirus as little more than Democratic hysteria to a deadly serious challenge that only Donald Trump could overcome. A right-wing media and social-media infrastructure reconciled the conflicting narratives through voicing contempt at liberal and scientific concerns over the spread of the virus. Trump, through Pence, assembled a task force including scientists; their expertise and independence only became targets of MAGA's ire. Its true function was to make Trump seem as if he was taking action against the virus after his inaction had all but ensured disaster. On May 3, a week before he declared victory and heralded a rapid reopening, the president assured the country that at worst, American deaths would total 100,000. The United States reached that total on May 27, and likely passed it even earlier. By mid-June, the country continued to average 24,000 new coronavirus cases daily, due in part to a rise in cases from reopened states, compared to 4,000 in the European Union. Trump himself caught the virus in late September, after attending White

House meetings honoring Supreme Court nominee Amy Coney Barrett and Gold Star families. He received first-rate treatment unavailable to the general public, as well as a sycophantic portrayal of his strength from physicians at Walter Reed Army Medical Center. Soon after, in echoes of Bush and the Iraq insurgency, Trump insisted that "we're rounding the corner" on confronting the virus he claimed in May to have defeated. By late November, the U.S. averaged 164,687 new cases daily. December 9 was the first day, but not the last, to exceed the 9/11 death toll.

Trump's wartime metaphor made sense, but not for the reason he had thought. Coronavirus was the public health equivalent of the War on Terror. The Bush administration had refused to consider that America's chosen role as global policeman had left it vulnerable to violent religious fanatics who refused U.S. hegemony. Trump and MAGA, reflecting their exceptionalism, could not imagine that America was actually susceptible to a widely predicted pandemic. Then he simply refused to do what was necessary to arrest the virus: rapid mass testing and tracing to isolate and treat the infected, while paying people to stay home so the resulting economic catastrophe could be brief and mitigated. Both measures were politically unthinkable, so America experienced the public-health version of neither peace nor victory.

A liberal's nightmare took shape as the public-health crisis went from preventable to inevitable because the government was controlled by people contemptuous of science. For many people, witnessing Washington's failure to respond to the pandemic was a radicalizing experience, pushing them toward left critiques about how the virus reflected and intensified America's extant socioeconomic cruelty. Ben Rhodes, Obama's leftmost foreign policy adviser, wrote in *The Atlantic* that COVID-19 revealed the emptiness of the previous decade. "Americans will have to rethink the current orientation of our own government and society, and move past our post-9/11 mindset," he urged, eliding the fact that Obama had accommodated it during his eight years in office.

Rhodes was correct in arguing that the coronavirus should have demonstrated, yet again, the folly of the 9/11 era. After all, the entire architecture of counterterrorism was predicated on the notion of stopping preventable deaths from becoming inevitable. That is what the coronavirus did, and what Trump was disinclined to stop. Yet the reality was that the 9/11 era *manifested* throughout the coronavirus's political, social, and cultural impacts.

Bush had neglected to heed the inconvenient warnings conveyed in the CIA's "Bin Laden Determined to Strike in U.S." briefing. It was Trump's first impulse as well. At the start of 2020, Grenell, Trump's loyalist acting director of national intelligence, delayed the only annual open briefing from the intelligence leadership. Later it would emerge that the intelligence agencies had, with some urgency, briefed Trump in January and February on the risks of the coronavirus erupting as a global pandemic. Publicly, however, Trump was saying as late as February 26 that "we're going to be pretty soon at only five people" exposed to the virus. When criticized later, Trump blamed his briefers, particularly the CIA's Beth Sanner, for not sufficiently impressing upon him that the coronavirus was a massive risk, much as Bush had faulted the Security State for not saying exactly when and where 9/11 would take place. The analysts drew the comparison themselves. "The system was blinking red," a U.S. official with intelligence access told *The Washington Post*, deliberately invoking George Tenet's famous phrase to the 9/11 Commission on the CIA's plethora of pre-9/11 warnings. The open intelligence briefing never happened, preventing the only chance at the start of the pandemic for the Security State to publicly assess the threat of the coronavirus.

Once the pandemic reached the United States, Trump adopted Bush's template. He spoke solemnly of an "invisible enemy" after he finally declared a national emergency on March 13. His purpose was not so much to deal with the outbreak as to reap the fealty the country awarded Bush after 9/11. "I view it as a, in a sense, a wartime president," Trump said. Mike Pence's coronavirus task force was a convenient vessel that Trump could use to frame a narrative of emergency leadership. "This is worse than the World

Trade Center," he accurately said. He intended the comment as a defense against charges of lethargy, without seeming to notice that being right only indicted him.

The surveillance apparatus the Security State had constructed since 9/11 to harvest global communications was useless in the face of the pandemic. While its algorithms were more than capable of conducting contact tracing, they depended on identifying precisely who had tested positive for COVID-19. Trump was slow to adopt any testing. He overpromised his ability to provide test kits by orders of magnitude. Even when rationed testing began in March, it was a perishable resource. The epidemiological purpose of the tests was to prevent a "community spread" that was already underway in Seattle and New York City. On June 20 in Tulsa, at Trump's first rally after the lockdowns ended, the president boasted of deliberately reducing the rate of tests in order to suppress an accurate portrayal of COVID-19 in America.

Yet many of the data tools that emerged from the counterterrorism surveillance apparatus could help the contractors involved in it seek new markets. Palantir, the data-mining giant started in 2004 with CIA seed money, became, in the Trump era, a major defense contractor. It owed its $800 million government windfall to its billionaire cofounder Peter Thiel, who had been Trump's ally in Silicon Valley. Thiel had once bemoaned what he considered the incompatibility of democracy and freedom—a crisis prompted by the people's insufficient enthusiasm for capitalism—and dreamed of seasteading his way out of America's dreadful politics to colonize a piece of the ocean where the richest people could be (even more) beyond the reach of any law. Now, during an economic shutdown, Palantir made a $25 million deal with FEMA and the Department of Health and Human Services for a data-management platform capable of crunching a stunning 187 data sets on coronavirus-related medical needs into a predictive picture of where health-care logistics would have to be directed. Palantir, as far as is known, didn't have access to Americans' medical records. But, apparently mindful of public distrust, it portrayed itself as having no access to any hospital data at all. In truth, emails showed FEMA instructing states to send their respirator data directly to Palantir. The company never explained if it was under any requirement to purge this windfall of publicly provided data—data that gave its owner a private portrait of which economies were safe to open or close.

Trump couldn't be a wartime president without a wartime enemy. But the "invisible enemy" couldn't be bombed. By the spring its domestic spread had become a threat to his presidency: he was losing the war. In another 9/11 pantomime, he sought to capture the loyalty afforded to Bush over the showdown with Saddam Hussein. This time the foreign threat was from China, with the virus as the WMD.

Already a MAGA target owing to Trump's trade war, China had the virtue of being the epicenter of the outbreak in December 2019, prompting an alarming lockdown of tens of millions of people in Wuhan Province even as the Chinese government assured the world that the coronavirus was manageable. The complication was that Trump, throughout his presidency, couldn't decide whether to flatter or demonize Xi Jinping. On January 24, the day after Sanner's intelligence briefing, he thanked Xi "on behalf of the American people" for China's vigilance "and transparency" in containing the virus. Pompeo ignored any such praise, and opted to refer to the "Wuhan Flu," a slur that became standard on the right. Blaming China for the virus quickly yielded the same result that blaming Muslims for 9/11 did. On March 14, a nineteen-year-old stabbed Bawi Cung and two of his young sons in the Midland, Texas, Sam's Club for what the FBI said was the assailant's belief that they were culpable for spreading coronavirus. A study of police statistics conducted by California State University found hate crimes against Asian Americans rose by 150 percent in 2020. There were at least twenty-eight assaults on Asian New Yorkers, an 833 percent increase from the three such attacks in 2019.

Like the Cheneyites before them, Trump officials pressed the intelligence agencies to substantiate the politically useful "Wuhan Flu" narrative. Pompeo, as well as top National Security Council official Matt Pottinger, pushed the Security State to investigate a discounted theory that the outbreak was the result of a virus that escaped from a Chinese lab. Under Grenell, intelligence analysts publicly concurred on April 30 "with the wide scientific consensus that the COVID-19 virus was not manmade or genetically modified"—but added that they would "rigorously examine emerging information" to determine if the lab-outbreak theory was valid. Paul Pillar, who had been a senior CIA Mideast analyst during the Iraq invasion, observed that the kind of politicization that had taken place prior to the war was happening again. It was the inevitable consequence of Trump turning the intelligence agencies into "just one more element of government to be pressed into supporting his own assertions." Grenell characterized Trump's skepticism in the coronavirus briefings not as dismissal, but a mark of superior intellect. "You see a president questioning the assumptions and using the opportunity to broaden the discussion to include real-world perspectives," he said, much as Cheney had portrayed his pressure to connect Saddam to al-Qaeda as the basic due diligence of asking "a hell of a lot of questions." Soon a dossier prepared by a Pentagon contractor circulated on Capitol Hill. It attempted to portray conclusively that the coronavirus did escape from a Wuhan lab—but used provably false data in a job as sloppy as the Cheneyites' manufactured alliance between Saddam and al-Qaeda.

Such stillborn efforts reflected MAGA's desperation. The economic agony that was the result of the belated March shutdown threatened Trump's hold on power. Many in Trump's base were inclined to disbelieve that coronavirus was an actual threat. Demographics abetted their delusion. The first wave of coronavirus deaths was disproportionately Black, brown, working class, and generally not the MAGA profile. New York's second devastation in a generation was this time not accompanied by national solidarity. Without an enemy to turn trauma into bloodlust, MAGA felt no need to hide its hatred. Florida governor Ron DeSantis, an important Trump ally, blamed New Yorkers for bringing to his state "unwittingly or not" a late-March surge in coronavirus cases. Trump, an amalgam of no less than four of the worst kinds of New Yorkers—Outerborough White

Racist, Wealth Vampire, Dignity-Free Media Striver, and Landlord—considered quarantining the entire tri-state area.

As the desperation turned vicious, MAGA, and particularly Fox News, distrusted the task-force expert Dr. Anthony Fauci for the same reasons the right had distrusted the U.N. weapons inspector Hans Blix in 2002: he represented a source of authority independent from the president. Fauci began to get enough death threats to prompt augmentation of his security detail. The same anger was soon directed at public health officials across the country. By June, *The Washington Post* noted, the pandemic was "fully entangled with ideological tribalism." That was imprecise: the lockdowns had substantial public support, with four out of five Americans seeing their value, or simply fearful of coronavirus. More precisely, MAGA viewed the virus as a threat to their conceptions of freedom. Small but persistent protests among right-wingers featured signs defending their right to have someone else cut their hair. In late May the Michigan Conservative Coalition orchestrated Operation Haircut, a barbering station protest outside the state capitol. The capitol itself had been shut down for weeks after white gunmen, unimpeded by police, intimidated the legislature into halting business. Respectable GOP officials began to echo the macabre themes of the jihadis they had considered uncivilized. The lieutenant governor of Texas, Dan Patrick, told Tucker Carlson that "lots of grandparents out there in this country like me" were prepared to die for the economy. "Don't sacrifice the country," Patrick implored. By late June coronavirus cases ticked sharply upward in Texas and DeSantis's Florida.

In another continuity with the 9/11 era, as the deaths accumulated, the Trump administration used the coronavirus to intensify its existing agenda. In March, after the president blocked entry to travelers from China and then the European Union, the State Department stopped visa services. The following month Trump halted all immigration for sixty days, contending it would be unfair to struggling native-born workers, even while immigrant labor powered "essential" services like health care and food production. By June he expanded the immigration freeze to apply to high-skilled workers, seasonal workers, executives, and scholars. Refugee admissions, already dec-imated by Trump, were suspended. Even as coronavirus spread through the United States, to the point of requiring the Army Corps of Engineers to aid in constructing additional hospital facilities, the corps doled out contracts for Trump's southern border wall worth $1.3 billion from late February through early April. The following month a MAGA-favorite firm from North Dakota, Fisher Sand and Gravel, won its very own $1.3 billion slice of the wall bounty, all while being under investigation by the Pentagon inspector general.

However cynical the immigration restrictions were, they ensured that immigrants held in ICE prisons were at the mercy of the invisible enemy. ICE refused entreaties to release the tens of thousands of people it detained who posed no public danger. With no way to social distance inside teeming detention centers, coronavirus outbreaks intensified. Edwin Tineo, detained during the early days of the pandemic in a New Jersey ICE facility where detainees lacked hand soap, toilet paper, and health information, called it "the most stressful thing I've ever experienced in my life." At Krome in Miami, which once held Adham Hassoun, ICE fed Muslim de-tainees pork while its chaplain shrugged, "It is what it is." Inside a for-profit ICE prison in Virginia called FarmVille, an intake of seventy-four out-of-state detainees skyrocketed a virus outbreak. The FarmVille guards re-sponded to protests with violence, including pepper sprayings and firing a noise round in a crowded dormitory. "We think we're going to die without seeing our families," a desperate detainee said in July. Weeks later, on Au-gust 5, a seventy-two-year-old Canadian detainee, James Hill, died of coro-navirus at the prison.

By April the ICE prison at Batavia became, however temporarily, ICE's leading coronavirus detention center. Adham Hassoun feared for his life. He started a hunger strike in early February to protest his now officially indefinite detention. Already weak and immunocompromised from a heart condition, he grew nervous when an ICE officer mentioned having come down with a flu. Soon he began experiencing body aches and felt as if he was burning up. Hassoun was wary of being taken to the local hospital for fear of exposure, so he remained inside, first in the Batavia clinic and then in the solitary cells known as the SHU. He recovered—it remains unclear if Hassoun actually contracted COVID-19—and being in the SHU may have spared his life, as it separated him from other Batavia coronavirus patients. By late June, forty-nine people at Batavia had contracted COVID-19, a total eclipsed by fourteen other ICE detention facilities. By November, at least eight people had died from the virus in ICE detention.

A lack of concern for the health of those on the front lines was as conspicuous for coronavirus health-care workers as it had been for troops in Iraq. The sloth of the Trump administration in equipping health-care workers rivaled the Rumsfeld Pentagon's laxity in equipping soldiers properly in Iraq. Both turned to "hillbilly armor." Just as the soldiers had dug through scrap piles to uparmor their Humvees, nurses wrapped themselves in garbage bags to fashion personal protective equipment.

Service in the wars turned into a preexisting condition for those veterans who had been exposed to the open-air burn pits of Iraq and Afghanistan. There, everything from furniture to human shit was disposed of in the flames, and the military insisted no one who breathed in the acrid smoke would suffer lasting harm. In reality, an army study never intended for public release found that exposure to the burn pits would likely lead to "reduced lung function or exacerbated chronic bronchitis, chronic obstructive pulmonary disease (COPD), asthma, atherosclerosis, or other cardiopulmonary diseases." When Elana Duffy, an Iraq and Afghanistan veteran in New York, began developing shortness of breath and a high fever on March 18, she suspected she knew why. A Veterans Affairs hospital turned her away without so much as administering a coronavirus test, "largely because the VA is slammed," Duffy explained. None of the two hundred thousand veterans who had signed up for the VA's burn-pit registry, created precisely for situations like this, received any guidance about what special precautions to take.

Coronavirus even had a General Shinseki. A navy captain named Brett Crozier helmed the USS *Theodore Roosevelt*, one of America's eleven aircraft carriers, when a coronavirus outbreak threatened it in March. "We're fucked," a *TR* sailor told a reporter, at a time when about a hundred of the forty-eight-hundred-member crew, docked off of Guam, had contracted the virus. Crozier was astonished to see his chain of command move with insufficient urgency to offload the entire crew into separate lodgings. He recognized the source of its inaction: a reluctance to shut down one of the most visible manifestations of American power. At the Pentagon, which did not order a redeployment pause until March 25, Mattis's successor Mark Esper emphasized "readiness" and insisted local commanders were better positioned to determine when to lock down. It was a position that suited Trump's political interests. Like Shinseki before the Iraq invasion, Crozier shamed his superiors for treating his sailors as an afterthought. On March 3 he wrote: "[W]e are not at war, and therefore cannot allow a single Sailor to perish as a result of this pandemic unnecessarily."

Rumsfeld humiliated Shinseki but did not strip him of command. The navy did both to Crozier. Acting Navy Secretary Thomas Modly—who would later claim to be sparing the navy another Eddie Gallagher–like debacle—flew to Guam to notify the sailors that Crozier was "too naïve or too stupid" for command. Defiantly, the ship's crew saw their captain off by chanting Crozier's name, and Modly eventually resigned. Even more shameful was Admiral Mike Gilday, the chief of naval operations. Gilday stood by as Modly fired Crozier, then recommended Crozier's reinstatement, only to reverse himself again after Esper refused. In June Gilday produced a report claiming that Crozier, and not the navy, had jeopardized the lives of the *TR* sailors. Meanwhile 1,273 sailors aboard the carrier contracted coronavirus, ten times more than at the point when Crozier tried to save them. On April 13, Aviation Ordnanceman Chief Petty Officer Charles Robert Thacker Jr. died of COVID, a death Crozier had warned his superiors was preventable.

As impeachment failed and coronavirus crested, liberals, panicked at the prospect of losing a winnable election by moving too far left, behaved as if it were 2004. In place of John Kerry, the Democrats chose as their presidential nominee Kerry's friend, ally, and fellow Iraq war champion Joe Biden. Biden, who had worried that his opposition to the bin Laden raid would doom his late-life presidential ambitions, entered the race after younger faces failed to decisively claim Obama's legacy. But in this contest, if Biden was Kerry, the unapologetic antiwar politics that Howard Dean championed was far more potent.

The entire Democratic field—even Biden himself—now vowed to "end endless wars." The ease with which Biden and the others took up the slogan spoke to how unclear its meaning had become. It represented a triumph of Obama's legacy: making the War on Terror sustainable through making it sufficiently inconspicuous to split the difference with abolition. "We must maintain our focus on counterterrorism, around the world and at home, but staying entrenched in unwinnable conflicts drains our capacity to lead on other issues that require our attention," Biden wrote in the midsection of a *Foreign Affairs* essay outlining his foreign policy.

Biden's political revival was hardly the result of a foreign policy debate. But his return was all the more striking since Bernie Sanders had found his geopolitical voice, and it was proudly abolitionist—both toward the War on Terror and against the American exceptionalism that fueled it. In *Foreign Affairs*, Sanders decried the *concept* of a War on Terror. Not only did it fail on its own terms, providing terror networks "exactly what they wanted" in terms of attention, but it had created an opportunity for American nativism. "There is a straight line," Sanders wrote, "from the decision to reorient U.S. national-security strategy around terrorism after 9/11 to placing migrant children in cages on our southern border." In the Senate, Sanders, guided by his adviser Matt Duss, pushed through a resolution to extricate the United States from the Saudi war in Yemen that Obama had supported; Trump, revealingly, vetoed it. Sanders said he regretted his vote for the Afghanistan war, unlike practically every other politician who had voted for it. With the help of Duss, Sanders finally elevated ending the War on Terror to a central position within his revolution. When he tied or won the first three primary contests, it seemed as if the abolitionist moment had arrived.

But the Democrats opted to regress to familiar 9/11-era patterns. After Biden secured the nomination, his allies dreamed of winning the endorsement of generals with the stature of a Mattis. By August, Biden had won the endorsement of a host of GOP-aligned Security Staters with deep legacies in the Forever War, such as Mike Hayden; Bush's first director of national intelligence, John Negroponte; and Colin Powell. For his transition planning team, Biden elevated Avril Haines to helm the foreign policy and national security teams, a position from which she would proceed to director of national intelligence. Haines, who had worked for Biden in the Senate, was an archetypal figure in the Sustainable War on Terror. As an attorney on the Obama NSC, she chaired the group reviewing the drone strikes and was a force for their restriction—though never their abolition—and at the CIA, she effectively absolved the agents who spied on Dan Jones. Her Obama administration colleagues considered Haines among their most thoughtful, lawful, and civilized peers. Trump sought a War on Terror stripped of any civilized veneer. Biden, who helped construct that veneer, wanted it reinstated.

The indifference, grift, dishonesty, incompetence, and distrust of expertise that characterized Trump's coronavirus response were all familiar. It was how the Coalition Provisional Authority had governed Iraq. Now it was standard operating procedure for a government facing an escalating crisis at home. No one with power could be trusted as the foundations of daily life neared collapse. As allies like Palantir and Fisher Sand and Gravel cashed in, Trump blamed everyone else for his failure, even responding to a question about the slowness in acquiring test kits, "I don't take responsibility at all."

With discontent boiling over as the summer approached, Trump reached for the legacy of the 9/11 era in a different way. He aimed the weapons of the Forever War at Americans protesting for their lives and their freedom.

———

"WHILE NO ONE CONDONES LOOTING," said Donald Rumsfeld, shortly after U.S. troops entered a Baghdad that was erupting into chaos, "on the other hand, one can understand the pent-up feelings that may result from decades of repression and people who've had members of their family killed by that regime, for them to be taking their feelings out on that regime."

On May 25, 2020, Minneapolis police officer Derek Chauvin knelt for eight minutes and forty-six seconds on the neck of George Floyd, whom a convenience store owner suspected of using a counterfeit twenty-dollar bill to buy cigarettes. It was part of an American police tradition, stretching back to white posses empowered by the Fugitive Slave Act, of executing Black people. Bystanders watched, filming, as Floyd, fearing he was about to die, cried out for his deceased mother. When paramedics arrived, Chauvin did not rise from Floyd's corpse for more than another minute. Floyd's brother Philonise later told Congress, "I'm tired of the pain I'm feeling now, and I'm tired of the pain I feel every time another Black person is killed for no reason."

He spoke for tens of millions. The protests that erupted on behalf of Floyd—and Breonna Taylor, slain in her own home by Louisville police executing a no-knock warrant, and Ahmaud Arbery, shot by a white father and son while out for a jog in Georgia's Glynn County—were unique in size and fury. *The New York Times* estimated that between 15 million and 26 million people mobilized in a single month, all without much organizational infrastructure or national leadership, all amid a global pandemic. That made the Black Lives Matter uprising of 2020 the largest mass movement in American history. The white reaction they prompted brought the War on Terror onto the streets like never before.

On May 28, Minneapolis demonstrators burned a police precinct station. New York City remembered its own Eric Garner, whom a police officer also suffocated to death over cigarettes, and ended its coronavirus-lockdown silence by flooding the streets. Cities across the country rapidly joined in.

Incidents of looting, burnt cars, smashed windows, and other property damage were anecdotal compared to the millions who spent the next several
weeks demanding an end to racist policing—as a thin wedge into a demand
for an end to white supremacy. Police nationwide treated the protests as a
challenge to their authority. The Saturday after Floyd's murder, two NYPD
vehicles drove through protesters on Brooklyn's Flatbush Avenue. The next
evening, just south of Union Square, an officer drew his gun on a group who
had made makeshift barricades on Broadway with trash and construction
barriers. As terrified protesters frantically fled, at least three cops nightsticked one who had fallen. Yet for the first week of its coverage of the unrest,
the media largely presented a narrative of protest violence, obscuring the
Trump-encouraged police rampage underway.

Trump passed the first Sunday of the protests in the underground bunker where Dick Cheney spent 9/11, despite never being in any danger. It
forecasted his reaction. "When the looting starts, the shooting starts," he
tweeted, echoing an infamous police response to protesters in the 1960s civil
rights movement. For generations, reactionaries had attributed demands for
Black liberation to "outside agitators," usually meaning left-wing radicals.
But since Occupy, Black Lives Matter, and the resistance to the nationalist
right in places like Charlottesville, the perspective of conservative politicians and media to left-wing radicals had become more militant. Outsized
in their imagination was antifascist action, or Antifa. In truth, antifascism
was a movement rather than any form of hierarchical organization, but to
Trump supporters like Representative Dan Crenshaw of Texas that sounded
like a Deep State excuse for "downplaying" an internal enemy. Antifa's
invisible org chart was, to them, little more than the latest version of leaderless jihad.

Trump responded to the protests in the spirit of 9/11, declaring on May 31
that he was designating Antifa "a terrorist organization." His decree was
a legal and bureaucratic impossibility. America's refusal to acknowledge its
own white homegrown terrorists, even after McVeigh and Oklahoma City,
meant there was no domestic terror statute to ban such a group, criminalize

its associates, and dry up its money. Even if there had been, the formless Antifa could not qualify. But that could be a weapon in the hands of the administration: there would be no way to prove a suspect *wasn't* Antifa. The legal category error around Antifa mattered less than the clear message that the administration was willing to use the power of the state to treat the left as terrorists. "Now that we clearly see Antifa as terrorists, can we hunt them down like we do those in the Middle East?" wondered Trumpist congressman Matt Gaetz.

It was Bill Barr's moment. Months before, the attorney general had delivered apocalyptic speeches warning that "militant secularists" were on a campaign of civilizational "organized destruction," assaulting Christianity so furiously that its end result would be to drain America of the "virtue" necessary for a free society. Now he had the opportunity to strike back. Barr announced that the Joint Terrorism Task Forces would train their considerable resources on "extremists, anarchists . . . agitators" taking part in the protests, to "identify people in the crowd, pull them out and prosecute them." He told puzzled state governors that all the intelligence necessary for the coming prosecutions would flow through the JTTFs. David Bowdich, the FBI's deputy director, concurred. In early June, in the face of what he called "a national crisis," Bowdich rallied his agents to crack down on the protesters in Forever War terms: "When 9/11 occurred, our folks did not quibble about whether there was danger ahead for them." But it proved difficult to cobble together prosecutable cases. With hundreds arrested in New York City, interrogators pressed those in custody for any connection to Antifa. Yet the first wave of twenty-two criminal complaints for violence in the protests included no mention of Antifa at all.

Where law enforcement seemed inadequate, the military was available. During a June 1 conference call Trump demanded that state governors take a hard-line approach, including deploying their National Guard. If they refused to do so, he threatened, he would invoke the nineteenth-century Insurrection Act, which empowered him to order the military to suppress unrest. Esper told the governors that the military stood prepared to "dominate the battlespace," by which he meant American cities, streets, and citizens. He would later brush off his comment as inoffensive military jargon.

During a protest that turned chaotic near the White House on the first weekend of the demonstrations, someone set a fire in the basement of the cherished St. John's Church. Trump used it as an opportunity for an operation spearheaded by Barr against a peaceful protest at Lafayette Square hours after the president's call with the governors. As Trump threatened at a press conference to use violence, Barr ordered the U.S. Park Police, backed by D.C. national guardsmen, to advance on the crowd that had gathered between Trump and the church. Panicked protesters fled an unprovoked burst of rubber bullets, pepper balls, and tear gas. The White House initially attempted to argue that the police never fired tear gas, but the Park Police later acknowledged using it. D.C. national guardsmen, all locals, reported agonizing over their forced complicity and felt compelled to defend the protesters. "I felt that we were more protecting the people from the police," said Specialist Isaiah Lynch.

Trump and his coterie strutted to the church. There, he waved a Bible and grinned for the cameras, pantomiming as a defender of a besieged Christianity. Accompanying him was not only Esper but the chairman of the Joint Chiefs of Staff, army general Mark Milley, dressed in his camouflage combat uniform. The Pentagon would later tell reporters that Milley thought he was going to inspect the guardsmen. But the chairman had sent an unmistakable message of military support for the crackdown Trump threatened. Trump had even said Milley, who by statute is not in the chain of command, was "in charge" of the government's response, something he quickly forgot. Yingling, who served under McMaster at Tal Afar more than a decade earlier, said Milley had "knowingly, willingly betrayed his oath."

With Milley's complicity, a week of chaos descended upon Washington. A D.C. Guard helicopter flew threateningly low over a nighttime crowd of protesters, a war-zone technique of "rotor washing" away a crowd with noise, dust, and fear. Trump persuaded allied governors to loan him some national guardsmen. The day after Lafayette Square, the Pentagon deployed an infantry battalion from Fort Bragg, dubbed Task Force 504, just beyond the Washington city limits. An army regiment in northern Virginia was issued bayonets in the event it was ordered into the city. Residents soon began to notice uniformed masked police massing around federal buildings, often without any identifying insignia. It took days to discover that Barr had essentially assembled a militia. An estimated thirteen hundred members of the Bureau of Prisons, Park Police, and loaned Homeland Security personnel from components like CBP became newly deputized U.S. marshals, under the ultimate command of Barr's Justice Department. In the city's northeast neighborhoods people spotted what they assumed was a drone overhead. It turned out that Washington was one of fifteen cities consumed by protests where CBP had flown drones and even manned surveillance flights.

Applauding it all was Trumpist senator Tom Cotton. While a lieutenant in Iraq, Cotton had demanded that *Times* journalists be imprisoned for exposing part of STELLARWIND. Now he advocated for the military to disperse the protests and give what he called "no quarter" to "antifa terrorists" and other protesters. The *Times* gave Cotton op-ed space to develop his ideas about using the military to suppress Americans. It prompted an internal backlash that yielded the resignation in disgrace of the *Times* opinions editor. Elite media recriminations tended to bemoan an allegedly censorious culture within mainstream journalism rather than that culture's willingness to permit a sitting senator to legitimize uniformed violence against nonwhite and left-wing protesters.

Then came a sudden backdown. Esper, a West Pointer seemingly pushed to the breaking point of his cronyism by Lafayette Square, announced on June 3 that he now opposed using the military against the protests. His public dissent ruined his standing with Trump. Before the week was over, a large group of retired generals and admirals, all figures marked by the War on Terror—including JSOC's Bill McRaven and Tony Thomas, John

Allen, Mike Mullen, and Vincent Brooks—denounced Trump for threatening to use the Insurrection Act. Chief among them was Mattis, who finally broke his silence to denounce Trump as a threat to the Constitution. After Mattis unsubtly implied that Milley had disgraced his uniform, the chairman apologized days later for appearing in Lafayette Square alongside Trump. By mid-June, Task Force 504 demobilized, the National Guard stood down, and Barr's posse disappeared from the city streets. In its place came an investigative task force Barr convened to hunt and prosecute "anti-government extremists." While the Pentagon saw its moral authority in jeopardy, Barr continued to wield law enforcement against what he viewed as a rising left-wing threat.

MAGA was already habituated to interpret civil disobedience on behalf of Black liberation as a threat. Those mobilizing across America were interlopers, Antifa, the terrorists Barr's task force would expose. Hadn't the media talking heads apologizing for these rioters *just* been insisting that everyone had to stay indoors to prevent the spread of coronavirus? They had been quick to demand a quarantine when it meant destroying the economy in a reelection year, MAGA reckoned, but not when Trump's enemies were on the streets. The protests were not about justice, just as the coronavirus was not about public health: they were both part of the same power grab by the left.

Tucker Carlson, the Iraq war cheerleader who styled himself an antiwar conservative after he came to see Iraqis as culturally unworthy, aimed the Forever War at Americans on his June 25 broadcast—the *entire* Forever War. Those in the streets, he stated, were "not protesters, not civil rights activists, not CNN contributors, but domestic terrorists." He urged Barr to "change the course of this country's future." All Barr had to do was round up "the leaders of antifa tomorrow, along with every single person caught on camera torching a building, destroying a monument, defacing a church, and put them all in shackles and then frog-marc[h] them in front of cameras like MS-13, and call them what they actually are, domestic terrorists."

Barr needed little encouragement from Fox pundits. The attorney general took control with the determination of someone watching Trump's reelection chances slipping away. He and his allies overruled career prosecutors to drop charges against Mike Flynn and reduce a recommended sentence for Roger Stone. Then, late on a Friday, Barr announced that he had accepted the resignation of acting U.S. attorney Geoffrey Berman of the Southern District of New York, who was investigating Rudy Giuliani and in whose jurisdiction a post-presidential Trump had considerable criminal exposure. Berman publicly stated he had never offered his resignation, and Barr had to temporarily appoint Berman's deputy as the price of his exit. Yet Barr knew he had a reliable MAGA phalanx in Congress. When former Stone prosecutor Aaron Zelinsky, a serving assistant U.S. attorney in Baltimore, denounced Barr's politicizing his office at a House Judiciary Committee hearing, a chorus of Republicans praised Barr for doing what Jim Jordan called "the Lord's work" in purging the Security State of Trump's enemies.

Barr's separate crackdown on the BLM protests was augmented by white supremacist vigilantes. Even before the protests exploded and Trump labeled Antifa a terrorist group, the FBI broke up what it said was a plot by three members of white supremacist group the Base to murder Antifa activists who had revealed their identities online. In the fall, the FBI arrested thirteen Michigan men, including some who had attended the anti-lockdown protests at the state capitol, on charges including conspiracy to kidnap the Democratic governor, Gretchen Whitmer. Once the protests broke out, an actual violent group exploited the unrest. They were the Boogaloo Boys, dressed in a flamboyant mixture of tactical gear and Hawaiian shirts to advertise the casual enthusiasm with which they sought to spark a second civil war, something many Boogs expected to be a race war. The Boogaloo was a meme that became a movement. But some of its members who confronted the police even came to see that Black Lives Matter had a point and expressed ambivalence about law enforcement. Lurking underneath the Boogaloo was an extremist's plea for *closure*, for an end to the

Forever War that America had become for them. Except this one they expected to win.

Unlike Antifa, Boogaloo Boys appeared in Barr's first protest charges. One case in Nevada alleged that three Boys had brought Molotov cocktails to a BLM protest. All had served in the military, an indication that the Boogaloo had some appeal to current and former service members, further vindicating the onetime DHS analyst Daryl Johnson. Counterprotesters used their cars to run demonstrators down at least eighteen times in a single month, following the path set in Charlottesville by James Fields and before that by al-Qaeda in the Arabian Peninsula. Other violence was more intimate. In late August seventeen-year-old Kyle Rittenhouse drove from his home in Illinois to Kenosha, Wisconsin, and shot dead two protesters demanding justice for Jacob Blake, whom police had shot in front of his children, leaving him paralyzed. After the shooting, Rittenhouse walked past the police, who permitted him to leave—they had been passing out water bottles and showing their appreciation to Rittenhouse's armed anti-BLM cohort, which saw itself as a police auxiliary—but he was later arrested in Illinois. Tucker Carlson defended Rittenhouse by saying he "had to maintain order when no one else would." For months afterward, MAGA treated Rittenhouse as a hero and a martyr. Talking points for the Department of Homeland Security defended "Kyle," who had gone to what it described as "the scene of the rioting to help defend small business owners." Right-wing donors, including the former child actor Ricky Schroder, rallied to post his $2 million bail in time for Thanksgiving.

On June 28, a BLM protest entered the Portland Place community in St. Louis to demand the mayor's resignation. When marchers walked peacefully past the mock Renaissance palazzo of one of the mayor's neighbors, out from the mansion emerged lawyers Mark and Patricia McCloskey. He, in a pink polo shirt and barefoot, waved an AR-15 to demand protesters "get out of my neighborhood." She, also shoeless, leveled her handgun and screamed at them. "It was like the storming of the Bastille," Mark told local reporters, claiming the protesters had forced entry into Portland Place, though video footage showed them walking through an open gate. The Republican National Convention gave the McCloskeys a speaking role, where Patricia warned, "What you saw happen to us could just as easily happen to any of you who are watching from quiet neighborhoods around our country."

What MAGA resented most about BLM was its demand to reckon with MAGA's cherished past, during which white supremacy was understood to be either meritocratic or natural. They claimed cultural besiegement when protesters dethroned Confederate monuments, and vindication when the rage of the protests toppled granite statues of liberal heroes like Ulysses S. Grant. "Our history is being erased," Matt Gaetz said at a House Judiciary Committee hearing about Zelinsky's accusations against Barr. The historical reckoning even extended into the army, where retired officers backed by David Petraeus belatedly endorsed renaming bases honoring Confederate generals. A furious Trump vowed to veto any defense bill that required renamings, and Congress had to override his objection to pass the bill into law.

A wartime attitude took hold. Protesters encountered white gun owners kitted out in "tacticool" gear like ballistic helmets, hard-knuckle gloves, and plate-carrier vests, playacting at being "warfighters." By midsummer 2020, they had shown up at BLM protests some five hundred times, committing sixty-four incidents of assault and even six shootings that killed three people. Trump, invited to condemn white supremacist violence during a presidential debate, told one of the most prominent right-wing gangs, the Proud Boys, to "stand back and stand by," which the group cheered. Like Rittenhouse, such organizations considered themselves adjuncts to a now-infuriated police. Unlike Rittenhouse, the Fred Perry–uniformed Proud Boys had for years grown proximate to mainstream MAGA figures like Nunes, Carlson, and Roger Stone.

One place police vented their rage was Buffalo. Martin Gugino, a seventy-five-year-old peace activist, approached a column of police during a march. One of them shoved him backward, fracturing his skull when he fell onto the concrete while they continued forward. Trump dismissed Gugino, who spent the next four weeks in the hospital, as an Antifa plant. All fifty-seven members of the Buffalo police emergency response team later resigned—out of disapproval not of their colleagues, but of officials *suspending* their colleagues. In Philadelphia, where protesters toppled the statue of infamous racist Mayor Frank Rizzo—and where Proud Boys and police had a warm relationship—a white-shirt cop named Joseph Bologna Jr. took a retractable baton to a protester's head. When he was suspended, the police union sold BOLOGNA STRONG T-shirts. In North Carolina two middle-aged police officers were caught on tape musing about "slaughtering" Black people in a second civil war. In Seattle, where protesters temporarily reclaimed part of their city from police, an officer in a gas mask was filmed encouraging his colleagues, "Don't kill 'em, but push 'em back . . . hit 'em hard." By then the NYPD union had endorsed Trump's reelection.

If the military was unwilling to suppress the protests, the Department of Homeland Security, the quintessential Forever War institution, was eager to take on the task. Alongside the U.S. Marshals Service, the department sent its tactical teams from CPD into Portland, the scene of sustained BLM protests, which had included vandalizing a federal courthouse. That was all the opening they needed. Barr and the DHS's acting leader, Chad Wolf—whom the Senate never confirmed and who had advocated for migrant child separation—portrayed vandalism as insurrection. Their minimally identified agents, kitted out in camouflage, body armor, and gas masks, seized Portland protesters without probable cause and placed them into unmarked vans—a taste for native-born whites of what DHS had done to migrants for years. They fired rubber bullets at protesters' heads, fracturing skulls, and doused them with pepper spray and tear gas. Their violence only prompted Portland protesters to escalate their nighttime resistance, sending firecrackers sailing into the federal courthouse, which the marshals and the DHS now held, leading one GOP congressman to compare the fireworks to IEDs. The marshals even referred to "violent extremists," the

Obama-era euphemism for terrorists, amid the protesters. Federal forces acted accordingly. The DHS created Iraq-war-like "baseball card" intelligence reports on arrested protesters and permitted its intelligence unit to "collect [intelligence] from incarcerated, detained, or arrested persons," as if they were wartime interrogators. Oregon's elected leaders demanded DHS withdraw its forces. Wolf indignantly refused. When Christopher David, a fifty-three-year-old navy veteran, approached the feds to ask why they weren't "honoring your oath to the Constitution," they broke his hand with batons.

The response to all of this from Security State veterans was at first muted. "While I am not in a position to second-guess decisions being made on the ground in Portland," said Jeh Johnson, the air force lawyer who was Obama's final DHS secretary, "I do know that if the mayor, governor, and both U.S. senators questioned the deployment of additional DHS law enforcement personnel in their state, I would, too." Trump reacted as he had always done in the absence of forceful opposition. In late July he announced the expansion of his crackdown against "crime" in "Democrat-run cities" to Chicago, Cleveland, Detroit, Milwaukee, and Albuquerque. He knew how to package his response: this was his Surge. Sounding like Bush talking about Iraq and Obama talking about Afghanistan, Trump marshaled the language of the Forever War to bring that war to American streets: "This will be hard, painstaking work, it will take time, the tide will not recede overnight."

It was inevitable that Trump would stoke his base's resentments. Black Lives Matter was guilty of "Treason, Sedition, Insurrection," he tweeted. In mid-June he announced a rally, his first since the appearance of the coronavirus, to be held on Juneteenth, the commemoration of Black liberation. It would be held in Tulsa, where ninety-nine years earlier a white pogrom had destroyed the city's Black Wall Street. Trump ultimately pushed the rally back from Juneteenth by a day. But the unsubtle message here was that Trump, who had been robbed of adulation by the pandemic, was returning to the city in triumph on a symbolic day. Days before, he actively encouraged violence among his supporters in the police department and among civilians. "Protesters, anarchists, agitators, looters or lowlifes" needed to "please understand" that they would face a "much different scene" than they had before. But while his campaign boasted of an anticipated record turnout, only eighty-six hundred showed up for the rally. Trump had to cancel a planned speech to an overflow crowd. No violence marked Tulsa. Lack of interest, which for Trump was a toxic reception, did.

Still, at a sparsely attended BOK Center, the president vented MAGA's expanding grievances. He mocked coronavirus as the "Kung Flu." The "unhinged left-wing mob . . . trying to vandalize our history" was another target. Trump portrayed it all as a war for civilization now underway. A toppled statue of Confederate general Albert Pike was a "beautiful piece of art." Black Lives Matter wanted to "demolish our heritage" and replace it with their "new oppressive regime." Trump spoke for the police and "our great people from ICE," and against enemies like Ilhan Omar, who "would like to make the government of our country just like the country from where she came, Somalia." He reminded Tulsa that he had brought about the deaths of both Baghdadi and Qassem Soleimani. While promising to keep out of "foolish, stupid, ridiculous foreign wars," Trump added that he would "never hesitate to kill America's terrorist enemies." They were now found closer to home. Trump had learned the foremost lesson of 9/11: the terrorists were whomever you said they were.

AS CORONAVIRUS SPREAD THROUGH BATAVIA, Adham Hassoun grew re-flective. Now fifty-eight, he had spent his middle age in one or another American prison, because he refused to become an informant, because he helped an unfortunate-seeming Jose Padilla remake himself in Egypt, because the PATRIOT Act allowed it. When his time grew short in the general population at Marion, where he felt the freest he had anywhere in captivity, Hassoun allowed himself to be goaded into challenging someone to fight him. The fight didn't happen, but his friends were angry he had jeopardized what they assumed would be his freedom. "I'm Palestinian and hardheaded," he explained. He kept his sanity in prison by knowing he hadn't dishonored himself.

Coronavirus threatened more than Hassoun's health. It delayed the all-important evidentiary hearing at which the Justice Department and DHS would have to present their case that Hassoun was actually the threat they claimed he was. His habeas judge, Elizabeth Wolford, kept ruling in his favor. Over the government's objections, she refused to permit FBI agents to summarize what their informants told them, and instead compelled the Justice Department to produce their witnesses for testimony and cross-examination. But the outbreak of the virus resulted in the April hearing getting postponed until June. Hassoun, steadying himself, remembered how often he had thought himself close to freedom. "I won't believe it until I see the sky above me and breathe the air and no one tells me to put my jumpsuit on," he said.

Wolford gave the Justice Department a simple mandate: prove that Hassoun posed a threat to the United States. Instead, in May, after the defense team confronted the government about the shattered credibility of its lead witness, the prosecution informed Judge Wolford that Hassoun was to be released on restrictions, pending the approval of DHS, which never manifested. That was a last chance for a face-saving exit. In June, prosecutors belatedly revealed that their witness, jailhouse informant Shane Ramsundar, had given near-identical testimony about another prisoner earlier. Wolford issued a scathing ruling striking his and another informant's testimonies and threatening sanctions for prosecutorial misconduct. In response the Justice Department conceded it could not meet what it called the "burden" Wolford had imposed and filed a motion to scrap the evidentiary hearing without a contest.

While the government's latest case against Hassoun had collapsed, its compulsion to imprison him had not. It petitioned Wolford to stay Hassoun's release while it appealed her decision. During a Zoom hearing, Wolford noted the awkwardness of ruling on a stay of release after she had rejected the entire case for keeping Hassoun imprisoned. Hassoun immediately agreed to a monitored release in the custody of his sister. But the administration was still unwilling to permit Hassoun to leave Batavia until it had exhausted all its options. None of its appeals depended on an alternative reading of its fabricated evidence. The government instead wanted a higher court to rule that it was not required to meet basic thresholds of admissibility, to include thresholds of witness credibility, against a man it had once convicted on a terrorism offense.

Everywhere Hassoun turned, the War on Terror created an obstacle to his release. Hassoun never would have been imprisoned had the government not lowered the standards for criminal association. The climate of fear ensured his conviction. But even with the material-support and conspiracy charges brought against him thanks to the PATRIOT Act, he had served his time. Now, three years into post-conviction detention, the government was unwilling to let Hassoun go free even after conceding its residual case against him couldn't withstand judicial scrutiny. The permanent, carceral impulses of the War on Terror inclined the government to reach again for its favorite tool: impunity. All it needed was a sufficiently submissive court to declare that judges had to stay out of the government's way on national security matters. The courts had obliged so often since 9/11.

The anxiety dream America made out of Adham Hassoun's life was one scene in an endless nightmare. In response to 9/11, America had invaded and occupied two countries, bombed four others for years, killed at least 801,000 people—a full total may never be known—terrified millions more, tortured hundreds, detained thousands, reserved unto itself the right to create a global surveillance dragnet, disposed of its veterans with cruel indifference, called an entire global religion criminal or treated it that way, made migration into a crime, and declared most of its actions to be legal and constitutional. It created at least 21 million refugees and spent as much as $6 trillion on its operations. Through it all, America said other people, the ones staring down the barrel of the War on Terror, were the barbarians.

Asked if these efforts had been worth it, Stanley McChrystal, the former

JSOC and Afghanistan war commander, replied, "It would be impossible to argue that it was. The outcome just hasn't been positive enough to argue that. I think that we can never know a counterfactual, we can never know what would have happened if we'd gone in and done things differently, so I can't argue it automatically would have been different. I think the things that were done were done with good intentions, mostly. But no. We just made so many fundamental mistakes in how we approached it that the question is, which again, you and I can't answer, had we gone in with a different mindset, a totally different approach, which would have been more of a counterinsurgency approach, building through the state, would it have worked? I can't say it would've, but I think it would have been a better approach."

Even after eighteen years of his ordeal, Hassoun thought he might be able to clear all this up if only Chad Wolf would talk with him. He had heard Wolf on the common-room radio talking about the injustice of George Floyd's murder. Hassoun wrote him talking about the injustice that he was right now enduring, an injustice Wolf could end. Hadn't Wolf been the one signing the six-month threat designations? Was it too much to expect he would read Hassoun's letter? "Here people are slammed with stupid stuff for life and it's a disgrace," he reflected. "The greatest country in the world cannot reach a point where it can be a little bit civilized in its justice system."

And not only in its justice system. The War on Terror, not the nationalist fantasy Trump spun in his inaugural address, was the real American carnage. It turned foreigners into nonpersons—Anti-Iraqi Forces, Military-Aged Males, Detainees. When necessary, it could turn Americans into foreigners, all through turning citizenship into a border that it militarized. Those deemed no longer worthy of constitutional protections, like Anwar al-Awlaki and his teenage son Abdulrahman, could outrun the drones for only so long. The longer America viewed itself as under siege, the easier it became to see enemies everywhere. The longer America found itself unable to resolve its agonizing failure to achieve peace and victory, the easier it became to blame the vulnerable at home, to see Black liberation as terror, to see nonwhite immigration as terror, to see protesters as terror, to see liberalism as the handmaiden of terror, to see everything as terror except the apparatus it had constructed to inflict terror on men like Adham Hassoun. As the War on Terror became permanent, it was inevitable that those confronted with the agonizing refutation of American exceptionalism would look for a satisfying, violent resolution. The answers liberals offered were to call the War on Terror something else, reconcile themselves to a diminished "sustainable" version, and posture as if that was as good as ending the war. Liberalism, like the Security State, would always be shocked to discover that such permanence empowered those who wanted America not to be a global police force for undeserving foreigners, but a domestic one guarding the ramparts of American civilization.

In late July 2020 the Trump administration and Adham Hassoun reached a deal. He could go free—but not in America. The arrangement suited Hassoun, who had grown weary of a country that would never have room for him anywhere but in a cage. He started a new life in Rwanda. It could hardly be considered a loss for the government. As long as the Justice Department didn't fail in court, it wouldn't have to foreclose on any Forever War authority. Retaining the war itself was more important than retaining any particular detainee. Accordingly, from his new Kigali home, Hassoun watched as Portland protesters were snatched off the street and put into vans. He recognized what he saw. "This is what America has become," he said. "You started out doing it to people like me. Aliens and Muslims are vulnerable. Once the persecutors perfect their game, they move up to target citizens." His disgust for the War on Terror does not extend to Americans. Hassoun "still considers the American people to be my people," he said.

Trump's political coalition would never reciprocate that sentiment. But by the November election, MAGA did not consider millions of Americans to be their people, either. While the Democrats may have reached for their 2004 template against a hated Republican president, it turned out that Biden was not Kerry and Trump was not Bush. Trump lost the election, but the Democrats did not defeat MAGA. The head of the Texas Republican Party, Allen West—who, when he was an army lieutenant colonel, had an Iraqi policeman tortured—made the party's slogan "We Are The Storm," echoing a QAnon cry, and suggested that secession was a legitimate goal after the Supreme Court declined to overturn Trump's loss. In Washington, where the Republicans gained House seats, one of the new GOP freshmen, Georgia's Marjorie Taylor Greene, was an outright QAnon believer who had called the previous Congress part of "an Islamic invasion of our government" and declared white men to be "the most mistreated group of people in the United States today." When she took her oath of office on January 3, Greene wore a TRUMP WON mask to the Capitol.

Greene reflected the general MAGA mood. Trump had learned another pivotal lesson of the War on Terror: failure was no more than an argument for escalation. He and his surrogates insisted that they had won the election, amplified it through their journalistic surrogates and across the surveillance-capitalism platforms of social media, and then set to work attempting to cobble together any evidence of mass voter fraud. It took them to absurd extremes—Grenell, a former acting director of national intelligence, performed Trump's sort of intelligence collection by groundlessly asserting that Nevada had covered up its fraudulent votes—and court after court rejected the campaign's allegations. But Trump's relentless, manufactured insistence that the election was stolen from him led substantial portions of the right to believe it. In December, 18 Republican state attorneys general, supported by over 125 members of Congress, backed a frivolous Texas lawsuit to invalidate the election. Some of that support was cynical. "What is the downside for humoring him for this little bit of time?" a senior Republican official wondered to *The Washington Post*. But there was also a sincere mood taking hold on the right that democracy itself was an obstacle to its agenda, as it empowered the wrong sorts of voters. "Democracy isn't the objective," tweeted Utah Republican Senator Mike Lee, "liberty, peace and prosperity are." No meaningful difference existed between a lost election and a stolen election. The only mark of a valid election was a right-wing victory. Anything else was a Flight 93 Election.

With Congress on the brink of certifying the results of the electoral college, Trump called for his MAGA followers to assemble in Washington on January 6, 2021, for a demonstration to make legislators "Stop The Steal." MAGA understood the implications of their leader's message. Their online fora exploded with messages to show up in D.C. with guns. "Yes, it's illegal," said one poster, "but this is war, and we're clearly in a post-legal phase of our society." Mike Flynn, arriving in D.C., had already called for martial law to prevent Biden's presidency; the day before the rally, he asked if Trump's loyalists were ready to "bleed" for their freedom. That night, MAGA skirmished with local police, prompting fury that the cops, whom MAGA had so fervently defended, could show such disloyalty. "We don't got your back no more! We're the business owners! We're the veterans!" one shouted. Angry MAGA devotees from around the country—some arriving by private jet—assembled the next day to hear Trump; amped by the un-likely motivational music of "Fortunate Son" and the 1980s pop of Laura Branigan's "Gloria," he told them to march on the Capitol. "You'll never take back your country with weakness. You have to show strength," he told them, deceitfully adding that "I'll be there with you" on the procession to Congress. A rising MAGA senator who was objecting to the certification, Josh Hawley of Missouri, raised his fist in salute when he saw the protest advancing.

With that, a MAGA mob, later estimated at around eight hundred peo-ple, stormed into the Capitol. Despite how thoroughly telegraphed the in-surrection had been, the Capitol's perimeter defenses were no match for the rioters, who forced down flimsy knee-high fencing and prompted Capitol police officers, not all of whom were in riot gear, to fall back to the build-ing. It was no use. Overwhelming the police, people in body armor and red MAGA hats smashed through exterior windows with poles, entered the Capitol, and let in their comrades. Some officers fought to keep the mob out: One shot dead Ashli Babbitt, a QAnoner who was also an Afghanistan and Iraq veteran, as a crowd she was in attempted to breach a barricaded door. Another, Officer Eugene Goodman, an army infantryman in Iraq during the apocalyptic years of 2005–2006, heroically utilized his knowledge of the chamber's layout to maneuver the mob away from legislators and may have saved the life of Vice President Mike Pence. But other cops took selfies with the insurrectionists, stood aside as they entered, and permitted all but fourteen insurrectionists to leave without arresting them. It would be unthinkable to afford Adham Hassoun such treatment, and Hassoun had never committed an act of violence.

For over four hours inside the Capitol, men wearing things like CAMP AUSCHWITZ sweatshirts and carrying zip ties useful for taking hostages ransacked offices, smeared shit through the halls, and, underscoring the meaning of the day, unfurled Confederate flags. Panicked lawmakers and staff barricaded office doors with furniture and sheltered for their lives. One man who broke into Nancy Pelosi's office, which he was unaware was empty, carried a 950,000-volt stun gun. Many of the rioters—in the main, people accustomed to not being policed—posted and livestreamed their involvement in an insurrection that ultimately left five people dead.

Unlike at the BLM protests of June, there was no phalanx of minimally marked Justice Department police to protect federal installations. Part of the reason was a conscious decision to avoid a replay of the crackdown. Washington mayor Muriel Bowser requested the D.C. National Guard on the streets, but not in an armed capacity, only to free up cops for crowd control. But the guard's commander, Major General William Walker, accused Trump's new Pentagon leadership of restricting his authority to respond to the Capitol Police's call for backup early in the insurrection; Acting Secretary of Defense Christopher Miller, a War on Terror Special Operations veteran, denied impropriety but took three hours and nineteen minutes to get the National Guard to the Capitol. The result was that no real relief arrived for the Capitol Police. Its quickly fired chief, Steven Sund, sounded like Bush in blaming the attack on an intelligence failure. Sund claimed "nothing . . . including intelligence provided by FBI, Secret Service, Department of Homeland Security (DHS) and D.C. Metropolitan Police (MPD)" had indicated "a well-coordinated, armed assault on the Capitol might occur on Jan. 6." That required ignoring weeks of calls by Trump to Stop The Steal and responses by MAGA pledging to show up in force.

The insurrectionists themselves vindicated Daryl Johnson once again. Present at the Capitol were blackshirt gangs and militias, including the Three Percenters, the Oath Keepers, and the Proud Boys, whom a *Wall Street Journal* investigation reported were "coordinating, instigating and leading some of the most pivotal moments" of the riot. But most conspicuous within the crowd were the veterans. Of the first 176 people charged with crimes related to the insurrection, 22 had military experience. One of them was Larry Rendell Brock, a retired air force lieutenant colonel who had deployed to Iraq and Afghanistan. Brock had carried flex cuffs, the sort used to subdue detainees by American police and servicemembers alike, onto the Senate floor. His plate carrier featured patches with the insignia of his 706th Fighter Squadron and the *Totenkopf* skull of the Marvel Comics vigilante killer known as the Punisher. Another was a former Navy SEAL named Adam Newbold, who posted a video boasting about "breaching" the Capitol, a term familiar from a generation of special operators forcing their way into buildings in pursuit of terrorists. A month earlier, he had posted that he would be prepared to stop a Communist uprising he considered imminent: "Once things start going violent, then I'm in my element." The FBI swiftly questioned Newbold, who insisted he was nothing like those the SEALs hunted. "I am not a terrorist," he told ABC News, later expressing remorse for his participation. An entire generation of war had taught people like Newbold that terrorists didn't look or worship as they did.

The senior U.S. attorney in D.C. pledged to aggressively prosecute the insurrectionists, including through "sedition and conspiracy" charges. But the first month's worth of charges fit a template familiar to observers of CIA torture. They were all people who answered the call to Stop The

Steal, not the powerful politicians who issued the call in the first place. Hawley and other lawmakers who stoked the lie that Trump won the election refused liberal demands for their resignation, and within weeks sat on oversight committees investigating the failures of the Security State—and only their's—on January 6. The House impeached Trump a second time, this time with ten Republican votes, but in the Senate, Mike Lee argued that Trump deserved a "mulligan" for his incitement.

Liberals and their Security State allies, restored to power in the Biden administration, reached once again for security solutions to a fundamentally political problem. Robert Grenier, a CIA Counterterrorism Center chief during the age of the black sites, argued that the insurrectionists represented an insurgency. "To remove the supportive environment in which they were able to live and flourish," as Grenier described the mission of the Afghanistan quagmire, is "the heart of what we need to deal with here." A career prosecutor who helmed the Justice Department's national security division under Obama, Mary McCord, advocated for new laws against domestic terrorism, including the power that Congress refused to grant after Oklahoma City: making domestic terrorism "an offense that people and organizations are prohibited from materially supporting." It fell to the democratic socialists in Congress, chiefly Alexandria Ocasio-Cortez and Ilhan Omar, to explain why that was unacceptable even beyond the plethora of existing laws available to prosecute the insurrectionists. "We should not lose sight of our disgust at the double standards employed against white protesters and Black ones, or against Muslims and non-Muslims," said Omar, who had hidden on January 6 from a mob that had been cued to hate her. "But at the same time, we must resist the very human desire for revenge—to simply see the tools that have oppressed Black and brown people expanded."

Another liberal response was to take the opportunity to declare that January 6 turned a page in American history. Elissa Slotkin spent the Forever War as a CIA analyst of the Middle East, deploying three times to Iraq, and served as a senior official in Obama's Pentagon. In 2018, she was elected to Congress to represent Michigan's Eighth District, home to several of the militiamen conspirators charged in the Gretchen Whitmer kidnapping plot. "The 'post-9/11' era, where our greatest threats to national security were external, is over," Slotkin declared. Given the difficulty, after bin Laden, of finding a material circumstance to indisputably resolve the war, January 6 had a plausibility to it. But while Slotkin's argument reflected the War on Terror's exhaustion, it also displayed a familiar liberal formalism. She made no effort to locate the path to January 6 that the American response to September 11 had paved. Nor did Slotkin argue that because the 9/11 era was supposedly over, the extraordinary security powers that characterized the era ought to end as well. Behind the declaration of finality was, as ever, continuity. Forty men remained imprisoned at Guantanamo after Slotkin said the 9/11 era was over.

Neither conservatives nor liberals wanted to face what nationalists and leftists knew: the War on Terror could sustain itself because of how deeply American it was. Its iconography, a gun wrapped in the flag, with a cross implied in the background, was no accident. It was there even before 9/11, at Oklahoma City, where Americans preferred blaming and then legislating against Muslims to recognizing that foundational American mythology bred terrorists like Timothy McVeigh. The reign of terror that America launched after 9/11 was familiar to nonwhites across four hundred years of American history, in both its violence and its insistence that such violence was for the ultimate benefit of civilization. It ensured that America would pay any price for what would prove a futile, self-destructive war. Paying that price, in blood, was what America had always valorized, what it had always justified. The War on Terror fit within American traditions of settler colonialism, observed New York University professor Nikhil Pal Singh, as it was a "reengagement with the more primal terms of American race war and the fantasy of national social and economic regeneration through (frontier) violence." Donald Trump saw the same thing. Except to MAGA, settler colonialism was how America made itself great. "You think our country's so innocent?" he had sneered at Bill O'Reilly.

After insisting that its role as a global hegemon bore no relationship to 9/11, America was left with a civilizational explanation for its generation-long sense of intolerable vulnerability. It could only understand the fanaticism of al-Qaeda, and then of ISIS, and whatever successor group emerges, through mass civilizational pathology. Jihadism was dangerous because it was so deeply rooted in Islam, Americans concluded. Islam attacked America because Islam was, in the final analysis, terror itself. Never would America acknowledge that the violent, reactionary dangers that it attributed to its enemies were also part of its own history. That was the meaning of Oklahoma City. It was the meaning of January 6. A white man with a flag and a gun, the man who had made America great, was not a terrorist. The 9/11 era said he was a counterterrorist. America had never been the sort of place that would tell him he was anything else. As the Forever War persisted, with Trump handing off to Biden a perpetual-motion engine of death powered by the worst of American history, its targets increasingly domestic and its final form still unachieved, it became increasingly difficult to see America as anything more than its War on Terror.

ACKNOWLEDGMENTS

Yes, I know this book is incomplete.

There's not enough in *Reign* about the pivotal role of the media in manu-facturing consent for the War on Terror. There's nowhere *near* enough about the economic forces driving the war, both specific and structural. Ultimately, I found that attempting either analysis swallowed the actual narrative events of the war and *still* felt superficial. These subjects require books in their own right—particularly one I'm tossing around in my head called *Capitalism and Terrorism*. (That book is the forum to go into the U.S.–Saudi relationship and its place in all this, I found . . . after failing to get it into *Reign* satisfactorily.) I chose to attempt to do one thing well instead of three things badly.

That leads to the second way *Reign* is incomplete. I had to make a lot of cuts. They were a function of *Reign*'s particular critique, as well as the un-avoidable reality that I have a twenty-year palette of events and a contractu-ally stipulated word limit. (Someone have me on their podcast to talk about Michelle Malkin bullying Dunkin' Donuts because she was mad Rachael Ray appeared in a commercial wearing a scarf that looked kind of like a kaffiyeh.) Even after all those cuts, at all times writing this book, a voice in my head objects that I'm presenting the "We Didn't Start the Fire" version of the Forever War. So if I didn't dwell long enough on events you think are crucial, know that I tried, and please research and write your own versions that outdo mine.

The third way *Reign* is incomplete is that much of what I write about remains an official secret. The façade of the War on Terror has been cracked, but we won't know what the war truly was for decades. I frankly don't think anything we discover will undermine the critique of *Reign*. I expect what we learn to reinforce my critique. Consider that at least eighteen hundred photographs of military torture have been barred from public release after a yearslong legal battle. Not even Dan Jones's torture report could tell the story of CIA renditions, operations that we know applied to more people than the CIA directly jailed and tortured. Some aspects of the War on Terror are likely lost to history forever.

The War on Terror has no shortage of excellent books about its component operations: surveillance (*Dark Mirror* by Bart Gellman, *Power Wars* by Charlie Savage, *The Watchers* by Shane Harris), torture (*The Dark Side* by Dana Priest), immigration (*We Are All Suspects Now* by Tram Nguyen, *All-American Nativism* by Daniel Denvir), detention (*Guantanamo's Child* by Michelle Shephard), occupation (*Imperial Life in the Emerald City* by Rajiv Chandrasekaran), secrecy and its impact on the rule of law (*Top Secret America* by Dana Priest and William Arkin, *Angler* by Gellman, *Power Wars* again), and the wars themselves (*Dirty Wars* by Jeremy Scahill, *Night Draws Near* by Anthony Shadid, *Fiasco* by Tom Ricks, *Relentless Strike* by Sean Naylor, *Shatter the Nations* by Mike Giglio, so many more). There's no point in trying to write a better exploration of Dick Cheney than Gellman did in *Angler*, nor in trying to outdo Scahill in exposing Blackwater. This is an attempt at doing something a bit different: surveying the entirety of the War on Terror and its impact on America. Ironically, that makes it difficult to go into everything I would have liked. That's probably also a function of the difficulty of writing about the previous twenty years, a period that's too old for journalism and too young for history. But very soon will come a wave of critical and political reappraisal of the War on Terror, each with its own focus, whose critiques intersect with, challenge, and bolster *Reign*'s. Some of these projects I'm aware of and excited about. My fondest ambition for *Reign of Terror* is that it be one work among many to confront and destroy both the War on Terror and the conditions that created it.

The writing of this book would have been impossible, in material and emotional ways, particularly in a pandemic, without the following people:

Laurie Liss at Sterling Lord put up with me for entire years when I had bad, unsellable ideas for books and did not make her any money. Shortly after Thanksgiving 2018 I came to her to say I had finally found my book and needed her help to see if I could sell it or if I should resign myself to not being an author. She challenged me to refine what it was I was talking about and to civilize myself for the purpose of getting out of the way of the story I wanted to tell. So did Rick Kot at Viking, who steered this book to be what I needed it to be. He put up with a lot of random texts, unfocused phone calls, and tens of thousands of self-indulgent words in my drafts. I am grateful to have worked with an editor of his caliber. Special thanks go out to Viking's Camille Leblanc, Louise Braverman, and Julia Rickard for their invaluable work making sure people see this book. My gratitude also goes out to Viking designer Lucia Bernard, production manager Fabi Van Arsdell, and managing editor Tricia Conley. Production editor Ryan Boyle put up with a lot of eleventh-hour changes, and I am grateful for his forbearance.

Andrew Ackerman taught me to love to read and to never leave myself exposed in an argument. Some of my favorite memories are of being ten years old walking around Bay Ridge listening to my father talk about pre-Norman English history or Hobbes versus Locke. Or at least they were. Now I cherish hearing his excitement for a book I really did not think he would find compelling, even if I can't convince him that executing Anwar al-Awlaki was wrong.

When I was seven years old, I met my cousin Sky Cohen for the first time. I have no siblings, but suddenly I had a little brother. It occurs to me that my life right now resembles what my preteen self assumed it would be: a household composed of me, my wife, our children, and you.

The person I admire most is Colin Asher, the singer of my teenage punk band and simply the most righteous person I know. When I was nineteen and Colin came back to New York for a summer after moving to California, we took one of the long walks we liked to take and I told him about interning at *New York Press*, which was the center of my world at the time. After I had gone on for long enough, Colin simply asked, "What is your journalism *for?*" I was mortified not to have an answer. Colin recently offered his own in the form of *Never a Lovely So Real*, his resurrection of the writer Nelson Algren. In that and in so much else, he inspires me.

It was at *New York Press* where I met Daria Vaisman, my sister. Daria was the research editor at the paper, not much older than me, her employee, and taught me a lot about how shambolic a human being you can be if you're also the wittiest and most erudite person in a weird alt-weekly newsroom. She is the sort of person I had hoped newsrooms cultivated, and being around her vindicated my decision to make this my life. I'm lucky she loves me, because I would not be equipped to withstand her. No one has believed in this project more or made me laugh harder. I miss reading aloud with you, and once we get the vaccines, we'll hold each other's babies.

Laura Hudson is my best creative partner. I was a fan of hers before we came to work together at *Wired*, and I sheepishly told her that over a proto-Slack office messaging program. The first time we met in person I was under the twin emotional pressures of the Snowden leaks and the death of my mother. I can't thank her enough for listening to me, throughout the years, and especially about *Reign*. Laura is one of the finest cultural writers and editors working, and I was afraid to show her parts of this book. I benefited so much from doing so.

I briefly became a conservative after years of being unable to beat Sam Goldman in arguments about politics. Sam and our friend Jesse Cannon are people who possess iron determination and impossibly high standards, and these are things that punk rock rewards. To be friends with them required me to get on their level. We put on a two-day, thirty-band music festival before Sam and I were out of high school, and, as I am fond of recalling, for weeks during the lead-up, Sam and Jesse were not speaking to each other. Jesse in particular has taught me a lifetime's worth about the programmatic aspects of and discipline behind creativity. Sam gave me the title of chapter nine—a dramatic improvement over my sorry idea to call it "9/11's Virus." I'm a much worse person in the best possible ways because of them.

I'm going to talk at some length about Michelle Shephard. As the national security correspondent of the *Toronto Star*, she fearlessly, rigorously, and without euphemism revealed Canada's contributions to the War on Terror and many aspects of the wars in Yemen and Somalia. Among her towering journalistic achievements is the definitive investigative and narrative portrait of the ordeal of Omar Khadr, the grievously wounded teenager who had to grow into adulthood inside Guantanamo Bay. For this she received predictable misogynistic attacks. I first encountered Michelle over the course of a week at Guantanamo bookended by her fighting a snake and the military ordering her expelled because she wrote someone's name that the Pentagon didn't want printed. She won both battles. Michelle has been a hero of mine ever since, and I'm honored to call her my friend. I could not have written this book without her enthusiasm, support, and guidance. More than that: if Michelle had winced at *Reign*, it would have convinced me I didn't really have anything here.

That leads me to another point we need to acknowledge. Women produce the lion's share of exceptional national security journalism. This book is only possible because of pioneering, relentless journalists like Jane Mayer, Dana Priest, Laura Poitras, Carol Rosenberg, Sharon Weinberger, Marcy Wheeler,

ACKNOWLEDGMENTS

Muna Shikaki, Nancy Youssef, Kashmir Hill, Dara Lind—one of the foremost immigration journalists, who has been crucial in walking me through arcana I should have already understood—Aura Bogado, Alexa O'Brien, Emma Graham-Harrison, Janet Reitman, Raya Jalabi, Talia Lavin, Julia Angwin, Tram Nguyen, Kim Zetter, Hannah Allam, Betsy Woodruff Swan, Erin Banco, Kelly Weill, Laila al-Arian, Azmat Khan, Betty Medsger, and so many others. The foremost theorist of surveillance capitalism, *the prophet who named it*, is Shoshana Zuboff.

If Michelle Shephard is the real-life Lois Lane, Janine Gibson is the real-life Perry White, as I learned less than a week into working for her. On a phone call hours before we published the first Snowden story, I listened as some of the most powerful men in the Security State told Janine to stop and asked to speak with her manager when she made clear that she wouldn't. When all that failed, one of them raised his voice at her, telling us we would have blood on our hands if we published. To be honest, I spent much of that phone call expecting her to fold, because much of my experience of working with editors had accustomed me to expect them to back down to power. But that was because I did not yet know Janine Gibson. Once we ended that call, I knew that I would do whatever she told me to do for as long as she told me to do it. She captained the most important story in the world and it was my privilege to play a part. It's a tragedy for the public in a time of global crisis that Janine isn't the editor of *The Guardian*. To paraphrase Jack Kirby, journalism will break your heart.

Whatever I've been able to achieve as a reporter is because of Noah Shachtman. Before I ever worked for him, Noah would GChat me for feedback on sections of his latest magazine piece, which would inevitably start out with widescreen accounts in media res of being pinned down with marines in Afghanistan and waiting interminably for air support to materialize. Whatever I would be writing would immediately seem nowhere near as vivid. When I started working for him at *Wired*, I failed again and again. My first couple FBI Islamophobia stories were so horrendously written that Noah had to take control; that National Magazine Award really is his as well. Noah (and John Abell) stood by me when *The Daily Caller* launched a chickenshit attempt at canceling journalists, including myself within weeks of starting at *Wired*. The most rational thing to do was to get rid of me, and he didn't. That's who he is and who he'll always be, and it's why there is an entire alumni network of reporters and editors who are forever loyal to him. If that wasn't enough, Noah is one of the last editors who put in the work as a reporter—a *freelance* reporter—before making the transition. No one has ever believed in me like Noah has, no one has ever pushed me as hard as he does, and I'll never be able to repay him. He is journalism's Patrick Ewing.

Every single day, for more years than I can remember, I'm guaranteed to talk to two people outside my family: Adam Serwer and Matt Bors. I was talking with them when I came up with this book, and they encouraged me to write it. They have been beside me during the journalistic and mental-health journeys of writing *Reign of Terror*, which is to say that they have put up with a tremendous amount. Imagine my luck at being able to call upon the talents of both the foremost political essayist *and* the foremost political cartoonist of our era. Imagine how much you have to prove when your closest friends coined The Cruelty Is The Point *and* We Should Improve Society Somewhat. To miss the excellence they consistently produce is to risk misunderstanding our present crises. I owe this book to them.

Sam Thielman, my work-husband at *The Guardian*, gave me invaluable guidance about his evangelical Christian faith. University of Wisconsin historian Suzanne Desan generously found the Alfred de Vigny quote for the epigraph. It won't ever stop being wild to me that I rambled through my book and the troubles I had writing it with Sam McPheeters, whose lyrics I quoted in my high school senior yearbook. Three cartographers lent their expertise to my attempt to find an American base of comparison for the area of tribal Pakistan that U.S. drones attacked: thanks to Eben Dennis, Graham Twibell, and David Maye. I'm also grateful for conversations I've had related to this book with scholars like Nikhil Pal Singh, Ruth Ben-Ghiat, and Jason Stanley; and with dear friends like Sasha Acosta-Cohen and Ryan Simons. Most importantly, thanks to everyone who ever trusted me to tell their stories. Whenever I have succeeded, it is because I stayed true to the legacy of my late mother, Bette Cohen, and whenever I have failed, it is because I lost sight of her.

In the fall of 2007, legislation to legalize much of STELLARWIND was moving on Capitol Hill, and I was following it for *Talking Points Memo*. Some development occurred late on a Friday afternoon and I needed a civil-libertarian reaction voice in my writeup. I called the press office of the ACLU's Washington outpost. The woman who answered said she'd have one of their lobbyists get back to me by my deadline, but before I left, she asked me if my ringtone was really "Guns of Brixton" by the Clash, as she had read on the internet. Surprised, I said it was, and she told me how much she also liked the Clash, and before I could stop myself I mentioned that I have a Clash tattoo. Mandy Simon dedicated her life to demanding justice for the War on Terror at the ACLU, the American Constitution Society, and Amnesty International. This is the legacy she provides for our two children. Somehow the thing in this world I hate the most gave me the people I love the most.

NOTES

Introduction: Neither Peace nor Victory

xi Miller's last-minute elevation: Spencer Ackerman, "Mark Esper, Who Flinched at Military Crackdown, Out at Pentagon," *Daily Beast*, November 9, 2020. Spencer Ackerman, "Infamous MAGA Figures Flood into Purged Pentagon," *Daily Beast*, November 10, 2020. Official biography of Acting Defense Secretary Christopher C. Miller, www.defense.gov/Our-Story/Biographies/Biography/Article/2111192/christopher-c-miller, accessed December 4, 2020.

xii Senator Tammy Duckworth: Spencer Ackerman and Asawin Suebsaeng, "A Cadre of Top Trumpists Is Pushing for Full Afghanistan Withdrawal," *Daily Beast*, November 17, 2020. Statement of Sen. Tammy Duckworth, "Duckworth Releases Statement in Response to Trump Administration's Plan to Withdraw Troops from Afghanistan and Iraq," press release, November 17, 2020, www.duckworth.senate.gov/news/press-releases/duckworth-releases-statement-in-response-to-trump-administrations-plan-to-withdraw-troops-from-afghanistan-and-iraq.

xii–xiii Trump's accelerated bombing: Spencer Ackerman, "Trump's Afghanistan Airstrikes Increased Civilian Deaths by 330 Percent, Brown Costs of War Study Shows," *Daily Beast*, December 7, 2020.

xiii Howard Stern's radio show: Donald Trump on *The Howard Stern Show*, September 11, 2002, soundcloud.com/buzzfeedandrew/trump-on-the-howard-stern-show-on-sept-11-2002#t=0:00, accessed August 9, 2020.

xvi suspend the Constitution: Spencer Ackerman and Kelly Weill, "'When the Bombs Fall, the Blood Is on Mike Flynn's Hands': Retired Officers Blast His Calls for Martial Law," *Daily Beast*, December 2, 2020.

xvii "A perpetual war": Barack Obama, "Remarks by the President at the National Defense University," May 23, 2013. Transcript available at https://obamawhitehouse .archives.gov/the-press-office/2013/05/23/remarks-president-national-defense-university.

xvii conducted widespread surveillance: Tim Elfrink, "Police Shot Portland Slaying Suspect without Warning or Trying to Arrest Him First, Witness Says," *Washington Post*, September 10, 2020.

xviii Aimé Césaire observed: Aimé Césaire, *Discourse on Colonialism* (1950), medium.com /religion-bites/discourse-on-colonialism-by-aim%C3%A9-c%C3%A9saire -793b291a0987, accessed December 3, 2020.

Prologue: The Worst Terrorist Attack in American History

2 "led the American radical right": This account of Elohim City is drawn from Somer Shook, Wesley Delano, and Robert W. Balch, "Elohim City: A Participant-Observer Study of a Christian Identity Community," *Nova Religio: The Journal of Alternative and Emergent Religions* 2, no. 2, April 1999. Tony Reinhart, "Suspicion Surrounds Sect Leader," *Kitchener-Waterloo Record*, May 9, 1997. Unbylined, "City of Secrets: Separatist Group at Elohim City, Oklahoma, May Have Ties to Timothy McVeigh and Other Anti-Government Extremists," *Dateline NBC*, May 30, 1997. Deborah Hastings, "Elohim City on Extremists' Underground Railroad," Associated Press, February 23, 1997. Gustav Niebuhr, "A Vision of an Apocalypse: The Religion of the Far Right," *New York Times*, May 22, 1995. Unbylined, "Changing of the Guard," Southern Poverty Law Center *Intelligence Report*, August 29, 2001. Also see the FBI's declassified file on Covenant, Sword and Arm of the Lord, which references Millar and Elohim City. The file includes a May 2, 1985, memo from an FBI official, J. W. Hicks, who laments that the FBI/ATF search on the CSA compound was shoddy: "[A] more careful processing of the crime scene would have produced a great deal more information regarding the CSA and its affiliates," vault.fbi.gov/The%20Covenant%20The%20Sword%20The%20Arm %20of%20the%20Lord%20/The%20Covenant%20The%20Sword%20The %20Arm%20of%20the%20Lord%20Part%201%20of%202/view, and https://vault .fbi.gov/The%20Covenant%20The%20Sword%20The%20Arm%20of%20the %20Lord%20/The%20Covenant%20The%20Sword%20The%20Arm%20of %20the%20Lord%20Part%202%20of%202/view, accessed September 5, 2019.

3 According to an informant: Julie DelCour, "Jurors Hear Howe's Testimony: Ex-Informant Says She Had Seen McVeigh at Elohim City in 1994," *Tulsa World*, December 11, 1997.

3 an "inspiration" to younger soldiers: Dale Russakoff and Serge F. Kovaleski, "An Ordinary Boy's Extraordinary Rage," *Washington Post*, July 2, 1995.

4 talking about avenging them: Andrew Gumbel and Roger G. Charles, *Oklahoma City: What the Investigation Missed—and Why It Still Matters* (New York: HarperLuxe, 2012), 123–24.

4 from *The Turner Diaries*: Kathleen Belew, *Bring the War Home: The White Power Movement and Paramilitary America* (Cambridge, MA: Harvard University Press, 2019), 222.

5 people McVeigh killed: Gumbel and Charles, *Oklahoma City*, 47, 78–79. Theresa Walker, "20 Years Later, OKC Bombing Victim Helped by Laguna Beach Has Found Peace," *Orange County Register*, April 18, 2015.

6 Cal Thomas agreed: Gumbel and Charles, *Oklahoma City*, 58. Robert Marquand, "Media Still Portray Muslims as Terrorists," *Christian Science Monitor*, January 22, 1996. Farhan Haq, "Anti-Muslim Backlash Feared," *Inter Press Service*, April 20, 1995. Walter Goodman, "Terror in Oklahoma City; TV Critic's Notebook; Wary Network Anchors Battle Dubious Scoops," *New York Times*, April 20, 1995. Mike Royko, "Time to Up the Ante Against Terrorism," *Chicago Tribune*, April 21, 1995.

6 "I'll never forget it": Norman Kempster, "Man Returned to United States Is Not a Suspect," *Los Angeles Times*, April 22, 1995. Marquand, "Media Still Portray."

6 Several Elohim City Residents: Belew, *Bring the War Home*, 226.

6 The need for a successful prosecution: Gumbel and Charles, *Oklahoma City*, 257–77.

6 ATF informant, Carol Howe: Ibid. David Pugliese, "Meet the Holiday Inn of Hate," *Ottawa Citizen*, April 15, 2000. Belew, *Bring the War Home*, 234.

7 Whether or not anyone at Elohim City: Belew, *Bring the War Home*, 210–16.

7 a broad disavowal: Laura Smith, "Armed Resistance, Lone Wolves and Media Messaging: Meet the Godfather of the Alt-Right," *Timeline*/Medium.com, November 6, 2017, timeline.com/louis-beam-white-supremacy-history-20d028315d, accessed September 12, 2019. Belew, *Bring the War Home*, 27–30.

8 even after McVeigh's conviction: Pugliese, "Meet the Holiday Inn of Hate."

8 A *Washington Post* profile: Ronald Brownstein, "Public Fears the Price of Security May Be Liberty," *Los Angeles Times*, April 30, 1995. Russakoff and Kovaleski, "An Ordinary Boy's Extraordinary Rage." Arthur Hirsch, "The Loner; Seeking Solitude; With So Many Individualists Out There Doing Terrible Things These Days, Is It Possible that an American Love Affair with the Strong Silent Type Is on the Rocks?" *Baltimore Sun*, April 24, 1996.

9 "McVeigh's enemies weren't blacks": Lou Michel and Dan Herbeck, *American Terrorist: Timothy McVeigh & the Oklahoma City Bombing* (New York: Harper, 2001), 86–89.

9 Not long before the bombing: Fox Butterfield, "Rifle Association Has Long Practice in Railing against Federal Agents," *New York Times*, May 8, 1995. Guy Gugliotta, "NRA, Backers Have Focused Ire on ATF," *Washington Post*, April 26, 1995.

9 At trial McVeigh's lawyers: Julie DelCour, "The Real McVeigh? Defense Describes Him as Pleasant, Polite," *Tulsa World*, September 12, 1996. Stephen Paulson, "Attorneys Portray McVeigh as Gulf War Hero," Associated Press, September 11, 1996. Sam Howe Verhovek, "The Emotional Politics of a Political Trial," *New York Times*, April 27, 1997.

10 Limbaugh called the president: Todd S. Purdham, "Shifting Debate to the Political Climate, Clinton Condemns 'Promoters of Paranoia,'" *New York Times*, April 25,

1995. Testimony of Gregory Nojeim, American Civil Liberties Union, to the House Judiciary Committee, June 12, 1995, available at https://fas.org/irp/congress/1995_hr/h950612-3n.htm.

10 **Congressional hearings on Waco and Ruby Ridge:** George Lardner Jr. and Pierre Thomas, "U.S. to Pay Family in FBI Idaho Raid," *Washington Post*, August 16, 1995.

11 **A *Los Angeles Times* poll:** Testimony of Gregory Nojeim, American Civil Liberties Union, House Judiciary Committee, June 12, 1995. Brownstein, "Public Fears the Price of Security May Be Liberty." "Blown Away? The Bill of Rights after Oklahoma City," *Harvard Law Review* 109, no. 8 (June 1996), 2074–91.

11 **"eviscerated the heart and soul":** Statement of President Bill Clinton on signing the Antiterrorism and Effective Death Penalty Act of 1996, April 24, 1996. Greg McDonald, "Terrorism Bill Loses Hard Edge," *Houston Chronicle*, March 14, 1996. Charles V. Zehren, "Unkept Promises: Still No Pact on Anti-Terror Bill," *Newsday*, April 15, 1996. Text of the 1996 Antiterrorism and Effective Death Penalty Act, www.govinfo.gov/content/pkg/PLAW-104publ132/html/PLAW-104publ132.htm, accessed September 19, 2019.

11 **making the American carceral state more lethal:** Elizabeth Bruenig, "The Fire Last Time," *New York Times*, January 18, 2021.

11 **For good measure, a bill:** Jordan E. Helton, "Construction of a Terrorist under the Material Support Statute, 18 USC 2339B," *American University Law Review* 67, no. 2, article 5. Jim Abrams, "A Year after Oklahoma City, Anti-Terrorism Bill Nears Completion," Associated Press, April 15, 1996. Liliana Segura, "Gutting Habeas Corpus: The Inside Story of How Bill Clinton Sacrificed Prisoners' Rights for Political Gain," *The Intercept*, May 4, 2016.

Chapter One: 9/11 and the Security State

14 **By August 6:** *Final Report of the National Commission on Terrorist Attacks Upon the United States*, 254–77.

14 **Yet the president responded:** Michael Morell, *The Great War of Our Time: The CIA's Fight against Terrorism—From al Qa'ida to ISIS* (New York: TwelveBooks, 2015), 41.

14 **"The Arabian Peninsula has never":** "Al-Qaeda's Declaration of War against Americans," *The al-Qaeda Reader*, ed. Raymond Ibrahim (New York: Crown, 2007), 11–14.

17 **He marveled at all:** Susan Sachs, "Below 14th Street, Silence but an Eerie Disquiet," *New York Times*, September 13, 2001. Mark Abadi, "Trump Had an Unusual Reaction to 9/11 Just Hours after the Attacks," *Business Insider*, September 11, 2019. Additionally, Trump speculated baselessly that al-Qaeda had planted bombs in the World Trade Center because "how could a plane . . . possibly go through the steel?"

17 **"They certainly found our American":** Zell Miller, September 12, 2001. Collected in *Zell Miller: A Senator Speaks Out on Patriotism, Values and Character* (Washington, D.C.: Monument Press, 2005), 78.

18 **"Think of the guilt":** Edward Snowden, *Permanent Record* (New York: Metropolitan Books, 2019), 80.

18 with energy if not enthusiasm: Michael Morell, a senior career CIA official at the time of the attacks who rose to become acting director, titled his reflections on the War on Terror *The Great War of Our Time*.

19 The fires at Ground Zero burned for one hundred days: Staff and agencies, "Ground Zero Stops Burning, after 100 Days," *Guardian*, December 20, 2001. Paul J. Lioy et al., "Characterization of the Dust/Smoke Aerosol that Settled East of the World Trade Center (WTC) after the Collapse of the WTC 11 September 2001," *Environmental Health Perspectives* 110, no. 7 (July 2002): 703–14. Robin Schulman, "Ex-EPA Chief Is Ruled Not Liable for 9/11 Safety Claims," *Washington Post*, April 23, 2008.

19 "He's bursting out all over": Peggy Noonan, "God Is Back," *Wall Street Journal*, September 28, 2001, available here: https://peggynoonan.com/154.

19 A thirty-three-year-old Palestinian-born: Tram Nguyen, *We Are All Suspects Now* (Boston: Beacon Press, 2005), 51.

19 Hate crimes against Muslims—or those, like Sikhs: Kuang Keng Kuek Ser, "Data: Hate Crimes Against Muslims Increased after 9/11," Public Radio International, September 12, 2016.

19–20 "Larry Silverstein, the owner of the WTC": Terry J. Allen, "The 9/11 Truth Conspiracy Is a Distraction from the Real Crimes of Our Government," *In These Times*, July 11, 2006.

20 Before September ended O'Reilly: Dennis Prager to Bill O'Reilly, *The O'Reilly Factor*, Fox News, September 19, 2001. Bill O'Reilly, *The O'Reilly Factor*, Fox News, September 29, 2001. Bill O'Reilly, "Man Whose Father Died in Trade Center Signs Anti-War Ad," *The O'Reilly Factor*, Fox News, February 4, 2003.

20 "All the time I would say": Author's interviews with Adham Amin Hassoun, May 30 and June 11, 2020.

20 college student, Monique Danison: Michael Elliott, "The Shoe Bomber's World," *Time*, February 16, 2002.

21 New York's reactionary mayor: *Talk* magazine, November 2001.

21 He echoed Whitman: Anthony DePalma, "Ground Zero Illnesses Clouding Giuliani's Legacy," *New York Times*, May 14, 2007. Wayne Barrett, "Rudy Giuliani's Five Big Lies About 9/11," *Village Voice*, July 31, 2007.

21 Supreme Court Justice Antonin Scalia: Peter Lattman, "Justice Scalia Hearts Jack Bauer," *Wall Street Journal*, June 20, 2007.

22 Bush urged people to go shopping: Todd S. Purdham, "Bush Warns of a Wrathful, Shadowy, Inventive War," *New York Times*, September 17, 2001.

22 "not going to give up my Botox": Ruth La Ferla, "When Times Get Tough, Some Go for Plastic Surgery," *New York Times*, October 21, 2001.

23 But rather than dismantling it: Susan Sontag, "Tuesday, and After," *The New Yorker*, September 17, 2001. Joan Didion, *Fixed Ideas: America Since 9.11* (New York: New York Review of Books, 2003), 13. Lawrence F. Kaplan, "No Choice," *The New Republic*, October 1, 2001. Even Sontag's biographer, Benjamin Moser, wrote about Sontag's 9/11

essay, "Behind her analysis was the lack of empathy that wrecked her relationships and trivialized many of her political observations." Benjamin Moser, *Sontag: Her Life and Work* (New York: Ecco, 2019), 662.

23 **"In the wake of a massacre"**: Charles Krauthammer, "Voices of Moral Obtuseness," *Washington Post*, September 21, 2001. Krauthammer wrote before an accurate tally of the dead was available.

23 **The Strokes, on the cusp**: *Billboard* staff, "Strokes Pull NYPD-Themed Song from Album," *Billboard*, September 20, 2001.

23 **In the months after 9/11, Didion**: Anne K. Kofol, "Yasin Delivers 'Jihad' Speech," *Harvard Crimson*, June 6, 2002. Didion, *Fixed Ideas*, 13–15.

24 **"a known al-Qaeda facility"**: Matt Wells, "Al-Jazeera Accuses U.S. of Bombing Its Kabul Office," *Guardian*, November 17, 2001. Committee to Protect Journalists, "U.S. Airstrike Destroys Al-Jazeera Office in Kabul," November 13, 2001. Committee to Protect Journalists, "Attacks on the Press 2001: Afghanistan," March 26, 2002.

24 **"One good thing"**: Roger Rosenblatt, "The Age of Irony Comes to an End," *Time*, September 24, 2001.

25 **On the rainy Friday after 9/11**: "Bush Leads Memorial Service for Victims of Terror Attack," *New York Times*, September 14, 2001.

25 **"[T]his war was so different"**: Quoted in Barton Gellman, *Angler: The Cheney Vice Presidency* (New York: Penguin Press, 2008), 139.

25 **The priority was to give**: Gregory D. Johnsen, "60 Words and a War without End: The Untold Story of the Most Dangerous Sentence in U.S. History," *BuzzFeed*, January 16, 2014. "Authorization for Use of Military Force in Response to the 9/11 Attacks (P.L. 107–40): Legislative History," Richard F. Grimmett, Congressional Research Service, updated January 18, 2017. Addington "mostly sat out . . . the Authorization for the Use of Military Force" drafting, according to Gellman in *Angler*, 139.

25 **Once granted, the president's**: Deputy Assistant Attorney General John C. Yoo to the deputy counsel to the president, "The President's Constitutional Authority to Conduct Military Operations Against Terrorists and Nations Supporting Them," U.S. Department of Justice, September 25, 2001 www.justice.gov/file/19151/download. See also discussion in Charlie Savage, *Takeover: The Return of The Imperial Presidency and the Subversion of American Democracy* (New York: Little, Brown and Company, 2007), 121–22.

26 **A deeply religious Christian**: George W. Bush, "Remarks by the President at the Islamic Center of Washington, D.C.," September 17, 2001. Transcript available at https://georgewbush-whitehouse.archives.gov/news/releases/2001/09/20010917-11.html.

26 **The result was a vague definition**: Purdham, "Bush Warns of a Wrathful, Shadowy, Inventive War." Peter Waldman and Hugh Pope, "'Crusade' Reference Reinforces Fears War on Terrorism Is against Muslims," *Wall Street Journal*, September 21, 2001.

27 Years later, after the consequences: Spencer Ackerman and Betsy Swan, "'Homeland Security' Ignores White Terror, DHS Veterans Say," *Daily Beast*, October 31, 2018.

28 The database would eventually: John Ashcroft, "Prepared Remarks on the National Security Entry-Exit Registration System," June 6, 2002. Rights Working Group, Penn State Law Immigrants' Rights Clinic, "The NSEERS Effect: A Decade of Racial Profiling, Fear and Secrecy," May 2002. Arab-American Anti-Discrimination Committee, "End the Shame of NSEERS" fact sheet. Leslie Bererstein Roja, "NSEERS and 'Special Registration' Are Gone, but Long-Term Effects Continue," KPCC, January 30, 2012, www.scpr.org/blogs/multiamerican/2012/01/30/8161/nseers-and-special-registration -are-gone-but-long-, accessed February 24, 2021.

28 That included cells equipped: Justice Department Office of the Inspector General, *The September 11 Detainees: A Review of the Treatment of Aliens Held on Immigration Charges in Connection with the Investigation of the September 11 Attacks*, June 2003. Testimony of Justice Department Inspector General Glenn Fine, Senate Judiciary Committee, June 25, 2003.

28 It remains unknown, nearly: Nguyen, *We Are All Suspects Now*, 8.

28 A San Antonio radiologist: Eric Lichtblau, *Bush's Law: The Remaking of American Justice* (New York: Anchor, 2009), 22.

29 But after 9/11 the roundups: Lichtblau, *Bush's Law*, Kindle location 235.

29 The cleric opted instead to flee: Jeremy Scahill, *Dirty Wars: The World Is a Battlefield* (New York: Nation Books, 2013), 31–47. Alexander Meleagrou-Hitchens, "As American as Apple Pie: How Anwar al-Awlaki Became the Face of Western Jihad," the International Centre for the Study of Radicalisation and Political Violence, 2011. J. M. Berger, "The Enduring Appeal of al-Awlaki's 'Constants on the Path of Jihad,'" Combatting Terrorism Center at West Point, October 2011. Scott Shane, *Objective Troy: A Terrorist, a President, and the Rise of the Drone* (New York: Tim Duggan Books, 2016), 82–105.

30 On October 25: Rep. Michael Oxley, comments at "Panel I of Hearing of the House Financial Services Committee; Subject: Terrorist Financing," September 19, 2002. Feingold's speech is posted at epic.org/privacy/terrorism/usapatriot/feingold.html, accessed July 20, 2020.

31 "Our reactions to Adham": Valdis Ozols, letter on behalf of Adham Hassoun, October 15, 2002.

31 Some operated in mosques: Author's interviews with Hassoun. Trevor Aaronsen, "The Informant," *Mother Jones*, September–October 2011. Maria Dinzeo, "Ninth Circuit Orders New Look at Mosque Surveillance Case," *Courthouse News*, February 28, 2019. Paul Harris, "The Ex-FBI Informant with a Change of Heart: 'There Is No Real Hunt. It's Fixed,'" *Guardian*, March 20, 2012.

32 Tenet told Bush and Cheney: Peter Baker, *Days of Fire: Bush and Cheney in the White House* (New York: Anchor, 2014), 163. The primary source for the next several paragraphs is a draft NSA inspector general history of STELLARWIND dated March 24,

2009. It was leaked by Edward Snowden. Available at www.theguardian.com/nsa -inspector-general-report-document-data-collection. "Although NSA had the capability to collect bulk telephony and internet metadata prior to the [program], its application was limited because NSA did not have the authority to collect communications in which one end [the number being called or the recipient address of an email] was in the United States," 13.

32 In his memoir, *Playing to the Edge*: Michael V. Hayden, *Playing to the Edge: American Intelligence in The Age of Terror* (New York: Penguin, 2017), 9.

33 A volume the size: Cited in Barton Gellman, *Dark Mirror: Edward Snowden and the American Surveillance State* (New York: Penguin Press, 2020), 111. It appears Schmidt's math may have been off in the service of a valid point. See Robert J. Moore, "Eric Schmidt's '5 Exabytes' Quote Is a Load of Crap," February 7, 2011, blog.rjmetrics.com /2011/02/07/eric-schmidts-5-exabytes-quote-is-a-load-of-crap, accessed July 21, 2020.

33 In 2004, the CIA's investment: Siobhan Gorman, "How Team of Geeks Cracked Spy Trade," *Wall Street Journal*, September 4, 2009.

33 Its sophistication increased: Shane Harris, *The Watchers: The Rise of America's Surveillance State* (New York: Penguin, 2011), 158, and Gellman, *Dark Mirror*, 166–81.

33 Hayden later observed: Alan Rusbridger, "The Snowden Leaks and the Public," *New York Review of Books*, November 21, 2013.

34 One internal memo: Glenn Greenwald and Murtaza Hussein, "Meet the Muslim-American Leaders the FBI and NSA Have Been Spying On," *The Intercept*, July 9, 2014, https://theintercept.com/2014/07/09/under-surveillance.

34 They interpreted Addington's authorization: NSA inspector general's draft report on STELLARWIND, March 24, 2009, 39.

35 Hayden nevertheless considered: Letter from Rep. Nancy Pelosi to NSA director Michael Hayden, October 11, 2001, declassified January 3, 2006, pelosi.house.gov /news/press-releases/pelosi-s-declassified-letter-on-nsa-activities. Letter from Sen. Jay Rockefeller to Vice President Dick Cheney, July 17, 2003, fas.org/irp/news/2005/12 /rock121905.pdf. Accessed July 21, 2020.

35 For good measure Barr: Testimony of William P. Barr, House Intelligence Committee, October 30, 2003. Transcript available at https://fas.org/irp/congress/2003_hr /103003barr.pdf.

35 The Justice Department prepared: Hayden, *Playing to the Edge*, 87. NSA draft internal STELLARWIND history, 38–39. Hayden appears to tell Bart Gellman in *Dark Mirror* that he only kept STELLARWIND going to fix it legally. That is not captured in the draft STELLARWIND history.

36 Comey warned Bush: James Comey, *A Higher Loyalty: Truth, Lies, and Leadership* (New York: Flatiron, 2018), 94–96. Gellman, *Angler*, 312–26.

36 Hayden accurately observed: Kollar-Kotelly, order from July 14, 2004, partially declassified by the Director of National Intelligence in November 2013: www.dni .gov/files/documents/1118/CLEANEDPRTT%201.pdf, accessed April 16, 2019. The

judge noted that the NSA's application "seeks a much broader type of collection than other pen register/trap and trace applications," but ultimately concluded that "the proposed collection involves a form of both pen register and trap and trace surveillance." NSA internal STELLARWIND history, 39. Hayden, *Playing to the Edge*, 90.

36 Such a simulacrum of law: Giorgio Agamben, *State of Exception*, trans. Kevin Attell (Chicago and London: The University of Chicago Press, 2005), 87.

37 If "we fail": "Testimony from the Joint Intelligence Committee," *New York Times*, October 17, 2002.

38 A White House staffer: Sean Naylor, *Relentless Strike: The Secret History of Joint Special Operations Command* (New York: St. Martin's Press, 2015), 89.

38 More than four thousand marines: James Dao, "American Marines Land Near Kandahar," *New York Times*, November 25, 2001. DOD News Briefing—Secretary Rumsfeld and Gen. Peter Pace, December 6, 2001, transcript available at https://ava lon.law.yale.edu/sept11/dod_brief114.asp. Spencer Ackerman, "The Afghan Taliban Peace Deal Might Have Been Had Many Years and Thousands of Lives Ago," *Daily Beast*, February 29, 2020.

39 Berntsen witnessed the: Gary Berntsen and Ralph Pezzullo, *Jawbreaker: The Attack on bin Laden and Al-Qaeda: A Personal Account by the CIA's Key Field Commander* (New York: Crown, 2006), Kindle location 7172.

39 Berntsen's ally at CIA headquarters: Baker, *Days of Fire*, 179–80.

39 Rather than concluding: Bergan, "The Account of How We Nearly Caught Bin Laden in 2001," *The New Republic*, December 30, 2009. Mary Anne Weaver, "Lost at Tora Bora," *New York Times Magazine*, September 11, 2005. Senate Foreign Relations Committee, *Tora Bora Revisited: How We Failed to Get Bin Laden and Why It Matters Now*, November 30, 2009. Bernten and Pezzullo, *Jawbreaker*, Kindle location 7128–8405.

40 He had provided the staff: Declassified executive summary, Senate Select Committee on Intelligence, "Committee Study of the Central Intelligence Agency's Detention and Interrogation Program" ("The Torture Report"), December 9, 2014, 54. Available at www.intelligence.senate.gov/sites/default/files/publications/CRPT-113srpt288.pdf. This is a principal source for this passage.

40 A man known as Abu Zubaydah: Abu Zubaydah denied being an associate of bin Laden in his March 27, 2007, Combatant Status Review Tribunal at Guantanamo Bay. He said instead that he was a facilitator for travel to a terrorist training camp in eastern Afghanistan ahead of 9/11, rather than al-Qaeda's commanding officer, as alleged against him in a nonjudicial proceeding. His lucidity, even through translation, makes it difficult to credit the portrait painted of Abu Zubaydah by Ron Suskind in his *One Percent Doctrine*, which claims Abu Zubaydah is borderline incapacitated mentally; Abu Zubaydah refers to himself having too "big [a] name" for al-Qaeda to have made him a soldier. Noteworthy as well is that official government papers on Abu Zubaydah would quietly back off claims that he was formally a member of al-Qaeda, consistent with his 2007 denial of the same. The transcript was partially declassified in 2016 and is available at www.nytimes.com/interactive/2016/06/15/world/docu ment-CSRT-transcripts-high-value-ACLU-FOIA.html, accessed April 19, 2019.

40 **One of the FBI interrogators:** Confirmed by James Mitchell in James Mitchell with Bill Harlow, *Enhanced Interrogation: Inside the Minds and Motives of the Islamic Terrorists Trying to Destroy America* (New York: Crown Forum, 2016), 37–41, where he also suggests Abu Zubaydah manipulated Soufan. Also see Michael Isikoff, "Spin Wars: How a Bitter Feud between the CIA and FBI Stoked the Torture Debate," Yahoo News, December 15, 2014.

41 **"Again and again":** Transcript of Abu Zubaydah's 2007 Combatant Status Review Tribunal, 23–26. See Senate torture report, 410.

41 **Headquarters staff quickly:** Senate Select Committee on Intelligence report, December 2014, 80–82.

42 **It made them rich:** Mitchell concedes holding the contract but contends that the profits he reaped on it were "in the small single digits" after defraying costs such as payroll for a hundred-person staff and insurance. Mitchell, *Enhanced Interrogation*, 287–88.

42 **Mitchell, in his memoir:** Julian Borger, "Chilling Role of 'The Preacher' Confirmed at CIA Waterboarding Hearing in Guantanamo," *Guardian*, January 25, 2020.

42 **He "looked into the eyes":** The establishment of Islam postdates the Iron Age in the Middle East by nearly a thousand years. The Iron Age ended there around 550 BC, though Christian/pagan northern Europe was still in the Iron Age until about AD 800, at which point Islam was nearly two hundred years old and had become, on the Iberian peninsula, the center of European intellectual development.

42 **Mitchell described Abu Zubaydah:** Mitchell, *Enhanced Interrogation*, 34. Mitchell does not pause to address how his comparison not only renders al-Qaeda on par with the Jedi, guardians of justice and freedom, but makes him either a Sith or part of the evil Empire.

42 **a mandate from Congress and Bush:** Statement of Cofer Black, fas.org/irp/congress /2002_hr/092602black.html.

42 **As Tenet indicated:** See Michael J. Morell, *The Great War of Our Time: The CIA's Fight against Terrorism—From al Qa'ida to ISIS* (New York: Twelve Books, 2015), 269, where Morell, a senior CIA analyst at the time, writes that when briefing congressional leadership on torture, "there was either approval or in some cases concern that CIA was not going far enough in trying to obtain information from detainees." While Morell's account serves the CIA's interest in distributing blame, and Sen. Dianne Feinstein would later establish that the Senate Intelligence Committee knew little of substance during the Bush administration, few members of the congressional intelligence leadership demonstrated concerns for the rights of the detainees whom it was publicly known the CIA was holding.

43 **The CIA could use several:** George Tenet, "Guidelines on Interrogations," January 28, 2003, www.thetorturedatabase.org/document/cia-director-memo-guidelines-inter rogations-conducted-pursuant-presidential-memorandum-noti?search_url=search /apachesolr_search&search_args=filters=tds_cck_field_doc_date:[2003-01 -01T00:00:00Z%20TO%202004-01-01T00:00:00Z]%20tds_cck_field_doc _date:[2003-01-01T00:00:00Z%20TO%202003-02-01T00:00:00Z]%20sm_cck

_field_doc_type:63%26solrsort=tds_cck_field_doc_release_date%20desc. It somehow averred that three-day diapering and three-day sleep deprivation were familiar FBI techniques.

43 **That left it with no choice:** Michael Scheuer, *Imperial Hubris: Why the West Is Losing the War on Terror* (Washington, D.C.: Potomac Books, 2004), 258.

44 **The CIA's executive director:** Senate Select Committee on Intelligence report, December 2014, 55.

44 **That was insufficient to reassure Tenet:** See 18 USC 2340(A)(a), cited in Spencer Ackerman, "'She Should Have Fought Back. Other People Did': Inside Gina Haspel's Black Site," *Daily Beast*, May 9, 2018.

44 **Jay Bybee indemnified the CIA:** Yoo's opinion, with Jay Bybee, was dated August 1, 2002. The CIA had begun interrogating Abu Zubaydah months earlier, in April.

44 **irreversible psychological damage:** Several ex-detainees, including Abu Zubaydah, surpassed that threshold. Mustafa al-Hawsawi in 2016 underwent corrective surgery for an anal prolapse stemming from what he says was his torture at the black sites. Khaled el-Masri, whom the CIA released on a case of mistaken identity after torturing him, has set fires and is said to have abandoned his family. Ammar al-Baluchi has told doctors at Guantanamo Bay of "terrifying anxiety" that prevents him from sleeping. No American court has recognized their right to seek redress, nor has the FBI or Justice Department, following Mueller's 2002 decision in overruling Soufan, arrested or brought charges against any of their torturers.

45 **The report records that Nashiri:** Cited in Ackerman, "'She Should Have Fought Back.'"

45 **Later Haspel took over:** See Senate Select Committee on Intelligence report, December 2014, 62–70. Spencer Ackerman, "Gina Haspel, Trump's Pick to Lead the CIA, 'Ran the Interrogation Program,' Former CIA Lawyer Wrote," *Daily Beast*, April 18, 2018. Rizzo is quoted in this story averring that the CIA official he wrote about in 2014, when it seemed to be unimportant, was Haspel. Two days after this story's publication, and in the midst of Haspel's nomination for CIA director, Rizzo publicly recanted that he had referenced Haspel at all and claimed a sudden burst of corrective memory.

46 **The CIA institutionalization:** Spencer Ackerman, "CIA Photographed Detainees Naked Before Sending Them to Be Tortured," *Guardian*, March 28, 2016. Thomas Frank, "Fatima Boudchar Was Bound, Gagged and Photographed Naked. John McCain Wants to Know If Gina Haspel's Okay with That," *BuzzFeed*, March 23, 2018.

46 **In February 2002, Bush:** George W. Bush, "Humane Treatment of al-Qaeda and Taliban Detainees," memo, February 7, 2002, available at https://nsarchive2.gwu.edu /torturingdemocracy/documents/20020207-2.pdf.

47 **By the fall of 2002:** Senate Armed Services Committee, "Inquiry into the Treatment of Detainees in U.S. Custody," April 22, 2009, xvii, www.armed-services.senate.gov /imo/media/doc/Detainee-Report-Final_April-22-2009.pdf. Hereafter "SASC report."

47 **"If the detainee dies":** SASC report, 54–55. Statement of Jonathan Fredman to the SASC, November 17, 2008, available at www.emptywheel.net/wp-content/uploads /2013/04/Jonathan-Fredman-to-SASC.pdf, accessed July 28, 2020.

47 Benita Johnson remembered: Spencer Ackerman, "How Chicago Police Condemned the Innocent: A Trail of Coerced Confessions," *Guardian*, February 19, 2015.

48 Another detainee was sexually humiliated: Army Lt. Gen. Randall M. Schmidt and Brig. Gen. John T. Furlow, "Investigation into FBI Allegations of Detainee Abuse at Guantanamo Bay, Cuba Detention Facility," April 1, 2005. Collected in *Administration of Torture: A Documentary Record from Washington to Abu Ghraib and Beyond*, eds. Jameel Jaffer and Amrit Singh (New York: Columbia University Press, 2007), 99–105.

48 Rumsfeld, who approved torture: SASC report, 96–98.

48 "If you make this exception": Jane Mayer, "The Memo," *The New Yorker*, February 20, 2006.

48 He claimed that the interrogators: Jamie Doward, Antony Barnett, Peter Beaumont, David Rose, and Mark Townsend, "The Leak that Revealed Bush's Deep Obsession with Al-Jazeera," *Guardian*, November 26, 2005.

49 "virtually unknown in U.S. media circles": Joel Campagna, "Sami al-Haj: The Enemy?" Committee to Protect Journalists, October 2006.

49 But the U.S. eventually brought a teenaged: Michelle Shephard, *Guantanamo's Child* (Toronto: Wiley, 2008). See also her *Toronto Star* articles "Report Slaps CSIS over Khadr," July 15, 2009, and "In His Own Words: Omar Khadr," projects.thestar.com /omar-khadr-in-his-own-words, accessed July 29, 2020.

49 Mora's insight was that: This is a riff off a line written by Adam Serwer: "Trumpism, Realized," *The Atlantic*, June 20, 2018.

Chapter Two: 9/11 and the Right

52 "To those who scare": Attorney General John Ashcroft, testimony to the Senate Judiciary Committee, December 6, 2001, transcript available at www.justice.gov/ar chive/ag/testimony/2001/1206transcriptsenatejudiciarycommittee.htm. See also Jim McGee, "Ex-FBI Officials Criticize Tactics on Terrorism," *Washington Post*, November 28, 2001. Fox Butterfield, "Police Are Split on Questioning of Mideast Men," *New York Times*, November 22, 2001. Unbylined, "Ashcroft Says to Question Thousands of Visitors," CNN, November 13, 2001. Statement of the ACLU to the Senate Judiciary Committee, November 28, 2001, available at www.aclu.org/other/aclu-statement -senate-judiciary-committee-concerning-department-justice-anti-terrorism. Statement of CAIR, "Interviews of 5,000 Visa Holders Are Concern to Muslim Group," press release, November 13, 2001, available at www.cair.com/press_releases/interviews-of -5000-visa-holders-are-concern-to-muslim-group.

53 Liberal and left dissent: Andrew Sullivan, *Times* (London), September 16, 2001, linked to on Sullivan's blog at web.archive.org/web/20090608041410/http://sullivan archives.theatlantic.com/index.php.dish_inc-archives.2001_09_01_dish_archive .html. See also Timothy Noah, "Al Gore, Andrew Sullivan, and 'Fifth Column,'" *Slate*, December 2, 2002. Sullivan would apologize, numerous times, for the inflammatory "fifth column" reference. Stephen Miller, "Unpatriotic Dissent," *Duke Chronicle*, February 6, 2006.

53 **"There is a religious war"**: See, among others, Charles Krauthammer, "Holiday from History," *Washington Post*, February 14, 2003. Pat Buchanan, speech to the Republican National Convention, August 17, 1992, transcript available at https://buchanan .org/blog/1992-republican-national-convention-speech-148.

53 **"Conservatives saw the savagery"**: Patrick D. Healy, "Rove Criticizes Liberals on 9/11," *New York Times*, June 23, 2005. Gallup, "Presidential Approval Ratings—George W. Bush," news.gallup.com/poll/116500/presidential-approval-ratings-george-bush.aspx, accessed August 7, 2020.

54 **"Victory in war"**: Frederick Kagan, "The New Bolsheviks," American Enterprise Institute, November 2005.

54 **"I will show how jihad violence"**: Robert Spencer, "CBS Blocks the Truth about Islam," *Human Events*, August 10, 2005.

56 **But in 1986:** Lois Romano and George Lardner Jr., "Bush's Life-Changing Year," *Washington Post*, July 25, 1999.

56 **EPA chief Whitman:** John F. Dickerson, "Confessions of a White House Survivor," *Time*, January 10, 2004. Ron Suskind, "Faith, Certainty, and the Presidency of George W. Bush," *New York Times Magazine*, October 17, 2004.

56 **Asked about it at a White House briefing:** "Press Briefing with Ari Fleischer," September 26, 2001, available at https://georgewbush-whitehouse.archives.gov/news /releases/2001/09/20010926-5.html.

56 **One such conception:** Draft 1992 Defense Planning Guidance, Undersecretary of Defense for Policy Paul Wolfowitz, partially available at https://nsarchive2.gwu.edu /nukevault/ebb245/doc03_extract_nytedit.pdf. Patrick E. Tyler, "U.S. Strategy Plan Calls for Ensuring No Rivals Develop," *New York Times*, March 8, 1992.

57 **Any objection to invading:** Neal B. Freeman, "*NR* Goes to War," *The American Spectator*, August 4, 2006. Michiko Kakutani, "Personality, Ideology and Bush's Terror Wars," *New York Times*, June 20, 2006.

57 **Essayist Max Boot:** Bernard Lewis, "The Revolt of Islam," *The New Yorker*, November 19, 2001. In a lengthy and discursive essay, Lewis contends that bin Laden's ire came not from any geopolitical or material condition, but from America satanically tempting Muslims away from fundamentalism. Lewis attributed 9/11 to a provocative weakness—America as a "paper tiger" in bin Laden's eyes—and argued for overthrowing two regimes uninvolved in it. "In two countries, Iraq and Iran, where the regimes are strongly anti-American, there are democratic oppositions capable of taking over and forming governments." When Lewis died, Secretary of State Mike Pompeo, a former CIA director, called Lewis a kindred spirit from whom "a great deal of my understanding of the Middle East" derived. Lewis "believed, as I do, that Americans must be more confident in the greatness of our country, not less," Pompeo said on May 20, 2018. Max Boot, "The Case for American Empire," *Weekly Standard*, October 15, 2001.

58 *National Review* **fired Coulter:** Roger D. McGrath, "The Great Somali Welfare Hunt," *The American Conservative*, November 18, 2002. Howard Kurtz, "*National Review* Cans Columnist Ann Coulter," *Washington Post*, October 2, 2001.

59 "If the Islamic law": Interview with James Dobson, *Larry King Live*, CNN, September 5, 2003.

59 CAIR's Ibrahim Hooper: Richard N. Ostling, "Jerry Falwell Calls Islam's Prophet a 'Terrorist' in Television Interview," Associated Press, October 3, 2002. "Anti-Islam," *Religion & Ethics Newsweekly*, December 20, 2002.

59 Boykin was never: Christianity Today editorial, "Outpaced by Islam?" *Christianity Today*, February 4, 2002, www.christianitytoday.com/ct/2002/february4/26.26.html. Richard Cimino, "'No God in Common': American Evangelical Discourse on Islam after 9/11," *Review of Religious Research* 47, no. 2 (December 2005), 162–74. Richard T. Cooper, "General Casts War in Religious Terms," *Los Angeles Times*, October 16, 2003. Ted Olsen, "Should Christians Be Banned from the Military?" *Christianity Today*, October 16, 2003.

60 Overthrowing the Taliban: Beth Henary, "Feminists v. the Taliban," *Weekly Standard*, October 7, 2001.

60 "What they abominate about 'the West'": Christopher Hitchens, "Against Rationalization," *The Nation*, September 20, 2001.

61 Jones lamented that evangelicals: Sandra Marquez, "FBI Says It Will Investigate Alleged Hate Crime in California," Associated Press, March 5, 2003. Eric Carpenter, "An O.C.-Born Arab-American Teen Is Beaten, Stabbed by a Group with Apparent Ethnic Animus," *Orange County Register*, March 4, 2003. Amanda Beck, "For All the Changes, Much Remains the Same; Teen Reaches Out to Community Groups, Rashid Alam Reflects on Life After February's Hate-Crime Beating," *Yorba Linda Star/Orange County Register*, October 16, 2003. Bob Jones, "Truth or CAIR,' *World* magazine, March 22, 2003.

62 For decades GOP politicians: Lou Marano, "Christians Rally for Israel in Washington," United Press International, October 13, 2002.

62 The Reverend Richard Cizik: Laurie Goldstein, "Seeing Islam as 'Evil' Faith, Evangelicals Seek Converts," *New York Times*, May 27, 2003.

62 Assistant Secretary Bill Burns: Warren P. Strobel, "Long-Classified Memo Surfaces Warning of 'Perfect Storm' from Invading Iraq," *Wall Street Journal*, March 13, 2019.

62 The burgeoning resistance: Warren P. Strobel and Jonathan S. Landay, "Intelligence Agencies Warned about Growing Local Insurgency in Late 2003," McClatchy, February 28, 2006.

63 "The CIA is a long way": Robert Novak, "The CIA vs. Bush," *Washington Post*, September 27, 2004.

64 "I know, I know": Julian Borger, "Washington's Hawk Trains Sights on Iraq," *Guardian*, September 25, 2001. Joel Roberts, "Plans for Attack on Iraq Began on 9/11," CBS News, September 4, 2002. Eric Lichtblau, "President Asked Aide to Explore Iraq Link to 9/11," *New York Times*, March 29, 2004.

64 Rumsfeld agreed to table Iraq: Patrick E. Tyler and Elaine Sciolino, "Bush's Advisers Split on Scope of Retaliation," *New York Times*, September 20, 2001.

64 **Three months later, national security adviser:** Robert Draper, *To Start a War: How the Bush Administration Took America into Iraq* (New York: Penguin Press, 2020), 49. Spencer Ackerman and Franklin Foer, "The Radical," *The New Republic*, December 1, 2003.

65 *Countdown: Iraq* **and a few months later canceled Phil Donahue's program:** Lisa de Moraes, "MSNBC Again Tinkering With Its Lineup," *Washington Post*, October 26, 2002. Bill Carter, "MSNBC Cancels the Phil Donahue Talk Show," *New York Times*, February 26, 2003.

65 **Carlson's guest that day:** James Carville and Tucker Carlson, "Should the U.S. Attack Iraq?" *Crossfire*, CNN, June 17, 2002.

65 **"You can't distinguish":** George W. Bush, remarks in a photo opportunity with Colombian President Uribe, Washington, D.C., September 25, 2002, available at https:// georgewbush-whitehouse.archives.gov/news/releases/2006/09/20060915-4.html.

65 **By September 2003:** Dana Milbank and Claudia Deane, "Hussein Link to 9/11 Lingers in Many Minds," *Washington Post*, September 6, 2003.

66 **Her successor, Mike Morell:** Spencer Ackerman, "The CIA's Failures," *The Nation*, June 26, 2008. Michael J. Morell, *The Great War of Our Time: The CIA's Fight against Terrorism—From al Qa'ida to ISIS* (New York: Twelve Books, 2015), 86–87.

66 **"The State Department and the Central Intelligence Agency":** Reuel Marc Gerecht, "Hardly Intelligent: How the CIA Unintentionally Aids Terrorism," *Weekly Standard*, June 10, 2002.

66 **Laurie Mylroie, a conspiracist:** Laurie Mylroie, *Washington Journal*, C-SPAN, December 24, 2003.

67 **Asked after 9/11:** Patrick E. Tyler and Elaine Sciolino, "Bush's Advisers Split on Scope of Retaliation," *New York Times*, September 20, 2001.

67 **Established in August 2002:** See comments of Abram Shulsky, director, Office of Special Plans: www.esd.whs.mil/Portals/54/Documents/FOID/Reading%20Room /Homeland_Defense/04-F-1702.pdf.

67 **As Wurmser explained:** Barton Gellman, *Angler: The Cheney Vice Presidency* (New York: Penguin Press, 2008), 215–33.

67 **By September Rumsfeld spoke:** Eric Schmitt, "Rumsfeld Says U.S. Has 'Bulletproof' Evidence of Iraq's Links to al-Qaeda," *New York Times*, September 28, 2002.

67 **"[I]ntelligence was misused publicly":** Paul R. Pillar, "Intelligence, Policy and the War in Iraq," *Foreign Affairs*, March/April 2006. And Pillar's interview with Terry Gross, "CIA Terror Expert Charges Politicized Intelligence," *Fresh Air*, NPR, February 16, 2006, https://freshairarchive.org/segments/cia-terror-expert-charges-politicized -intelligence.

67 **That was also the impression:** Douglas Jehl, "British Memo on Iraq War Decision Rouses Bush Critics in U.S.," *International Herald-Tribune*, May 21, 2005. Michael Smith initially published the Dearlove memo in the *Times* of London, May 1, 2005.

68 Curveball later admitted: Martin Chulov and Helen Pidd, "Defector Admits to WMD Lies that Triggered Iraq War," *Guardian*, February 15, 2011. Mark Mazzetti, "Pre-War Intelligence Ignored, Former CIA Official Says," *New York Times*, April 22, 2006. Spencer Ackerman and John Judis, "The Operator," *The New Republic*, September 21, 2003.

68 And the Iraq WMD: Ackerman, "The CIA's Failures."

68 Rove had urged Republicans: Joe Conason, "Rove Waves Flag for GOP Candidates," *New York Observer*, January 28, 2002.

68 "Some people seem to think": Mary Orndorff, "Bush Builds Iraq Case; Promises to Get Congress' Approval to Strike at Saddam," *Birmingham News*, September 5, 2002.

69 Stern asked if Trump: Donald Trump on *The Howard Stern Show*, September 11, 2002, soundcloud.com/buzzfeedandrew/trump-on-the-howard-stern-show-on-sept-11 -2002#t=0:00, accessed August 9, 2020.

69 The Iraqi émigrés: Lewis, "The Revolt of Islam."

69 Wolfowitz spoke in the Arab American: "Paul Wolfowitz Speaks in Dearborn," CNN, March 11, 2003. Michael Dobbs, "For Wolfowitz, a Vision May Be Realized," *Washington Post*, April 7, 2003.

69 "Are millions of men": George W. Bush, "Remarks by the President at the 20th Anniversary of the National Endowment for Democracies," November 6, 2003. Transcript available at https://georgewbush-whitehouse.archives.gov/news/releases/2003/11 /20031106-2.html.

69 "As I've watched these men and women": Sean Coughlin, "House Cafeterias Change Names for 'French' Fries and 'French' Toast," CNN, March 12, 2003.

70 Those who practiced: David Frum, "Unpatriotic Conservatives," *National Review*, March 25, 2003.

71 That was the work of CIA torture: It failed. The U.S. rendered Libi to Egypt, where he was tortured further. Senate Intelligence Committee, "Postwar Findings about Iraq's WMD Programs and Links to Terrorism and How They Compare to Prewar Assessments," September 8, 2006, 76–82.

71 The month of Powell's speech: Eric Schmitt, "Army Chief Raises Estimate of G.I.'s Needed in Postwar Iraq," *New York Times*, February 25, 2003. Schmitt, "Pentagon Contradicts General on Iraq Occupation Force's Size," *New York Times*, February 28, 2003.

72 "What choice did I have?": "Colin Powell Rejects Iraq War Intelligence," Al Jazeera, September 11, 2011. Robert Draper, "Colin Powell Still Wants Answers," *New York Times Magazine*, July 16, 2020. Draper, *To Start a War*, 396–97. Jason M. Breslow, "Colin Powell: U.N. Speech 'Was a Great Intelligence Failure,'" *Frontline*, PBS, May 17, 2016.

72 "If they killed him": Jason M. Breslow, "Nada Bakos: How Zarqawi Went from Thug to ISIS Founder," *Frontline*, PBS, May 17, 2006.

72 **Surveying the intellectual landscape:** David Brooks, "The Collapse of the Dream Palaces," *Weekly Standard*, April 28, 2003.

72 **Baghdad neighborhood Yarmouk:** Anthony Shadid, *Night Draws Near: Iraq's People in the Shadow of America's War* (New York: Henry Holt & Co., 2005), 197–210.

73 **"What kind of people loot dirt?":** Daniel Williams and Rajiv Chandrasekaran, "U.S. Troops Frustrated with Role in Iraq; Soldiers Say They Are Ill-Equipped for Peacekeeping," *Washington Post*, June 20, 2003.

74 **They permitted the looting:** Sean Loughlin, "Rumsfeld on Looting in Iraq: 'Stuff Happens,'" CNN, April 12, 2003.

74 **One of them, KBR:** Ed Harriman, "Where Has All the Money Gone?" *London Review of Books*, July 7, 2005.

74 **It hired individuals:** Ariana Eunjung Cha, "In Iraq, the Job Opportunity of a Lifetime," *Washington Post*, May 23, 2004.

74 **An experienced diplomat:** Thomas E. Ricks, *Fiasco: The American Military Adventure in Iraq* (New York: Penguin, 2006), 204.

74 **Iraq could indeed:** Estimates of the exact size of the Green Zone mysteriously vary. This one comes from Stanley McChrystal, *My Share of the Task: A Memoir* (New York: Portfolio/Penguin, 2013), 100. It corresponds with my recollections of the Green Zone from 2007.

74 **Described in 2004 as home:** William Langewiesche, "Welcome to the Green Zone," *The Atlantic*, November 2004.

74 **a playpen for Americans:** Ricks, *Fiasco*, 206–9.

75 **CPA buildings, protected:** See Rajiv Chandrasekaran, interview with *Frontline*, PBS, August 9, 2006.

75 **In the Red Zone, Iraqis looking:** Anderson Cooper, Christiane Amanpour, Paula Zahn, Jane Arraf, John Zarrella, David Mattingly, Alex Quade, Rusty Dornin, and Judy Woodruff, "Iraq Votes," CNN, January 27, 2005.

75 **The war allowed a retired:** Spencer Ackerman, "Ain't No Party Like a Blackwater Party, 'Cause a Blackwater Party Got Coke, 'Roids and AKs," *Wired*, September 23, 2010.

75 **Before sunrise Blackwater staff:** Spencer Ackerman, "$265 Bomb, $300 Billion War: The Economics of the 9/11 Era's Signature Weapon," *Wired*, September 8, 2011.

75 **"You Americans can put a man":** Eric Schmitt, "For G.I.'s, Pride in War Efforts but Doubts About Iraq's Future," *New York Times*, January 4, 2004. Petraeus was a rare officer who recognized that the U.S. lived in Iraq on borrowed time but sought to borrow more.

76 **He issued cards:** Dexter Filkins, "Tough New Tactics by U.S. Tighten Grip on Iraqi Towns," *New York Times*, December 7, 2003.

76 **Sassaman later covered up:** Ricks, *Fiasco*, 232–40. Dexter Filkins, "The Fall of the Warrior King," *New York Times Magazine*, October 23, 2005.

NOTES

76 **Major General Ray Odierno:** Unbylined, "U.S. Officer Fined for Harsh Interrogation Tactics," CNN, December 13, 2003. Deborah Sontag, "How Colonel Risked His Career by Menacing Detainee and Lost," *New York Times,* May 27, 2004.

76 **"if we had had weapons":** "Violent Response: The U.S. Army in Falluja," Human Rights Watch, June 16, 2003. Ian Fisher, "U.S. Troops Fire on Iraqi Protesters, Leaving 15 Dead," *New York Times,* April 29, 2003.

77 **"Our combat against the Americans":** Letter of Abu Musab al-Zarqawi, translated by the Coalition Provisional Authority, February 2004, 2001-2009.state.gov/p/nea/rls /31694.htm, accessed May 16, 2019.

77 **Footage of the carnage:** Unbylined, "Bodies Mutilated in Iraq Attack," BBC, March 31, 2004. Colin Freeman, "Bodies Dragged through Street, Hung from Bridge," *San Francisco Chronicle,* April 1, 2004.

77 **According to a memo that two British Labour Party members:** David Leigh and Richard Norton-Taylor, "MPs Leaked Bush Plan to Hit al-Jazeera," *Guardian,* January 9, 2006. Jamie Doward, Antony Barnett, Peter Beaumont, David Rose, and Mark Townsend, "The Leak that Revealed Bush's Deep Obsession with al-Jazeera," *Guardian,* November 26, 2005.

78 **While Fallujah passed:** Ricks, *Fiasco,* 330–46. Paul Wood, "Iraq's Hardest Fight: The U.S. Battle for Fallujah 2004," BBC, November 10, 2014. Orly Halpern, "Hate for U.S. Unites Rival Muslims," *Globe and Mail* (Toronto), April 9, 2004. Deborah Horan, "Fallujah Lull Lets Women, Children Flee," *Chicago Tribune,* April 10, 2004. Dan Lamothe, "Remembering the Iraq War's Bloodiest Battle, 10 Years Later," *Washington Post,* November 4, 2014.

78 **massive open-air incinerators:** Katie Drummond, "Combat 'Burn Pits' Ruin Immune Systems, Study Shows," *WIRED,* May 23, 2012.

78 **"You go to war with the army you have":** Eric Schmitt, "Iraq-Bound Troops Confront Rumsfeld Over Lack of Armor," *New York Times,* December 8, 2004.

79 **Iraq convinced McChrystal:** McChrystal, *My Share of the Task,* 90–91. Author's interview with Stanley McChrystal, May 5, 2020.

79 **The regimen, modified and implemented:** Senate Armed Services Committee report on detentions, April 22, 2009, 205.

79 **The prison where this would unfold:** Brig. Gen. Janis Karpinski interview, *Frontline,* PBS, August 5, 2005, www.pbs.org/wgbh/pages/frontline/torture/interviews/karpinski .html#3, accessed April 23, 2019.

79 **Abu Ghraib soon became:** Report of Lt. Gen. Anthony Jones and Maj. Gen. George Fay, "Investigation of Intelligence Activities at Abu Ghraib," 4, available at https:// apps.dtic.mil/dtic/tr/fulltext/u2/a429125.pdf.

79 **Graner photographed his assaults:** Ibid., 71–95.

79 **the responsibility wasn't theirs:** Julian Borger, "Pentagon Blamed over Jail 'Sadism,'" *Guardian,* August 24, 2004.

80 **In these cases:** Jones and Fay, "Investigation of Intelligence Activities at Abu Ghraib," 3.

80 **If Rumsfeld resigned:** Eric Schmitt, "Abuse Panel Says Rules on Inmates Need Overhaul," *New York Times*, August 25, 2004.

80 **"promoting policies to abuse prisoners":** Sarah Wildman, "Closed Sessions," *The New Republic*, December 30, 2002. Kwame Holman, *The NewsHour with Jim Lehrer*, PBS, October 6, 2005.

81 **"The only way this effort":** Secretary of Defense Donald Rumsfeld and General Peter Pace, Vice Chairman, Joint Chiefs of Staff, press briefing, June 17, 2004.

81 **The Democratic senator who on 9/12:** Text of Zell Miller's Republican National Convention speech, CBS News, September 1, 2004, https://www.cbsnews.com/news/text-of-zell-millers-rnc-speech.

81 **"Iraq will either be":** Remarks of George W. Bush in a news conference, April 14, 2004. Available through *The New York Times*, "Transcript of Bush's Remarks on Iraq: 'We Will Finish the Work of the Fallen,'" April 14, 2004.

81 **Six months later:** Shaoni Bhattacharya, "Civilian Death Toll in Iraq Nears 100,000," *New Scientist*, October 29, 2004. Fred Barnes, "The Bumpy Road to Democracy in Iraq," *Weekly Standard*, April 11, 2004.

82 **A military source:** Michael Hirsch and John Barry, "The Salvador Option," *Newsweek*, January 8, 2005.

82 **"shut the fuck up and obey":** Cited in Michael Brice-Saddler and Eli Rosenberg, "Fox News Host Tucker Carlson Uses Racist, Homophobic Language in Second Set of Recordings," *Washington Post*, March 11, 2019.

82 **Neocon defense theorist:** Danielle Pletka, "There's No Freedom Gene," *New York Times*, March 18, 2008.

82 **Evangelicals were reaching:** Abdul Wahed Wafa, "Preachers in Kabul Urge Execution of Convert to Christianity," *New York Times*, March 25, 2006. Doug Bandow, "Christians in the Crosshairs," *The American Conservative*, October 23, 2006.

82 **One of the confirmed desecrations:** Josh White and Dan Eggen, "U.S. Admits Koran Abuse at Cuba Base," reprinted in *The Guardian*, June 4, 2005. Lloyd Vries, "U.S. Confirms Some Quran Abuse," CBS News, May 27, 2005.

82 **Barnes, speaking on Fox News:** Fred Barnes, *Special Report with Brit Hume*, Fox News, June 9, 2005.

82 **The next time the captain:** Scott Johnson, "A Fateful Letter to the Editor of the *New York Times*," *Powerline Blog*, October 23, 2012.

83 **"sometimes to the point of discomfort":** "Final Report of the Commission on the Intelligence Capabilities of the United States Regarding Weapons of Mass Destruction," 4. Available at https://fas.org/irp/offdocs/wmdcomm.html.

83 **Goss brought in a coterie:** Spencer Ackerman, "Shooting the Messenger," *Salon*, November 16, 2004.

83 Goss's GOP replacement: Spencer Ackerman, "Mole People," *The New Republic*, July 31, 2006.

83 It was his key: Quadrennial Defense Review, Office of the Secretary of Defense, February 6, 2006. Available at https://archive.defense.gov/pubs/pdfs/QDR20060203.pdf.

84 Bush's speech was simultaneously: George W. Bush, "President Discusses War on Terror at National Endowment for Democracy," October 6, 2005. Transcript available at https://georgewbush-whitehouse.archives.gov/news/releases/2005/10/20051006-3.html.

84 Bush's former security: Comments of Richard Falkenrath, *NewsHour with Jim Lehrer*, PBS, October 7, 2005.

84 "If we don't take the enemy": Comments of Dan Bartlett, *Scarborough Country*, NBC, November 11, 2005.

84 The Republican chairman: Comments of Ed Royce, House Subcommittee on International Terrorism and Nonproliferation, October 27, 2005, available at http://commdocs.house.gov/committees/intlrel/hfa24203.000/hfa24203_0f.htm.

84 Bay Buchanan, Pat's sister: Comments of Bay Buchanan, CNN, October 7, 2005.

84 On Fox, Barnes similarly exulted: Comments of Fred Barnes, *Special Report with Brit Hume*, Fox News, October 6, 2005.

84 Bush and his aides: Comments of Tucker Carlson, *The Situation with Tucker Carlson*, MSNBC, November 25, 2005.

84 Stanley McChrystal, by this time: Author's interview with Stanley McChrystal, May 5, 2020.

85 The president praised: George W. Bush speech on immigration, May 15, 2006, transcription by *The New York Times*.

85 "calling out the National Guard": "U.S. Sen. Jeff Sessions Reacts to Bush Immigration Address," press release, May 15, 2006. Available at www.judiciary.senate.gov/imo/media/doc/12a%20Appendix.pdf.

Chapter Three: Liberal Complicity in the War on Terror

87 "Governor Ridge obviously": John Gibson, "Inside Afghanistan," Fox News, October 11, 2001.

88 Lieberman's proposed new cabinet: Ari Fleischer, White House press briefing, March 19, 2002. Available at https://georgewbush-whitehouse.archives.gov/news/releases/2002/06/20020619-13.html.

88 "bold organizational change": Senate Government Affairs Committee hearing, "Legislation to Establish a Department of National Homeland Security and a White House Office to Combat Terrorism," April 11, 2002, www.govinfo.gov/content/pkg/CHRG-107shrg79889/html/CHRG-107shrg79889.htm.

NOTES

88 Tom Daschle, the Senate: Nick Andersen, "Bush Gets a Democratic Push on U.S. Homeland Security Bill," *Houston Chronicle*, June 14, 2002.

88 House Democrats rejected: "H.R. 5005 (107th): Homeland Security Act of 2002," United States House of Representatives, July 26, 2002. "On Passage of the Bill (H.R. 5005, as amended)," United States Senate, November 19, 2002.

88 Senator Russ Feingold, who: Unbylined, "Senate Approves Homeland Bill," CNN, November 20, 2002.

89 unavoidably politically advantageous: Spencer Ackerman, "Home Office," *The New Republic*, August 19–26, 2002.

90 "The real importance of this bill": Senate Government Affairs Committee hearing, "Creation of Department of Homeland Security," April 11, 2002.

90 California senator Dianne Feinstein said: Hearing of the Senate Judiciary Committee, "Protecting the Homeland: The President's Proposal for Reorganizing Our Homeland Security Infrastructure," June 25, 2002. The bill reassigned dispensation and care for children and teenagers who cross the border alone to the Office of Refugee Resettlement in the Department of Health and Human Services. But as was inevitable, DHS takes initial custody of those minors.

90 "exercise in disruption": Nomination hearing for Michael J. Garcia for Assistant Secretary of Homeland Security for Immigration and Customs Enforcement, Senate Judiciary Committee, 108th Congress, July 8, 2003.

90 Under cover of homeland security: U.S. House of Representatives Subcommittee on Workplace Protection, Committee on Education and Labor, 110th Congress, Second Session, "ICE Workplace Raids: Their Impact on U.S. Children, Families and Their Communities," May 20, 2008, available at www.govinfo.gov/content/pkg/CHRG-110hhrg42334/html/CHRG-110hhrg42334.htm. Maria Politzer, "Most Immigrants Arrested in 'Operation Return to Sender' Had No Criminal Record," *Phoenix New Times*, November 5, 2009. Jesse McKinley, "San Francisco Bay Area Reacts Angrily to Series of Immigration Raids," *New York Times,* April 28, 2007.

91 remembered hiding for a week: Yvonne Abraham and Brian R. Ballou, "350 Are Held in Immigration Raid," *Boston Globe*, March 7, 2007. Dan Adams, "Six Years Later, New Bedford Raid Still Stings," *Boston Globe*, March 10, 2013.

92 But there could be no doubt: Joseph Lieberman, "The Theological Iron Curtain," *The National Interest,* September 1, 2003.

92 Dean Acheson, a Cold War: Dean Acheson, *Present at the Creation: My Years at the State Department* (New York: W. W. Norton & Co., 1969), 355–70.

93 California's Maxine Waters: Rep. Maxine Waters to Tucker Carlson, CNN, September 20, 2001.

93 *Newsweek*'s Jonathan Alter: Jonathan Alter, "Blame America at Your Peril," *Newsweek*, October 15, 2001.

NOTES

94 editor of *The New Republic*: MoveOn.org bulletin, "Can Democracy Survive an Endless 'War'?" July 20, 2002. Peter Beinart, "A Fighting Faith," *The New Republic*, December 13, 2004.

94 House Democratic leader, Dick Gephardt: Dick Gephardt, Democratic response to the 2002 State of the Union, www.npr.org/news/specials/sou/2002/020129.demotext .html, accessed June 10, 2019.

94 When DeLay called: Ron Fournier, "Fears of Terrorism Trigger 'Shadow Government' Plan," Associated Press via *Chicago Sun-Times*, March 1, 2002.

94 Some detained Taliban: Joe Biden to Wolf Blitzer, "Interim Leader of Afghanistan Visits U.S.," CNN, January 28, 2002.

94 Given the choice: Unbylined, "Feinstein: Detainees Not Treated Harshly; Senator Says Jail's Conditions Worse," *Oakland Tribune*, January 29, 2002.

95 writers like Arundhati Roy: Arundhati Roy, "The Algebra of Infinite Justice," *Guardian*, September 29, 2001.

96 Clinton, a former first lady: Ed Pilkington and Andrea Bernstein, "9/11 Tapes Reveal Raw and Emotional Hillary Clinton," *Guardian*, September 9, 2016. Andrea Bernstein, "Who Hillary Clinton Really Helped after 9/11," WNYC, November 17, 2015. Frank Bruni, "Show Us the Money," *New York Times Magazine*, December 16, 2001.

96 Aides would later: Mark Landler, "How Hillary Clinton Became a Hawk," *New York Times Magazine,* April 21, 2016.

96 His concern was that: Wire services, "Senator Visits Afghan Leader," *Lexington Herald-Leader*, January 13, 2001.

97 His concerns on Iraq: "Hearings to Examine Threats, Responses, and Regional Considerations Surrounding Iraq," Senate Committee on Foreign Relations, 107th Congress, July 31–August 1, 2002, S. Hrg. 107–658. Joseph R. Biden Jr. and Richard Lugar, "Debating Iraq," *New York Times*, July 31, 2002.

98 Richard Holbrooke, urged: Testimony of Ambs. Madeleine Albright and Richard Holbrooke, Senate Foreign Relations Committee, September 25, 2002. Holbrooke's "collective action" was in truth a unilateral war with cosmetic allied contributions, though he assailed such an accurate description as a calumny against Tony Blair and "the indispensable NATO ally" Turkey, which did not, as envisioned, permit the U.S. to stage an invasion from its soil.

98 Ted Kennedy and Al Gore: Richard L. Berke, "Bush 'Is My Commander,' Gore Declares in Call for Unity," *New York Times*, September 30, 2001.

98 endorsed regime change: Al Gore, speech to the Commonwealth Club, September 23, 2002, transcript available at http://p2004.org/gore/gore092302sp.html. Ted Kennedy, speech to the Johns Hopkins University School of Advanced International Studies, September 27, 2002, transcript available at www.emkinstitute.org/resources/speech -against-invasion-iraq. Bill Clinton, *Larry King Live*, CNN, September 4, 2002. Dan Collins, "Bill Clinton Weighs In on Iraq," CBS News, September 6, 2002.

99 Biden echoed the sentiment: Senator Joseph Biden, "Authorization of the Use of United States Armed Forces against Iraq," Congressional Record, October 10, 2002, available at www.govinfo.gov/content/pkg/CREC-2002-10-10/html/CREC-2002-10 -10-pt1-PgS10233-7.htm.

100 George Packer, a leading liberal: George Packer, "Smart-Mobbing the War," *New York Times Magazine*, March 9, 2003.

100 Leon Wieseltier, the driving intellectual force: Leon Wieseltier, "Against Innocence," *The New Republic*, March 3, 2003, https://newrepublic.com/article/66773/iraq-liberal -bush-imperial. Lloyd Grove, "The Very Busy, Very Unproductive Life of Leon Wieseltier," *Vanity Fair*, March 1995, www.vanityfair.com/style/2017/10/leon-wieseltier -profile-1995.

100 Thomas Friedman, the *Times* foreign policy columnist: Thomas Friedman interview, *The Charlie Rose Show*, May 29, 2003.

100 Bill Keller of *The New York Times*: Bill Keller, "The I-Can't-Believe-I'm-a-Hawk Club," *New York Times*, February 8, 2003. For an anticipation of the applications toward Islam of such a tradition, see Pankaj Mishra, *Age of Anger: A History of the Present* (New York: Farrar, Straus and Giroux, 2017), 102–3, 128.

100 Kerry played War on Terror politics: Michael Janofsky, "Kerry Says Dean Is 'Imploding,'" *New York Times*, September 20, 2003.

101 it took Kerry "40 minutes": David Halbfinger, "Kerry Still Nagged by Questions on Vote to Authorize Iraq War," *New York Times*, October 24, 2003.

101 repealing Bush's hated tax cuts: Robert Draper, *Dead Certain: The Presidency of George W. Bush* (New York: Free Press, 2008), 236–38.

101 Kerry, stung by the critique: Jodi Wilgoren, "Kerry Says His Vote on Iraq Would Be the Same Today," *New York Times*, August 10, 2004.

102 "prevent another Manhattan": Transcript of Osama bin Laden videotape, October 30, 2004, Al Jazeera, www.aljazeera.com/archive/2004/11/200849163336457223.html, accessed June 14, 2004.

103 Israeli shipping company executive: "New York Senator Wants to Halt Ports Deal," *All Things Considered*, NPR, February 22, 2006. Frank J. Gaffney, Jr., "Company Policy," *National Review*, February 22, 2006. Carol Lin, Wolf Blitzer, Jeanne Meserve, and Satinder Bindra, "Israeli-Based Company Endorses Dubai Ports World," March 2, 2006, transcript available at http://transcripts.cnn.com/TRANSCRIPTS/0603/02/lt.03.html.

103 The company promptly: David E. Sanger, "Under Pressure, Dubai Company Drops Ports Deal," *New York Times*, March 10, 2006. Heather Timmons, "Dubai Port Company Sells Its U.S. Holdings to A.I.G.," *New York Times*, December 12, 2006.

104 Nihad Awad, under surveillance: Glenn Greenwald and Murtaza Hussein, "Meet the Muslim-American Leaders the NSA and FBI Have Been Spying On," *The Intercept*, July 9, 2014.

104 "The second part of 2004": Author's interview with Adham Hassoun, June 14, 2020. *U.S. v. Hassoun et al.*, Fourth Superseding Indictment, November 17, 2005.

105 **Ahmed Omar Abu Ali:** Brian Knowlton, "U.S. Man Charged with Aiding Qaeda," *New York Times*, February 25, 2005. David Stout, "Student from Virginia Is Convicted of Plotting with al-Qaeda to Assassinate Bush," *New York Times*, November 23, 2005. Spencer Ackerman, "Suspect Policy," *The New Republic*, March 14, 2005.

106 **bin Laden CNN interview:** *U.S. v. Hassoun et al.*, trial transcript, June 19, 2007.

106 **U.S. attorney, Alex Acosta:** "Government's Omnibus Response to Defendants' Fed. R. Crim. P29 Motion for Judgment of Acquittal," *U.S. v. Hassoun et al.*, October 29, 2007.

106 **the FBI claimed:** *U.S. v. Hassoun et al.*, trial transcript, June 8, 2007.

106 **Hassoun, Padilla, and Jayyousi:** "Government's Omnibus Response," October 29, 2007.

107 **"casualty of war":** Author's interview with Adham Hassoun, June 21, 2020.

108 **flattered American exceptionalism:** Joseph R. Biden Jr. and Leslie H. Gelb, "Unity through Autonomy in Iraq," *New York Times*, May 1, 2006. Ned Parker and Raheem Salman, "U.S. Vote Unites Iraqis in Anger," *Los Angeles Times*, October 1, 2007.

109 **They had won esteem:** George Packer, "Know Your Enemy," *The New Yorker*, December 10, 2006.

109 **Petraeus, a professorial soldier:** Dept. of the Army, FM 3-24, *Counterinsurgency*, December 2006. General Charles C. Krulak, "The Strategic Corporal: Victory in the Three-Block War," *Marines* magazine, January 1999.

109 **In Baghdad he instructed:** Tom Ricks, "Gen. Petraeus Warns against Using Torture," *Washington Post*, May 11, 2007.

109 **"Just because they sympathize":** Spencer Ackerman, "Training Iraq's Death Squads," *The Nation*, May 17, 2007.

109 **Abu Wail, the religious leader:** Stanley McChrystal, *My Share of the Task: A Memoir* (New York: Portfolio/Penguin, 2013), 240–48.

110 **"Korea was cited":** Author's interview with a retired senior U.S. military officer, May 5, 2020. Author's interview with Emma Sky, June 5, 2020.

110 **cult of Petraeus:** Spencer Ackerman, "How I Was Drawn into the Cult of David Petraeus," *Wired*, November 11, 2012.

110 **produced data showing:** By the spring of 2008, as the surge wound down, Petraeus's command reported reducing violence to 2005 levels, which had been at the time unacceptable to the American public. Spencer Ackerman, "King David," *Washington Independent*, May 6, 2008, now defunct but republished in *HuffPost*, where Petraeus discussed "the Martyr Sadr" and co-optation of ex-guerrillas.

110 **post-surge violence:** Steve Coll, "The General's Dilemma," *The New Yorker*, August 13, 2008.

110 **He clashed with CIA officials:** Karen DeYoung, "Experts Doubt Drop in Violence in Iraq; Military Statistics Called into Question," *Washington Post*, September 4, 2007. National Intelligence Estimate, "Prospects for Iraq's Stability: Some Security Progress

NOTES

but Political Reconciliation Elusive," August 2007, available at https://www.hsdl
.org/?abstract&did=478001.

110 **"a little bit of significant progress"**: Nomination hearing for Gen. David H. Petraeus
and Lt. Gen. Raymond T. Odierno, Senate Armed Services Committee, May 22, 2008.

111 **His attitude conflicted**: David Stout, "House Passes Iraq Resolution with 17 Votes
from G.O.P.," *New York Times*, February 16, 2007.

112 **why Obama didn't**: Author's interview with Ben Rhodes, July 13, 2020.

112 **He told Condoleezza Rice**: Senate Foreign Relations Committee hearing, January 19,
2005. Available at https://www.c-span.org/video/?185220-1/secretary-state-nomination
-hearing-day-2.

112 **a "very, very narrow exception"**: Ben Smith, "McCain Team Mocks Hil Torture Loophole," New York *Daily News*, October 16, 2006.

112 **Obama voted against**: William Neikirk and Andrew Zajac, "Tribunal Bill OK'd by
Senate; Bush's Legislative Victory Comes amid Concerns," *Chicago Tribune*, September 26, 2006.

112 **When the *Times* revealed**: Wolf Blitzer et al., "Senate Panel Approves Torture Bill
Opposed by President Bush," *The Situation Room*, CNN, September 24, 2006.

113 **mildest of rebukes**: Barack Obama, "A Way Forward in Iraq," Chicago Council on
Foreign Relations, November 20, 2006.

113 **Months before, Senate Democrats**: Shailagh Murray, "Iraq Vote in Senate Blocked by
GOP," *Washington Post*, February 18, 2007.

113 **His army mentor**: John Bresnahan, "Believing Petraeus and Crocker Requires 'Will-
ing Suspension of Disbelief,'" *Politico*, September 11, 2007. Thomas E. Ricks, *The
Gamble: General Petraeus and the American Military Adventure in Iraq* (New York:
Penguin Press, 2009), 250. Landler, "How Hillary Clinton Became a Hawk."

114 **reiterating a phrase**: Democratic presidential debate, Des Moines, Iowa, December 13,
2007. Available at www.c-span.org/video/?203026-1/iowa-democratic-presidential
-candidates-debate.

114 **he would not stop**: Democratic presidential debate, Los Angeles, Calif., January 30,
2007.

115 **But it was conspicuous**: Barack Obama, *A Promised Land* (New York: Crown, 2020),
305, 447.

116 **Brennan's CIA tribalism**: Spencer Ackerman, "The Obama Doctrine," *The American
Prospect*, March 2008. Ackerman, "Experts Differ on How to End Iraq War," *Wash-
ington Independent*, April 11, 2008. Eli Lake, "Contra Expectations," *The New Republic*,
July 30, 2008.

116 **Obama broke with a constituency**: Eric Lichtblau, "Senate Approves Bill to Broaden
Wiretap Powers," *New York Times*, July 10, 2008.

116 **Obama belatedly rebuked MoveOn**: Alexander Mooney, "Obama Takes Swipe at
MoveOn," CNN, July 1, 2008.

NOTES

116 **Maliki's spokesman endorsed:** Richard A. Oppel Jr. and Alissa J. Rubin, "Obama Meets Iraqi Prime Minister in Baghdad," *New York Times*, July 22, 2008. Bush had wanted a U.S. presence through 2015, but Maliki successfully pressed for 2010. Peter Baker, *Days of Fire: Bush and Cheney in the White House* (New York: Anchor, 2014), 619–20.

117 **"Foreign policy is about protecting America":** Michael Finnegan, "Giuliani Stumps in Central Valley," *Los Angeles Times*, February 14, 2007. Chris Reiter, "Romney, Giuliani Terrorism Comments Draw Criticism," Reuters, May 16, 2007. Andy Sullivan, "Candidate Paul Assigns Reading to Giuliani," Reuters, May 24, 2007.

118 **endorsement of John Hagee:** Amy Goodman, "McCain Embraces Endorsement from Anti-Catholic, Anti-Gay, Anti-Muslim Televangelist John Hagee," *Democracy Now!*, March 7, 2008.

118 **W. James Antle III:** W. James Antle III, "The War Party," *The American Conservative*, April 23, 2007.

118 **Clinton herself spoke:** Kate Philips, "Clinton Touts White Support," *New York Times*, May 8, 2008.

119 **Islamophobic Clarion Fund:** Deborah Feyerick and Sheila Steffen, "Muslim DVD Rattles Voters in Key Battleground States," *American Morning*, CNN, October 15, 2008. Ben Smith, "McCain Camp: Obama Is 'Radical,' Pals Around with Terrorists," *Politico*, October 4, 2008.

119 **"terrorist fist jab":** Wajahat Ali, Eli Clifton, Matthew Duss, Lee Fang, Scott Keyes, and Faiz Shakir, *Islamophobia Inc.*, Center for American Progress, August 2011. Mark Sweeney, "Fox News Anchor Taken Off Air after Obama 'Terrorist Fist Jab' Gaffe," *Guardian*, June 13, 2008.

119 **Rallygoers told McCain:** Nico Pitney, "Obama Hatred on Display Again at Palin Rally, Supporter Screams, 'Treason!,'" *HuffPost*, November 7, 2007. Matthew Quirk, "More Racism, Please," *The Atlantic*, October 2008.

119 **respectable *New Republic*:** Naples Daily News staff, "Sheriff Scott's Use of Obama's Middle Name Causes National Stir," *Naples* (Fla.) *Daily News*, October 6, 2008. Scott Conroy, "Defending the 'Hussein' Game," CBS News, October 9, 2008. Eli Lake, "Jihadists for Obama," *The New Republic*, November 10, 2008.

119 **appalled Colin Powell:** Jonathan Martin, "Powell Embarrassed by the Obama-Is-a-Muslim Stuff,'" *Politico*, October 19, 2008.

120 **"a decent, family man":** "McCain Counters Obama 'Arab' Question," Associated Press video, October 11, 2008. Laura Meckler, "McCain Asks Supporters to Show Obama Respect," *Wall Street Journal*, October 12, 2008.

Chapter Four: Obama and the "Sustainable" War on Terror

122 **Obama and his officials:** Barack Obama, "Remarks by the President on National Security," May 21, 2009, transcript available at https://obamawhitehouse.archives.gov /the-press-office/remarks-president-national-security-5-21-09. Barack Obama, "Remarks by the President on the Administration's Approach to Counterterrorism," De-

cember 6, 2016, transcript available at https://obamawhitehouse.archives.gov/the -press-office/2016/12/06/remarks-president-administrations-approach-counterter rorism.

123 **the guided missile:** Jo Becker and Scott Shane, "Secret 'Kill List' Proves a Test of Obama's Principles and Will," *New York Times*, May 29, 2012.

123 **As much as torture:** Senate Select Committee on Intelligence, "Committee Study of the Central Intelligence Agency's Detention and Interrogation Program" ("The Tor ture Report"), December 9, 2014, 16. Available at www.intelligence.senate.gov/sites /default/files/publications/CRPT-113srpt288.pdf.

124 **Obama's relationship with progressives:** Noah Shachtman, "CIA Chief: Drones 'Only Game in Town' for Stopping Al Qaeda," *Wired*, May 19, 2009.

125 **Obama's closest counterterrorism adviser:** Scott Shane, "CIA Is Disputed on Civilian Toll in Drone Strikes," *New York Times*, August 11, 2011.

125 **Admiral Dennis Blair:** Jeremy Scahill, *Dirty Wars: The World Is a Battlefield* (New York: Nation Books, 2013), 353.

125 **During Obama's second year:** Obama launched at least 122 drone strikes in 2010, according to statistics tallied by the New America Foundation: www.newamerica.org /international-security/reports/americas-counterterrorism-wars/the-drone-war-in -pakistan. The author would like to thank cartographers Eben Dennis, Graham Twi bell, and David Mayer for their help.

126 **"a list of tyrants":** Spencer Ackerman, "Victim of Obama's First Drone Strike: 'I Am the Living Example of What Drones Are,'" *Guardian*, January 23, 2016. Ackerman, "After Drones: The Indelible Mark of America's Remote Control Warfare," *Guardian*, April 21, 2016.

126 **interrogations of suspected high-ranking terrorists:** Spencer Ackerman, "Obama Task Force on Torture Considers CIA-FBI Interrogation Teams," *Washington Indepen dent*, June 24, 2009.

126 **the closure of Guantanamo Bay:** Executive Orders 13491 and 13492, January 22, 2009, www.archives.gov/federal-register/executive-orders/2009-obama.html, accessed July 10, 2019.

127 **If waterboarding was deemed:** "The Dark Side," interview with John Brennan, *Front line*, PBS, March 6, 2006. *The Early Show*, CBS News, November 2, 2007.

127 **"extraordinarily talented" CIA officials:** David Johnson and Charlie Savage, "Obama Reluctant to Look into Bush Programs," *New York Times*, January 11, 2009.

127 **Rahm Emanuel, told ABC News:** *This Week with George Stephanopoulos*, ABC News, April 19, 2009.

128 **Bikowsky misrepresented a report:** Matthew Cole, "Bin Laden Expert Accused of Shap ing CIA Deception on 'Torture' Program," NBC News, December 18, 2014. Marcy Wheeler, "Should Alfreda Bitkowsky's Lawyer Really Be in Charge of Declassifying the Torture Report?" *Emptywheel*, August 27, 2004. Glenn Greenwald and Peter Maass,

NOTES

"Meet Alfreda Bikowsky, the Senior Officer at the Center of the CIA's Torture Scandals," *The Intercept*, December 19, 2014. Jane Mayer, "The Unidentified Queen of Torture," *The New Yorker*, December 18, 2014. The CIA does not confirm or deny Bikowsky's name despite considerable public reporting. John Rizzo's book *Company Man: Thirty Years of Controversy and Crisis in the CIA* (New York: Scribner, 2014) refers to "96" videotapes, but most other sources, including the CIA's 2004 inspector general report on the matter, say the CIA destroyed ninety-two videotapes. Spencer Ackerman, "Ex-CIA Official Says Some Torture Videotapes May Still Exist," *Daily Beast*, May 1, 2018.

128 *Washington Post* **identified:** Greg Miller, "CIA Official Who Directed Hunt for Bin Laden Is Being Removed from Post," *Washington Post*, March 25, 2015. Matthew Rosenberg and Adam Goldman, "CIA Names 'the Dark Prince' to Run Iran Operations, Signaling a Tougher Stance," *New York Times*, June 2, 2017.

129 **immediately backed down:** Statement of Sen. Mitch McConnell, "Releasing Guantanamo Detainees into the U.S. Will Not Make America Safer," April 24, 2009. Peter Finn and Anne E. Kornblut, "Guantanamo Bay: How the White House Lost the Fight to Close It," *Washington Post*, April 23, 2011. Spencer Ackerman, "Uighur Men Held for 12 Years Leave Guantanamo Bay for Slovakia," *Guardian*, December 31, 2013.

129 **Bernie Sanders was among:** Mitch McConnell, "There Are No Good Alternatives to Guantanamo," *Washington Post*, March 15, 2009. Helene Cooper and David Johnston, "Obama Tells Prison to Take Detainees," *New York Times*, December 15, 2009. Spencer Ackerman, "'No One but Himself to Blame': How Obama's Guantanamo Plans Fell Through," *Guardian*, February 24, 2016. Roll Call vote, 111th Congress— 1st Session, On the Amendment (Inouye Amdt. No. 1133), May 20, 2009.

129 **dozens of these people:** Charlie Savage, *Power Wars: The Relentless Rise of Presidential Authority and Secrecy* (New York: Little, Brown & Co., 2015), 117.

129 **Ben Rhodes wrote:** Author's interview with Ben Rhodes, July 13, 2020.

130 **Pentagon's top lawyer, Jeh Johnson:** Spencer Ackerman, "Johnson Opens the Door to Post-Acquittal Detentions," *Washington Independent,* July 7, 2009.

130 **An effort predicated:** Barack Obama, "Remarks by the President on National Security," May 21, 2009. Transcript available at obamawhitehouse.archives.gov/the-press -office/remarks-president-national-security-5-21-09, accessed July 10, 2019.

131 **a bureaucratic death:** Savage, *Power Wars*, 295–99, 309.

131 **McRaven fired a shot:** Spencer Ackerman, "Drift: How This Ship Became a Floating Gitmo," *Wired*, July 6, 2011. Savage, *Power Wars*, 339–40.

131 **a security inconvenience:** It was hysterical because months earlier, the Southern District of New York successfully prosecuted a different Guantanamo and black-site denizen without any such calamity or expense. Spencer Ackerman, "Bloomberg Killed the Best Chance for Justice for the 9/11 Attacks," *Daily Beast*, February 23, 2020.

132 **The detentions disaster:** Author's interview with Ben Rhodes, July 13, 2020.

133 **Abdulmutallab was not:** An invaluable resource for our knowledge about Awlaki and Abdulmutallab are Abdulmutallab's interviews, or 302s, with the FBI in 2010, most

importantly in January and February. Disclosure of those 302s we owe to *The New York Times*, reporter Scott Shane, and the ACLU. They were not released until 2017, long after the U.S. executed Awlaki.

133 **Hasan had also emailed Awlaki:** Scahill, *Dirty Wars*, 40–41.

133 **The series was enormously popular:** There remains an uncertainty about the U.S. timeline for hunting Awlaki. Two missile strikes on Yemen in December 2009 predate Abdulmutallab's identification of Awlaki as a figure within the AQAP chain of command. At least one of them, ironically on Christmas, is believed to have targeted him. Morten Storm, a jihadi defector and a premier CIA informant on AQAP, records in his memoir *Agent Storm: My Life Inside Al Qaeda and the CIA* (New York: Grove, 2015) that his CIA handler, "Jed," sought to kill Awlaki in December 2009. Jeremy Scahill's reporting in *Dirty Wars* presents a similar account. Charlie Savage, in his *Power Wars*, finds that the Obama administration did not decide on killing Awlaki until after interviewing Abdulmutallab. My reporting over the years does not decisively settle the question. Official alarm about Awlaki existed for years, particularly after he left the United States, gathered after he released "Constants on the Path of Jihad," and crested after Canadian court documents indicated his role inspiring the "Toronto 18." Sources with CIA counterterrorism experience, in conversation, tend to emphasize Awlaki's *incitement* as the heart of the threat he posed, with his operational role taken for granted—further blurring the lines. While it remains possible that the CIA considered Awlaki a target of opportunity before the Abdulmutallab incident, the administration apparatus that both consigned Awlaki to death and created legal justification for it began deliberations after Abdulmutallab's first Mirandized FBI interview on January 29, 2010.

134 **Holder would later say:** Adam Martin, "Attorney General Holder: Due Process Doesn't Necessarily Mean a Courtroom," *The Atlantic*, March 5, 2012.

134 **Charlie Savage of *The New York Times*:** Savage, *Power Wars*, 235–36. Abdulmutallab, who began his search for Awlaki on Wikipedia, was not the only one able to get close to him. The white jihadi turned CIA informant Morten Storm met with Awlaki several times in Yemen; see his *Agent Storm*, 90–109. As well, the CIA and JSOC all but directed Yemen's security apparatus.

134 **Judge John Bates:** Evan Perez, "Judge Dismisses Targeted Killing Suit," *Wall Street Journal*, December 8, 2010.

135 **ACLU attorney Jameel Jaffer:** Terry Frieden, "Judge Throws Out Assassination Lawsuit," CNN, December 7, 2010. Press release, "Court Dismisses Targeted Killing Case on Procedural Grounds without Addressing Merits," Center for Constitutional Rights, December 7, 2010.

135 **The loudest objection:** Spencer Ackerman, "11 Years On, Senate Wakes Up to War on Terror's 'Battlefield America,'" *Wired*, March 6, 2013.

135 **a military authorization bill:** Fiscal 2012 National Defense Authorization Act, December 31, 2011, www.congress.gov/112/plaws/publ81/PLAW-112publ81.pdf.

135 **Obama had intended:** Barack Obama, "Remarks by the President at Cairo University," June 4, 2009. Transcript available at https://obamawhitehouse.archives.gov/the -press-office/remarks-president-cairo-university-6-04-09.

136 **"killed some militants":** Ackerman, "Victim of Obama's First Drone Strike."

136 **Penn State Law report:** Office of the Inspector General, Department of Homeland Security, "Information Sharing on Foreign Nationals: Border Security (Redacted)," February 2012, available at https://www.oig.dhs.gov/assets/Mgmt/2012/OIGr_12-39 _Feb12.pdf. Rights Working Group, Penn State Law Immigrants' Rights Clinic, "The NSEERS Effect: A Decade of Racial Profiling, Fear and Secrecy," *Center for Immigrants' Rights Clinic Publications* 11, May 2012, https://elibrary.law.psu.edu/irc _pubs/11.

137 **broader goals of his counterterrorism:** Barack Obama, "Remarks by President Obama at Cairo University," June 4, 2009.

136 **Obama's approach, formalized:** "Empowering Local Partners to Prevent Violent Extremism in the United States," August 2011, available at www.dhs.gov/sites/default /files/publications/empowering_local_partners.pdf. "Strategic Implementation Plan for Empowering Local Partners to Prevent Violent Extremism in the United States," December 2011, available at https://obamawhitehouse.archives.gov/sites/default/files /sip-final.pdf.

137 **white supremacists were infiltrating:** FBI Intelligence Assessment, "White Supremacist Infiltration of Law Enforcement," October 17, 2006. Available at https://oversight .house.gov/sites/democrats.oversight.house.gov/files/White_Supremacist_Infiltra tion_of_Law_Enforcement.pdf.

137 **Janet Napolitano, quietly dismantled:** U.S. Department of Homeland Security, "Right-wing Extremism: Current Economic and Political Climate Fueling Resurgence in Radicalization and Recruitment," April 2009, fas.org/irp/eprint/rightwing.pdf, accessed July 23, 2019. U.S. Department of Homeland Security, statement of Janet Napolitano "on the threat of right-wing extremism," April 15, 2009. R. Jeffrey Smith, "Homeland Security Department Curtails Home-Grown Terror Analysis," *Washington Post*, June 7, 2011. Spencer Ackerman, "DHS Crushed This Analyst for Warning about Far-Right Terror," *Wired*, August 7, 2012.

139 **Enduring and effective counterterrorism:** Spencer Ackerman, "FBI Teaches Agents 'Mainstream' Muslims Are 'Violent, Radical,'" *Wired*, September 14, 2011. Ackerman and Noah Shachtman, "Video: FBI Trainer Says Forget 'Irrelevant' al-Qaida, Target Islam," *Wired*, September 20, 2011. Ackerman, "New Evidence of Anti-Islam Bias Underscores Deep Challenges for FBI's Reform Pledge," *Wired*, September 23, 2011.

139 **Obama's horrified White House:** Spencer Ackerman, "FBI Purges Hundreds of Terrorism Documents in Islamophobia Probe," *Wired*, February 15, 2012.

139 **Dooley told the officers:** Noah Shachtman and Spencer Ackerman, "U.S. Military Taught Officers: Use 'Hiroshima' Tactics for 'Total War' on Islam," *Wired*, May 10, 2012.

139 **Student officers gave:** Spencer Ackerman, "Exclusive: Senior U.S. General Orders Top-to-Bottom Review of Military's Islam Training," *Wired*, April 24, 2012.

139 Ordering a thorough review: Spencer Ackerman, "Top U.S. Officer: Stop This 'Total War' on Islam Talk," *Wired*, May 10, 2012.

140 Dempsey's review didn't recommend: Spencer Ackerman and Noah Shachtman, "'Institutional Failures' Led Military to Teach War on Islam," *Wired*, June 20, 2012. Kurtis Lee and Jenny Jarvie, "Anti-Sharia Rallies around the U.S. Denounce Islam While Stoking Concerns among Muslim Groups," *Los Angeles Times*, June 10, 2017.

141 Alpha Cavalry Troop: Spencer Ackerman, "Hunt for Weapons Cache Continues," *Washington Independent*, September 16, 2008. I am referring to "Sergeant Rob," rather than using his full name, at his wife's request.

142 "fifty times more important": Steve Coll, *Directorate S: The C.I.A. and America's Secret Wars in Afghanistan and Pakistan* (New York: Penguin, 2019), 352.

143 "very much a counterinsurgency approach": Spencer Ackerman, "The Making of Michèle Flournoy," *Washingtonian*, September 2011.

143 In December, Obama: Barack Obama, "Remarks by the President in Address to the Nation on the Way Forward in Afghanistan and Pakistan," December 1, 2009. Transcript available at https://obamawhitehouse.archives.gov/the-press-office/remarks -president-address-nation-way-forward-afghanistan-and-pakistan.

144 suspended the use: C. J. Chivers and Rod Norland, "Errant U.S. Rocket Strike Killed Civilians in Afghanistan," *New York Times*, February 14, 2010.

144 the Taliban continued: Fred Kaplan, *The Insurgents: David Petraeus and the Plot to Change the American Way of War* (New York: Simon & Schuster, 2014), 329–32.

144 he called Marja: Michael Hastings, "The Runaway General," *Rolling Stone*, July 8, 2010.

144 "We aren't putting fear": Ibid.

145 He dismissed questions: Spencer Ackerman, "Drones Surge, Special Ops Strike in Petraeus Campaign Plan," *Wired*, August 16, 2010.

145 Petraeus removed McChrystal's: Noah Shachtman, "U.S. Escalates Air War over Afghanistan," *Wired*, August 30, 2010.

145 He remembered telling the village elders: Spencer Ackerman, "'Why I Flattened Three Afghan Villages,'" *Wired*, February 1, 2011. Ackerman, "25 Tons of Bombs Wipe Afghan Town off Map," *Wired*, January 19, 2011.

145 "We're being forced": Spencer Ackerman, "Petraeus Team: Taliban Made Us Wipe Out Village," *Wired*, January 20, 2011.

145 forty-seven-year-old Niaz Mohammed: Kevin Sieff, "Years Later, a Flattened Afghan Village Reflects on U.S. Bombardment," *Washington Post*, August 25, 2013.

146 The 3/5 marines: Tom Bowman, "Afghan Success Comes at High Price for Commander," NPR, October 30, 2011.

146 General David Rodriguez: Robert Gates, *Duty: Memoirs of a Secretary at War* (New York: Knopf, 2014), 560.

146 Gates made Kelly: Greg Jaffe, "Lt. Gen. John Kelly, Who Lost Son to War, Says U.S. Largely Unaware of Sacrifice," *Washington Post*, March 2, 2011.

147 **an open secret:** Spencer Ackerman, "Troops Wonder: WTF Are We Doing in Afghanistan, Again?" *Wired*, August 26, 2010. Mark Boal, "The Kill Team," *Rolling Stone*, March 28, 2011.

147 **Staff Sergeant Robert Bales:** Brendan Vaughan, "Robert Bales Speaks: Confessions of America's Most Notorious War Criminal," *GQ*, October 21, 2015.

147 **suffered lasting scars:** Greg Jaffe, "The Cursed Platoon," *Washington Post*, July 2 and 3, 2020.

147 **an outraged Karzai:** BBC News, "Afghanistan's Taliban Suspend Peace Talks with U.S.," March 15, 2012. Coll, *Directorate S*, 581–85.

148 **As Sergeant Rob died:** Tom Sileo, "Go Get 'Em: Soldier's Final Words Still Ring," *Bowling Green Daily News*, February 2, 2014.

148 *New Yorker* **writer Peter Maass:** Peter Maass, "Celebrating the Celebrations," *The New Yorker*, May 4, 2011.

148 **Annabel Hogg, three years older:** Sam Fulwood III, "Osama's Death Unites Americans that Came of Age After 9/11," Center for American Progress, May 3, 2011.

149 **Brennan also claimed:** "Press Briefing by Press Secretary Jay Carney and Assistant to the President for Homeland Security and Counterterrorism John Brennan," May 2, 2011, transcript available at https://obamawhitehouse.archives.gov/the-press-office/2011/05/02/press-briefing-press-secretary-jay-carney-and-assistant-president-homela. Josh Gerstein and Matt Negrin, "W.H. Changes bin Laden Account," *Politico*, May 4, 2011. "How the CIA's Fake Vaccination Campaign Endangers Us All," *Scientific American*, May 1, 2013.

149 **bin Laden's death offered:** Barack Obama, *A Promised Land* (New York: Crown, 2020), 698.

150 **"I'm going to plead":** *U.S. v. Faisal Shahzad*, U.S. Southern District Court of New York, plea transcript, June 21, 2010.

152 **Restricted Counterterrorism Security Group:** Redactions and current disclosures at the time of this writing conceal the other members, as well as the entire membership of the Interagency Disposition Planning Group.

152 **Obama's order states:** May 22, 2013, Presidential Planning Guidance, reprinted in Jameel Jaffer, *The Drone Memos: Targeted Killing, Secrecy and the Law* (New York and London: The New Press, 2016). The process generated extraordinary amounts of record-keeping, but all by the "National Security Staff," i.e., White House officials, whose records are exempt from the Freedom of Information Act. It remains unknown if or how often Obama delegated life-and-death decisions. Nor is it clear whether Obama ratified decisions functionally made at lower levels. "When operations are proposed in Yemen, Somalia or elsewhere, it is Brennan alone who takes the recommendations to Obama for a final sign-off": Karen DeYoung, "CIA Veteran John Brennan Has Transformed U.S. Counterterrorism Policy," *Washington Post*, October 24, 2012.

153 **wage a war of regime change:** Spencer Ackerman, "What Happened in Benghazi Was a Battle," *Wired*, September 12, 2012.

Chapter Five: The Right vs. Obama's War on Terror

155 **"There is nothing holy"**: John Brennan, speech to the Center for Strategic and International Studies, May 26, 2010. Brennan, addressing an audience question, lamented that terms like "terrorism" had cemented themselves within the post-9/11 "American lexicon," despite their shortcomings. Available at www.c-span.org/video/?293739-1/john -brennan-remarks-national-security.

156 **On Fox News Charles Krauthammer**: Charles Krauthammer et al., *Fox News All-Stars*, Fox News, May 28, 2010.

156 *The Washington Times* **editorialized**: Editorial, "Terrorists Are the Real Victims? Obama Legitimizes the Terrorist Viewpoint," *Washington Times*, June 14, 2010.

156 **An anti-Islam activist**: Pamela Geller, "Obama's Counterterror Adviser Calls Jihad 'Legitimate Tenet' of Islam," *Atlas Shrugs*, May 27, 2010. Doug Chandler, "The Passions (and Perils) of Pamela Geller," *New York Jewish Week*, September 1, 2010.

157 **Islam in Cairo**: Nile Gardner and Morgan Lorraine Roach, "Barack Obama's Top 10 Apologies: How the President Has Humiliated a Superpower," Heritage Foundation, June 2, 2009.

157 **Dick Cheney explained**: Bill Hoffman, "Cheney to NewsMax: 'Obama Doesn't Believe in an Exceptional America," *NewsMax*, September 2, 2005.

158 **Yusef Salaam recalled**: Oliver Laughland, "Donald Trump and the Central Park Five: The Racially Charged Rise of a Demagogue," *Guardian*, February 17, 2016. Donald Trump, "Donald Trump: Central Park Five Settlement Is a 'Disgrace,'" New York *Daily News*, June 21, 2014.

158 **"I don't agree"**: Glenn Kessler, "A Look at Trump's 'Birther' Statements," *Washington Post*, April 28, 2011. Ari Melber, "The Nation: Confronting Trump's Coded Racism," NPR, April 27, 2011.

159 **Islamophobic think tank**: Spencer Ackerman, "The Islamists Have Brainwashed General Petraeus!," *Wired*, April 28, 2011.

159 **Far from Washington**: "Anti-Sharia Law Bills in the United States," Southern Poverty Law Center, February 5, 2018.

159 **Brian Michael Jenkins**: Brian Michael Jenkins, "Would-Be Warriors: Incidents of Jihadist Terrorist Radicalization in the United States Since September 11, 2001," RAND Corporation, 2010, vii.

160 **native son Moses Maimonides**: Ira M. Lapidus, *A History of Islamic Societies*, 3rd ed. (New York: Cambridge University Press, 2014), 378–89. Herbert A. Davidson, *Moses Maimonides: The Man and His Works* (New York: Oxford University Press, 2005), 11–17. Maimonides did not seek refuge in Christian Europe but in Muslim Egypt.

160 **Rauf delivered a moving address**: "Message delivered by Imam Feisal Abdul Rauf," Daniel Pearl Memorial, B'Nai Jeshurun, February 23, 2003, www.bj.org/wp-content /uploads/2010/08/daniel_pearl_memorial.pdf, accessed August 13, 2019.

161 "We strive for a 'new Córdoba'": Faisal Abdul Rauf, *What's Right with Islam: A New Vision for Muslims and the West* (New York: HarperOne, 2005), 1–32.

161 Rauf had been preaching: Anne Barnard, "In Lower Manhattan, Two Mosques Have Firm Roots," *New York Times*, August 13, 2010.

161 Rauf and his wife: Ralph Blumenthal and Sharaf Mowjood, "Muslim Prayers and Renewal Near Ground Zero," *New York Times*, December 8, 2009.

161 explained to the committee: Christian Salazar, "Building Damaged in 9/11 to Be Mosque for NYC Muslims," Associated Press, May 5, 2010.

161 a "monster mosque": Anne Barnard and Alan Feuer, "Outraged, and Outrageous," *New York Times*, October 8, 2010.

162 Geller was also a birther: Chandler, "The Passions (and Perils) of Pamela Geller." Pamela Geller, "How Could Stanley Ann Dunham Have Delivered Barack Hussein Obama Jr. in August of 1961 in Honolulu, When Official University of Washington Records Show Her 2680 Miles Away in Seattle Attending Classes the Same Month?" *Atlas Shrugs*, October 24, 2008. The theory, which defies summarization, is attributed to Rudy Schultz as a "more plausible" explanation for the question animating Geller's headline, which relies foundationally on a confusion between *enrollment* records and *attendance* records.

162 Stop Islamization of America: Michelle Boorstein, "In Flap over Mosque Near Ground Zero, Conservative Bloggers Gaining Influence," *Washington Post,* August 19, 2010.

162 *New York Post* ran columns: Andrea Peyser, "Mosque Madness at Ground Zero," *New York Post*, May 13, 2010.

162 El-Gamal described the: Javier C. Hernandez, "Vote Endorses Muslim Center Near Ground Zero," *New York Times*, May 26, 2010. "The Man Behind the Mosque," *Frontline*, PBS, September 27, 2011.

162 Rudy Giuliani told a radio host: Maggie Haberman, "Rudy: GZ Mosque Is a 'Desecration,' 'Decent' Muslims Won't Be Offended," *Politico*, August 2, 2010. Javier C. Hernandez, "Giuliani Says Mosque Near Ground Zero Is Offensive," *New York Times*, August 19, 2010.

162 A Republican candidate: Ben Smith, "Hedge Fund Figure Financed Mosque Campaign," *Politico*, January 18, 2011.

162 a shakedown artist: Sumathi Reddy and Tarek El-Ghobashy, "Trump Offers to Buy Out Islamic Center Investor," *Wall Street Journal*, September 9, 2010.

162–163 signs reading SHARIA: Michael M. Grynbaum, "Proposed Muslim Center Draws Opposing Protests," *New York Times*, August 22, 2010.

163 twenty-five-year-old nephew: Erik Badia, Kate Nocera, and Simone Weichselbaum, "Anti-'Ground Zero Mosque' Protesters Descend on Downtown Park51 Site," New York *Daily News*, August 22, 2010.

163 cabbie named Ahmed Sharif: N. R. Kleinfield, "Rider Asks If Cabby Is Muslim, Then Stabs Him," *New York Times*, August 25, 2010. Jonathan Allen, "Student Pleads

Guilty to Stabbing Muslim Cabbie in New York," Reuters, June 11, 2013. "Violence against Muslims," Human Rights First, March 2011, available at https://silo.tips /download/violence-against-muslims.

163 Islam's premier persecutor: Wilders's September 11, 2010, remarks are posted at www.geertwilders.nl/index2.php?option=com_content&do_pdf=1&id=1712, accessed August 14, 2019.

163 a CBS poll: Ishaan Tharoor, "Mosque Protests Add Note of Discord to 9/11 Remembrances," *Time*, September 11, 2010. "Poll: Most Americans Oppose Ground Zero Mosque," CBS News, August 26, 2010. Josh Marshall, "Brings It All into Focus," *Talking Points Memo*, September 11, 2010. Pamela Geller, "America Speaks! Historic 9/11 Rally Draws 40,000," *Atlas Shrugged*, September 11, 2010. Amber Sutherland, Douglas Montero, and Sabrina Ford, "Rallies Rage in Downtown Duel; Cops Keep Order amid a Raucous Mosque Battle," *New York Post*, September 12, 2010. *Contra* Geller, the *Post* tallied the attendees at fewer than six thousand, with counterprotesters slightly outnumbering the protesters.

163 Three Democratic congressmen: Russell Goldman, "Sen. Harry Reid Breaks with Obama over 'Ground Zero Mosque,'" ABC News, August 16, 2010. Maggie Haberman, "NY Members in Swing Districts Coming Out against Mosque," *Politico*, August 17, 2010.

164 Rauf's project reflected: Sue Fishoff and Ami Eden, "Will the Real Imam Rauf Please Stand Up?" *Jewish Telegraph Agency*, August 24, 2010. Paul Vitello, "For High Holy Days, Rabbis Weigh Their Words on Proposed Islamic Center," *New York Times*, September 8, 2010.

164 El-Gamal deemphasized and: Rosemary R. Corbett, *Making Moderate Islam: Sufism, Service and the 'Ground Zero Mosque' Controversy* (Stanford, CA: Stanford University Press, 2016), 183–209. David Jeans, "Behind a $10M Construction Showdown at Sharif El-Gamal's 45 Park," *The Real Deal*, April 30, 2019.

164 "promote fear and antagonism": Daniel Burke, "Q&A with Imam Feisal Abdul Rauf," Religion News Service, August 29, 2012, reprinted at www.washingtonpost .com/national/on-faith/qanda-with-imam-feisal-abdul-rauf/2012/08/29/1c1c701c -f21f-11e1-b74c-84ed55e0300b_story.html, accessed August 9, 2019.

165 was "accommodating sharia": Robert Spencer in his video *The Ground Zero Mosque: Second Wave of the 9/11 Attacks*, directed by Pamela Geller (Goldfish Pictures, 2011).

165 anxiety among local non-Muslims: Diane Macedo, "Plans to Build Massive Islamic Centers Raise Concerns in Tennessee," Fox News, August 9, 2010.

165 assailants poured gas: CBS/Associated Press, "Fire at Tenn. Mosque Building Site Ruled Arson," CBS News, August 28, 2010.

165 CNN filmed a segment: Robbie Brown, "Incidents at Mosque in Tenn. Spread Fear," *New York Times*, August 30, 2010.

166 To bolster their case: Travis Loller, "Mosque Hearing Puts Islam on Trial," Associated Press, November 12, 2010. "An Uncivil Action: Middle Tennessee Puts Islam on Trial,"

The Economist, November 18, 2010. Christian Grantham, "Murfreesboro Mosque Opponents Appear in Chancery Court," *Murfreesboro Post*, September 27, 2010.

166 **menace came from powerful figures:** Islamic Center of Murfreesboro and Dr. Ossama Bahloul, Plaintiffs' Memorandum of Law in Support of Plaintiffs' Application for a Temporary Restraining Order or Preliminary Injunction, U.S. District Court, Middle Tennessee District, July 17, 2012. Soledad O'Brien, "Unwelcome: The Muslims Next Door," *CNN Presents*, CNN, August 18, 2012. Tim Murphy, "The Craziest GOP House Race of the Year," *Mother Jones*, July 30, 2012.

166 **the target of suspicion:** Bob Smietana/Religion News Service, "Murfreesboro Mosque Fight Laid to Rest after Supreme Court Ruling," *Washington Post*, June 3, 2014. Nancy DeGennaro, "Islamic Center of Murfreesboro Tells Vandals, 'We Forgive You,'" *Daily News Journal* (Tenn.), March 9, 2018.

166 **Tennessee Republican lawmaker:** Resolution of the House of Delegates of the American Bar Association, August 8–9, 2011. Beenish Ahmed, "Intimidating Muslims One Sharia Ban at a Time," *The American Prospect*, March 3, 2011.

167 **reduced civic space for Muslims:** Mark Olalde and Dustin Gardiner, "The Network Behind State Bills 'Countering' Sharia Law and Terrorism," Center for Public Integrity, July 18, 2019.

167 **infamous 2008 *Washington Times* column:** Frank Gaffney, "The Jihadist Vote," *Washington Times*, October 14, 2008.

168 **It referenced Muslim:** Center for Security Policy, "Shariah: The Threat to America, An Exercise in Competitive Analysis—Report of Team B II," 2010, esp. 8, 18–22. Available at www.centerforsecuritypolicy.org/wp-content/uploads/2010/09/Shariah -The-Threat-to-America-Team-B-Report-Web-09292010.pdf.

168 **Adlouni's memo implored:** Bridge Initiative Team, "'Civilization Jihad': Debunking the Conspiracy Theory," February 2, 2016.

169 **Islamophobic FBI training:** Frank Gaffney, "Remarks to the Western Conservative Summit," June 30, 2012.

169 **received $40 million:** Suzanne Goldenberg, "Secret Funding Helped Build Vast Network of Climate Denial Think Tanks," *Guardian*, February 14, 2013.

169 **the Bradleys' largesse:** This is a conservative calculation. It does not include fifty thousand dollars the documents record the Bradleys giving the Center for Security Policy on November 13, 2001, on the assumption that the donation was solicited before 9/11. Internal Bradley Foundation grant request documents acquired by the author.

170 **The Scaife foundations:** Wajahat Ali, Eli Clifton, Matthew Duss, Lee Fang, Scott Keyes, and Faiz Shakir, "Fear, Inc.," Center for American Progress, August 2011.

171 **Leitner's warning against:** Spencer Ackerman, "After Oslo, Group Accuses Thousands of Being Homegrown Terrorists," *Wired*, July 25, 2011. Tim Murphy, "Rep. Allen West's (Very, Very) Stealth Jihad," *Mother Jones*, July 26, 2011.

171 **Southern Poverty Law Center reported:** Mark Potok, "Rage on the Right," Southern Poverty Law Center *Intelligence Report*, March 2, 2010.

171 **"an orchestrated effort":** Andy Barr, "Ariz. Targets 'Anchor Baby' Citizenship," *Politico*, June 14, 2010.

171 **al-Qaeda wives would travel:** Joe Tacopino, "Texas Rep. Louie Gohmert Warns of Baby-Making Terrorists Coming to U.S.," New York *Daily News*, June 27, 2010.

171 **Gohmert was eviscerated:** Anderson Cooper, "Interview with Rep. Louie Gohmert," *Anderson Cooper 360*, August 12, 2010.

172 **Anwar al-Awlaki, the center claimed:** "W. D. Reasoner" (a pseudonym), "Birthright Citizenship for the Children of Visitors: A National Security Problem in the Making?" Center for Immigration Studies, March 9, 2011. Available at https://cis.org/Report /Birthright-Citizenship-Children-Visitors.

172 **Corruption within CBP:** Nina Bernstein, "Border Sweeps in North Reach Miles into U.S.," *New York Times*, August 29, 2010. Neena Satija, "Feds Tight-Lipped on Weeding Out Corrupt Border Agents," *Texas Tribune*, July 10, 2016.

172 **1 million deportations:** DHS counts *deportations*, not *people deported*. Since the same person might be deported more than once, a certain imprecision exists when discussing deportations in terms of people. Molly O'Toole, "Analysis: Obama Deportations Raise Immigration Policy Questions," Reuters, September 18, 2011.

172–173 **For much of his first term:** U.S. Immigration and Customs Enforcement, U.S. Department of Homeland Security, "ICE Enforcement and Removals Operations Report, Fiscal Year 2015," Homeland Security Digital Library, December 22, 2015, 8, www.hsdl.org/?abstract&did=789209.

173 **DHS considered misdemeanor offenses:** Laura Meckler, "5 Things to Know about Obama's Record on Deportations," *Wall Street Journal*, May 2, 2014.

173 **Separating the family:** Ken McLaughlin, "San Mateo Family Struggles to Stay Together as U.S. Deports Dad, Tries to Deport Mom," *San Jose Mercury News*, September 10, 2010.

173 **children languished in foster care:** Seth Freed Wessler, "U.S. Deports 46K Parents of Citizen Kids in Just Six Months," *Colorlines*, November 3, 2011. Robert Mackey, "Worried Girl Asks Michelle Obama If Her Mother Will Be Deported," *New York Times*, May 19, 2010.

174 **the task force held:** Homeland Security Advisory Council, "Report of the Task Force on Secure Communities: Findings and Recommendations," U.S. Department of Homeland Security, September 2011. Available at www.dhs.gov/xlibrary/assets/hsac-task -force-on-secure-communities-findings-and-recommendations-report.pdf.

174 **Ashcroft's immigration crackdown:** Scott Wong and Sheila Toelitz, "DREAM Act Dies in Senate," *Politico*, December 18, 2010. Kris W. Kobach, "Why Arizona Drew a Line," *New York Times*, April 28, 2010.

175 **Tea Party congressman Joe Walsh:** Joe Walsh YouTube channel via CNSNews YouTube channel, www.youtube.com/watch?v=oRYqYJhyVVI, accessed August 29, 2019.

175 **his accelerated deportations:** "Obama's Remarks on Immigration," *New York Times*, May 10, 2011.

NOTES

175 **Representative Peter King:** House Homeland Security Committee, "Visa Overstays: Can They Be Eliminated?" March 25, 2010.

175 **Texas Representative Lamar Smith:** House Judiciary Committee hearing with Attorney General Eric Holder, May 13, 2010.

175 **tougher on undocumented people:** Anderson Cooper, "Battle on the Border," *Anderson Cooper 360*, CNN, August 6, 2010.

176 **Frank Gaffney's radio show:** Daniel W. Reilly, "Rep. Peter King: There Are 'Too Many Mosques in This Country,'" *Politico*, September 19, 2007. Scott Keyes, "Rep. Peter King: '80 Percent of Mosques in This Country Are Controlled by Radical Imams,'" *ThinkProgress*, January 25, 2011. Lee Fang, "Rep. Peter King Says Muslims Aren't 'American' When It Comes to War," *ThinkProgress*, January 11, 2011. Raymond Hernandez, "Muslim 'Radicalization' Is Focus of Planned Inquiry," *New York Times*, December 16, 2010.

176 **"political correctness at its worst":** "Interfaith Alliance and Colleagues Raise Concerns about Rep. Peter King's Planned Hearings on 'Radicalization of the American Muslim Community,'" press release and accompanying open letter, February 1, 2011, available at https://interfaithalliance.org/interfaith-alliance-and-colleagues-raise-concerns-about-rep-peter-kings-planned-hearings-on-radicalization-of-the-ameri can-muslim-community. Laurie Goodmartin, "Muslims to Be Congressional Hearings' Main Focus," *New York Times*, February 7, 2011.

177 **Mississippi's Bennie Thompson:** Thomas Clouse, "Suspect in MLK Bomb Tied to Racist Movement," *Spokane Spokesman-Review*, March 9, 2011. Unbylined, "Neo-Nazi Pleads Guilty in Attempted MLK Bombing," Southern Poverty Law Center *Intelligence Report*, November 2011.

177 **Both warned of a disaster:** Senate Armed Services Committee hearing, "U.S. Policy Toward Iraq," February 3, 2011. Transcript available at www.congress.gov/event/112th-congress/senate-event/LC2860/text?s=1&r=1948.

177 **surge architect Jack Keane:** Rowan Scarborough, "Key General: Iraq Pullout Plan a 'Disaster,'" *Washington Times*, October 23, 2011.

178 **"clash of civilization theory":** Maggie Haberman, "Burlingame on Symbol and Reality," *Politico*, August 15, 2010.

178 **Keep America Safe ran:** Peter Baker, *Days of Fire: Bush and Cheney in the White House* (New York: Anchor, 2014), 641–42. Justin Elliott, "ABA Blasts Liz Cheney Ad as 'Divisive and Diversionary,'" *Talking Points Memo*, March 4, 2010. Scott Horton, "Keep America Safe," *Harper's*, October 14, 2009. Josh Rogin, "Graham Blasts Cheney on 'al-Qaeda Seven' Ad," *Foreign Policy*, March 9, 2010. Spencer Ackerman, "Latest Conservative Smear Calls Justice Dept. Lawyers Terror-Sympathizers," *Washington Independent*, February 26, 2010.

178 **"bringing bin Laden to justice":** Catalina Camia, "Reacting to the Death of Osama bin Laden," *USA Today*, May 2, 2011.

179 **Mark Boal and Kathryn Bigelow:** Spencer Ackerman, "Surveillance, Not Torture, Led to bin Laden," *Wired*, May 3, 2011. Greg Sargent, "John McCain to Bush

Apologists: Stop Lying about Bin Laden and Torture," *Washington Post*, May 12, 2011. Daniel Halper, "Keep America Safe: 'Justice Has Been Done,'" *Washington Examiner*, May 2, 2011. Jason Burke and Paul Harris, "Osama bin Laden Death 'Justifies' Torture of Terror Suspects, Former Bush Aides Claim," *Guardian*, May 3, 2011.

179 **Mubarak was not a dictator:** Jim Lehrer, "Exclusive: Biden: Mubarak Not a Dictator, but People Have a Right to Protest," *PBS NewsHour*, January 27, 2011.

179 **"a lot of differences":** Devin Dwyer, "Republican Presidential Hopefuls Critique Obama on Egypt," ABC News, February 2, 2011.

180 **Hannity cried, "They're voting":** *Fox News All-Stars*, December 5, 2011. Sean Hannity, "Interview with Imam Faisal Abdul Rauf," *Hannity*, May 24, 2012.

180 THE BROTHERHOOD'S PENETRATION: Stephanie Samuel, "Gingrich Says 'Arab Spring' Is Really 'Anti-Christian Spring,'" *Christian Post*, October 31, 2011. For a contrary view, Erich Bridges reported for the *Baptist Press* a feeling of freedom among North African Christians now that *secular* regimes that repressed Christianity had fallen. Erich Bridges,"Whatever Happened to the 'Arab Spring'?" *Baptist Press*, June 13, 2012. Sean Hannity, "Interview with Ron Paul," *Hannity*, October 25, 2011. Mark Landler, "Obama Ordered Secret Report on Unrest in the Arab World," *New York Times*, February 16, 2011. Frank Gaffney, "Remarks to the Western Conservative Summit," June 30, 2012.

181 **Libyan jihadist targets:** Spencer Ackerman, "While Libya War Grows, Obama Team Denies It's a War," *Wired*, March 24, 2011. Ackerman, "GatesFAIL: How Hope Became Military's Plan in Libya," *Wired*, March 30, 2011. Caroline D. Krass, "Authority to Use Military Force in Libya," Justice Department Office of Legal Counsel Memorandum, April 1, 2011, available at https://fas.org/irp/agency/doj/olc/libya.pdf. Ackerman, Chris Stephen, and Ewen MacAskill, "U.S. Launches Airstrikes Against ISIS in Libya," *Guardian*, August 1, 2016.

181–182 **"Who's going to own Libya":** Hugh Hewitt, "Mitt Romney's Analysis of Barack Obama's Libyan Policy," Hughhewitt.com, March 21, 2011. Mitt Romney, "Mission Muddle in Libya," *National Review*, April 21, 2011. Jake Tapper, "Where Is Mitt Romney on Libya?" ABC News, October 20, 2011.

182 **his ambition and his decency:** Scott Shane, "In Islamic Law, Gingrich Sees a Mortal Threat to U.S.," *New York Times*, December 21, 2011.

182 **to "self-deport":** Lucy Madison, "Romney on Immigration: I'm for 'Self-Deportation,'" CBS News, January 24, 2012. Felicia Sonmez, "Russell Pearce, Arizona Immigration Law Author, Says Romney's Policy Is 'Identical to Mine,'" *Washington Post*, April 5, 2012.

182 **straddling the respectable balance:** Bill Kristol, "A Real War & a Phony War," *Weekly Standard*, September 10, 2012. Spencer Ackerman, "What Obama Won't Say in Charlotte: War on Terror Is Done," *Wired*, September 4, 2012.

183 **His first statement:** David Weigel, "The Accidental Tourist," *Slate*, September 12, 2012.

183 **moderator Candy Crowley:** Dylan Byers, "Crowley Fact-Checks Mitt," *Politico*, October 17, 2012.

183 **Romney's advisers, Gabriel Schoenfeld:** Zeke J. Miller, "Campaign Insider Book Argues Mitt Romney Lost Because of Benghazi," *Time*, May 8, 2013.

183 **mainstream members of the party:** Garance Franke-Ruta, "What You Need to Read in the GOP Autopsy Report," *The Atlantic*, March 13, 2013.

184 **"It looked so false":** Greta Van Susteren, "Donald Trump, CEO, Trump Organization Is Interviewed on Fox News," transcript via Financial Markets Regulatory Wire, August 20, 2013.

184 **shot twelve times:** Associated Press, "Stories of the Six Killed in Sunday's Sikh Temple Shooting; Sikh Temple President Tried to Stab Gunman with Butter Knife," August 7, 2012. Stephen Yaccino, Michael Schwirtz, and Marc Santora, "Gunman Kills 6 at Sikh Temple Near Milwaukee," *New York Times*, August 5, 2012. Sara Sidner and Traci Tamura, "Terror in Wisconsin: How One Cop Survived 15 Gunshots," CNN, April 6, 2017.

184 **turned his gun:** Chris McGreal/wire services, "Wisconsin Temple Gunman Died of Self-Inflicted Wound after Shot by Police," *Guardian*, August 8, 2012.

185 **"the American Anders Breivik":** Marilyn Elias, "Sikh Temple Killer Wade Michael Page Radicalized in Army," Southern Poverty Law Center *Intelligence Report*, November 11, 2012. Aziz Haniffa, "'Page Almost Certainly Mistook Sikhs for Muslims,'" *India Abroad*, August 17, 2012. Spencer Ackerman, "DHS Crushed This Analyst for Warning about Far-Right Terror," *Wired*, August 7, 2012.

185 **acquire the chemicals:** Asne Seierstad, *One of Us: The Story of a Massacre in Norway—and Its Aftermath* (New York: Farrar, Straus and Giroux, 2015), 151–53, 190–208, 237, 246.

185 **After killing seventy-seven people:** Ibid., 375. My account of Breivik owes a debt to Seierstad's authoritative, emotionally wrenching book.

186 **The manifesto quoted Spencer:** Scott Shane, "Killings in Norway Spotlight Anti-Muslim Thought in U.S.," *New York Times*, July 24, 2011. Eli Clifton, "CHART: Oslo Terrorist's Manifesto Cited Many Islamophobic Pundits and Bloggers," *ThinkProgress*, July 25, 2011.

186 **"incited him to violence":** Bruce Bawer, "Inside the Mind of the Oslo Murderer," *Wall Street Journal*, July 25, 2011. Adam Serwer, "In Response to Norway Attacks, Right-Wing Bloggers Suddenly Demand Nuance," *Washington Post*, July 25, 2011. Serwer, "Professional Islamophobe Angry the FBI Discontinued Anti-Muslim Training," *Mother Jones*, September 19, 2011. Shane, "Killings in Norway Spotlight Anti-Muslim Thought in U.S."

Chapter Six: The Left vs. Obama's War on Terror

187 **largest single-day protest:** Phyllis Bennis, "February 15, 2003: The Day the World Said No to War," Institute for Policy Studies, February 15, 2013.

188 **seminal 2010 filibuster:** Sen. Bernie Sanders statement, "Sanders Votes against PATRIOT Act Extension," May 26, 2011, available at www.sanders.senate.gov/press

-releases/sanders-votes-against-patriot-act-extension. Sen. Bernie Sanders, "Full Congressional Record Transcript of Sanders' Filibuster: 'The Economy,'" December 10, 2010, available at www.c-span.org/video/?297021-5/senator-sanders-filibuster.

189 **The United Nations called:** Mike Allen and Josh Gerstein, "Crowley Resigns over WikiLeaks Flap," *Politico*, March 13, 2011. Ed Pilkington, "Bradley Manning's Treatment Was Cruel and Inhuman, UN Torture Chief Rules," *Guardian*, March 12, 2012.

191 **Ilyse Hogue of MoveOn:** James Dao, "American Antiwar Movement Plans an Autumn Campaign against Policies on Afghanistan," *New York Times*, August 29, 2009.

191 **same argument as its predecessor:** John Schwartz, "Obama Backs Off a Reversal on Secrets," *New York Times*, February 9, 2009. Marc Ambinder, "Obama DoJ Asserts 'State Secrets': ACLU Blasts Obama," *The Atlantic*, February 9, 2009.

191 **Disclosure and accountability:** Ian Williams, "Seeking the Truth about the Bush Years," *Guardian*, March 5, 2009. Caroline Fredrickson, "Reconciling Senator Leahy's Independent Commission Proposal," ACLU, February 10, 2009.

192 **"You only want to":** Daniel Klaidman, "Independent's Day," *Newsweek*, July 20, 2009. Wil S. Hylton, "Hope. Change. Reality," *GQ*, November 11, 2010.

192 **ACLU's executive director:** Unbylined, "Top Prosecutor Orders Probe into Interrogations; Obama Shifts Onus," CNN, August 24, 2009.

192 **agendas of Bush and Obama:** Center for Constitutional Rights statement, "Human Rights Group Denounces End of Torture Investigation," press release, August 30, 2012, available at https://ccrjustice.org/home/press-center/press-releases/human-rights-group-denounces-end-torture-investigation.

192 **meeting with civil libertarians:** David Axelrod, *Believer: My 40 Years in Politics* (New York: Penguin, 2016), 400.

193 **"war porn", she later called them:** Nick Davis and David Leigh, "Afghanistan War Logs: Massive Leak of Secret Files Exposes Truth of Occupation," *Guardian*, July 25, 2010. Nick Davies, Jonathan Steele, and David Leigh, "Iraq War Logs: Secret Files Show How U.S. Ignored Torture," *Guardian*, October 22, 2010.

194 **chose the handle "Mendax":** Julian Assange, "I Am—Like All Hackers—a Little Bit Autistic," *Independent*, September 22, 2011.

195 **army's Criminal Investigation Division:** Kim Zetter and Kevin Poulsen, "U.S. Intelligence Analyst Arrested in WikiLeaks Video Probe," *Wired*, June 6, 2010.

195 **insightful counterinsurgency critic:** "The War Logs: Reaction to Disclosure of Military Documents on Afghan War," *New York Times*, July 25, 2010, atwar.blogs .nytimes.com/2010/07/25/the-war-logs, accessed February 26, 2020.

196 **Torture Euphemism Generator:** Rob Beschizza, "The New York Times Torture Euphemism Generator!" *BoingBoing*, October 22, 2010. Danny Schechter, "Media War: WikiLeaks vs. the Pentagon," Al Jazeera, October 26, 2010.

196 **fully redact names:** Matthew Weaver, "Afghanistan War Logs: WikiLeaks Urged to Remove Thousands of Names," *Guardian*, August 10, 2010.

196 German tech activist Daniel Domscheit-Berg: Kim Zetter and Kevin Poulsen, "Unpublished Iraq War Logs Trigger Internal WikiLeaks Revolt," *Wired*, September 27, 2010. Mark Hosenball, "Swedish Sex Probes of WikiLeaks Founder May Be Closed This Week," *Newsweek*, August 23, 2010. Kim Zetter, "WikiLeaks Defector Slams Assange in Tell-All Book," *Wired*, February 10, 2011.

196 "the blood of some young soldier": Spencer Ackerman, "Top U.S. Officer: WikiLeaks Might Have 'Blood on Its Hands,'" *Wired*, July 29, 2010.

196 State Department's Harold Koh: Josh Rogin, "State Department Refuses to Negotiate with WikiLeaks," *Foreign Policy*, November 28, 2010.

196 Joe Biden called Assange: Ewen MacAskill, "Julian Assange Like a Hi-Tech Terrorist, Says Joe Biden," *Guardian*, December 19, 2010.

197 The Pentagon expanded: Spencer Ackerman, "DARPA's Star Hacker Looks to WikiLeak-Proof the Pentagon," *Wired*, August 31, 2010. Michael O'Brien, "Republican Wants WikiLeaks Labeled as Terrorist Group," *The Hill*, November 29, 2010.

197 The pretext for this cruelty: Chelsea Manning, "The Years Since I Was Jailed for Releasing the 'War Diaries' Have Been a Roller Coaster," *Guardian*, May 27, 2015. Ed Pilkington, "Bradley Manning: Stripping Me of All My Clothing Is Without Justification," *Guardian*, March 11, 2011. Charlie Savage, "WikiLeaks Case Lawyer Chides Marine Jailers on Manning's Treatment," *New York Times*, December 11, 2012.

197 Philippa Thomas, a BBC journalist: Philippa Thomas, "The State Department Spokesman and the Prisoner in the Brig," *Philippa Thomas Online*, March 10, 2011, philippathomas.wordpress.com/2011/03/10/the-state-department-spokesman-and-the-prisoner-in-the-brig, accessed February 29, 2020.

198 Obama lectured the protesters: Scott Shane, "Obama Defends Detention Conditions for Soldier Accused in WikiLeaks Case," *New York Times*, March 11, 2011. Carrie Budoff Brown, "Obama Gets a Singing Rebuke," *Politico*, April 21, 2011. MJ Lee and Abby Phillip, "Obama Says Manning 'Broke the Law,'" *Politico*, April 22, 2011.

198 Bill O'Reilly called Manning: Bill O'Reilly, "There Are Traitors in America," Fox News, November 29, 2010.

198 UN special rapporteur: Jason Leopold, "Secret Report Contradicts U.S. Position on Chelsea Manning Leaks," *BuzzFeed*, June 20, 2017. Ed Pilkington, "Bradley Manning's Treatment Was Cruel and Inhuman, U.N. Torture Chief Rules," *Guardian*, March 12, 2012. Ed Pilkington, "Bradley Manning Leak Did Not Result in Deaths by Enemy Forces, Court Hears," *Guardian*, July 31, 2013.

199 "these dynamics were artificial": Alexa O'Brien, "Transcript: US v Pfc. Manning, Pfc. Manning's Statement for the Providence Inquiry, 2/28/13," alexaobrien.com /archives/985, accessed February 24, 2020. Spencer Ackerman, "Bradley Manning Takes 'Full Responsibility' for Giving WikiLeaks Huge Government Data Trove," *Wired*, February 28, 2013. In her chats with Adrian Lamo in May 2010, Manning refers to her WikiLeaks interlocutor as "Assange." Kim Zetter and Kevin Poulsen, "'I Can't Believe What I'm Confessing to You': The WikiLeaks Chats," *Wired*, June 10, 2010.

200 data empires of these Silicon Valley: Glenn Greenwald and Ewen MacAskill, "NSA PRISM Program Taps into User Data of Apple, Google and Others," *Guardian*, June 7, 2013. Documents released by Edward Snowden, including an April 2013 overview of PRISM, note that PRISM actually began before the 2008 law, under its 2007 predecessor, the "Protect America Act." Conspicuous in the PRISM document is a lack of reference to Amazon.

201 the codename MUSCULAR: Barton Gellman and Ashkan Soltani, "NSA Infiltrates Links to Yahoo, Google Data Centers Worldwide, Snowden Documents Say," *Washington Post*, October 30, 2013.

201 the lawlessness of UPSTREAM: Spencer Ackerman, "NSA Illegally Collected Thousands of Emails Before FISA Court Halted Program," *Guardian,* August 21, 2013. Electronic Frontier Foundation, "Jewel v. NSA" overview, available at www.eff.org /cases/jewel, accessed March 3, 2020. Trevor Aaronson, "NSA Secretly Helped Convict Defendants in U.S. Courts, Classified Documents Reveal," *The Intercept,* November 30, 2017. John J. Bates, October 3, 2011, opinion, www.dni.gov/files/documents /0716/October-2011-Bates-Opinion-and%20Order-20140716.pdf, accessed March 3, 2020. Bates wrote that "the sheer volume of transactions acquired by NSA through its upstream collection is such that any meaningful review of the entire body of the transactions is not feasible," 31 of the opinion. See also Charlie Savage, "Don't Cite the Prism v. Upstream Collection Numbers from Judge Bates' 2011 FISC Opinion Anymore," September 17, 2017, charliesavage.com/?p=1714. Savage provides a thorough caveating of statistics cited by Bates that seem to quantify the 702 surveillance but end up complicating it.

202 "the greatest regret of my life": Edward Snowden, *Permanent Record* (New York: Metropolitan, 2019), 69–101, 2.

202 Dixie Cups through chain-link fences: Snowden, *Permanent Record*, 80.

203 indexing tool called Boundless Informant: Boundless Informant is less famous than these other programs, but it catalogs the country of origin of NSA's intercepts. Its existence complicates the stated position of the NSA that estimating how many Americans have their surveillance caught in its dragnets is impossible. However, just because an intercept emerges from America does not make it American, due to the America-centric architecture of the internet. Glenn Greenwald and Ewen MacAskill, "Boundless Informant: The NSA's Secret Tool to Track Global Surveillance Data," *Guardian*, June 11, 2013.

203 His greatest fear: Glenn Greenwald, Ewen MacAskill, and Laura Poitras, "Edward Snowden: The Whistleblower behind the NSA Surveillance Revelations," *Guardian*, June 11, 2013. The original version of the article appeared Sunday, June 9, 2013. Snowden's explanation for the Verax handle is on 251 of *Permanent Record*.

203 an "act of treason": Jeremy Herb and Justin Sink, "Sen. Feinstein Calls Snowden's NSA Leaks an 'Act of Treason,'" *The Hill*, June 10, 2013.

204 Nancy Pelosi and John Boehner: Spencer Ackerman, "NSA Surveillance: Narrow Defeat for Amendment to Restrict Data Collection," *Guardian*, July 25, 2013.

204 **retained NSA's mass surveillance:** Wholesale domestic internet metadata collection, such as email records and web search histories, was the exception. Clapper's spokesman said in 2013 the program was "discontinued in 2011 for operational and resource reasons." Glenn Greenwald and Spencer Ackerman, "NSA Collected U.S. Email Records in Bulk for Two Years under Obama," *Guardian*, June 27, 2013. It was later disclosed that the NSA replicated much of the same collection through targeting internet infrastructure overseas "with less oversight by the Foreign Intelligence Surveillance Court." Charlie Savage, "File Says NSA Found Way to Replace Email Program," *New York Times*, November 19, 2015. Author interview with Ben Rhodes, July 13, 2020.

204 **"no support for the agency":** *Washington Post* staff, "TRANSCRIPT: President Obama's August 9, 2013, News Conference at the White House," August 9, 2013, www.washingtonpost.com/politics/transcript-president-obamas-august-9-2013-news-conference-at-the-white-house/2013/08/09/5a6c21e8-011c-11e3-9a3e-916d e805f65d_story.html, accessed March 2, 2020. Shane Harris, "NSA Veterans: The White House Is Hanging Us Out to Dry," *Foreign Policy*, October 11, 2013.

204 **the "least untruthful" answer:** Spencer Ackerman, "Clapper: I Gave 'Erroneous' Answer Because I Forgot about Patriot Act," *Guardian*, July 2, 2013.

204 **Clapper denounced Snowden's revelations:** Harris, "NSA Veterans: The White House Is Hanging Us Out to Dry."

205 **"human relations database":** A. J. Vicens, "Stopping the 'Ever-Expanding Surveillance State,'" *Mother Jones*, July 31, 2013.

205 **prevented any terrorism:** Spencer Ackerman, "NSA Chief Claims 'Focused' Surveillance Disrupted More Than 50 Terror Plots," *Guardian*, June 19, 2013. *Ars* staff, "NSA Director Addresses Black Hat, Says There Have Been 'Zero Abuses' of Data," *Ars Technica*, July 31, 2013.

205 **searched through them:** Usually this querying occurs by algorithm, rather than a person performing the search.

205 **Bates secretly found:** Bates, October 3, 2011, 33 of opinion. See Ackerman, "NSA Illegally Collected Thousands of Emails."

206 **"the whole haystack":** House Permanent Select Committee on Intelligence hearing, "Potential Changes to Intelligence Surveillance Act (FISA)," October 29, 2013. Available at www.hsdl.org/?view&did=747348.

206 **The general was left to insist:** Janus Kopfstein, "NSA Director Heckled as He Pleads with Hackers to Put 'Facts on the Table,'" *The Verge*, July 31, 2013.

206 **"Eddie Snowden supporters":** Chuck Hagel, "Secretary of Defense Chuck Hagel Delivers Remarks at Retirement Ceremony for General Keith Alexander," Fort George Meade, Maryland, March 28, 2014. Transcript available at www.defense.gov/observe/photo-gallery/igphoto/2001126886.

206 **one Snowden had been catastrophic:** Spencer Ackerman, "DARPA's Star Hacker Looks to WikiLeak-Proof Pentagon," *Wired*, August 31, 2010.

207 **Snowden's discomfort with Assange:** In *Permanent Record*, 301–2, Snowden calls Assange "vain, moody and even bullying," as well as referencing "a sharp disagreement
just a month after our first, text-based conversation" that caused him to cease contact
with Assange. He writes, "I never was, and never would be, a source" for WikiLeaks.

208 **Snowden was a "paranoid libertarian":** Sean Wilentz, "Would You Feel Differently
about Snowden, Greenwald and Assange If You Knew What They Really Thought?"
The New Republic, January 19, 2014.

208 **"I don't get into making comments":** Vicens, "Stopping the 'Ever-Expanding Surveillance State.'"

208 **An exception was Bernie Sanders:** Jim Sciutto, Brian Todd, Barbara Starr, and Wolf
Blitzer, "Interview with Vermont Senator Bernie Sanders," *The Situation Room*, CNN,
January 6, 2014.

208 **ban on the bulk collection:** Spencer Ackerman, "NSA Admits It Improperly Collected
a Huge Amount of Americans' Call Records," *Daily Beast*, June 29, 2018.

208 **tech giants disclaimed responsibility:** Casey Newton, "Mark Zuckerberg on NSA
Spying: 'The Government Blew It,'" *The Verge*, September 11, 2013. Steven Levy,
"How the NSA Almost Killed the Internet," *Wired*, January 17, 2014.

210 **lead Senate torture investigator:** Unless otherwise noted, the primary sources for this
section, including all quotations, come from "The Insider," a three-part series I
reported for *The Guardian* in 2016 after extensive interviews with Jones. Spencer Ackerman, "Crossing the Bridge: Inside the Fight to Reveal the CIA's Torture Secrets,"
September 9, 2016. Ackerman, "'A Constitutional Crisis': The CIA Turns on the
Senate," September 10, 2016. Ackerman, "No Looking Back: The CIA Torture Report's Aftermath," September 11, 2016.

213 **"The Public Roll-Out":** Senate Select Committee on Intelligence, "Committee Study
of the Central Intelligence Agency's Detention and Interrogation Program" ("The
Torture Report"), December 9, 2014, 378, endnote 2137. Available at www.intelli
gence.senate.gov/sites/default/files/publications/CRPT-113srpt288.pdf.

214 **a book called *Rebuttal*:** Ewen MacAskill, "Former CIA Leaders Go on Offensive to
Deny Claim Torture Was Ineffective," *Guardian*, December 10, 2014.

214 **Brennan's clash with the Senate:** Greg Miller and Julie Tate, "CIA Director Faces a
Quandary over Clandestine Service Appointment," *Washington Post*, March 26, 2013.
John Hudson, "CIA's New Clandestine Service Chief Remains Undercover," *Foreign
Policy*, May 7, 2013.

214 **"We're always the ones left":** Spencer Ackerman, "No Looking Back: The CIA Torture Report's Aftermath," *Guardian*, September 11, 2016.

214 **"lack of violence":** Spencer Ackerman, "'A Constitutional Crisis': The CIA Turns on
The Senate," *Guardian*, September 10, 2016.

215 **antiwar perspectives and values:** The author would like to thank Daniel Denvir for
sharpening his thinking on this point.

215 **BLM had been born:** Jelani Cobb, "Some Answers, More Questions in Ferguson," *The New Yorker*, August 15, 2014. Ryan Devereaux, "A Complete Guide to the Shooting of Michael Brown by Darren Wilson," *The Intercept*, November 20, 2014. Unbylined, "Ferguson Cop Darren Wilson Not Indicted in Shooting of Michael Brown," NBC News, November 24, 2014. Department of Justice Civil Rights Division, *Investigation of the Ferguson Police Department*, March 4, 2015, 10: "City, police, and court officials for years have worked in concert to maximize revenue at every stage of the enforcement process, beginning with how fines and fine enforcement processes are established." Jelani Cobb, "The Matter of Black Lives," *The New Yorker*, March 7, 2016.

216 **police would claim there were gunshots:** Two Ferguson police officers were shot, but not until the following year. Unbylined, "Ferguson Police Shot During Protest," BBC, March 12, 2015.

216 **flash-bang grenades:** Robert Patrick and Joel Currier, "Ferguson Highlights Police Use of Military Gear and Tactics," *St. Louis Post-Dispatch*, August 15, 2014. Yasmine Hafiz, "Ferguson Police Reportedly Shot Pastor Renita Lamkin with Rubber Bullet During Protest," *HuffPost*, August 14, 2014. Amnesty International, "On the Streets of America: Human Rights Abuses in Ferguson," October 23, 2014. Mark Berman, "Holder Criticizes Police Response in Ferguson, Says He Is 'Deeply Concerned' about Use of Military Equipment," *Washington Post*, August 14, 2014. Mark Berman and Wesley Lowery, "Justice Dept. Criticizes Police Response to Ferguson Protests," *Washington Post*, June 30, 2015.

217 **"dangers of militarizing the police":** Amnesty International, "On the Streets of America." Luke Harding, Patrick Kingsley, and Shaun Walker, "From Cairo to Moscow: How the World Reacted to Ferguson," *Guardian*, November 25, 2014. Author's interview with Mandy Simon, the author's wife, August 23–24, 2020.

217 **Journalist Radley Balko:** Radley Balko, *Rise of the Warrior Cop: The Militarization of America's Police Forces* (New York: PublicAffairs, 2013), 301.

217 **Thanks to a 2007 law:** Spencer Ackerman, "US Police Given Billions from Homeland Security for 'Tactical' Equipment," *Guardian*, August 20, 2014. Jon Swaine, Spencer Ackerman, and Sabrina Siddiqui, "Ferguson Forced to Return Humvees as US Military Gear Still Flows to Local Police," *Guardian*, August 11, 2015.

217 **three-day-long instruction:** Mark Bell, "Three-Day Anti-Terror Training Scrutinized," Murfreesboro *Daily News Journal*, February 15, 2012. Mark Bell, "SEG President Defends Anti-Terror Law Training," Murfreesboro *Daily News Journal*, February 16, 2012.

218 **regretted his participation:** Michael Powell, "In Shift, Police Say Leader Helped with Anti-Islam Film and Now Regrets It," *New York Times*, January 24, 2012.

218 **Journalist George Joseph:** Spencer Ackerman, "DHS Uses Wartime Mega-Camera to Watch Border," *Wired*, April 2, 2012. Spencer Ackerman, "To Protect and Observe," *Playboy*, December 2011. George Joseph, "Racial Disparities in Police 'Stingray' Surveillance, Mapped," *Bloomberg CityLab*, October 18, 2016.

219 ***When They Call You a Terrorist*:** Tyler Estep, "Gwinnett Sheriff Issues Scathing Statement: 'All Lives Matter,'" *Atlanta Journal-Constitution*, May 15, 2015. *Fox & Friends*,

October 23, 2015. WECT News-6 Staff, "Ex-Police Chief Responds to Retirement after 'Black Lives Matter' Post: 'I Have Done Nothing Wrong,'" WECT News-6, September 15, 2015. "MPD Union Leader: 'Black Lives Matter Is a Terrorist Organization,'" CBS-4 WCCO Minnesota, June 1, 2016.

219 **"turn-key tyranny":** Greenwald, MacAskill, and Poitras, "Edward Snowden."

Chapter Seven: The Decadent Phase of the War on Terror and the Rise of Trump

222 **One detainee, Obaidullah:** Paul Harris, Tracy McVeigh, and Mark Townsend, "How Guantánamo's Horror Forced Inmates to Hunger Strike," *Guardian*, May 4, 2013.

222 **Rumsfeld Pentagon holdover:** Carol Rosenberg, "Qurans at Crux of Guantanamo Hunger Strike," *Miami Herald*, April 5, 2013.

222 **lubricated with olive oil:** Spencer Ackerman, "Guantanamo Use of Olive Oil in Force Feedings 'Astonishing,' Doctor Tells Court," *Guardian*, October 7, 2014.

222 **inserted a catheter:** Samir Naji al Hasan Moqbel, "Gitmo Is Killing Me," *New York Times*, April 14, 2013.

223 **a war of national survival:** Andrew DeGrandpre, "Gen. John Kelly, SOUTHCOM Chief and Gold-Star Dad, to Retire," *Military Times*, October 25, 2015.

223 **Lietzau warned Kelly:** Bill Chappell, "Violence Hits Guantanamo Bay as Inmates Continue Hunger Strike," NPR, April 14, 2013. Reprieve press release, "Tear Gas and Shotguns—Guantanamo Detainee Gives First Inside Account of Raid," May 2, 2013. SOUTHCOM press release, "Commander Orders Single-Cell Detention at Guantanamo Bay for Continued Health and Safety," April 13, 2013. Charlie Savage, "Mounting Tensions Escalate into Violence at Guantanamo Bay," *New York Times*, April 13, 2013. Paul Harris, Tracy McVeigh, and Mark Townsend, "How Guantanamo's Horror Forced Inmates to Hunger Strike," *Guardian*, May 4, 2013. A senior defense official who worked with Kelly shared recollections with the author.

224 **explained the blackout:** Charlie Savage, "Guantanamo Hunger Strike Is Largely Over, U.S. Says," *New York Times*, September 23, 2013. Carol Rosenberg, "Military Imposes Blackout on Guantanamo Hunger-Striker Figures," *Miami Herald*, December 3, 2013.

224 **Neglect favored the Guantanamo status quo:** Nancy Youssef, "General Hides Gitmo Detainees," *Daily Beast*, December 15, 2015.

224 **unsubtle as Kelly was:** Charles Levinson and David Rohde, "Special Report: Pentagon Thwarts Obama's Effort to Close Guantanamo," Reuters, December 29, 2015.

225 **1 million Iraqis:** Physicians for Social Responsibility, *Body Count* (Washington, D.C., Berlin, Ottawa: International Physicians for the Prevention of Nuclear War, 2015), 15. Available at www.ippnw.de/commonFiles/pdfs/Frieden/Body_Count_first_international_edition_2015_final.pdf.

225 **more intrusive Security State:** Spencer Ackerman, "Top U.S. Spy: Don't Blame Us for Boston," *Wired*, April 25, 2013.

226 **Representative Steve King:** David M. Herszenhorn, "Delegates Visit Moscow for Insight on Boston Attack," *New York Times*, June 2, 2013.

226 **purging the Islamophobic training material:** Robert Spencer, "The Human Cost of Jihad Denial," *FrontPage*, May 1, 2013. The piece ends with a plea: "How many more have to die before the bloody legacy of Farhana Khera, John Brennan, Spencer Ackerman and Barack Obama is decisively rejected?"

226 **"put on weight":** Unbylined, "GOP Rep.: 'No Crisis' at Gitmo, Detainees Have 'Put on Weight,'" MSNBC, May 26, 2013.

226 **Pompeo's point was to dictate:** Rep. Mike Pompeo, "The Silence of Muslim Leaders Is Deafening," 113th Congress, 1st Session, *Congressional Record* 159, no. 82, June 11, 2013. Kevin Eckstrom, "Muslim Leaders: We Stand Against Terrorism," Religion News Service/*Washington Post*, April 19, 2013. CAIR California, "Boston Bombing: Islam Condemns Violence, Muslim Leader Reiterates," April 19, 2013.

226 **"Is the Boston killer eligible":** Donald Trump (@realdonaldtrump), "Is the Boston killer eligible for Obama Care to bring him back to health?" Twitter, April 19, 2013, 9 P.M., https://twitter.com/realdonaldtrump/status/325413682379120640, accessed March 21, 2020.

227 **thwart FOIA lawsuits:** Spencer Ackerman, "No Looking Back: The CIA Torture Report's Aftermath," *Guardian*, September 11, 2016. Jason Leopold, "GOP Senator Wants to Make Sure the Full Torture Report Never Sees the Light of Day," *Vice*, January 21, 2015. Mark Mazzetti and Matt Apuzzo, "Classified Report on the CIA's Secret Prisons Is Caught in Limbo," *New York Times*, November 9, 2015.

227 **misstatements "Flynn facts":** Nicholas Schmidle, "Michael Flynn, General Chaos," *The New Yorker*, February 18, 2017.

228 **Saudi royal family:** In Maqdisi's 1989 work *al-Kawashif al-Jaliyya fi Kufr al-Dawla al-Saudiyya*. The author wishes to thank Maqdisi scholar Joas Wagemakers for this reference and this timeline.

228 **Camp Bucca's commanding officer:** Michael Daly, "ISIS Leader: 'See You in New York,'" *Daily Beast*, June 14, 2014.

228 **Their theology was heavy:** Hassan Hassan, "The Sectarianism of the Islamic State: Ideological Roots and Political Context," Carnegie Endowment for International Peace, June 13, 2016.

228 **Baghdadi marched his:** Ehab Zahriyeh, "How ISIL Became a Major Force with Only a Few Thousand Fighters," Al Jazeera, June 19, 2014.

229 **Committed jihadis were apoplectic:** Reuters staff, "Al Qaeda Splinter Group Declares Islamic 'Caliphate,'" Reuters, June 29, 2014.

229 **"The gangs of al-Baghdadi":** Associated Press via *Guardian* liveblog, June 30, 2014, www.theguardian.com/world/middle-east-live/2014/jun/30/isis-declares-caliphate -in-iraq-and-syria-live-updates, accessed March 26, 2020.

229 "accept the Islamic project": Hassan, "The Sectarianism of the Islamic State," citing Michael Weiss and Hassan Hassan, *ISIS: Inside the Army of Terror* (New York: Regan Arts, 2016), 222.

230 The 9/11 hijackers: Peter Bergen and Swati Pandey, "The Madrassa Myth," *New York Times*, June 14, 2005.

230 "The actions in New York": Shiv Malik, Mustafa Khalili, Spencer Ackerman, and Ali Younes, "How ISIS Crippled al-Qaeda," *Guardian*, June 10, 2015. Malik, Khalili, Younes, and Ackerman, "The Race to Save Peter Kassig," *Guardian*, December 18, 2014. Mike Giglio, *Shatter the Nations: ISIS and The War for The Caliphate* (New York: PublicAffairs, 2019), 80, 89.

231 twenty-three hundred U.S.-made Humvees: Nicola Smith, "ISIS Waterboards Hostages Who Try to Escape, Says Cantlie," *Times* (London), October 26, 2014. Rukmini Callimachi, "The Horror Before the Beheadings," *New York Times*, October 25, 2014. Agence France-Presse, "Iraq Lost 2,300 Humvee Armoured Vehicles in Mosul: PM," May 31, 2015.

231 "jayvee squad [in] Lakers uniforms": David Remnick, "Going the Distance," *The New Yorker*, January 20, 2014. Mark Landler and Eric Schmitt, "U.S. Scrambles to Help Iraq Fight Off Militants as Iraq Is Threatened," *New York Times*, June 12, 2014.

232 a tacit accommodation: Spencer Ackerman, "U.S. Warplanes Begin Airstrikes on ISIS in Iraqi City of Tikrit," *Guardian*, May 25, 2015.

232 an exhausted United States: Author's interview with Ben Rhodes, July 13, 2020. Rhodes credits Dempsey, chair of the Joint Chiefs of Staff, as the architect of By, With, and Through. Interviews with senior U.S. diplomats for Iraq contemporaneous with the ISIS campaign corroborate Rhodes, December 18 and 22, 2020, though they also credit then-general Lloyd Austin for embracing the concept.

232 with the aid of Joe Biden: Loveday Morris and Liz Sly, "Iran Endorses Haidar al-Abadi as Iraq's New Prime Minister, Spurning Nouri al-Maliki," *Washington Post*, August 12, 2014. Michael R. Gordon, "New Iraqi Premier Backs U.S. Air Campaign, within Limits," *New York Times*, September 25, 2014.

232 count its membership: Spencer Ackerman, "U.S. Has Trained 'Four or Five' Syrian Fighters against ISIS, Top General Testifies," *Guardian*, September 16, 2015.

233 recast his humiliation: Michael Flynn, "The Military Fired Me for Calling Our Enemies Radical Jihadis," *New York Post*, July 9, 2016.

233 Petraeus's army mentor and surge architect: Ashley Killough, "Strong Reaction to Obama Statement: 'ISIL Is Not Islamic,'" CNN, September 11, 2014. Senate Armed Services Committee, "Global Challenges and the U.S. National Security Strategy," January 27, 2015, available at www.armed-services.senate.gov/hearings/15-01-27-global-challenges-and-us-national-security-strategy.

234 "its profound distrust": Moni Basu, "A Gunman Killed His Brother. Now Farris Barakat Is on an American Journey," CNN, February 9, 2018. Margaret Talbot, "The Story of a Hate Crime," *The New Yorker*, June 22, 2015.

NOTES

234 67 percent rise in hate crimes: Mazin Sidahmed, "FBI Reports Hate Crimes against Muslims Surged by 67 Percent in 2015," *Guardian*, November 14, 2016.

234 scheduled CVE summit: Spencer Ackerman, "Documents Support Fears of Muslim Surveillance by Obama-Era Program," *Guardian*, March 16, 2017.

235 September 2014 press conference: Pamela Constable, "U.S. Muslim Leaders Denounce Islamic State, Pledge to Dissuade Youth from Joining," *Washington Post*, September 10, 2014.

235 convinced her to convert: Rukmini Callimachi, "ISIS and the Lonely American," *New York Times*, June 28, 2015.

235 counterterrorism chief, Michael B. Steinbach: Eric Lichtblau, "FBI Steps Up Use of Stings in ISIS Cases," *New York Times*, June 7, 2016.

235 Comey and his allies: Spencer Ackerman, "James Comey Remained at Justice Department as Monitoring Went On," *Guardian*, June 27, 2013.

235–236 ISIS's social-media presence: Pierre Thomas, Mike Levine, Jack Date, and Jack Cloherty, "ISIS: Potentially 'Thousands' of Online Followers inside U.S. Homeland, FBI Chief Warns," ABC News, May 7, 2015.

236 Before a judge: Spencer Ackerman and Danny Yadron, "FBI May Have Found Way to Unlock San Bernardino Shooter's iPhone without Apple," *Guardian*, March 22, 2016.

237 south of Paris: Adam Nossiter, Aurelien Breeden, and Katrin Bennhold, "Three Teams of Coordinated Attackers Carried Out Assault on Paris, Officials Say; Hollande Blames ISIS," *New York Times*, November 14, 2015. "Three Hours in Paris, Moment by Moment," *New York Times*, updated November 9, 2016, www.nytimes.com/interactive /2015/11/13/world/europe/paris-shooting-attacks.html, accessed April 3, 2020.

237 white nativist appetite: Adam Weinstein, "Breitbart.com Is Sure This Adidas Shirt Is an Islamo-Mexican Terror Rug," *Gawker*, July 10, 2014.

237 "The front line with ISIS": W. James Antle III, "How Immigration Became the Latest Front in the War on Terror," *Washington Examiner*, January 23, 2016. Sessions/Cruz press release, "Chairmen Sessions, Cruz Ask Feds to Provide Immigration Histories of Terrorists Operating Inside U.S.," August 12, 2015. Southern Poverty Law Center, "Stephen Miller's Affinity for White Nationalism Revealed in Leaked Emails," November 12, 2019.

238 migrants from "Somalia": Stephen Dinan and Dave Boyer, "U.S. General Warns Ebola Could Cross Southern Border," *Washington Times*, October 9, 2014. Posture Statement of General John F. Kelly, USMC, Commander, U.S. Southern Command, before the 114th Congress Senate Armed Services Committee, March 12, 2015. Nick Carey, "U.S. Republicans Look to Gain Election Ground on Ebola," Reuters, October 21, 2014. Tom Jacobs, "Ebola Fears Helped the GOP in 2014 Election," *Pacific Standard*, June 14, 2017.

238 CIA's Zarqawi targeters: Spencer Ackerman, "Obama Maintains al-Qaida and ISIS Are 'One and the Same' despite Evidence of Schism," *Guardian*, October 2, 2014.

238 Sanders called for a vote: Statement of Bernie Sanders on Iraq and Syria, September 8, 2014. The air strikes began on August 8, sixty days shy of the limit set for unilateral military strikes under the 1973 War Powers Resolution.

240 **Brennan's deputy Avril Haines:** Carol Morello, "U.S. Surpasses Syrian Refugee Goal Set by Obama, Expects More Next Year," *Washington Post*, September 27, 2016. Spencer Ackerman, "The Proxy War over a Top Biden Adviser," *Daily Beast*, July 7, 2020.

240 **"Texas will not accept any Syrian":** Ashley Fantz and Ben Brumfield, "More Than Half the Nation's Governors Say Syrian Refugees Not Welcome," CNN, November 19, 2015.

241 **sink Iranian boat swarms:** Daniela Diaz and Jeremy Diamond, "Donald Trump on Iran Ship Behavior: 'They Will Be Shot out of the Water,'" CNN, September 9, 2016.

242 **analysis applies equally:** "Full Text: Donald Trump Announces a Presidential Bid," *Washington Post*, June 16, 2015. Eliza Relman, "The 25 Women Who Have Accused Donald Trump of Sexual Misconduct," *Business Insider*, October 9, 2019. Daniel Denvir, *All-American Nativism: How the Bipartisan War on Immigrants Explains Politics as We Know It* (London and New York: Verso 2020), 256.

242 **Stephen Miller was so excited:** Imtiyaz Delawaya, "What ABC News Footage Shows of 9/11 Celebrations," ABC News, December 4, 2015. Nick Gass, "Trump: We Have to Take Out ISIL Members' Families," *Politico*, December 2, 2015. Tim Haines, "Trump's Updated ISIS Plan: 'Bomb the Shit Out of Them,' Send in Exxon to Rebuild," *Real Clear Politics*, November 13, 2015. Matthew Weaver and Spencer Ackerman, "Trump Says Torture 'Absolutely' Works but Experts Warn of Its 'Potentially Existential' Costs," *Guardian*, January 25, 2017. David Weigel, "Trump: Maybe Cuba Should Take Over Guantanamo 'and Reimburse Us,'" *Washington Post*, February 23, 2016. Tom McCarthy, "Donald Trump: I'd Bring Back 'a Hell of a Lot Worse than Waterboarding,'" *Guardian*, February 7, 2016. Nick Gass, "Trump: 'Absolutely No Choice' but to Close Mosques," *Politico*, November 18, 2015. Jessica Taylor, "Trump Calls for 'Total and Complete Shutdown of Muslims Entering' the U.S.," NPR, December 7, 2015. Robert Costa, "Top Sessions Aide Joins Trump Campaign," *Washington Post*, January 25, 2016.

242 **Even Bill O'Reilly was discomfited:** Jeremy Diamond, "Trump Lavishes Praise on 'Leader' Putin," CNN, December 18, 2015. Sophie Tatum, "Trump Defends Putin: 'You Think Our Country's So Innocent?'" CNN, February 6, 2017.

243 **"the radical right suddenly felt":** Joe Helm, "This White Nationalist Who Shoved a Trump Protester May Be the Next David Duke," *Washington Post*, April 12, 2016. Adrian Florido, "The White Nationalist Origins of the Term 'Alt-Right'—and the Debate around It," NPR, November 27, 2016. Cassie Miller and Howard Graves, "When the 'Alt-Right' Hit the Streets: Far Right Political Rallies in the Trump Era," Southern Poverty Law Center, August 10, 2020.

243 **"Donald the Dove":** Maureen Dowd, "Donald the Dove, Hillary the Hawk," *New York Times*, April 30, 2012.

244 **Sean MacFarland, a Petraeus-favored officer:** Spencer Ackerman, "U.S. Military Commander in Iraq and Syria Rejects GOP Pledges to 'Carpet-Bomb' ISIS," *Guardian*, February 1, 2016.

244 **self-reflection from signatories:** "Open Letter on Donald Trump from GOP National Security Leaders," *War on the Rocks*, March 2, 2016. David E. Sanger and Maggie

Haberman, "50 GOP Officials Warn Trump Would Put Nation's Security 'At Risk,'" *New York Times*, August 8, 2016.

244 **"tough and smart"**: Donald J. Trump (@realdonaldtrump), "A suicide bomber has just killed U.S. troops in Afghanistan. When will our leaders get tough and smart. We are being led to slaughter!" Twitter, December 21, 2015, 1:08 P.M., https://twitter.com /realdonaldtrump/status/679000573241393154?lang=en, accessed April 22, 2020.

246 **BLM cofounder Patrisse Khan-Cullors**: Fernando Alfonso III, "4Chan Pranksters Are Behind Petition to Label Black Lives Matter a Terrorist Organization," *Forbes*, July 12, 2016. Patrisse Khan-Cullors and Asha Bandele, *When They Call You a Terrorist: A Black Lives Matter Memoir* (New York: St. Martin's Press, 2017), 7.

246 **"I will never let you down"**: Eric Bradner, "Trump Praises 9/11 Truther's 'Amazing' Reputation," CNN, December 2, 2015.

247 **played "Real American"**: Ben Schreckinger, "A Tale of Two Rallies: My Summer with Bernie and Trump," *Politico*, August 23, 2015.

247 **marathon Benghazi session**: Jon Cohen and Aaron Blake, "Hillary Clinton Reaches New Heights of Political Popularity," *Washington Post*, January 23, 2013.

248 **Saudi Arabia wasn't paying**: Andrew Prokop, "Read Bernie Sanders' Speech on Democratic Socialism in the United States" *Vox,* November 19, 2015.

249 **"part of our homeland security"**: Mohamed Hassan, "Muslim Americans Express Disappointment over 2016 Debate Rhetoric Tying Muslims to Terrorism," NBC News, October 10, 2016. Ryan Teague Beckwith, "Transcript: Read Hillary Clinton's Speech on Fighting ISIS," *Time*, November 19, 2015.

249 **"Hillary Clinton's more muscular brand"**: Mark Landler, "How Hillary Clinton Became a Hawk," *New York Times Magazine*, April 21, 2016.

249 **explicitly prohibiting use**: Josh Gerstein, "Clinton Private Email Violated 'Clear Cut' State Dept. Rules," *Politico*, March 5, 2015.

250 **Russian intelligence sent messages**: Robert S. Mueller, *Report on the Investigation into Russian Interference in the 2016 Presidential Election* (Washington, D.C.: US Department of Justice, 2019), 49 (hereafter "Mueller Report").

250 **"a grave counterintelligence threat"**: Sharon LaFraniere and Julian E. Barnes, "Report Details Manafort's Ties During 2016 Trump Campaign to a Russian Agent," *New York Times*, August 18, 2020.

250 **from Russia to Clinton**: Mueller Report, 67–120.

251 **stolen DNC user credentials**: Ellen Nakashima, "Russian Government Hackers Penetrated DNC, Stole Opposition Research on Trump," *Washington Post*, June 14, 2016.

251 **Assange denied it**: Mueller Report, 36–49. Raffi Katchadourian, "Julian Assange, a Man without a Country," *The New Yorker*, August 14, 2017. Kevin Poulsen and Spencer Ackerman, "'Lone DNC Hacker' Guccifer 2.0 Slipped Up and Revealed He Was a Russian Intelligence Officer," *Daily Beast*, March 22, 2018.

251 **impersonated an American Muslim group**: Spencer Ackerman, "Russia Is Exploiting American White Supremacy Over and Over Again," *Daily Beast,* October 9, 2018.

Kevin Poulsen, Ben Collins, and Spencer Ackerman, "Russia Used Facebook Events to Organize Anti-Immigrant Rallies on U.S. Soil," *Daily Beast,* September 13, 2017. Kevin Poulsen, Spencer Ackeman, and Ben Collins, "Russians Impersonated Real American Muslims to Stir Up Chaos on Facebook and Instagram," *Daily Beast,* September 27, 2017.

251 **Tens of millions of American accounts:** Mueller Report, 26.

252 **consigliere Roger Stone:** Roger Stone, "Dear Hillary: DNC Hack Solved, So Stop Blaming Russia," *Breitbart,* August 5, 2016.

252 **Downer reported the conversation:** Sharon LaFraniere, Mark Mazetti, and Matt Apuzzo, "How the Russia Inquiry Began: A Campaign Aide, Drinks and Talks of Political Dirt," *New York Times,* December 30, 2017.

252 **When Page wondered:** Department of Justice Inspector General, "A Review of Various Actions by the Federal Bureau of Investigation and Department of Justice in Advance of the 2016 Election," 404.

252 **A veteran of the office:** Spencer Ackerman, "'The FBI Is Trumpland': Anti-Clinton Atmosphere Spurred Leaking, Sources Say," *Guardian,* November 4, 2016. Matt Apuzzo, Michael S. Schmidt, Adam Goldman, and William S. Rashbaum, "FBI's Email Disclosure Broke a Pattern Followed Even This Summer," *New York Times,* November 1, 2016. Wayne Barrett, "Meet Donald Trump's Top FBI Fanboy," *Daily Beast,* November 3, 2016.

253 **Comey loudly drove:** Mark Landler and Eric Lichtblau, "FBI Director James Comey Recommends No Charges for Hillary Clinton on Email," *New York Times,* July 5, 2016.

254 **issued a stronger warning:** Greg Miller, Ellen Nakashima, and Adam Entous, "Obama's Secret Struggle to Punish Russia for Putin's Election Assault," *Washington Post,* June 23, 2017. Adam Entous, Ellen Nakashima, and Greg Miller, "Secret CIA Assessment Says Russia Was Trying to Help Trump Win White House," *Washington Post,* December 9, 2016.

254 **"Islam is a political ideology":** Ismat Sarah Mangla, "'Islam Is a 'Malignant Cancer': The Hateful Rhetoric of Trump's New National Security Adviser," *Quartz,* November 18, 2016. Peter Baker and Matthew Rosenberg, "Michael Flynn Was Paid to Represent Turkey's Interests during Trump Campaign," *New York Times,* March 10, 2017. Ken Dilanian, "Russians Paid Mike Flynn $45,000 for Moscow Speech, Documents Show," NBN News, March 16, 2017.

255 **Assange DM'd Guccifer 2.0:** Mueller Report, 45.

255 **"Russian Roulette with a semi-auto":** Michael Anton, writing under the pretentious pseudonym Publius Decius Mus, "The Flight 93 Election," *Claremont Review of Books,* September 5, 2016.

Chapter Eight: Making the War on Terror Great Again

258 **"We're locked in":** Author's interview with Adham Hassoun, July 5, 2020. Author's interview with Andy Stepanian, July 9, 2020.

259 **ICE agents waited:** Julie Carey, "ICE Agents Arrest Men Leaving Fairfax County Church Shelter," NBC News-4, February 15, 2017.

259 **By March 2019 ICE's prisons:** Spencer Ackerman, "ICE Is Detaining 50,000 People, an All-Time High," *Daily Beast,* March 8, 2019.

259 **Trump never fulfilled his promise:** At the time of this writing, if this occurred, it hasn't leaked yet, and a *lot* about the Trump administration's national security policies has leaked.

259 **Mariee was dead:** Human Rights Watch, "In the Freezer: Abusive Conditions for Women and Children in US Immigration Holding Cells," February 28, 2018. Todd J. Gilman, "'My Daughter Is Gone': House Hearing on 'Kids in Cages' Spotlights Infant Who Died after ICE Custody," *Dallas Morning News,* July 10, 2019. Taylor Dolven and Kathleen Caulderwood, "This Toddler Got Sick in ICE Detention. Two Months Later She Was Dead," *Vice,* August 27, 2018. Julia Webster, "Her 19-Month-Old Daughter Died after Being Held in an ICE Facility. Here's What Yazmin Juarez Told Congress," *Time,* July 11, 2019.

260 **having "vomited feces":** Monsy Alvarado, Ashley Balcerzak, Stacey Barchenger, et al., "Deaths in Custody. Sexual Violence. Hunger Strikes. What We Uncovered inside ICE Facilities across the US," *USA Today,* December 19, 2019.

260 **237 reports of sexual abuse:** Alvarado et al., "Deaths in Custody," *USA Today,* December 22, 2019. Alice Speri, "Detained, Then Violated," *The Intercept,* April 11, 2018. Robert Moore, "Gay, Transgender Detainees Allege Abuse at ICE Facility in New Mexico," *Washington Post,* March 25, 2019. Victoria Lopez and Sandra Park, "ICE Detention Center Says It's Not Responsible for Staff's Sexual Abuse of Detainees," ACLU, November 6, 2018. American Oversight, "DHS Records Relating to Family Separation from 2017 to 2019," Records Received from January 2020 to March 2020, 636, www.americanoversight.org/document/dhs-records-relating-to-family-separation-from-2018-to-2019, accessed May 28, 2020.

260 **the "uterus collector":** Project South/Institute for the Elimination of Poverty & Genocide, whistleblower complaint of Dawn Wooten, September 14, 2020.

261 **an *Arizona Republic* reporter:** Michael Kiefer, "First Peek: Immigrant Children Flood Detention Center," *Arizona Republic,* June 18, 2014.

261 **the practice began under Kelly:** Daniella Diaz, "Kelly: DHS Is Considering Separating Undocumented Children from Their Parents at the Border," CNN, March 7, 2017. Michael Garcia Bochenek, "Trump's Family Separation Affected 'Thousands' More Children Than Previously Known," Human Rights Watch, January 18, 2019.

261 **suffering chest pains:** Office of the Inspector General, Department of Health and Human Services, "Care Provider Facilities Described Challenges Addressing Mental Health Needs of Children in HHS Custody," September 2019. Available at https://oig.hhs.gov/oei/reports/oei-09-18-00431.asp.

262 **"foster care, or whatever":** "Transcript: White House Chief of Staff John Kelly's Interview with NPR," NPR, May 11, 2018. Juan Guzman, "What I Witnessed at Casa Padre Detention Center," Alliance for Childrens' Rights, July 24, 2018. Jasmine

Aguilera, "Everything You Need to Know about the Status of Family Separation at the U.S. Border, Which Isn't Nearly Over," *Time*, September 20, 2019. Caitlin Dickerson, "Parents of 545 Children Separated at the Border Cannot Be Found," *New York Times*, October 21, 2020.

263 **Six Senate Democrats:** Roll Call Vote, 115th Congress, Second Session, On The Confirmation of Gina Haspel to be Director, Central Intelligence Agency, May 17, 2018, www.senate.gov/legislative/LIS/roll_call_lists/roll_call_vote_cfm.cfm?congress =115&session=2&vote=00101.

264 **trying to obtain a visa:** Spencer Ackerman, "Iraqis Lament Trump Travel Ban that Disregards Their Service to America," *Guardian,* January 29, 2017.

264 **Bolton emerged as an obstacle:** Aaron Klein, "McMaster Worked at Think Tank Backed by Soros-Funded Group that Helped Obama Sell Iran Nuclear Deal," *Breitbart*, August 7, 2017. Justin Baragona, "Lou Dobbs Slams Staunch Conservative John Bolton as 'Tool for Radical Dems,'" *Daily Beast*, January 27, 2020.

265 **Obama made no move:** Barack Obama, "Remarks by the President on the Administration's Approach to Counterterrorism," December 6, 2016, transcript available at https:// obamawhitehouse.archives.gov/the-press-office/2016/12/06/remarks-president -administrations-approach-counterterrorism. Spencer Ackerman, "Obama Will Not Restrict Drone Strike 'Playbook' before Trump Takes Office," *Guardian*, November 15, 2016.

266 **"They lost Ryan":** Spencer Ackerman, "Eight-Year-Old American Girl 'Killed in Yemen Raid Approved by Trump,'" *Guardian*, February 1, 2017. Abby Phillip, "Trump Passes Blame for Yemen Raid to His Generals: 'They Lost Ryan,'" *Washington Post*, February 28, 2017. Cynthia McFadden, William Arkin, and Tim Uehlinger, "How the Trump Team's First Military Raid in Yemen Went Wrong," NBC, October 1, 2017. Bureau of Investigative Journalism, www.thebureauinvestigates.com/drone -war/data/yemen-reported-us-covert-actions-2017#strike-4397, accessed May 19, 2020.

266 **authority for lethal air strikes:** Charlie Savage and Eric Schmitt, "Trump Poised to Drop Some Limits on Drone Strikes and Commando Raids," *New York Times*, September 21, 2017.

266 **air force statistics:** Spencer Ackerman and Sune Engel Rasmussen, "36 ISIS Militants Killed in US 'Mother of All Bombs' Attack, Afghan Ministry Says," *Guardian*, April 14, 2017.

267 **"You're going to say":** Spencer Ackerman and Sabrina Siddiqui, "Donald Trump Speech at CIA Memorial Risks Fueling Intelligence Feud," *Guardian*, January 21, 2017. Philip Rucker, John Wagner, and Greg Miller, "Trump, in CIA Visit, Attacks Media for Coverage of His Inaugural Crowds," *Washington Post*, January 21, 2017.

267 **"sycophantic and obsequious":** Susan Glasser, "Mike Pompeo, the Secretary of Trump," *The New Yorker*, August 19, 2019.

267 **Gina Haspel, the avatar:** Brigitte Gabriel, ACT for America, web.archive.org/web /20170610105418/https://www.actforamerica.org/bgeoy, accessed May 17, 2020. Mark

Mazetti, "New Head of CIA's Clandestine Service Is Picked, as Acting Chief Is Passed Over," *New York Times*, May 7, 2013.

267 **welcomed WikiLeaks' campaign:** Michael Pompeo, "Director Pompeo Delivers Remarks at CSIS," CIA, April 13, 2017. Andrew Kaczynski, "CIA Director Mike Pompeo Repeatedly Cited WikiLeaks to Attack Clinton during Campaign," CNN, April 24, 2017. *United States of America v. Julian Paul Assange*, indictment (Virginia, District Court for the Eastern District of Virginia, March 6, 2018), https://www.justice.gov/opa/press-release/file/1153486/download, accessed February 24, 2021. Department of Justice Office of Public Affairs, "WikiLeaks Founder Julian Assange Charged in 18-Count Superseding Indictment," press release no. 19-575, May 23, 2019, www.justice.gov/opa/pr/wikileaks-founder-julian-assange-charged-18-count-superseding-indictment, accessed February 24, 2021.

267 **as Trump reviewed footage:** Greg Jaffe, "For Trump and His Generals, 'Victory' Has Different Meanings," *Washington Post*, April 5, 2018.

268 **"The big problem":** Spencer Ackerman, "Trump Ramped Up Drone Strikes in America's Shadow Wars," *Daily Beast*, November 25, 2018. In a later piece—Spencer Ackerman and Matt Bors, "The Truth about Trump's Drone War: 'All I Saw Was Death,'" *Daily Beast*, May 26, 2019—I cite that by the end of 2018, Trump's totals rose to 253. But I've lost my notes for that piece and think it's safer to stand by my total in "Ramped Up Drone Strikes." As well, in the cartoon piece, I erroneously mistransposed the earlier 238 *Trump* total to *Obama*. It's my mistake, not Matt Bors's, and we've corrected it in *The Nib*, where it was also published.

268 **war in Somalia:** Stanley McChrystal, *My Share of The Task: A Memoir* (New York: Portfolio/Penguin, 2013), 250. Author's conversation with House staffer, June 13, 2018.

269 **AFRICOM knew it:** Christina Goldbaum, "Strong Evidence that U.S. Special Operations Forces Massacred Civilians in Somalia," *Daily Beast*, November 29, 2017. John Vandiver, "AFRICOM Ends 2019 with Record Number of Strikes in Somalia," *Stars & Stripes*, December 30, 2019. Hamza Mohamed, "A Family Mourns as U.S. Drone Attacks Continue," Al Jazeera, April 1, 2020. "Somalia: Zero Accountability as Civilian Deaths Mount from U.S. Air Strikes," Amnesty International, April 1, 2020. Nick Turse, "U.S. Military Is Severely Undercounting Civilian Casualties in Somalia," *The Intercept*, February 25, 2020.

269 **fight West African jihadists:** Robbie Gramer and Chloe Havadas, "Coup Plotters in Mali Were Trained by U.S. Military," *Foreign Policy*, August 21, 2020.

269–270 **Sergeant La David Johnson:** Spencer Ackerman, "Slain U.S. Soldier Was Missing for Over Two Days," *Daily Beast*, October 7, 2017. Helene Cooper, Thomas Gibbons-Neff, and Eric Schmitt, "Military Inquiry Finds Soldiers Were Unprepared in Deadly Niger Ambush," *New York Times*, May 10, 2018.

270 **"General Kelly needs counseling":** Amanda Holpuch, "Trump Bickers with Soldier's Widow over Condolence Call," *Guardian*, October 24, 2017. Anne Gearan and Kristine Phillips, "Fallen Soldier's Mother: 'Trump Did Disrespect My Son,'" *Washington Post*, October 18, 2017. Alex Daugherty, "Frederica Wilson Never Got an Apology from John Kelly. She Got Nooses from Critics," *Miami Herald*, December 10, 2018.

NOTES

271 **U.S.–Russian military:** Spencer Ackerman, "White House 'Muslim Ban' Man Pushes for Even More Power," *Daily Beast,* June 2, 2017. Ackerman, "White House Official Floated Withdrawing U.S. Forces to Please Putin," *Daily Beast,* January 10, 2018. Ackerman, "Mike Flynn Had a Plan to Work with Russia. It Wasn't Exactly Legal," *Daily Beast,* June 7, 2017.

272 **The Taliban could be beaten:** Kim Sengupta, "Exclusive: Blackwater Founder's Plan to Privatize America's $76 Billion, 17-Year War in Afghanistan," *Independent,* July 10, 2018.

272 **Flynn had assured:** Spencer Ackerman and Erin Banco, "Mike Flynn Asked Russian for Alliance against 'Radical Islamists' on Infamous Phone Call," *Daily Beast,* May 29, 2020. Spencer S. Hsu, Devlin Barrett, and Matt Zapotsky, "Justice Department Moves to Drop Case Against Michael Flynn," *Washington Post,* May 7, 2020.

273 **redoubt against the nativists:** H. R. McMaster and Gary Cohn, "America First Doesn't Mean America Alone," *Wall Street Journal,* May 30, 2017.

274 **announced the escalation:** Kimberley Dozier and Spencer Ackerman, "Team Trump Worried He'll Change His Mind Again on Afghanistan War Plan," *Daily Beast,* August 21, 2017.

275 **remarkable confidence from someone:** Maj. Thomas D. Arnold and Maj. Nicolas Fiore, "Five Operational Lessons from the Battle for Mosul," *Military Review,* January–February 2019. Martin Chulov, "The Fall of Raqqa: Hunting the Last Jihadists in ISIS' Capitol of Cruelty," *Guardian,* October 6, 2017. Jason Burke, "Rise and Fall of ISIS: Its Dream of a Caliphate Is Over, So What Now?" *Guardian/Observer,* October 21, 2017. Tim Arango and Michael R. Gordon, "Iraqi Prime Minister Arrives in Mosul to Declare Victory over ISIS," *New York Times,* July 9, 2017. Mike Giglio, *Shatter the Nations: ISIS and the War for the Caliphate* (New York: PublicAffairs, 2019), 177–278. Amnesty International, "Iraq: New Reports Place Mosul Civilian Death Toll at More Than Ten Times Official Estimates," December 20, 2017. Jared Malsin, "A U.S. Commander's Year on the Front Line against ISIS in Iraq and Syria," *Time,* September 7, 2017.

276 **Multiple lawsuits did not dissuade:** Trudy Ring, "Trump Sticking with Trans Military Ban," *The Advocate,* March 23, 2018.

277 **after Mattis's departure:** Richard Gonzales and Tom Bowman, "Pentagon Considers Canceling Program that Recruits Immigrant Soldiers," NPR, July 3, 2017. Javonte Anderson, "'I'm Just Overwhelmed': Deported Army Veteran Miguel Perez Jr. Says after Being Granted Citizenship," *Chicago Tribune,* October 4, 2019. Alex Horton, "The Military Is Kicking Out Foreign Recruits—for Having Foreign Ties," *Washington Post,* July 30, 2019. Dave Phillips, "Army Suspends Its Purge of Immigrant Recruits," *New York Times,* August 9, 2018. Meghann Myers, "ICE Is Supposed to Consider Service When Deporting Veterans. It Hasn't Been," *Military Times,* June 12, 2019.

277 **the administration manufactured:** Linda Qiu, "Border Crossings Have Been Declining for Years, Despite Claims of a 'Crisis of Illegal Immigration,'" *New York Times,* June 20, 2018.

277 Trump also lied: Elana Schor, "Trump Concedes 'No Proof' of Middle Easterners in Caravan," *Politico*, October 23, 2018.

277 the nebulous mission: Pentagon pool report, "Remarks by Secretary Mattis at an Armed Forces Full Honor Arrival Welcoming Republic of Korea Minister of National Defense Jeong to the Pentagon," October 31, 2018, available at www.defense.gov/Newsroom/Transcripts/Transcript/Article/1678582/remarks-by-secretary-mattis-at-an-armed-forces-full-honor-arrival-welcoming-rep. Associated Press, "Mattis Visits Border Troops, Defends Use of Military on U.S.-Mexico Line," November 14, 2018.

278 reminiscent of 2002: John Walcott, "Officials Doubt Mike Pompeo's Claim that Iran Is Collaborating with al-Qaeda," *Time*, May 21, 2019.

279 Security Staters like Jim Clapper: Spencer Ackerman and Kimberly Dozier, "Bolton's Hawkish Syria Plan Backfired, Pushing Trump to Get Out," *Daily Beast*, December 22, 2018. Ackerman, "Trump Finally Gets the National Security Adviser McMaster Tried to Prevent," *Daily Beast*, March 22, 2018. Mark Landler, Helene Cooper, and Eric Schmitt, "Trump to Withdraw U.S. Forces from Syria, Declaring, 'We Have Won' against ISIS,'" *New York Times*, December 19, 2018. Ackerman, "U.S. Officials Try to Slow Trump's 'Everybody Out of Syria' Order," *Daily Beast*, December 19, 2018.

279 "participation in hostage-taking": Spencer Ackerman and James LaPorta, "Detention Camps on Military Bases 'Smacks of Totalitarianism,' Troops Say," *Daily Beast*, June 25, 2018. Defense Department press release, "Statement on Request of Department of Homeland Security for Assistance," May 22, 2019.

280 McGurk told an Abu Dhabi conference: Ryan Browne, Holmes Lybrand, and Tara Subramaniam, "Fact Checking Trump's Claim that Kurds Are Releasing ISIS Prisoners on Purpose," CNN, October 14, 2019. *Middle East Eye* staff and agencies, "American Soldiers Pelted with Fruit and Vegetables as They Exit Northern Syria," *Middle East Eye*, October 21, 2019. Christopher Dickey and Spencer Ackerman, "The U.S. Spoiled a Deal that Might Have Saved the Kurds, Former Top Official Says," *Daily Beast*, October 13, 2019.

281 view Baghdadi as anything: Donald Trump, "Remarks of President Trump on the Death of ISIS Leader Abu Bakr al-Baghdadi," White House, October 27, 2019, transcript available at www.voanews.com/usa/text-trumps-statement-death-baghdadi. Eric Schmitt, Helene Cooper, and Julian E. Barnes, "Trump's Syria Troop Withdrawal Complicated Plans for al-Baghdadi Raid," *New York Times*, October 27, 2019. Daniel Estrin and Lama al-Arian, "Syrians Say U.S. Helicopter Fire Killed Civilians during the Raid on Baghdadi," NPR, December 3, 2019.

281 "three great warriors": Dave Phillips, "Anguish and Anger from the Navy SEALs Who Turned in Edward Gallagher," *New York Times*, December 27, 2019. Andrew Dyer, "Retired Navy SEAL Eddie Gallagher Strikes Back at SEALs Who Testified against Him," *San Diego Union-Tribune*, January 27, 2020. Ashley Parker and Dan Lamothe, "Navy Secretary Forced Out by Pentagon Chief over Handling of Navy SEAL's War Crimes Case," *Washington Post*, November 29, 2019. Asawin Suebsaeng and Spencer Ackerman, "Trump Tells Allies He Wants Absolved War Criminals to Campaign for Him," *Daily Beast*, November 25, 2019. Julie Watson and Brian Melley,

"Witnesses: Eddie Gallagher Shot Civilians in Iraq," Associated Press, June 21, 2019. John Fritze, "Trump Ramps Up Attacks on 'Deep State,' Focuses on Pentagon amid Gallagher Controversy," *USA Today*, November 27, 2019.

282 **Flynn appointee on the NSC:** Jana Winter and Elias Groll, "Here's the Memo that Blew Up the NSC," *Foreign Policy*, August 10, 2017. Damien Paletta, Robert Costa, and Josh Dawsey, "The Partisan Warrior Leading the White House's Shutdown Response," *Washington Post*, January 8, 2019. Andrew Kaczynski and Nathan McDermott, "More Anti-Muslim, Conspiratorial Tweets Emerge from Trump's Pick for Top U.N. Migration Job," CNN, March 22, 2018. Andrew Kaczynski, "HHS Official Listed Work for Anti-Islam Show, Conspiracy Website on Resume," CNN, June 22, 2018. Andrew Kaczynski, "Top Trump Appointee at Veterans Affairs Spread Conspiracy Theories, Made Anti-Muslim Comments," CNN, July 24, 2018. Josh Rogin, "New USAID Religious-Freedom Adviser Has History of Anti-Islam Comments," *Washington Post*, May 27, 2020. Eli Rosenberg and Amar Nadhir, "After Drubbing by Media, Trump's Ambassador to the Netherlands Apologizes for Anti-Muslim Remarks," *Washington Post*, January 12, 2008.

283 **Smear campaigns circulated:** Amanda Seitz, "Photograph Does Not Show Rep. Omar with a Gun at a Military Camp," Associated Press, August 22, 2019. Lauren Aratani, "How Trump Distorts Facts to Make Ilhan Omar Seem Like an Enemy to the U.S.," *Guardian*, July 18, 2019. Lateshia Beachum, "Rep. Ilhan Omar Wants Compassion for Trump Supporter Convicted of Making Death Threats against Her," *Washington Post*, November 19, 2019.

283 **singled out Omar:** Tom McCarthy, "Trump Rally Chants 'Send Her Back' after President Attacks Ilhan Omar," *Guardian,* July 18, 2019. Bianca Quilantan and David Cohen, "Trump Tells Dem Congresswomen: Go Back Where You Came From," *Politico*, July 14, 2019.

284 **"very fine people":** Cassie Miller and Howard Graves, "When the Alt-Right Hit the Streets: Far Right Rallies in the Trump Era," Southern Poverty Law Center, August 10, 2020. "Remarks by President Trump on Infrastructure," August 15, 2017. Glenn Kessler, "The 'Very Fine People' at Charlottesville: Who Were They?" *Washington Post*, May 8, 2020.

284 **an active-duty marine:** A. C. Thompson, Ali Winston, and Jake Hanrahan, "Ranks of Notorious Hate Group Include Active-Duty Military," *ProPublica*, May 3, 2018.

284 **drove his Dodge Challenger:** Joe Heim, Ellie Silverman, T. Rees Shapiro, and Emma Brown, "One Dead as Car Strikes Crowds amid Protests of White Supremacist Gathering in Charlottesville," *Washington Post*, August 13, 2017. Ian Shapira, "The Parking Garage Beating Lasted 10 Seconds. DeAndre Harris Still Lives with the Damage," *Washington Post*, September 16, 2019. Christine Hauser, "DeAndre Harris, Beaten by White Supremacists in Charlottesville, Is Found Not Guilty of Assault," *New York Times*, March 16, 2018. Mitch Smith, "James Fields Sentenced to Life in Prison for Death of Heather Heyer in Charlottesville," *New York Times*, June 28, 2019.

284 **The leader of the Base, Rinaldo Nazzaro:** Ben Makuch, "Department of Homeland Security Confirms Neo-Nazi Leader Used to Work for It," *Vice*, February 17, 2021,

www.vice.com/en/article/epd7wa/department-of-homeland-security-confirms-neo
-nazi-leader-used-to-work-for-it.

284 **far quicker to ban jihadists:** Janet Reitman, "All-American Nazis," *Rolling Stone*, May 2, 2018.

285 **Crusius left a manifesto:** Campbell Robertson, Christopher Mele, and Sabrina Tavernise, "11 Killed in Synagogue Massacre; Suspect Charged with 29 Counts," *New York Times*, October 27, 2018. Minyvonne Burke, "What We Know about the Pipe Bomb Scare and Suspect Cesar Sayoc's Arrest," *NBC News*, October 26, 2018. Tim Arango, Nicholas Bogel-Burroughs, and Katie Benner, "Minutes before El Paso Killing, Hate-Filled Manifesto Appears Online," *New York Times*, August 3, 2019.

285 **Scheuer knew the Security State:** Michael Scheuer, "Racism, Hate, Power-Lust, and Greed Are Part of Human Nature; They Can Be Restrained, Not Ended; Trying to Do So Means War," *Non-Intervention*, July 20, 2020. Scheuer, "Trump Moves Closer to the Meaning of America First by Killing Soleimani," *Non-Intervention*, January 5, 2020. Scheuer, "Must Martial Law Be Applied against the Insurrection in 2020?" *Non-Intervention*, December 29, 2019. Scheuer, "Those Who Do Not Believe QANON Will Be Mighty Surprised," *Non-Intervention*, December 7, 2019.

287 **Running the Justice Department:** Lachlan Markay and Spencer Ackerman, "Team Trump Cooks Terror Stats for Bogus Immigration Argument," *Daily Beast*, January 16, 2018. Adam Serwer, "Jeff Sessions' Blind Eye," *The Atlantic*, April 5, 2017.

288 **Comey leaked his accounts:** Eric Tucker and Hope Yen, "AP Fact Check: Trump's Baseless Claim of Fudged NBC Tape," Associated Press, August 30, 2018.

288 **kill Section 702:** Matthew Rosenberg, Maggie Haberman, and Adam Goldman, "2 White House Officials Helped Give Nunes Intelligence Reports," *New York Times*, March 30, 2017. Spencer Ackerman and Sabrina Siddiqui, "Trump v US Intelligence: Growing Feud Puts NSA's Legislative Authority at Risk," *Guardian*, March 7, 2017.

289 **stunning amount of "overcollection":** Spencer Ackerman, "NSA Admits It Improperly Collected a Huge Amount of Americans' Call Records," *Daily Beast*, July 28, 2018.

289 **FBI's backdoor searches:** Spencer Ackerman, "Secret Court: FBI Warrantless Searches Were Illegal," *Daily Beast*, October 8, 2019. Charlie Savage, "National Security Surveillance on U.S. Soil Fell amid Scrutiny of Russia Inquiry," *New York Times*, April 30, 2020.

290 **"get the documents":** Spencer Ackerman, "Republicans Won't Say If Spying on Carter Page Was Wrong," *Daily Beast*, February 9, 2018.

291 **Mike Morell vouched:** "What They Are Saying: Widespread Praise for Gina Haspel, President Trump's Nominee for CIA Director," www.whitehouse.gov/briefings-statements/wtas-widespread-praise-gina-haspel-president-trumps-nominee-cia-director, May 2, 2018, accessed June 8, 2020.

291 **unexpectedly threatened Haspel:** Spencer Ackerman, "Gina Haspel, Trump's Nominee to Lead the CIA, 'Ran the Interrogation Program,' Former CIA Lawyer Wrote," *Daily Beast*, April 18, 2018.

292 legal wing of the #Resistance: Neema Singh Giuliani and Brian Tashman, "William Barr Helped Build America's Surveillance State," ACLU, January 9, 2019.

292 "A very decent outcome": Benjamin Wittes (@benjaminwittes), "Ok, folks, I know Barr has said some bad stuff, but let me express the perhaps unpopular view that say that this would be a very decent outcome. Barr was a very fine AG. He knows and values the department's traditions and supervised at least two special prosecutor investigations," Twitter, December 6, 2018, 2:47 P.M., https://twitter.com/benjaminwittes/status/1070766732904722434.

292 "Complete and Total EXONERATION": Mark Mazzetti and Michael S. Schmidt, "When the Mueller Investigation Ended, the Battle over Its Conclusions Began," *New York Times*, May 1, 2019.

293 "quid pro quo": Rachel Bade, Aaron C. Davis, and Matt Zapatowsky, "Sondland Acknowledges Ukraine 'Quid Pro Quo,' Implicates Trump, Pence, Pompeo and Others," *Washington Post*, November 21, 2019.

293 "necessity for vengeance": Michael Scheuer, "The Time and Necessity for Vengeance Is Upon Us," *Non-Intervention*, February 2, 2020.

294 theatrically baseless defenses: "Rep. John Ratcliffe Statement on Vote against Trump Impeachment," December 19, 2019, txktoday.com/news/rep-ratcliffe-statement-on-vote-against-trump-impeachment, accessed June 9, 2020.

294 Allies of the president: Spencer Ackerman, Sam Brodey, and Adam Rawnsley, "Devin Nunes Aide Is Leaking the Ukraine Whistleblower's Name, Sources Say," *Daily Beast*, October 28, 2019. Robert Mackey, "Republicans Accuse Colonel Vindman, a Jew Who Fled Soviet Persecution, of Dual Loyalty," *The Intercept*, October 29, 2019.

294 "full-blown national security crisis": Spencer Ackerman, Betsy Swan, Erin Banco, and Sam Stein, "Russia Is Helping Elect Trump Again, Intel Official Says," *Daily Beast*, February 20, 2020. Eddy Rodriguez, "Former CIA Director Criticizes Trump's Recent Intel Moves as a 'Virtual Decapitation of the Intelligence Community,'" *Newsweek*, February 21, 2020.

294 Grenell used his appointment: Matt Zapotosky and Shane Harris, "'Unmasking' Probe Commissioned by Barr Concludes without Charges or Any Public Report," *Washington Post*, October 13, 2020.

295 Grenell's obvious cronyism: Brooke Singman, "Newly Declassified Intel Document Noted Steele Dossier Claims Had 'Limited Corroboration,'" Fox News, June 11, 2020.

295 deemphasized threat assessments: Whistleblower complaint from Brian Murphy to the Office of the Inspector General, Department of Homeland Security, September 8, 2020, intelligence.house.gov/uploadedfiles/murphy_wb_dhs_oig_complaint9.8.20.pdf, accessed September 9, 2020.

295 "The bottom line from the White House": Spencer Ackerman, "FBI Sits on Report Detailing White-Supremacist Terror Threat," *The Daily Beast*, October 26, 2020.

296 "He dishonestly mischaracterized": Spencer Ackerman, "Democrats Working with Trumpsters to Re-Up the PATRIOT Act," *Daily Beast*, March 10, 2020. Charlie

Savage, "House to Vote on Limiting FBI Power to Collect Americans' Internet Data," *New York Times*, May 26, 2020. Davidson to author, May 29, 2020.

297 **twenty errors in each:** Office of the Inspector General, Department of Justice, "Management Advisory Memorandum for the Director of the Federal Bureau of Investigation Regarding the Execution of Woods Procedures for Applications Filed with the Foreign Intelligence Surveillance Court Relating to U.S. Persons," March 31, 2020, 8. Available at https://oig.justice.gov/sites/default/files/reports/a20047.pdf.

298 **keep Hassoun in such cages forever:** Charlie Savage, "Testing Novel Power, Trump Administration Detains Palestinian after Sentence Ends," *New York Times*, March 26, 2019. Spencer Ackerman, "Trump Is First to Use PATRIOT Act to Detain a Man Forever," *Daily Beast*, November 29, 2019.

298 **"This is the USA":** Author's interview with Adham Hassoun, May 21, 2020.

Chapter Nine: The Invisible Enemy

299 **air cover for Iraqi Shiite militias:** Renad Mansour and Faleh A. Jabar, "The Popular Mobilization Forces and Iraq's Future," Carnegie Endowment for International Peace, April 28, 2017.

300 **Iraqi militia Kata'ib Hezbollah:** Sawsan Morrar and Sam Stanton, "U.S. Contractor Killed in Iraq, Which Led to Strike on Iranian General, Buried in Sacramento," *Sacramento Bee*, January 7, 2020. Thomas Gibbons-Neff and Eric Schmitt, "Despite Vow to End 'Endless Wars,' Here's Where About 200,000 U.S. Troops Remain," *New York Times*, October 21, 2019. Anita Chabria, Laila Miller, and Sarah Parvini, "Defense Contractor from California Whose Death Sparked U.S.-Iran Conflict Is Mourned," *Los Angeles Times*, January 9, 2020.

300 **his Mar-a-Lago resort:** Spencer Ackerman, Asawin Suebsaeng, Erin Banco, and Betsy Swan, "Trump Told Mar-a-Lago Pals to Expect 'Big' Iran Action 'Soon,'" *Daily Beast,* January 3, 2020.

301 **ever-expanding target list:** Spencer Ackerman, "Leaked Audio Shows an Iranian Gambit to Control Iraq Failing," *Daily Beast*, October 5, 2018. Helene Cooper, Eric Schmitt, Maggie Haberman, and Rukmini Callimachi, "As Tensions with Iran Escalated, Trump Opted for Most Extreme Measure," *New York Times*, January 4, 2020. Philip Rucker, John Hudson, Shane Harris, and Josh Dawsey, "'Four Embassies': The Anatomy of Trump's Unfounded Claim about Iran," *Washington Post*, January 13, 2020.

301 **lack of carnage:** Jane Arraf, "The Aftermath of Iran's Missile Attack on an Iraqi Base Housing U.S. Troops," NPR, January 14, 2020. Ariel Zilber, "Iraqi Prime Minister Says Qassem Soleimani Was in Iraq to 'Discuss De-escalating Tensions between Iran and Saudis' When He Was Killed—and Claims Trump Had Asked for Help Mediating Talks after Embassy Attack," *Daily Mail*, January 5, 2020. Idrees Ali and Phil Stewart, "More than 100 U.S. Troops Diagnosed with Brain Injuries from Iran Attack," Reuters, February 10, 2020. Bobby Allyn and Jane Arraf, "In a Day of Turmoil, Repercussions of Soleimani Killing Grow More Widespread," NPR, January 5, 2020.

302 **Trump portrayed Soleimani:** "Qasem Soleimani: Strike Was to 'Stop a War,' Says Trump," BBC, January 4, 2020. Rucker, Hudson, Harris and Dawsey, "'Four Embassies.'" Spencer Ackerman, "Trump, Iran and Where the Forever War Was Always Headed," *Daily Beast,* January 7, 2020. The Pentagon's first statement after killing Soleimani spoke not of "imminent" attacks, but instead of Soleimani "actively developing plans to attack" Americans in the region. U.S. Department of Defense, "Statement by the Department of Defense," press release, January 2, 2020, 9:46 P.M. Available at www.defense.gov/Newsroom/Releases/Release/Article/2049534/statement-by-the -department-of-defense.

302 **twenty-five hundred troops in Iraq:** Spencer Ackerman, Erin Banco, and Asawin Suebsaeng, "Trump Is Handing Iran Its Biggest Strategic Objective: Iraq," *Daily Beast,* January 10, 2020. Alissa J. Rubin and Eric Schmitt, "Rocket Attack Kills Three U.S. Coalition Members in Iraq," *New York Times,* March 11, 2020. Associated Press, "4 Rockets Hit Baghdad's Green Zone in Challenge to Iraqi PM," June 19, 2020. Spencer Ackerman and Asawin Suebsaeng, "A Cadre of Top Trumpists Is Pushing for Full Afghanistan Withdrawal," *Daily Beast,* November 17, 2020.

303 **demonstration of the white anger:** Carol Thompson, "Michigan Capitol Building Will Be Closed During Protest Because Legislature Won't Meet," *Lansing State Journal,* May 13, 2020.

304 **At least 260,000:** Kate Taylor, "The U.S. Reaches 20 Million Cases," *New York Times,* December 31, 2020.

304 **deny the novel coronavirus:** Maggie Haberman, "Trump Admits Downplaying the Virus Knowing It Was 'Deadly Stuff,'" *New York Times,* September 9, 2020.

304 **as late as March 24:** Philip Bump, "Trump Again Downplays Coronavirus by Comparing It to the Seasonal Flu. It's Not a Fair Comparison," *Washington Post,* March 24, 2020. Haberman, "Trump Admits Downplaying the Virus."

305 **received first-rate treatment:** Spencer Ackerman, Erin Banco, Asawin Suebsaeng, and Sam Stein, "White House Quietly Told Vets Group It Might Have Exposed Them to COVID," *Daily Beast,* October 7, 2020. Sam Gringlas and Barbara Sprunt, "Timeline: What We Know of President Trump's COVID Diagnosis, Treatment," NPR, October 5, 2020. Matthew Impeli, "Fact Check: Is U.S. 'Rounding the Turn' on COVID, as Trump Claims?" *Newsweek,* October 26, 2020.

305 **new cases daily:** Rick Noack, "In Countries Keeping the Coronavirus at Bay, Experts Watch U.S. Case Numbers with Alarm," *Washington Post,* June 19, 2020. Peter Baker, "Trump Foresees Virus Death Toll as High as 100,000 in The United States," *New York Times,* May 3, 2020. Denise Lu, "The True Coronavirus Total in the U.S. Has Already Surpassed 200,000," *New York Times,* August 13, 2020. *New York Times,* "COVID in the U.S.: Latest Map and Case Count," www.nytimes.com/interactive /2020/us/coronavirus-us-cases.html, accessed November 27, 2020.

305 **December 9 was the first day:** Carolyn Crist, "COVID-19 Deaths Surpass 9/11 Deaths in Single Day," WebMD, December 10, 2020.

305 **"post-9/11 mindset":** Ben Rhodes, "The 9/11 Era Is Over," *The Atlantic,* April 6, 2020.

306 **pre-9/11 warnings:** Shane Harris, Greg Miller, Josh Dawsey, and Ellen Nakashima, "U.S. Intelligence Reports from January and February Warned of a Likely Pandemic," *Washington Post*, March 20, 2020. "Remarks by President Trump, Vice President Pence and Members of the Coronavirus Task Force in Press Conference," Whitehouse .gov, February 26, 2020, available at https://ge.usembassy.gov/remarks-by-president -trump-vice-president-pence-and-members-of-the-coronavirus-task-force-in-press -conference-february-26. Julian E. Barnes and Adam Goldman, "For Spy Agencies, Briefing Trump Is a Test of His Attention," *New York Times*, May 21, 2020.

306 **a narrative of emergency leadership:** David Smith, "Trump Talks Himself Up as 'Wartime President' to Lead America through a Crisis," *Guardian*, March 22, 2020. Ebony Bowden, "Trump Says Coronavirus Pandemic 'Worse than Pearl Harbor . . . World Trade Center,'" *New York Post*, May 6, 2020.

307 **at Trump's first rally:** Benjamin Fearnow, "White House Promised 27 Million Coronavirus Test Kits by End of March, but U.S. Just Hit 1 Million," *Newsweek*, March 31, 2020. Spencer Ackerman, "It's Probably Too Late to Use South Korea's Trick for Tracking Coronavirus," *Daily Beast*, March 26, 2020. Maeve Reston, "Trump Says He Wanted Testing Slowed Down, Uses Racist Term for Coronavirus," CNN, June 21, 2020.

308 **purge this windfall:** Spencer Ackerman, "FEMA Tells States to Hand Public Health Data to Palantir," *Daily Beast*, May 21, 2020.

308 **hate crimes against Asian Americans:** Julia Reinstein, "A Man Who Allegedly Tried to Kill an Asian-American Family Because of the Coronavirus Could Face Federal Hate-Crimes Charges," *BuzzFeed*, April 1, 2020. Matt Lofman, "Asian Americans Describe 'Gut Punch' of Racist Attacks during Coronavirus Pandemic," *PBS News-Hour*, April 7, 2020. Myah Ward, "15 Times Trump Praised China as Coronavirus Was Spreading across the Globe," *Politico*, April 15, 2020. Barnes and Goldman, "For Spy Agencies, Briefing Trump Is a Test." Kimmy Yam, "Anti-Asian Hate Crimes Increased by Nearly 150% in 2020, Mostly in N.Y. and L.A., New Report Says," NBC News, March 9, 2021.

309 **to portray conclusively:** Mark Mazetti, Julian E. Barnes, Edward Wong, and Adam Goldman, "Trump Officials Are Said to Press Spies to Link Virus and Wuhan Labs," *New York Times*, May 14, 2020. Office of the Director of National Intelligence, "Intelligence Community Statement on Origins of COVID-19," ODNI news release no. 11-20, April 30, 2020, available at www.dni.gov/index.php/newsroom/press-releases /item/2112-intelligence-community-statement-on-origins-of-covid-19. Paul R. Pillar, "The Trump Administration's Politicization of Coronavirus Intelligence," *The National Interest*, May 4, 2020. Erin Banco, Adam Rawnsley, and Lachlan Cartwright, "Busted: Pentagon Contractors' Report on 'Wuhan Lab' Origin of Virus Is Bogus," *Daily Beast*, May 17, 2020.

309 **first wave of coronavirus deaths:** Centers for Disease Control, "COVID-19 in Racial and Ethnic Minority Groups," www.cdc.gov/coronavirus/2019-ncov/need-extra-pre cautions/racial-ethnic-minorities.html, accessed June 23, 2020. Vanessa Williams,

"Disproportionately Black Counties Account for Over Half of Coronavirus Cases in the U.S. and Nearly 60 Percent of Deaths, Study Finds," *Washington Post*, May 6, 2020.

309 **Florida governor Ron DeSantis:** Mark Joseph Stern, "Ron DeSantis Is Facing a Coronavirus Catastrophe," *Slate*, March 30, 2020.

310 **"Don't sacrifice the country":** Isaac Stanley-Becker, Yasmeen Abutaleb, and Devlin Barrett, "Anthony Fauci's Security Is Stepped Up as Doctor and Face of U.S. Coronavirus Response Receives Threats," *Washington Post*, April 1, 2020. Nate Chute, "See What the 'Operation Haircut' Protest at the Michigan Capitol Looked Like," *Lansing State Journal*, May 20, 2020. Lois Beckett, "Older People Would Rather Die than Let COVID-19 Harm US Economy: Texas Official," *Guardian*, March 24, 2020. Rachel Weiner and Ariana Eunjung Cha, "Amid Threats and Political Pushback, Public Health Officials Are Leaving Their Posts," *Washington Post*, June 22, 2020.

311 **a MAGA-favorite firm:** Jackie Northam, "State Department Halts Routine Visa Services Worldwide," NPR, March 20, 2020. Nick Miroff, Maria Sacchetti, and Tracy Jan, "Trump to Suspend Immigration to U.S. for 60 Days, Citing Coronavirus Crisis and Jobs Shortage, but Will Allow Some Workers," *Washington Post*, April 21, 2020. Molly O'Toole, "Trump Announces New Visa Restrictions on Immigrant Workers, but Exempts Agriculture, Food Service, Health," *Los Angeles Times*, June 22, 2020. Linda Chavez and Scott Roehm, "Trump's Coronavirus Order Scapegoats Immigrants and Doesn't Make Us Safer," *USA Today*, April 28, 2020. Muzaffar Chishti and Sarah Pierce, "Crisis within a Crisis: Immigration in the United States in a Time of COVID-19," Migration Policy Institute, March 26, 2020. Spencer Ackerman and William Bredderman, "Trump's Favorite Is Under Investigation—and Getting Big Bucks to Build the Wall," *Daily Beast*, April 21, 2020. Nick Miroff, "Trump's Preferred Construction Firm Lands $1.3 Billion Border Wall Contract, the Biggest So Far," *Washington Post*, May 19, 2020.

311 **a desperate detainee:** Spencer Ackerman, "ICE Dodged Orders to Free Detainees— and Triggered an Outbreak," *Daily Beast*, July 19, 2020. Tu Thanh Ha, "Canadian Dies after Being Held in U.S. Immigration Detention Center with COVID-19 Outbreak," *Globe and Mail* (Toronto), August 6, 2020. Muslim Advocates, Letter to DHS and ICE, August 19, 2020, available at https://muslimadvocates.org/wp-content/uploads/2020/08/2020.08.18-Krome-Letter-FINAL.pdf.

312 **died from the virus in ICE detention:** Spencer Ackerman, "ICE: No Plan to Free Immigrants in Jail, but Will Arrest Fewer Due to Pandemic," *Daily Beast*, March 19, 2020. Tammy La Gorce, "'Everybody Was Sick': Inside an ICE Detention Center," *New York Times*, May 15, 2020. Ryan Devereaux, "'Burials Are Cheaper than Deportations': Virus Unleashes Terror at a Troubled ICE Detention Center," *The Intercept*, April 12, 2020. Author's interview with Adham Hassoun, May 21, 2020. "COVID-19 ICE Detainee Statistics by Facility," www.ice.gov/coronavirus, accessed June 23, 2020. Ryan Devereaux, "ICE Detainee Who Died of COVID-19 Suffered Horrifying Neglect," *The Intercept*, May 24, 2020. Jeremy Redmon, "ICE Detainee Held in South Georgia Dies from COVID-19," *Atlanta Journal-Constitution*, May 25, 2020. "ICE Guidance on COVID-19," www.ice.gov/coronavirus, accessed November 27, 2020.

312 VA's burn-pit registry: Spencer Ackerman, "Military 'Burn Pits' Trashed These Veterans' Lungs. Then the Virus Hit," *Daily Beast*, April 16, 2020.

313 Crozier shamed his superiors: James LaPorta and Spencer Ackerman, "'We're Fucked': Aircraft Carrier Outbreak Sends Troops Scrambling," *Daily Beast*, March 26, 2020. Spencer Ackerman, "Military Imposes 60-Day Coronavirus Ban on Troops Coming Home from Overseas," *Daily Beast*, March 25, 2020. CDR Salamander, "We Are Not at War. Sailors Do Not Need to Die," *US Naval Institute Blog*, April 1, 2020.

313 Aviation Ordnanceman Chief Petty Officer: David Ignatius, "Acting Navy Chief Fired Crozier for 'Panicking'—and Before Trump Could Intervene," *Washington Post*, April 5, 2020. Spencer Ackerman, "The Navy Is Blaming the Captain It Fired for Accurate COVID-19 Warning," *Daily Beast*, June 19, 2020.

314 "end endless wars": Tyler Bellstrom, "Ending 'Endless War' Can't Just Become an Empty Slogan," *Jacobin*, February 20, 2020.

314 "maintain our focus": Joseph R. Biden Jr., "Why America Must Lead," *Foreign Affairs*, March–April 2020.

314 regretted his vote: Bernie Sanders, "Ending America's Endless War," *Foreign Affairs*, June 24, 2019. Jamie Ross, "Trump Blocks Measure to End U.S. Involvement in Yemen," *Daily Beast*, April 19, 2019. The Fix Team, "Transcript: The December Democratic Debate," *Washington Post*, December 19, 2019.

315 construct that veneer: Tim Reid, "Exclusive: Dozens of Republican Former U.S. National Security Officials to Back Biden," Reuters, June 23, 2020. David Sanger, "Top Republican National Security Officials Say They Will Vote for Biden," *New York Times*, August 20, 2020. Mike Memoli, "Biden Builds Out His Presidential Transition Operation," NBC News, June 20, 2020. Charlie Savage, *Power Wars: The Relentless Rise of Presidential Authority and Secrecy* (New York: Little, Brown & Co., 2015), ch. 4, subch. 13. Karen DeYoung and Greg Miller, "CIA's Deputy Director to Be Replaced by White House Lawyer," *Washington Post*, June 12, 2013. Spencer Ackerman, "The Proxy War over a Top Biden Adviser," *Daily Beast*, July 6, 2020.

315 Trump blamed everyone: Caitlin Oprysko, "'I Don't Take Responsibility at All': Trump Deflects Blame for Coronavirus Testing Fumble," *Politico*, March 13, 2020.

316 "NO ONE CONDONES LOOTING": Sean Loughlin, "Rumsfeld on Looting in Iraq: 'Stuff Happens,'" CNN, April 12, 2003.

316 Floyd's brother Philonise: Evan Hill, Ainara Tiefenthaler, Christiaan Triebert, Drew Jordan, Haley Wills, and Robin Stein, "How George Floyd Was Killed in Police Custody," *New York Times*, May 31, 2020. Lauren Gambino, "'Make It Stop': George Floyd's Brother Calls on Congress to Act over Police Violence," *Guardian*, June 10, 2020.

316 largest mass movement: Larry Buchanan, Quoctrung Bui, and Jugal K. Patel, "Black Lives Matter May Be the Largest Movement in U.S. History," *New York Times*, July 3, 2020.

317 three cops nightsticked: The author observed the nightsticking at Broadway and West Twelfth Street on May 31, 2020.

NOTES

317 in the underground bunker: Peter Baker and Maggie Haberman, "As Protests and Violence Spill Over, Trump Shrinks Back," *New York Times*, May 31, 2020.

317 "When the looting starts": Barbara Sprunt, "The History Behind 'When the Looting Starts, the Shooting Starts,'" NPR, May 29, 2020.

317 In truth, antifascism was a movement: Spencer Ackerman, "FBI is Investigating Regional 'Nodes' of Antifa, Director Christopher Wray Says," *Daily Beast*, September 17, 2020.

318 the formless Antifa: Kelly Weill and Spencer Ackerman, "Trump's 'ANTIFA' Threat Is Total Bullshit—And Totally Dangerous," *Daily Beast,* May 31, 2020.

318 delivered apocalyptic speeches: William Barr, "Attorney General William P. Barr Delivers Remarks to the Law School and the de Nicola Center for Ethics and Culture at the University of Notre Dame," Department of Justice, October 11, 2019. Transcript available at www.justice.gov/opa/speech/attorney-general-william-p-barr-delivers-re marks-law-school-and-de-nicola-center-ethics.

318 Bowdich rallied his agents: Zolan Kanno-Youngs, Sergio Olmos, Mike Baker, and Adam Goldman, "From the Start, Federal Agents Demanded a Role in Suppressing Anti-Racism Protests," *New York Times*, July 28, 2020.

318 no mention of Antifa: Erin Banco and Spencer Ackerman, "Bill Barr Promises to Sic Terror-Hunters on Protesters," *Daily Beast*, June 1, 2020. William Bredderman and Spencer Ackerman, "'Antifa' Is Literally Never Mentioned in the First Prosecutions of Protest Violence," *Daily Beast*, June 5, 2020. Ryan Devereaux, "What Law Did We Break? How the NYPD Weaponized a Curfew against Protesters and Residents," *The Intercept*, June 28, 2020.

319 their forced complicity: Alex Ward, "U.S. Park Police Said Using 'Tear Gas' in a Statement Was a Mistake. It Just Used the Term Again," *Vox*, June 5, 2020. Daniel Lippman, "'What I Saw Was Just Absolutely Wrong': National Guardsmen Struggle with Their Role in Containing Protests," *Politico*, June 9, 2020.

319 "knowingly, willingly betrayed his oath": Spencer Ackerman, "Joint Chiefs Chairman Blasted as Uniformed 'Prop' for Trump's 'Fascist Political Stunt,'" *Daily Beast,* June 2, 2020.

320 CBP had flown drones: Spencer Ackerman and Erin Banco, "Justice Department Deputized Border Patrol as U.S. Marshals for Protest Response," *Daily Beast*, June 9, 2020. Zolan Kanno-Youngs, "U.S. Watched George Floyd Protests in 15 Cities Using Aerial Surveillance," *New York Times*, June 19, 2020.

320 advocated for the military: Tom Cotton (@TomCottonAr), "And, if necessary, the 10th Mountain, 82nd Airborne, 1st Cav, 3rd Infantry—whatever it takes to restore order. No quarter for insurrectionists, anarchists, rioters, and looters," Twitter, June 1, 2020, 10:14 A.M., https://twitter.com/tomcottonar/status/1267459561675468800.

321 the chairman apologized: Hanna Trudo, Spencer Ackerman, and Sam Brodey, "These Generals Turned on Trump. Will They Go for Biden?" *Daily Beast,* June 13, 2020.

Helene Cooper, "Milley Apologizes for Role in Trump Photo Op: 'I Should Not Have Been There,'" *New York Times*, June 11, 2020. Brooks, by 2020 a rare Black four-star general, was, not coincidentally, the officer more inclined to discuss the righteousness of the protests than the risk of damaging civil-military relations.

321 **moral authority in jeopardy:** Matt Zapotosky, "Barr Forms Task Force to Counter 'Anti-Government Extremists,'" *Washington Post*, June 26, 2020.

321 **round up "the leaders of antifa":** Media Matters staff, "Tucker Carlson Unleashes Deranged Rant Calling for Protesters to Be Labeled Domestic Terrorists, Arrested and Paraded 'in Front of Cameras Like MS-13,'" *Media Matters*, June 26, 2020.

322 **denounced Barr's politicizing:** Spencer Ackerman, "'The Lord's Work': House Republicans Unite behind Bill Barr amid Corruption Claims," *Daily Beast*, June 24, 2020. Harry Siegel, Asawin Suebsaeng, and Erin Banco, "Berman Leaves SDNY in Trusted Hands after Bill Barr Fucks Up His Ouster," *Daily Beast*, June 20, 2020.

322 **FBI broke up:** Derek Hawkins and Hannah Knowles, "Alleged Members of White Supremacy Group 'The Base' Charged with Plotting to Kill Antifa Couple," *Washington Post*, January 18, 2020.

322 **thirteen Michigan men:** Tom Perkins, Kelly Weill, Will Sommer, and William Bredderman, "The 'Wolverine Watchmen' Accused of Targeting Michigan Guv Spooked Their Neighbors," *Daily Beast*, October 8, 2020.

323 **Counterprotesters used their cars:** Hannah Allam, "Vehicle Attacks Rise as Extremists Target Protesters," NPR, June 21, 2020. Spencer Ackerman, "Qaeda Pushes Snack Attacks, 'Ultimate Mowing Machine,'" *Wired*, October 12, 2020.

323 **Right-wing donors:** *Guardian* staff, "Tucker Carlson Defends Actions of Teen Charged in Killings of Kenosha Protesters," *Guardian*, August 26, 2020. Mark Guarino, Mark Berman, Jaclyn Peiser, and Griff Witte, "17-Year Old Charged with Homicide after Shootings during Kenosha Protests, Authorities Say," *Washington Post*, August 26, 2020. Teo Armus, Mark Berman, and Griff Witte, "Before a Fatal Shooting, Teenage Kenosha Suspect Idolized the Police," *Washington Post*, August 27, 2020. Julia Ainsley, "Internal Document Shows Trump Officials Were Told to Make Comments Sympathetic to Kyle Rittenhouse," NBC News, October 1, 2020. Hannah Allam, "Kyle Rittenhouse, Accused in Kenosha, Wis., Shooting Deaths, Is Released on Bail," NPR, November 25, 2020. Jorge Fitz-Gibbon, "Ricky Schroder Defends Helping Bail Out Kenosha Gunman Kyle Rittenhouse," *New York Post*, November 24, 2020.

323 **"the storming of the Bastille":** Alexis Zotos, "Experts Examine Whether It Was Legal for St. Louis Couple to Point Guns at Protesters," KMOV-4 St. Louis, June 30, 2020. Stefene Russell, "A Decades-Long Renovation Returns a Midwestern Palazzo to Its Original Glory," *St. Louis Magazine*, August 16, 2018. Chris King, "McCloskeys Were 'Opposed to Cultural Diversity' in Directions to Nanny in '90s," *St. Louis American*, July 2, 2020.

324 **shown up at BLM protests:** Christopher Mathias, "White Vigilantes Have Always Had a Friend in Police," *HuffPost*, August 28, 2020.

324 **"stand back and stand by"**: Kelly Weill, "Trump's Crew of Far-Right Vigilante Poll Watchers Is Coming," *Daily Beast*, September 30, 2020.

324 **Nunes, Carlson, and Roger Stone**: Kelly Weill and Will Sommer, "Republicans are Adopting the Proud Boys," *Daily Beast*, Octover 16, 2018.

325 **Proud Boys and police**: Kelly Weill, "Video Exposes Proud Boys and 'Extra Friendly' Philly Cops," *Daily Beast*, October 16, 2020.

325 **encouraging his colleagues**: Jamie Ross, "Trump Spreads Baseless Conspiracy Theory that Video of Cops Shoving Elderly Man Was Antifa 'Setup,'" *Daily Beast*, June 9, 2020. House Committee on the Judiciary, "Oversight of the Department of Justice: Political Interference and Threats to Prosecutorial Independence," June 24, 2020, available at https://judiciary.house.gov/calendar/eventsingle.aspx?EventID=3034. Jay Croft and Elizabeth Hartfield, "Buffalo Officers Quit Special Team after 2 Officers Are Suspended for Shoving a 75-year-old Protester," CNN, June 6, 2020. Jacqueline Rose, Allen Kim, and Elizabeth Johnson, "Buffalo Protester Martin Gugino Has Been Released from the Hospital," CNN, June 30, 2020. Katie Shepherd, "Philadelphia Police Suspend Joseph Bologna, Who Beat Protesters in Viral Videos. The Union Is Selling 'Bologna Strong' Shirts," *Washington Post*, June 10, 2020. Hayley Fowler, "NC Cops Fired for Racist Remarks Had Been Demoted or Terminated Before, Records Show," June 26, 2020. Spencer Ackerman (@attackerman), "Like the Guantanamo field-grade officer who jotted notes during a briefing from a CIA lawyer that read "if the detainee dies, you're doing it wrong," Twitter, June 3, 2020, 8:40 A.M., https://twitter.com/attackerman/status/1268160564502638594.

325 **advocated for migrant child separation**: Zolan Kanno-Youngs and Jesse McKinley, "Meet the Official Accused of Helping Trump Politicize Homeland Security," *New York Times*, August 4, 2020.

325 **escalate their nighttime resistance**: House Judiciary Committee oversight hearing with Attorney General William Barr, July 28, 2020, comments of Rep. Kelly Armstrong (R-ND). Available at www.c-span.org/video/?473384-1/attorney-general-barr-testifies-justice-department-mission-programs.

326 **"baseball card" intelligence reports**: Shane Harris, "DHS Compiled 'Intelligence Reports' on Journalists Who Published Leaked Documents," *Washington Post*, July 30, 2020. Letter from Senate Intelligence Committee Democrats to Acting Undersecretary for Homeland Security Brian Murphy, July 31, 2020. Available at www.bennet.senate.gov/public/_cache/files/a/6/a6814d23-9fce-4e2d-9e82-94646b2fd36e/ED2E77294EBA1BFD9767F2FE281B17CC.intelligence-to-ia-murphy-letter.pdf.

326 **broke his hand with batons**: Sam Brodey and Spencer Ackerman, "Barr Calls Portland Protests 'an Assault' in Testy Hearing," *Daily Beast*, July 28, 2020. Spencer Ackerman and Winston Ross, "Inside the Creepy Crackdown on Portland Protesters," July 17, 2020. Statement of Drew Wade, spokesperson, U.S. Marshal Service, July 27, 2020. Marissa J. Long, "A Navy Vet Asked Federal Officers in Portland to Remember Their Oaths. Then They Broke His Hand," *Washington Post*, July 20, 2020.

326 **Jeh Johnson, the air force lawyer**: Spencer Ackerman, Erin Banco, and Asawin Suebsaeng, "Trump Administration Plots Crackdown by Feds on Cities Nationwide,"

Daily Beast, July 20, 2020. Former DHS official Juliette Kayyem warned of anti-DHS *overreaction* in "Trump Is the Problem. The Organizational Chart Doesn't Matter," *The Atlantic*, July 23, 2020. An exception came from Richard Clarke, the former Clinton/Bush counterterrorism czar, in his "Dismantle the Department of Homeland Security," *Washington Post*, July 30, 2020.

326 **Trump marshaled the language:** Spencer Ackerman, "Trump 'Surges' Feds to Chicago Like It's a War Zone," *Daily Beast*, July 22, 2020.

327 **promising to keep out:** Colby Itkowitz, "Trump Lashes Out at Black Lives Matter, Accuses One Member of 'Treason,'" *Washington Post*, June 25, 2020. Transcript, Trump rally in Oklahoma, June 21, 2020, www.rev.com/blog/transcripts/donald -trump-tulsa-oklahoma-rally-speech-transcript, accessed July 3, 2020.

329 **may never be known:** The Costs of War Project at Brown University assesses at least 801,000 dead "due to direct war violence, including armed forces on all sides of the conflicts, contractors, civilians, journalists, and humanitarian workers." It continues: "It is likely that many times more have died indirectly in these wars, due to malnutrition, damaged infrastructure, and environmental degradation." Costs of War, "Summary of Findings," Watson Institute for International and Public Affairs, Brown University, https://watson.brown.edu/costsofwar/papers/summary.

329–330 **Stanley McChrystal, the former JSOC:** Author's interview with Stanley McChrystal, May 5, 2020.

330 **"stupid stuff for life":** Spencer Ackerman, "Government Case Collapses against Man Jailed Indefinitely under Patriot Act," *Daily Beast*, June 22, 2020. Author's interviews with Adham Hassoun, June 21, July 5, 2020.

331 **Hassoun "still considers":** Author's interview with Adham Hassoun, July 28, 2020. Spencer Ackerman, "Man Trump Detained Indefinitely under Patriot Act Is Free," *Daily Beast,* July 22, 2020.

332 **The head of the Texas Republican Party:** Matthew Rosenberg and Maggie Haberman, "The Republican Embrace of QAnon Goes Far beyond Trump," *New York Times*, August 20, 2020. Republican Party of Texas Staff, "Chairman Allen West's Response to SCOTUS Decision," press release, December 11, 2020, www.texasgop.org/chairman -allen-wests-response-to-scotus-decision, accessed February 10, 2021.

332 **"an Islamic invasion":** Ally Mutnick and Melanie Zanona, "House Republican Leaders Condemn GOP Candidate Who Made Racist Videos," *Politico*, June 17, 2020.

332 **When she took her oath:** Marjorie Taylor Greene (@mtgreenee), "Just sworn in!! It's an honor to represent the people of Northwest Georgia! Time to get to work," Twitter, January 3, 2021, 6:49 P.M., https://twitter.com/mtgreenee/status/13458799424841 35940.

332 **Nevada had covered up:** Graig Graziosi, "Trump Spokesman Lashes Out at Journalists Asking for Evidence behind Nevada Fraud Case: 'You're Here to Take in Information,'" *Independent*, November 5, 2020.

332 **In December, 18 Republican state attorneys general:** Spencer Ackerman, "The GOP's Replaying the Conspiracy that Predicted Rome's Fall," *Daily Beast,* January 7, 2021.

332 **"What is the downside":** Amy Gardner, Ashley Parker, Josh Dawsey, and Emma Brown, "Top Republicans Back Trump's Efforts to Challenge Election Results," *Washington Post*, November 9, 2020.

332 **"Democracy isn't the objective":** David Morgan, "'Democracy Isn't the Objective': Republican U.S. Senator Draws Democrats' Ire," *Reuters*, October 8, 2020.

333 **"Yes, it's illegal":** Craig Timberg and Drew Harwell, "Pro-Trump Forums Erupt with Violent Threats Ahead of Wednesday's Rally Against the 2020 Election," *Washington Post*, January 5, 2021.

333 **"bleed" for their freedom:** Spencer Ackerman and Kelly Weill, "'When the Bombs Go Off, the Blood Is on Mike Flynn's Hands': Retired Officers Blast His Calls for Martial Law," *Daily Beast*, December 2, 2020. Dan Barry, Mike McIntire, and Matthew Rosenberg, "'Our President Wants Us Here': The Mob that Stormed the Capitol," *New York Times*, January 9, 2021.

333 **"We don't got your back":** Bob Price, "Watch: Violence Breaks Out as Cops Block Pro-Trump Protesters From BLM Plaza," *Breitbart*, January 5, 2021.

333 **some arriving by private jet:** Abigail Rosenthal, "The Texas Woman Who Took a Private Jet to D.C. to 'Storm the Capitol' Has Been Charged," *Houston Chronicle*, January 8, 2021.

333 **"You'll never take back your country":** Antonio Fins, "What Trump Said in Rally Speech to Spark U.S. Capitol Storming," *Palm Beach Post*, January 6, 2021.

333 **A rising MAGA senator:** Katie Bernard, "A Photographer and a Fist Pump. The Story behind the Image that Will Haunt Josh Hawley," *Kansas City Star,* January 7, 2021.

333 **With that, a MAGA mob:** Tom Jackman, "Numerous Capitol Police Officers Who Responded to Riot Test Positive for Coronavirus," *Washington Post*, January 23, 2021.

334 **One shot dead Ashli Babbitt:** Spencer Ackerman, "Why the 'Blue Lives Matter' Thugs Were So Quick to Kill a Cop," *Daily Beast*, January 8, 2021.

334 **But other cops took selfies:** Carol D. Leonnig, Aaron C. Davis, Dan Lamothe, and David Farenthold, "Capitol Breach Prompts Urgent Questions about Security Failures," *Washington Post*, January 7, 2021. Spencer Ackerman and Adam Rawnsley, "Capitol Police Chief Quits after Pelosi Demanded He Be Fired for MAGA Riot," *Daily Beast*, January 8, 2021. United States Capitol Police, "U.S. Capitol Police Arrests —January 6, 2021" press release, January 7, 2021, www.uscp.gov/media-center/press -releases/us-capitol-police-arrests-january-6-2021, accessed February 11, 2021.

334 **smeared shit through the halls:** Chris Sommerfeldt, "Pro-Trump Rioters Smeared Poop in Capitol Hallways during Belligerent Attack," New York *Daily News*, January 7, 2021.

334 **a 950,000-volt stun gun:** Josiah Ryan, "The Man Seen in Viral Photograph at Pelosi's Desk Was Carrying a 950,000 Volt Stun Gun," CNN, February 10, 2021.

334 **Washington mayor Muriel Bowser:** Alex Marquardt, Barbara Starr, Alison Main, and Devan Cole, "Pentagon Approves D.C. Mayor's Request to Deploy National Guard for Upcoming Demonstrations," CNN, January 4, 2021.

334 Major General William Walker: Paul Sonne, "Pentagon Restricted Commander of D.C. Guard Ahead of Capitol Riot," *Washington Post*, January 26, 2021.

334–335 Sund claimed "nothing": Mark Mazzetti and Adam Goldman, "Hazy Warnings Missed Extent of Capitol Plot," *The New York Times*, February 5, 2021.

335 "coordinating, instigating and leading": Unbylined, "Video Investigation: Proud Boys Were Key Instigators in Capitol Riot," *Wall Street Journal*, January 26, 2021.

335 Of the first 176 people charged: Jennifer Valentino-DeVries, Grace Ashford, Denise Lu, Eleanor Lutz, Alex Leeds Matthews, and Karen Yourish, "Arrested in Riot: Organized Militants and a Mob of Radicals," *New York Times*, February 6, 2021.

335 Brock had carried flex cuffs: Ronan Farrow, "An Air Force Combat Veteran Breached the Senate," *The New Yorker*, January 9, 2021.

335 "I am not a terrorist": James Gordon Meek and Catherine Sanz, "'I Am Not a Terrorist': Retired Navy SEAL Speaks after Capitol Siege," ABC News, January 12, 2021. Dave Phillips, "From Navy SEAL to Part of the Angry Mob Outside the Capitol," *New York Times*, January 26, 2021.

336 Trump deserved a "mulligan": Glenn Thrush, "Mike Lee Suggests Trump Should Get a 'Mulligan' for Capitol Riot Day Speech," *New York Times*, February 9, 2021.

336 "To remove the supportive environment": Mary Louise Kelly, "Former CIA Officer: Treat Domestic Extremism as an Insurgency," NPR, February 2, 2021.

336 "an offense that people and organizations": Masood Farivar, "Why Domestic Terrorism Is Not Specifically Designated a Crime in US," Voice of America, February 10, 2021.

336 "But at the same time, we must resist": Spencer Ackerman, "The Last Thing We Need Is Another War on Terror," *Daily Beast*, January 13, 2021.

337 "The 'post-9/11' era": Elissa Slotkin, "Slotkin to Take on Domestic Terrorism as Head of Counterterrorism Subcommittee," press release, February 1, 2021, https://slotkin.house.gov/media/press-releases/slotkin-take-domestic-terrorism-head-counterterrorism-subcommittee, accessed February 11, 2021.

337 New York University professor Nikhil Pal Singh: Nikhil Pal Singh, *Race and America's Long War* (Oakland, California: University of California Press, 2019), Kindle location 496.

INDEX